UNSETTLING QUEER ANTHROPOLOGY

UNSETTLING QUEEN ANTHROPOLOGY

Edited by Margot Weiss

UNSETTLING QUEER ANTHROPOLOGY

Foundations, Reorientations, and Departures

DUKE UNIVERSITY PRESS
Durham and London
2024

© 2024 DUKE UNIVERSITY PRESS
All rights reserved
Printed and bound by CPI Group (UK) Ltd, Croydon, CR0 4YY
Project Editor: Bird Williams
Designed by A. Mattson Gallagher
Typeset in Untitled Serif by Westchester Publishing Services

Library of Congress Cataloging-in-Publication Data
Names: Weiss, Margot Danielle, [date] editor.
Title: Unsettling queer anthropology : foundations,
reorientations, and departures / edited by Margot Weiss.
Description: Durham : Duke University Press, 2024. | Includes
bibliographical references and index.
Identifiers: LCCN 2023037617 (print)
LCCN 2023037618 (ebook)
ISBN 9781478030386 (paperback)
ISBN 9781478026150 (hardcover)
ISBN 9781478059400 (ebook)
Subjects: LCSH: Ethnology. | Anthropology—Philosophy. | Queer
theory. | Feminist anthropology. | Settler colonialism. | BISAC:
SOCIAL SCIENCE / Anthropology / Cultural & Social | SOCIAL
SCIENCE / LGBTQ Studies / General
Classification: LCC GN345 .U57 2024 (print)
LCC GN345 (ebook)
DCC 306.7601—dc23/eng/20231026
LC record available at https://lccn.loc.gov/2023037617
LC ebook record available at https://lccn.loc.gov/2023037618

Cover art: Julie Mehretu, *Dissident Score* (detail), 2019–2021.
Ink and acrylic on canvas, 108 × 120 in. (274.3 × 304.8 cm).
Courtesy of the artist and Marian Goodman Gallery,
© Julie Mehretu. Photo: Tom Powel Imaging.

CONTENTS

ix   Preface

you're invited: *a playlist for errant ethnographers*

Savannah Shange

xiii   Acknowledgments

1   INTRODUCTION

Queer Anthropology

Foundations, Reorientations, and Departures

Margot Weiss

PART I   FOUNDATIONS

Queer Anthropology's Contested Genealogies

31   **1**   **The Anthropology of "What Is Utterly Precious"**

Black Feminist Habits of Mind and the Object (and Ends) of Anthropology

Jafari Sinclaire Allen

53 **2 Queer Theories from Somewhere**

Situated Knowledges and Other Queer Empiricisms

Margot Weiss

77 **3 Intimate Methods**

Reflections on Racial and Colonial Legacies within Sexual Social Science

Scott L. Morgensen

PART II REORIENTATIONS
Queering the Anthropological Canon

99 **4 Kinship and Kinmaking Otherwise**

Lucinda Ramberg

116 **5 Pronoun Trouble**

Notes on Radical Gender Inclusion in English

Tom Boellstorff

133 **6 Stylization in the Flesh**

Queer Anthropology and Performance

Brian A. Horton

152 **7 Worldly Power and Local Alterity**

Transnational Queer Anthropology

Ara Wilson

169 **8 Queer States**

Geopolitics and Queer Anthropology

Sima Shakhsari

PART III   DEPARTURES
Reworlding Queer Anthropology

191 **9** **Black Queer Anthropology Roundtable**
Speculations on Activating Ethnographic
Practice in and for Community

Shaka McGlotten and Lyndon Gill, Marshall Green,
Nikki Lane, and Kwame Otu

209 **10** **The Subject of Trans Lives and Vitalities**
Queer and Trans Anthropological
Object-Making

Elijah Adiv Edelman

227 **11** **Doing It Together**
A Queer Case for Cripping Ethnography

Erin L. Durban

247 **12** **When Our Tulips Speak Together**
More-Than-Human Queer Natures

Juno Salazar Parreñas

266 **13** **Queer (Re)generations**
Disrupting Apocalypse Time

Anne Spice

283 **14** **The Queer Endotic**
Experiments on the Infra-ordinary
(Or seeds for a worlding)

Martin F. Manalansan IV

299 Contributors

305 Index

PREFACE   Savannah Shange

you're invited

a playlist for errant ethnographers

now playing: "i'm coming out," diana ross, 1980
"i'm coming out / i want the world to know / got to let it show"

come sip with us

we pregame with riggs and rubin and lorde and fresh mint and lavender tea, spiked for some with honey and others with rum. we take turns crowding in the too-small mirror, brushing waves forward and slicking edges back. unscented shea butter smooths over our rough elbows and frayed nerves—it's been such a long time. reluctant and resolute, we pawn the sweet solitude of books and cats and apps for the heady promise of a good time.

now playing: "you make me feel (mighty real)," sylvester, 1978
"i feel real / when you touch me"

come stand with us

this is when the doubts creep in, standing in line outside the club with a hundred other queermos freezing in their saturday night best. i shift my weight from one foot to the other, envious of the bulky jacket we all told you to leave in the trunk. self-satisfied but not smug, you let us all huddle around your fluffy mustard faux fur, a goosepimpled nest of relation, swaying almost imperceptibly in anticipation.

now playing: "woman is a word," empress of, 2016
"i'm only a woman if woman is a word"

come strut with us

finally in, we are wordless and intent on the first circuit around the club. like a school of fish or thought, we wind around the perimeter of the dance floor and past both bars, drinking in the vibe as we pour ourselves into it. looking at everyone and no one in particular, we surveil our kin and commit the mood to memory. this, too, is fieldwork.

now playing: "ima read," zebra katz featuring njena reddd foxxx, 2012
"school's in—ima read that bitch / ima write a dissertation to excuse my shit"

come shake with us

before we can make it back to the bar to lean and preen, a subterranean bass lick hits and scatters us onto the dance floor, limbs akimbo. hips sway a bit too hard, knees creak and pop and settle in. we flock into a formation that is ancient but not ahistorical, flexing and vibrating our asses to the collective beat. we read the fuck out of each other. this is epistemology.

now playing: "CINDERELLA parts i and ii," chika, 2021
"what she doin' at a party like this?"

come swoon with us

in line again, this time for the bathroom. you nudge me excitedly and tell me not to look. i look. they're unkempt and nervous and fucking perfect, just like you. i wave them over, feigning familiarity to act like we were kin before this moment, this night, this life produced us as such. they slide between us with only a nanosecond's hesitation, meeting your twinkle with their own. what do you call a flock of wingwomen?

now playing: "everybody everybody," black box, 1990
"own my own / so free / sad and free"

come scream with us

like ants in a sudden downpour, we burrow back to the dance floor, ready for rupture. this is it—the rite has begun. the bassline hits and an infectious "owww" ad lib calls us to ceremony. stylized and deliberate improvisation gives way to collectivized movement—anthems are no good for solos. it seems like we are lip syncing 'til the DJ cuts the music out and "everybodyyy!" crescendos naked and triumphant against the dank walls, echoing our release in a way that eludes representation.

now playing: "MONTERO (call me by your name)," lil nas x, 2021
"if eve ain't in your garden / you know that you're kin"

come sweat with us

lubricated joints carve shapes in space; repetition gives us a container for play. i hit my favorite high-knee triple step and a loose bouncy cipher forms around me and another aging club kid. i don't recognize their face, but i know their steps. a telltale right-toe wiggle invites me to mirror, and my breath catches as we lock damp hands and hit the kid 'n play duet spin in rhythm. *it's been so long.* breaking the meniscus of my own desire, i turn outward to the onlookers and grab two folks into dance with us, while you

PREFACE **xi**

do the same. the circle breaks into a crowd. i scan the faces for yours, worried for a moment until i see your dazed smile and sweaty torso pinned to the wall by thighs too thick for description.

now playing: "both hands (live)," ani difranco, 1997
"i am writing graffiti on your body / i am drawing the story of how hard we tried"

come suck with us

you grab your (now somehow sticky?!) jacket with your right hand and interlace their warm thick fingers with your left. [i know we look very buttoned up scurrying down the halls between the AQA business meeting and presidential sessions, and queer seems almost totally abstracted from sex by this point, but "almost" is the key word here—we still like to fuck.] stall door, train door, bedroom door. jaw held shut and then gaping ajar. scuffed knees, smudged lipstick, the flat scent of silicone, accidental elbow to the eye—are you okay?
   is this okay?

now playing: "chanel," frank ocean, 2017
"my guy pretty like a girl / and he got fight stories to tell"

come slip away with us

we may not be able to escape representation, but we can escape. together. let's keep the party going at the after-hours spot or hit the twenty-four-hour donut shop that has vegan crullers. then we could watch the sunrise behind the condos that used to be homes. or we could just sit back to back on the el and read theory out loud to each other 'til the sun comes up.

listen at https://apple.co/3Gf7mdx

ACKNOWLEDGMENTS

To gesture toward the future of queer anthropology means first thanking those who blazed the trail and made it all possible: Esther Newton, Gayle Rubin, Ellen Lewin, Gloria Wekker, Kath Weston, Evie Blackwood, Elizabeth Lapovsky Kennedy, Lisa Rofel, and so many others. Work on a volume like this also invites reflection on those who made my own path possible. Thank you to Gil Herdt for first introducing me to queer anthropology (and Michel Foucault) when I was a curious, confused undergraduate at the University of Chicago in the 1990s. Though I did not know its name at the time, that brush with queer anthropology changed everything. In graduate school, Antonio Viego and Robyn Wiegman schooled me in a relentlessly critical, reflexive, but always pleasurable queer theory. I have been obsessed with combining queer theory and anthropology, for better or worse, ever since, and I try to kindle a little of the same for my students now.

My greatest gratitude to each of the contributors to this book, who wrote brilliant chapters during a pandemic that made most everything impossible. You all kept this project going through ups and downs both personal and professional—I am deeply thankful to have been able to work with these geniuses. Special thanks to Shaka McGlotten, a co-conspirator for many years: I think you and I first talked about a queer anthropology volume back in 2017, in the hallway at the AAAs—was it in Denver? Who can remember? Thank you for being up for it, and also for saying "why not talk to Duke?" Special thanks to Scott Morgensen, who made my solo editing a lot less solo: thank you for your excellent advice throughout the volume's twists and turns. I am always blown away by your conscientious care and ability to proffer bracing critique with deep respect.

We were able to meet in person only once, at the 2022 AAA meetings; thank you to the authors who participated in that roundtable: Tom Boellstorff, Erin Durban, Shaka McGlotten, Scott Morgensen, Kwame Otu, Juno Salazar Parreñas, Lucinda Ramberg, Anne Spice, and Ara Wilson, and those in the audience who contributed to a dynamic conversation about the multiple futures of queer anthropology. Thank you to Vanessa Agard-Jones, Jenny Davis, Dredge Byung'chu Kang, Karen Nakamura, and Lal Zimman, who lent their brilliance to the initial formulation of this project. Thank you to Nais Dave, Dána-Ain Davis, Jenny Davis, Matt Garrett, J. Kēhaulani Kauanui, Ellen Lewin, Courtney Lewis, and Joey Weiss for sage advice and crucial feedback at critical junctures.

There are many queer anthropologies, and I have learned so much over the years from mentors, collaborators, comrades, and friends. I joined AQA (then SOLGA) in 2001, presenting my first AAA paper (with the very 1990s title "Queering Race and Sex/uality: SM and the [Im]possibilities of a Queer Anthropology") as a still-in-the-field and very nervous graduate student. In the years since, from Yale to Stockholm to Milan, with all the AAA meetings in between, I am grateful to Vanessa Agard-Jones, Jafari Allen, Tom Boellstorff, Christa Craven, Serena Owusua Dankwa, Nais Dave, Elijah Edelman, Elisabeth Engebretsen, Nessette Falu, Rudi Gaudio, Mary Gray, Bill Leap, Ellen Lewin, Sarah Luna, Martin Manalansan, Michelle Marzullo, Jeff Maskovsky, Shaka McGlotten, Greg Mitchell, Scott Morgensen, David A. B. Murray, Karen Nakamura, Marcia Ochoa, Silvia Posocco, Savannah Shange, Jay Sosa, David Valentine, and so many others for the queer conversations, provocations, and intellectual community.

Bringing a book like this into the world is a collaborative endeavor—intellectually and materially. Ken Wissoker, you have been an amazing editor. Your steady hand and perfectly calibrated advice through every stage of this project kept it (and me!) going. I am very grateful for the two anonymous reviewers whose attentive and engaged suggestions strengthened the volume as a whole and all of its chapters. Thank you to Josh Gutterman Tranen and Ryan Kendall, whose editorial assistance kept everything on track; to Chris Dahlin for expertly editing the manuscript; and to Bird Williams, who kept the final production process moving smoothly—no small feat! Thank you to Natasha Korda and the Center for the Humanities; dean of the Social

Sciences, Mary-Jane Rubenstein; and Megan Glick and the Department of American Studies at Wesleyan University for generously providing subvention funds for the brilliant index, compiled by "Ideas on Fire." And a final thanks to A. Mattson Gallagher, who designed this book and its brilliant cover—helping to bring our queerness to life.

Margot Weiss

INTRODUCTION

Queer Anthropology

Foundations, Reorientations, and Departures

In 2010, the Society of Lesbian and Gay Anthropologists (SOLGA)—a section of the American Association of Anthropology (AAA)—officially changed its name to Association for Queer Anthropology (AQA). I was on the task force charged with navigating this transition; at the annual meeting and on the listserv, there had been vigorous debate, mostly around the word *queer*. To some, *queer* could never shed its origins as a slur or insult; to others, it could never adequately or appropriately describe those to whom it was applied. Many more embraced the change, in part to reposition the section away from what seemed to some an identitarian and exclusionary *lesbian* and *gay*, and in part to align with newer queer and trans anthropology. Indeed, some recall a (transphobic) thread in the debates concerning the place of *trans* in LGBT/queer anthropology.[1] AQA'S new mission statement emphasized intersectional queer and trans anthropology, linking "culturally-constructed categories of gender and sexuality" with "race, class, disability, nationality, colonialism and globalization."

Was this the start of queer anthropology? Indeed, no, not by any reckoning.

The first use I have found of the phrase "queer anthropology" was in 1994, in Florence Babb's published reflection on teaching her course, "Teaching Anthropologies and Sexualities." Babb distinguished between two approaches to the anthropology of sexuality: one more ethnocarto-graphic (in Kath Weston's [1993] term) that sought "descriptions of sexual variability" in cultures around the world; the other a *queer* "analysis of the social construction of sexuality" (Babb 1994, 126). For Babb, *queer* meant "nondominant sexualities that have been marginalized," and *queer anthropology* was anthropology "informed by queer theory and analysis and attentive to cultural difference" (1994, 122–23).

Babb's reflections provide one snapshot of early 1990s queer anthropology. One year before, in 1993, in a review of what she was still ambivalently calling "gay and lesbian anthropology," Kath Weston took a stand for queer anthropology, writing, "In the wake of the deconstruction of homosexuality as an analytic category, the field I have called 'lesbian/gay studies in anthropology' looks much more like queer studies than gay studies as conventionally conceived. If lesbian and gay take a fixed sexual identity, or at least a 'thing' called homosexuality, as their starting point, queer defines itself by its difference from hegemonic ideologies of gender and sexuality" (1993, 348).

Babb and Weston were not alone—many anthropologists embraced the new *queer*. In 1993, for instance, a mere two years after the first use of "queer theory" in print, the T-shirt SOLGA sold at the AAA annual meeting was emblazoned with "QUEER THEORY" above a "cute little queer kinship chart," available in black, white, "pretty in pink," or "lesbian purple" (see figure I.1).

As it emerged in the 1990s across the humanities and humanistic social sciences like anthropology, queer studies heralded a profound skepticism toward stable, cross-historical or cross-cultural identity categories (like "gay"). It advanced a multifaceted analysis of sexuality as it intersected with multiple modes of power, from the most granular level of subject formation to the broadest level of global power and political economy. In anthropology, scholars deconstructed sex, gender, and sexuality across cultures; took up antifoundational critiques of the categories "gay," "lesbian," and "homosexual"; queried the multiple modes of subjectivity that may or may

1993 SOLGA T-SHIRT: QUEER THEORY

ALSO AVAILABLE: THESE NATIVES CAN SPEAK FOR THEMSELVES

INDICATE BELOW: DESIGN (QUEER THEORY, OR THESE NATIVES)
                         SIZE (MED, LG, XL, XXL)
                         QUANTITY (1-?)

colors	design	size	quantity
basic black (white lettering)	_____	_____	_____
basic white (black lettering)	_____	_____	_____
pretty in pink (white lettering)	_____	_____	_____
lesbian purple (white lettering)	_____	_____	_____

I.1   SOLGA's T-shirt order form for the 1993 "QUEER THEORY" shirt and the 1992 "THESE NATIVES . . ." shirt. (*Society of Lesbian and Gay Anthropologists Newsletter* 16[2]: 32)

not rest on sexed and gendered difference; and theorized the challenges of linguistic categorization as concepts, representations, and practices moved across borders.

The first flush of queer anthropology in the 1990s includes Martin Manalansan's (1993, 1995) postcolonial and transnational challenge to "gay" Filipino subjectivities; Gloria Wekker's (1993) analysis of nation, diaspora, and class in Afro-Surinamese *Mati* work; Elizabeth Lapovsky Kennedy and Madeline D. Davis's (1993) oral history of working-class butch/fem lesbians in Buffalo, New York; Rosalind Morris's (1994) critique of Orientalism and Thai sex/gender systems; Deborah Elliston's (1995) antifoundational critique of the category "homosexual" in Melanesia; Lawrence Cohen's (1995) articulation of desire against hetero/homo categorization, inflected through a West/rest binary in India; and David Valentine and Riki Anne Wilchins's (1997) analysis of the queer visibility politics of trans embodiment in the United States (see also Rofel 1999; Kulick 1998; Boellstorff 1999).[2] It includes work on the queer erotics of fieldwork (Newton 1993; Seizer 1995) and volumes such as *Taboo* (Kulick and Willson 1995), *Queerly Phrased* (Livia and Hall 1997), *Female Desires* (Blackwood and Wieringa 1999), and Ellen Lewin and William Leap's canonical trilogy, especially the slightly later *Out in Theory* (2002)—even when their editors explicitly rejected the term *queer* (e.g.,

INTRODUCTION   3

Blackwood and Wieringa 1999, 20–21; Lewin and Leap 2002, 10–12). In the 1990s, *queer*, for many anthropologists, seemed to offer a new way to consider the "wide range of genders, sexualities, and oppositional identities that are emerging in various post-colonial contexts," as Deborah Amory put it (1997, 10 see also Bustos-Aguilar 1995; Povinelli 1994).

Fast forward to today: it is safe to say that queer anthropology has arrived. From courses to book prizes to AQA itself, queer anthropology is a dynamic and growing subfield of contemporary anthropology in and beyond the United States—even as the book you are reading is the first edited volume of its kind.[3] Yet, as the AQA debate might suggest, queer anthropology has its own contested histories and formations, inclusions and exclusions, digressions and deviations. "Far from being a monolithic field of inquiry," Martin Manalansan writes, queer anthropology is "characterized by messy genealogies, incomplete and uncomfortable transitions, divergent strands, and contentious debates" (2016, 596). This volume invites you into the diverse foundations, reorientations, and departures shaping queer anthropology today.

Unsettling Queer: Orientation Points

Why *queer*? As a student of queer theory in the late 1990s, I am partial to Eve Kosofsky Sedgwick's classic definition of queer as "the open mesh of possibilities, gaps, overlaps, dissonances and resonances, lapses and excesses of meaning when the constituent elements of anyone's gender, of anyone's sexuality aren't made (or *can't be* made) to signify monolithically" (1993, 8). My own investments in queer were shaped in relation to these possibilities, excesses, and dissonances—elaborated by José Esteban Muñoz's reading of queer as "that thing that lets us feel that this world is not enough, that indeed something is missing," "the rejection of a here and now and an insistence on potentiality for another world" (2009, 1).

Queer was meant to point beyond or beside identity—specifically gay and lesbian—and instead signify transgression of, resistance to, or exclusion from normativity, especially but not exclusively heteronormativity. From Michael Warner's insight into queer as "resistant to regimes of the normal" (including the "normal business of the academy" [1993, xxvi]) to Cathy Cohen's rereading of queer as a site of racialized and classed deviance (1997), queer focalizes the problem of normativity—sexual/gendered, but also the boundaries of racialization, embodiment, class, and nation—in relation to shifting social institutions. The paradoxes of queer's antinormativities emerge in important analytics like Lisa Duggan's "homonormativity" (2002), Robert McRuer's "crip theory" (2006), Jasbir Puar's "homonationalism" (2007), Scott Morgensen's "settler homonationalism" (2010), C. Riley Snorton's Black/trans (2017), and Zakiyyah Iman Jackson's rereading of the human in an anti-Black world (2020), to name just a few.

Thinking this way, *queer* is less an object of study (a *who* we might study) than an analytic (a *how* to think sexual/gendered norms and power). It is not shorthand or a substitute for LGBTQIIA+ but rather a lens, a provocation, a horizon, or a way of reading. As David Eng, Jack Halberstam, and José Esteban Muñoz note, there is no "proper subject *of* or object *for*" queer studies; it has "no fixed political referent" (2005, 3; see also Eng and Puar 2020). Instead, queer is epistemological: a desire to trouble taken-for-granted assumptions and normativities. As I've written elsewhere, queer, like anthropology, is a project of defamiliarization—it seeks to provide an opening or way to think differently (Weiss 2016a). And yet, even as it has this aspirational orientation toward new, Muñozian queer horizons, queer continues to refer back to its core foundational objects: sex, gender, and sexuality. In this way, queer anthropology can be read both as a critique of gay and lesbian anthropology and as its continuation, especially when it centers same-sex desires, gender transgression, and other forms of queer anti- or nonnormativity rooted in gender and sex/sexuality.[4]

This volume does not straighten out what *queer* can or should mean. Rather, it embraces these divergent threads as what makes queer anthropology *queer*—an intellectually dynamic area of inquiry. *Unsettling Queer Anthropology* is grounded in queer's challenge to identitarian logics that take sexuality as a singular and self-evident category; and it insists that racialization, gender, Indigeneity, nation, and disability are co-constitutive formations. The following chapters show how the *queer* in queer anthropology has served as a provocation to reinvigorate canonical anthropological problematics like kinship, subjectivity, language, and human "nature," while also querying/queering the boundaries of anthropology's proper forms, methodologies, and objects of study. Queer is (or can be) a call to reimagine normative anthropological ways of knowing—to center analyses of how power moves through sex, gender, and sexuality as contingent historical, political, and embodied cultural formations, shaped and reshaped by colonialism, capitalism, and globalization.

INTRODUCTION   5

Even as *Unsettling Queer Anthropology* celebrates three decades—or more—of innovative work in queer anthropology, it also grapples with the ways that queer anthropology—like queer studies and anthropology more broadly—rests on white supremacist and colonial epistemes. As Jenny L. Davis and Krystal A. Smalls write, "As long as our field(s) do not account for anti/Blackness and anti/Nativeness, for colonialism and slavery, for White Supremacy, we are not only analytically and theoretically incomplete but we also enable the perpetuation of these foundational structures by default. So, the question is not, 'are they connected?' but 'how?' and 'since they are connected (and always have been) how do we (anthropologists) dismantle what we have helped create?'" (2021, 277).

This volume takes up queer anthropology—our field and its histories—as a site of *both* queer innovation and possibility *and* coloniality and white supremacy. Some of the threads of this history can be glimpsed in the story of the T-shirt that SOLGA sold in 1992, the one proclaiming THESE NA-TIVES CAN SPEAK FOR THEMSELVES (see figure I.1). The slogan was part of SOLGA's vibrant protest of a panel at the 1992 AAA in San Francisco called "AIDS and the Social Imaginary," which featured "star" anthropologists yet excluded LGBT/queer anthropologists, people with AIDS, and AIDS researchers—in other words, those who had dared study AIDS, sexuality, and queerness before it was acceptable (facing years of homophobia and scholarly delegitimation, including career precarity, harassment, professional scorning, even suicide). As the SOLGA cochairs at the time, Jeffrey Dickemann and Ralph Bolton, wrote in a letter to the AAA president and executive director after the meetings, "The elitism of famous anthropologists arrogating to themselves the role of legitimizing the issues of AIDS for anthropologists, in ignorance or disregard of all the work already undertaken and in process by qualified AIDS researchers, is unconscionable. To our knowledge, none of the participants listed had done work on AIDS, nor were any of the impacted populations represented. . . . Where were the voices of the 'natives' in this session?" They continue:

> It is hard to imagine that in 1992, a session addressing social problems that impact Native Americans or African Americans would have been planned without some participation of members of those groups. Most members of our profession have finally recognized that the "informant," as well as the specialist, has a critical contribution to make to our discourse. But gays and transgendered members of the

discipline have not yet been granted that recognition, a fact reflected in the discrimination against us in anthropological professional life. The "natives" in this case were not only in the discipline, and at the Meetings, but in the very room. And once again we were denied the opportunity to speak for ourselves.[5]

Looking back at this controversy today, it is striking how some of the same problems of power and knowledge are with us, still: from the heteronormativity and white saviorism that bolster anthropology's "star" system; to how whiteness (as queer exceptionalism) undergirds analogical slides from Indigenous to Black to queer; to questions of who might speak "for" whom, and whose knowledge counts as "expert."[6] Grappling with this history might prompt us to explore how the ways we produce our knowledges, even in politically motivated, marginalized, sensitive, and breathtakingly innovative fields like queer anthropology, can continue to work with and within white supremacist and colonial logics that normalize some forms of objectifying and colonial representation, even as they contest others.

In 1993, in the aftermath of the panel and protest, Deb Amory curated a series of reflections on "the future" of queer anthropology in SOLGA's newsletter, asking, in part, "What would a queer critique of anthropology look like?"[7] *Unsettling Queer Anthropology* takes up this question thirty years later. In the context of newly (re)vitalized calls to reckon with the white supremacy and settler logics that continue to shape our discipline, this volume considers both a queer critique of anthropology and a critical queer anthropology.

What does that queer critique look like?[8] In the chapters that follow, although each chapter takes a critical approach to queer anthropology, there is no single line on what that might mean. Some contributors reach back to what Jafari S. Allen (2016) has called the "decolonizing stream" of Black, Indigenous, feminist/queer anthropology, which finds an important precedent in Faye V. Harrison's (1991) volume *Decolonizing Anthropology*. Some explore the edges of what Savannah Shange (2019) has called "abolition anthropology," a call for an anthropology so transformed as to no longer *be* anthropology. Some take up antifoundational critiques of "anthropology of" epistemologies, queering ethnographic method and practice to refuse knowledge projects of extraction and the objectification of our "objects of study." Some explore what queer anthropology looks like when it centers different political-intellectual genealogies, including Black feminism, transnational postcolonial theory, Indigenous critique, crip of color critique, and

INTRODUCTION   7

feminist nature/culture theory. Others consider a queer anthropology that might refuse English and Euro-American hegemonic epistemes; follow Black theory to reconsider relationality; foreground anthropology's political responsibility to our interlocutors and communities; take up queer, postcolonial, and Indigenous critiques of the nation-state; and highlight vitality or the unruliness of life against static or objectifying epistemologies. Decades after Kath Weston's crucial critique of "ethnocartography," which marked a turn toward a *queer* anthropology (see below), many authors critically reappraise problematics of difference/sameness: how queer anthropology wrestles with its legacy of providing exotic/erotic difference that might be thickly described for others.[9] These are not discrete endeavors; many contributors take up both/and to surface other ways of doing anthropology that might be in better alignment with our political, ethical, and intellectual desires, and perhaps do (more) justice to our objects of study (see Wiegman 2012). *Queer* and *anthropology* take many forms in the chapters that follow, but each contributor, in different ways, seeks to disrupt the normalized racism and settler colonial logics that undergird our epistemologies—to unsettle the grounds of a white- and US-centered theory and practice of anthropology.

In my invitation to each contributor, I shared my desire for a volume that would center critical, queer of color, and decolonizing approaches to queer anthropology.[10] While the resulting volume explores the contours of queer and trans lives in Cuba, Canada, India, China, Brazil, Indonesia, the Philippines, Thailand, Iran, Turkey, Ghana, Haiti, Wet'suwet'en First Nation, and the United States, among other locales, my focus was not on representational regional expertise, world atlas-style. Instead, I invited anthropologists whose work attends to the ways sex, gender, and sexuality retain multiple relations to power—including the normative operations of the discipline, which often marginalizes critical perspectives from Black, Indigenous, and other anthropologists of color, and from scholars working in postcolonial, feminist, crip, and trans studies. And even as I hoped to refuse queer anthropology as usual, I also hoped each chapter would reimagine crucial topics and analytics—not so much to "review" them as to rethink what *queer* can do—in ways useful, provocative, and generative to budding and experienced queer anthropologists alike. *Queer* as topic, theme, approach, method, way of reading, way of being, refusal, politics, ethics, pleasure, field of contestation—these multiple, overlapping models of *queer*, grounded in feminist, postcolonial, Indigenous, Black, and queer of color critique, unsettle the grounds of queer anthropology. The resulting volume shows how *queer* and *anthropology* both contest and perpetuate colonialism, racism, capitalism, xenophobia, heteropatriarchy, ableism, and cisnormativity. Its chapters illuminate queer anthropology's brilliance, its interventions and insights, even as they emphasize the need for queer anthropology to continue to reckon with legacies of white supremacy, settler colonialism, extractive modes of knowledge production, and normative assumptions of embodiment within anthropology and beyond it.

From "Flora and Fauna" to Queer: Queer Anthropology's Prehistories

Before we dive in, however, I'll back up to give a brief history of queer anthropology's prehistory—the crucial context for this volume. Following Andrew Lyons and Harriet Lyons's (2004) history of the anthropology of sexuality, I start the story before the founding of anthropology proper, with Victorian-era social evolutionism and scientific racism, in which fantasies of "primitive sexuality" and concerns about "miscegenation" guided colonial governmental, ethnological, medical, and missionary reports about "sexuality." What Kath Weston characterized as the "flora and fauna" approaches of colonial-era anthropology (1998) located the core of inferiority in the "exotic sexual customs" of purportedly "primitive" Others (Fitzgerald 1977, 386). As anthropology institutionalized in the academy between 1880 and 1910, what Michel Foucault (1990) would call a *scientia sexualis* took up and transformed earlier understandings of "primitive sexuality." Work such as Edward Carpenter's (1914) *Intermediate Types among Primitive Folk*, or "Homosexual Love" (1917) by Edward Westermarck (Bronislaw Malinowski's teacher) simultaneously challenged a singular understanding of sex, gender, and sexuality *and* relied on and bolstered colonial racist typologies that projected ideas about promiscuity, inversion, and morality onto Others elsewhere.

In the 1920s and 1930s, a brief flourishing of interest in sexuality and gender included well-known scholarship like Margaret Mead's (1928) *Coming of Age in Samoa*, Malinowski's (1929) *The Sexual Life of Savages in North-Western Melanesia*, and E. E. Evans-Pritchard's 1920s research on woman-woman marriage among the Azande (published in 1970), as well as work by others such as Ruth Benedict, Ruth Landes, Georges Devereux, and Cora Du Bois. As "flora and fauna" approaches waned, cross-cultural surveys of sexual behavior emphasized sexual variation beyond Euro-American norms. Not yet an autonomous "field," studies of "sex" or "sexuality" (often as gender) appeared in a range of approaches—British functionalist, American culture and personality, ethnopsychiatric, structuralist—sometimes, as Fitzgerald put it, as "titillating bits of sexual esoterica . . . to spice up an otherwise 'dry' research report" (1977, 391). Simultaneously groundbreaking, conceptually sophisticated, essentialist, and colonialist, this work tended to view "homosexuality" or "sex drive" as universal and transhistorical in essence (see Vance 1991), even as it attended to a range of "exotic" sexual customs or attitudes in ways paradigmatic of what Michel-Rolph Trouillot called the "savage slot" as a foil of "Western" sexuality, morality, and civilization (2003).

Lyons and Lyons describe the 1930s through the 1960s as a relatively quiet period, during which studies of sexuality (and gender) were "subsumed into other projects," such as kinship or culture and personality studies (2011, 5). Vance (1991) and Weston (1998) similarly argue that, in this period, sexuality became an unrecognized center of canonical "non-sexual" anthropological topics—a form of what queer theorist Eve Kosofsky Sedgwick (1990) would later characterize as queer's minoritizing/universalizing dynamic. In these years, those who focused on the study of (homo)sexuality or trans/gender expressions more centrally—especially LGBT anthropologists—were subject to professional scorn and virulent homo- and transphobia.

It was in this context that the organization now called AQA was founded. As AQA notes on its website:

> Folk narratives place the very first beginnings at San Diego, in 1970. It was an era when academic conventions across the country were characterized by protests, walk outs, sit ins and demonstrations. In 1970, women's rights, Chicano rights, and homosexual rights were all topics of resolutions at the AAA annual meeting. According to reports, Clark Taylor stood in the business meeting, chained to another man, and announced a resolution on homosexuality.

In 1971, three resolutions were passed, demands that the AAA recognize the "legitimacy and immediate importance" of research on homosexuality and stand against homophobia ("homoerotophobia").[11] Informal organizing gave way to the formal founding of ARGOH—Anthropology Research Group on Homosexuality—in 1979. ARGOH's first convener and chair was Kenneth

Read; its mission was to advance and legitimate research on homosexuality and counter the heteronormativity of the discipline. While founded by and dominated by men for its first few years, early members included luminaries of lesbian/queer and feminist anthropology: Ellen Lewin, Esther Newton, Carole Vance, Unni Wikan, Liz Kennedy, Gayle Rubin, and Evelyn Blackwood. Blackwood was the first woman cochair of ARGOH; her groundbreaking (1985) collection *Anthropology and Homosexual Behavior* sought to advance anthropological analysis of the "cultural construction of homosexual behavior," noting that substantive "ethnographic and theoretical analysis" was lacking—especially of women and lesbians (2).

Through these interventions, the cross-cultural study of homosexuality, long treated with a combination of prurient titillation and scholarly contempt, became, in the 1980s, both a (quasi)valid research area within anthropology and potentially useful outside of it, fodder to "directly address contemporary gay political issues" at home (Lyons and Lyons 2004, 293–94). Illustrating the prevalence of same-sex sexualities and gender nonnormative roles through cross-cultural comparison had an impact on nascent gay and trans activism and political imaginations in the United States (and beyond). And yet, as Kath Weston argues, some work in what would become "gay and lesbian anthropology" in the 1980s tended toward "ethnocartography": "looking for evidence of same-sex sexuality and gendered ambiguity in 'other societies,'" an approach that treated concepts like "homosexuality" as stable, portable, and universal (1993, 341). At the same time, throughout the 1970s and 1980s, there were important debates within gay and lesbian anthropology on the relationship between gender and sex/sexuality, feminist critiques of the anthropology of sexuality, and warnings about the relevance of Euro-American terms like "homosexuality" to non-Western societies.[12] Lyons and Lyons locate the transformation of ARGOH to SOLGA (the Society of Lesbian and Gay Anthropologists) in 1987 as part of this shift away from the more clinical, "objective" or "scientific" language of "homosexuality" toward a more political stance informed by feminist and gay and lesbian rights movements.

We might pause here, at the dawn of the 1990s and what would become queer anthropology. As Weston writes, the 1990s saw the "deconstruction of homosexuality as an analytic category," leaving questions about what it is we mean by *sexuality* and *gender* as deeply cultural classifications that connect to power, normativities, erotics, practices, and more (1993, 348). As an aspirational intervention, *queer* was meant to break from what

INTRODUCTION   11

Weston called ethnocartography and what Tom Boellstorff calls the "logic of enumeration"—the presumption "that concepts name preexisting entities and relations" (2007b, 19). Both are knowing-as-owning colonialist epistemologies (ethnocartography is mapping as knowing; the logic of enumeration is naming as knowing); and both regularize the anthropologist's gaze on an "Other" as object and frontier: "data on the half shell," as Weston put it, "pure content" awaiting our discovery and collection like "driftwood on the beach" (1998, 21). *Queer*, instead, opens up sexuality itself as a contested field of power and knowledge. As we consider the transition from ARGOH (a more detached study *on* homosexuality) to SOLGA (a more political and identitarian society *of* lesbian and gay anthropologists) to, finally, AQA (an association *for* queer anthropology), we see a move into queer as not only a break with "on" and "of," but also into the aspirational desire "for" a queer(er) anthropology.

And yet one danger of rendering over one hundred years into a linear capsule history is that it might seem to present queer anthropology as the apex of progress—a shining future in which we have left behind the racisms of our past. What of colonial-era object-making, complex transits between "us" and "other," or the use/abuse of comparative exotica today? Where are the political investments in *queer* working with, and against, this history? How and when must we revisit earlier work to find resonances and legacies with which we must still reckon?

Kadji Amin (2020) argues that as long as we seek to move beyond queer theory's formative exclusions without working through them, we will be doomed to repeat them. I think, too, about Michael Hames-García's critique of queer theory's canonical origin story, one that consolidates the whiteness of *queer* by locating Black, postcolonial, and women of color interventions as derivative or peripheral, rather than preceding and formative. Amin and Hames-García foreground how genealogies are political and how revisiting their legacies might give rise to different futures. And so although I have provided a more or less canonical history of queer anthropology— moving from colonial era pre-anthropology flora and fauna, to anthropology of homosexuality, to gay and lesbian anthropology, and then finally to queer—that straight narrative is bent in the volume that follows. Contributors attend to different critical genealogies that open other possibilities for queer anthropology's futures—sometimes leaning in to the break that *queer* seeks, sometimes finding *queer* elsewhere and otherwise.

Volume Overview

This volume has three sections: (1) "Foundations: Queer Anthropology's Contested Genealogies"; (2) "Reorientations: Queering the Anthropological Canon"; and (3) "Departures: Reworlding Queer Anthropology." The three chapters in "Foundations" explore queer anthropology's multiple and contested genealogies, including legacies often obscured. They consider histories of queer anthropology beyond or beside canonical frameworks, as well as the displacements and racial and colonial legacies that queer anthropology has inherited. The five chapters in "Reorientations" put a queer spin on some of cultural anthropology's most enduring topics and thematics: kinship and family, cross-cultural comparison, language, culturally constructed gender, performance/performativity, the culture concept and the transnational turn, the scape/scale of globalization, nationalism and geopolitics, and human rights and the state. They show both what queer anthropology has contributed to these canonical topics and how queer critique might reorient, challenge, and transform them. The six chapters in "Departures" experiment with queer reworldings and relations beyond the normative parameters of ethnography. They consider how a queer anthropology grounded in Black/queer study, trans vitalities, crip epistemologies, more-than-human queer ecologies, Indigenous sovereignty and land activism, and the unfinished edges of the infra-ordinary might reshape ethnographic praxis toward community accountability, horizontality, and collaboration with wider webs of relation beyond the field, the discipline, or the university.

Foundations: Queer Anthropology's Contested Genealogies

The volume opens with Jafari Sinclaire Allen's "The Anthropology of 'What Is Utterly Precious': Black Feminist Habits of Mind and the Object (and Ends) of Anthropology." Allen shows how the Black intellectual tradition, and in particular radical Black feminist and lesbian intellectuals, artists, and activists, offer an alternative methodology, analysis, and theorization of anthropology as what Marlon Riggs called "the unending search for what is utterly precious." This is an embodied, intersectional, ethical ethnography outside of the disciplinary enclosure of professionalized "Anthropology" and its Eurocentric canon, in solidarity with Black queer lives across borders.

The next chapter is my own, "Queer Theories from Somewhere: Situated Knowledges and Other Queer Empiricisms." I reframe the canonical origin story of queer anthropology by disrupting the hierarchical binary of queer theory (from the humanities, and purportedly universal, unsituated, portable) and ethnographic data (from the social sciences, and particular, emplaced, a-theoretical) to show not only that queer theory depends on prior queer anthropology, but also that queer theory's disavowal of empiricism has effaced both its own historical situatedness and its accountability to its subjects and sources. Aiming to dislodge the universalist aspirations that produce queer theory's canonical white- and American-ness, I read a genealogy of situated, queerly empirical theory back in to queer theory.

The final chapter in "Foundations" moves further back into the social science of sexuality. Scott L. Morgensen's "Intimate Methods: Reflections on Racial and Colonial Legacies within Sexual Social Science" shows how, even as a primitivist, racializing, and colonialist ethnocartography gave way to a deracialized modernist ethnography, the "intimacies" of sexuality, social science, race, and colonialism (in Lisa Lowe's terms [2015]) continued to produce a white, gay, Western/Euro-American liberal sexual subject as the subject of freedom. Morgensen explores the obscured intimacies of racism, white supremacy, class, and colonialism that condition and inflect the very formation of the category "sexuality" and its modern subject.

Each "Foundations" chapter tells a different part of the story of queer anthropology. Allen explores how Black gay and lesbian radical intellectual traditions in and outside the academy that predate the 1990s "queer turn" might offer better collective, ethical, and aesthetic models for anthropological attention, engagement, and representation. My chapter challenges the displacements embedded in the commonly told origin story that queer anthropology emerged from anthropologists' application of 1990s humanities-based queer theory to our particular ethnographic locales, and rereads queer theory as grounded in queer empiricism. Morgensen's chapter shows how queer anthropology must reckon with the racial and colonial epistemological legacies of sexual social science methodologies that produce modern sexual subjectivity as what Roderick Ferguson has called the "one dimensional queer" (2019). Taken together, the section reexamines queer anthropology's foundations, displacing some canonical histories and legacies to enact other formations.

Reorientations: Queering the Anthropological Canon

The five chapters in "Reorientations" explore queer critiques of canonical topics and approaches in anthropology. The section starts from the insight that sex and sexuality have been central to anthropology since its inception; as Cymene Howe writes, "anthropology has always been a little bit 'queer'" (2015, 752). Yet if sexuality/gender is at the heart of foundational anthropological concepts like kinship, subjectivity, age grade, religion, morality, primitive versus civilized, and cultural difference/variation (see also Weston 1998), "one could also argue that the discipline of anthropology has been quite un-queer" (Howe 2015, 752). Howe is pointing to the illegitimacy faced by scholars who work more directly on queer and trans topics (as discussed above), but we might wish to consider as "un-queer" the normative orientations of these fields of study: often heteropatriarchal, cisnormative, ablebodied, ethnocartographic or voyeuristic, colonialist, white, and American- and Western-centered. This section asks: How might queer critique reorient these canonical areas?

The section starts with Lucinda Ramberg's "Kinship and Kinmaking Otherwise." Ramberg gives new life to the "tired" topic of kinship, rethinking relatedness beyond the intelligible. Beginning from the insight that the classificatory schemas of kinship have long been central to discourses of "civilization," Ramberg denaturalizes a white, colonial, and heterosexual matrix to illuminate kinmaking as a social and material practice intimately intertwined with race, gender, and sexuality. Putting contemporary interventions from Black, feminist, queer, postcolonial, and Indigenous critiques into critical conversation with canonical figures, Ramberg reorients the study of kinmaking as a site of both exclusion and queer worldmaking.

The next chapter, "Pronoun Trouble: Notes on Radical Gender Inclusion in English," by Tom Boellstorff, outlines—in a playful, provisional list form—a queer/feminist argument for replacing *she* and *he* pronouns with the epicene (nongendered) *they*. Boellstorff queers one of anthropology's longest-standing analytics—the comparative method—to denaturalize a political horizon dominated by English-language hegemony. Combining intralinguistic comparison (including the long history of the epicene *they* in English) and interlinguistic comparison (between English and the many epicene languages, including Chinese, Finnish, Ojibwe, and Indonesian), Boellstorff's provocation brings structural linguistics into conversation with queer/feminist theory to challenge contemporary gender exclusionary politics.

Brian A. Horton's "Stylization in the Flesh: Queer Anthropology and Performance" takes up performance as the stylized and embodied cultural construction of gender. Thinking across performance studies, queer of color critique, and anthropology, Horton emphasizes self-presentation and -determination: how people endure, play with, make beauty from, and live categories of race, class, gender, and sexuality. Following queer of color critique, Horton calls for accountability to the material lives of our interlocutors, rejecting the discursive figuration of dissident genders and sexualities (like the *travesti*, *hijra*, or drag queen) as symbols of transgression, and instead reorienting queer ethnographers toward performance as a grounded repertoire of embodied critique.

In "Worldly Power and Local Alterity: Transnational Queer Anthropology," Ara Wilson unpacks the "transnational" in transnational queer studies, considering the spatial scales of sexual/gendered variation beyond ideas of "culture" as discrete, local, or bounded by nation-states. Wilson explores the multiplicity of queer and trans life on the ground—attending to scales, spaces, and circulations, including the archipelagic, diasporic, and regional. Against work in queer studies that risks reproducing Western hegemony *through* a critique of its domination (via flows of Euro-American capital, media, activism, etc.), she considers transnational queer alterity beyond both Western *and* non-Western hegemonic constructions.

The final chapter in this section, Sima Shakhsari's "Queer States: Geopolitics and Queer Anthropology," focuses on the civilizational narratives of international human rights and refugee regimes. Shakhsari shows how the geopolitical deployment of sexuality in the name of purportedly universal LGBT rights reifies liberal and Eurocentric sexual/gender identities, vilifying "queered" third world states as unruly and sexually perverse. They call for a queer postcolonial anthropology of the state that decouples "queer" from LGBT identity and attends to homonational geopolitics, revealing the contradictions of interventions (such as sanctions and wars) that, in seeking to straighten queered states in the name of LGBT rights, punish their most marginalized populations.

The chapters in "Reorientations" highlight the contributions queer anthropology makes to foundational anthropological problematics: kinship, comparison, gender, culture, difference, nationalism, geopolitics, West/rest. They open up fresh new interpretations of these thematics by reorientating them toward feminist and queer of color, postcolonial, and transnational/ Global South critiques grounded in non-Euro-American, non-white epistemologies of queerness. As a whole, the section decenters purportedly universal concepts and configurations of difference while advancing a distinctively *queer* anthropology.

Departures: Reworlding Queer Anthropology

The six chapters in "Departures" queer ethnographic epistemology, considering relational practices, accountabilities, and worlds beyond anthropology's normative model of knowledge production: the anthropologist (distanced, disciplined, autonomous, expert) and their (human, bounded, subordinate) object of study. The section starts with "Black Queer Anthropology Roundtable: Speculations on Activating Ethnographic Practice in and for Community," curated by Shaka McGlotten and featuring Black queer anthropologists Lyndon Gill, Marshall Green, Nikki Lane, and Kwame Otu. In this wide-ranging conversation about art, activism, and Black study (Moten and Harney 2013) as abolitionist practice, McGlotten, Gill, Green, Lane, and Otu consider the possibilities of a Black queer anthropology beyond the enclosures of the neoliberal academy and beyond ethnography as a method of capture/consumption of queer, racialized difference. They look toward a Black/queer nonuniversity: open to the world, in relation with and accountable to community.

In "The Subject of Trans Lives and Vitalities: Queer and Trans Anthropological Object-Making," Elijah Adiv Edelman challenges "transgender" as an object of study in academic research and global LGBT rights activism. Edelman argues for "trans vitalities" as a model of participatory, activist, and coalitional research that centers lived experience at the intersection of race and class as the basis for knowledge, and forefronts the messy contradictions of trans life-making, rather than neat, researcher-derived categories like "the trans community." Arguing that research and activism "on" trans play a powerful role in categorizing lives as either livable or disposable, Edelman argues that trans knowledges must benefit and be held accountable to their subjects.

Erin L. Durban's "Doing It Together: A Queer Case for Cripping Ethnography" takes up anthropology's ableism, noting that while disability sometimes shows up as an object of study or theoretical insight, traditional ethnographic fieldwork relies on a normate bodymind and an ableist, white, colonialist model of anthropological knowledge production: "a single researcher using their own hypermobility to navigate informants' immobilities." Durban makes the case for a more promiscuous queer/crip methodology, providing examples of accessible, mixed-ability, collaborative ethnography. They argue that challenging *how* we do our work, making space for queer disabled anthropologists, is a necessary step toward a decolonial, antiracist, anticapitalist, feminist, *and* anti-ableist anthropology.

In "When Our Tulips Speak Together: More-Than-Human Queer Natures," Juno Salazar Parreñas considers multispecies ethnography as a way into sexual/gender diversity among nonhuman life forms: queer sexualities, trans embodiments, and asexual modes of reproduction among tulips, apes, slime mold, starfish, bears, primates, and more. Parreñas urges queer and feminist anthropology to move beyond a suspicion of biology and instead consider how thinking with nonhuman life forms opens up new critiques of hetero- and cisnormativity. Parreñas pursues queer ecology without biological essentialism, an approach to more-than-human life that revels in the queer diversity of life forms on earth.

Anne Spice's "Queer (Re)generations: Disrupting Apocalypse Time" considers the Indigenous land defense movement against oil and gas pipelines as a site of relations beyond compulsory heterosexual monogamy and the straight time of extractive capitalism and settler colonialism. Grounded in her ethnography/activism at the Unist'ot'en Camp on Wet'suwet'en Territory, Spice explores intersections of queer and Indigenous temporality as they point to alternative futures "at the end of the world." Linking ethnography and activism, Spice finds land defenders and water protectors model a sovereign, queer, Indigenous future that centers reciprocity, accountability, and responsibility to the land, earth, and plant and animal kin, against the straight, capitalist/colonial time of resource extraction.

Finally, Martin F. Manalansan IV's "The Queer Endotic: Experiments on the Infra-ordinary (Or seeds for a worlding)," the last chapter in this volume, considers the small, the fleeting, and the infra-ordinary as modes of attention that might reworld queer anthropology. Manalansan attends to the unfinished form of queerness, the affective, visceral, embodied modes of attention that shape not only queer anthropology, but also ordinary queer lives (our own included). Manalansan's attention to process, affect, and form grounds queer anthropology in the quotidian rather than a more spectacular exotic, offering less a "finished, complete set of methods, concepts, theories, and arguments, and more an experimental and inspirational resource for thinking, building, and living" in our precarious present and toward our uncertain future.

These six chapters imagine the practice of queer anthropology otherwise, resituated in a mesh of relations and responsibilities that exceed the field or discipline, the academy, or a human-centered community. Drawing from the undercommons of Black/queer study, reckoning with accountability for trans life-making, exploring collaborative crip methods that decenter the lone (white, able-bodied, male) fieldworker, celebrating other-than-human queer life forms, living toward Indigenous nonheteronormative futures, and reflecting on quotidian forms of queer life, this section shows how a Black, trans, crip, feminist, Indigenous, queer of color-centered queer anthropology provides models for reworlding anthropology.

As I make the final edits on this introduction, I note that *Unsettling Queer Anthropology* was written and edited between January 2020 and May 2023, high pandemic times. The real costs of our labors were evident in its making, for every one of its queer contributors, and especially for disabled, Black, Indigenous, and trans scholars, scholars who are parents and transnational immigrants, and others who face uneven burdens of carework in and out of the academy. This time of crisis ordinary and exceptional impacted all those who wrote for the volume, as well as those who needed to bow out partway through, and those who regretfully were unable to accept my invitation. I'll end this introduction as Manalansan begins his chapter—"I aim to offer an embodied sense of queerness as a vulnerable refuge, a refusal, a placeless nowhere-ishness, and a hopeful elsewhere-ishness . . . a queerness that is tacitly embedded in these uncertain scenes and precarious times"—in the hopes that such an "unfinished and open-ended" queer anthropology might, as Manalansan writes, serve as a "resource for thinking, building, and living."

Unsettling Queer Anthropology is part of an ongoing conversation about queer anthropology's histories and futures. In its pages, you will find interventions, disagreements, passionate engagements, reorientations, refusals, deviations, and departures. Let this be an invitation to all those who desire another *queer* anthropology.

Notes

1 The role of *trans* vis-à-vis *queer* has a longer and complex history in anthropology, where (often Indigenous) gender "inversion" *was* queerness. Thomas Fitzgerald writes in his 1977 review of "anthropological research on homosexuality" that previous scholars took a "disproportionate" interest in "the so-called berdache (loosely defined as any individual who assumes the role and/or status of the opposite sex)," an interest that, to Fitzgerald, reflected analytical confusion between gender and sexuality (387, 389). For more on the misuse of Indigenous gender categories within anthropology, see Towle and Morgan 2002, Morgensen 2011, Davis 2014, and Laing 2021. David Sonenschein, ten years earlier (and pointing at Alfred Kroeber), wrote that "some speak of berdache, transvestitism, and homosexuality as all one and the same thing" (1966, 76). Even as the model of "inversion" waned, questions around cross-cultural "trans" categories—sometimes glossed as "cross-dressing," "third gender," "transvestitism," or "effeminacy"—remained a (if not the) central topic in the (still quite sparse) anthropology of homosexuality. As David Valentine shows, this reflects a larger cultural history of the relationship between sex, gender, and sexuality, where "queer" *is* simultaneously "trans" and yet "trans" is the secondary, excluded category (2007; see also Edelman 2021).

2 As I hope will become clear, there is not a strict dividing line between the "gay and lesbian" anthropology of the 1980s and the "queer" anthropology of the 1990s, and certainly some earlier work—for instance, Esther Newton's (1972) *Mother Camp* or Gayle Rubin's (1993; originally published in 1984) "Thinking Sex" (both of which I take up in chapter 2)—might be considered "queer." Yet, for the purposes of an initial timeline, I focus on queer after 1990.

3 For prior reviews and analysis of queer anthropology, see Weston 1993, 1998; Morris 1995; Boellstorff 2007a, 2007b; Howe 2015; Weiss 2016a, 2016b, 2022; and Wilson 2019. For a short introduction, see Society for Cultural Anthropology's (2018) podcast "AnthroBites: What Is Queer Anthropology?" See also *Cultural Anthropology*'s two special sections on queer anthropology (Boellstorff and Howe 2015; Manalansan 2016).

4 I've characterized this as queer's constitutive polarity in Weiss 2022. Crucial analyses of the tension between a more expansive (racialized, classed, gendered, national) queer and a narrower (sex/gender) queer include C. Cohen 1997, Hames-García 2011, Mikdashi and Puar 2016, Gill 2018, and Ferguson 2019.

5 Letter from January 19, 1993, reprinted in a 1993 issue of *Society of Lesbian and Gay Anthropologists Newsletter* 15(1): 21–23.

6   For more on the panel and protest, see especially Deb Amory's feature story "The 1992 AAA Panel from Hell: AIDS and the Social Imaginary" (1993), in *Society of Lesbian and Gay Anthropologists Newsletter* 15(1): 20–32. The analogical slide of Native:queer should be read in conversation with concurrent complaints about SOLGA's whiteness. These are issues with which SOLGA had long wrestled—in the pages of its newsletter, at meetings, and at moments such as when Karen Nakamura (as a graduate student) ran for cochair of SOLGA first as the "male cochair" and then as the "female cochair" to "emphasize issues of inclusiveness for bisexuals, people of color, and people with disabilities," asking, "What steps will it take for the organization to be more inclusive?" (*Society of Lesbian and Gay Anthropologists Newsletter* 19(2): 3).

7   *Society of Lesbian and Gay Anthropologists Newsletter* 15(2): 26.

8   I take "critique" as generative, mobilizing—not what Ryan Cecil Jobson called a liberal "fix," where queerness elides or excuses coloniality and white supremacy (2020; see also Morgensen 2011). Indeed, these chapters illuminate "intimacy" (Lowe 2015) with global, historical interrelations as a way to contend with, rather than refuse, the complicities that shape our research, writing, and work (see also Allen and Jobson 2016).

9   For a critique of Geertzian "thick description" as a form of ethnographic mastery, see J. Jackson 2013. Queer anthropology is both central to the history of exotic/erotic representations of difference or Otherness and, because of its relationship to gay and lesbian anthropology, historically shaped by a search for others "like us"—a projected sameness that is sometimes appropriated into political projects at "home." Work on "sex in the field" has taken up this sameness/difference paradox; for recent takes, see Martin and Haller 2019 and Weiss 2020.

10 I cautiously use "decolonizing" to refer to work in line with the approaches outlined above (and in this volume)—both acknowledging that, as Eve Tuck and Wayne Yang (2012) argue, "decolonizing" is too often an empty promise without a commitment to Indigenous sovereignty or institutional change *and* that the project of decolonizing anthropology has a long genealogy in work by Black, Indigenous, queer, disabled, trans, and feminist anthropologists of color, which should not be sidelined (even as some have refused anthropology as a site for such work).

11 The full text of all three AAA resolutions are in *Anthropology News* 12(1) (1971), as well as the first issue of the *Society of Lesbian and Gay Anthropologists Newsletter* (1979). Resolution 11 encouraged research and training about homosexuality; Resolution 12 opposed homophobia within the discipline and discussed heteronormativity as "ethnocentrism"; and Resolution

13 put AAA "on record as urging the immediate legalization of all consensual sexual acts."

12 Important reviews and collections of gay and lesbian anthropology from various time periods include Lewin and Leap 1996, 2002, 2009; Robertson 2005; Fitzgerald 1977; Blackwood 1985; Weston 1993, 1998; Blackwood and Wieringa 1999; Rubin 2002; and Boellstorff 2007b. See also note 3.

References

Allen, Jafari Sinclaire. 2016. "One View from a Deterritorialized Realm: How Black/Queer Renarrativizes Anthropological Analysis." *Cultural Anthropology* 31(4): 617–26.

Allen, Jafari Sinclaire, and Ryan Cecil Jobson. 2016. "The Decolonizing Generation: (Race and) Theory in Anthropology since the Eighties." *Current Anthropology* 57(2): 129–48.

Amin, Kadji. 2020. "Genealogies of Queer Theory." In *The Cambridge Companion to Queer Studies*, edited by Siobhan B. Somerville, 17–29. Cambridge: Cambridge University Press.

Amory, Deborah P. 1997. "'Homosexuality' in Africa: Issues and Debates." *Issue: A Journal of Opinion* 25(1): 5–10.

Babb, Florence E. 1994. "Teaching Anthropologies and Sexualities." *Feminist Teacher* 8(3): 119–26.

Blackwood, Evelyn, ed. 1985. *Anthropology and Homosexual Behavior*. New York: Haworth.

Blackwood, Evelyn, and Saskia Wieringa. 1999. *Female Desires: Same-Sex Relations and Transgender Practices across Cultures*. New York: Columbia University Press.

Boellstorff, Tom, 1999. "The Perfect Path: Gay Men, Marriage, Indonesia." *GLQ: A Journal of Lesbian and Gay Studies* 5(4): 475–509.

Boellstorff, Tom. 2007a. *A Coincidence of Desires: Anthropology, Queer Studies, Indonesia*. Durham, NC: Duke University Press.

Boellstorff, Tom. 2007b. "Queer Studies in the House of Anthropology." *Annual Review of Anthropology* 36(1): 17–35.

Boellstorff, Tom, and Cymene Howe. 2015, July 21. "Queer Futures." Theorizing the Contemporary, *Cultural Anthropology* Fieldsights. https://culanth.org/fieldsights/series/queer-futures.

Bustos-Aguilar, Pedro. 1995. "Mister Don't Touch the Banana: Notes on the Popularity of the Ethnosexed Body South of the Border." *Critique of Anthropology* 15(2): 149–70.

Carpenter, Edward. 1914. *Intermediate Types among Primitive Folk: A Study in Social Evolution*. London: G. Allen.

Cohen, Cathy J. 1997. "Punks, Bulldaggers, and Welfare Queens: The Radical Potential of Queer Politics?" *GLQ: A Journal of Lesbian and Gay Studies* 3(4): 437–65.

Cohen, Lawrence. 1995. "Holi in Banaras and the *Mahaland* of Modernity." *GLQ: A Journal of Lesbian and Gay Studies* 2(4): 399–424.

Davis, Jenny L. 2014. "'More Than Just 'Gay Indians': Intersecting Articulations of Two-Spirit Gender, Sexuality, and Indigenousness." In *Queer Excursions: Retheorizing Binaries in Language, Gender, and Sexuality*, edited by Jenny Davis, Joshua Raclaw, and Lal Zimman, 62–80. Oxford: Oxford University Press.

Davis, Jenny L., and Krystal A. Smalls. 2021. "Dis/possession Afoot: American (Anthropological) Traditions of Anti-Blackness and Coloniality." *Journal of Linguistic Anthropology* 31(2): 275–82.

Duggan, Lisa. 2002. "The New Homonormativity: The Sexual Politics of Neoliberalism." In *Materializing Democracy: Toward a Revitalized Cultural Politics*, edited by Russ Castronovo and Dana D. Nelson, 175–94. Durham, NC: Duke University Press.

Edelman, Elijah Adiv. 2021. *Trans Vitalities: Mapping Ethnographies of Trans Social and Political Coalitions*. London: Routledge.

Elliston, Deborah A. 1995. "Erotic Anthropology: 'Ritualized Homosexuality' in Melanesia and Beyond." *American Ethnologist* 22(4): 848–67.

Eng, David L., and Jasbir K. Puar. 2020. "Introduction: Left of Queer." *Social Text* 38(4): 1–24.

Eng, David L., Jack Halberstam, and José Esteban Muñoz. 2005. "Introduction: What's Queer about Queer Studies Now?" *Social Text* 23 (3–4 [84–85]): 1–17.

Evans-Pritchard, Edward E. 1970. "Sexual Inversion among the Azande." *American Anthropologist* 72(6): 1428–34.

Ferguson, Roderick. 2019. *One Dimensional Queer*. Cambridge: Polity Press.

Fitzgerald, Thomas K. 1977. "A Critique of Anthropological Research on Homosexuality." *Journal of Homosexuality* 2(4): 385–97.

Foucault, Michel. 1990. *The History of Sexuality: An Introduction*. Translated by R. Hurley. New York: Vintage.

Gill, Lyndon K. 2018. *Erotic Islands: Art and Activism in the Queer Caribbean*. Durham, NC: Duke University Press.

Hames-García, Michael. 2011. "Queer Theory Revisited." In *Gay Latino Studies: A Critical Reader*, edited by Michael Hames-García and Ernesto Javier Martínez, 19–45. Durham, NC: Duke University Press.

Harrison, Faye V., ed. 1991. *Decolonizing Anthropology: Moving Further toward an Anthropology for Liberation*. Washington, DC: American Anthropological Association.

Howe, Cymene. 2015. "Queer Anthropology." In *International Encyclopedia of the Social and Behavioral Sciences*, 2nd edition, edited by James D. Wright, 752–58. Amsterdam: Elsevier.

Jackson, John L., Jr. 2013. *Thin Description: Ethnography and the African Hebrew Israelites of Jerusalem*. Cambridge, MA: Harvard University Press.

Jackson, Zakiyyah Iman. 2020. *Becoming Human: Matter and Meaning in an Antiblack World*. New York: New York University Press.

Jobson, Ryan C. 2020. "The Case for Letting Anthropology Burn: Sociocultural Anthropology in 2019." *American Anthropologist* 122(2): 259–71.

Kennedy, Elizabeth Lapovsky, and Madeline D. Davis. 1993. *Boots of Leather, Slippers of Gold: The History of a Lesbian Community*. New York: Routledge.

Kulick, Don. 1998. *Travesti: Sex, Gender, and Culture among Brazilian Transgendered Prostitutes*. Chicago: University of Chicago Press.

Kulick, Don, and Margaret Willson. 1995. *Taboo: Sex, Identity and Erotic Subjectivity in Anthropological Fieldwork*. New York: Routledge.

Laing, Marie. 2021. *Urban Indigenous Youth Reframing Two-Spirit*. New York: Routledge.

Lewin, Ellen, and William Leap. 1996. *Out in the Field: Reflections of Lesbian and Gay Anthropologists*. Urbana: University of Illinois Press.

Lewin, Ellen, and William Leap. 2002. *Out in Theory: The Emergence of Lesbian and Gay Anthropology*. Urbana: University of Illinois Press.

Lewin, Ellen, and William Leap. 2009. *Out in Public: Reinventing Lesbian/Gay Anthropology in a Globalizing World*. Hoboken, NJ: John Wiley and Sons.

Livia, Anna, and Kira Hall. 1997. *Queerly Phrased: Language, Gender, and Sexuality*. Oxford: Oxford University Press.

Lowe, Lisa. 2015. *The Intimacies of Four Continents*. Durham, NC: Duke University Press.

Lyons, Andrew P., and Harriet Lyons. 2004. *Irregular Connections: A History of Anthropology and Sexuality*. Lincoln: University of Nebraska Press.

Lyons, Andrew P., and Harriet D. Lyons, eds. 2011. *Sexualities in Anthropology: A Reader*. Malden, MA: Wiley-Blackwell.

Malinowski, Bronislaw. 1929. *The Sexual Life of Savages in North-Western Melanesia: An Ethnographic Account of Courtship, Marriage and Family Life among the Natives of the Trobriand Islands, British New Guinea*. New York / London: H. Liveright / G. Routledge and Sons.

Manalansan, Martin F., IV. 1993. "(Re)locating the Gay Filipino." *Journal of Homosexuality* 26(2–3): 53–72.

Manalansan, Martin F., IV. 1995. "In the Shadows of Stonewall: Examining Gay Transnational Politics and the Diasporic Dilemma." *GLQ: A Journal of Lesbian and Gay Studies* 2(4): 425–38.

Manalansan, Martin F., IV. 2016. "Queer Anthropology: An Introduction." *Cultural Anthropology* 31(4): 595–97.

Martin, Richard Joseph, and Dieter Haller, eds. 2019. *Sex: Ethnographic Encounters*. New York: Bloomsbury.

McRuer, Robert. 2006. *Crip Theory: Cultural Signs of Queerness and Disability*. New York: New York University Press.

Mead, Margaret. 1928. *Coming of Age in Samoa: A Psychological Study of Primitive Youth for Western Civilization*. New York: William Morrow.

Mikdashi, Maya, and Jasbir K. Puar. 2016. "Queer Theory and Permanent War." *GLQ: A Journal of Lesbian and Gay Studies* 22(2): 215–22.

Morgensen, Scott Lauria. 2010. "Settler Homonationalism: Theorizing Settler Colonialism within Queer Modernities." *GLQ: A Journal of Lesbian and Gay Studies* 16(1–2): 105–31.

Morgensen, Scott Lauria. 2011. *Spaces between Us: Queer Settler Colonialism and Indigenous Decolonization*. Minneapolis: University of Minnesota Press.

Morris, Rosalind C. 1994. "Three Sexes and Four Sexualities: Redressing the Discourses on Gender and Sexuality in Contemporary Thailand." *positions: east asian cultural critique* 2(1): 15–43.

Morris, Rosalind C. 1995. "All Made Up: Performance Theory and the New Anthropology of Sex and Gender." *Annual Review of Anthropology* 24: 567–92.

Moten, Fred, and Stefano Harney. 2013. *The Undercommons: Fugitive Planning and Black Study*. New York: Autonomedia.

Muñoz, José Esteban. 2009. *Cruising Utopia: The Then and There of Queer Futurity*. New York: New York University Press.

Newton, Esther. 1972. *Mother Camp: Female Impersonators in America*. Chicago: University of Chicago Press.

Newton, Esther. 1993. "My Best Informant's Dress: The Erotic Equation in Fieldwork." *Cultural Anthropology* 8(1): 3–23.

Povinelli, Elizabeth A. 1994. "Sexual Savages, Sexual Sovereignty: Australian Colonial Texts and the Post-colonial Politics of Nationalism." *Diacritics: A Review of Contemporary Criticism* 24: 122–50.

Puar, Jasbir K. 2007. *Terrorist Assemblages: Homonationalism in Queer Times*. Durham, NC: Duke University Press.

Robertson, Jennifer, ed. 2005. *Same-Sex Cultures and Sexualities: An Anthropological Reader*. London: Blackwell.

Rofel, Lisa. 1999. "Qualities of Desire: Imagining Gay Identities in China." *GLQ: A Journal of Lesbian and Gay Studies* 5(4): 451–74.

Rubin, Gayle. 1993. "Thinking Sex: Notes for a Radical Theory of the Politics of Sexuality." In *The Lesbian and Gay Studies Reader*, edited by Henry Abelove, Michele Barale, and David Halperin, 3–44. New York: Routledge. Originally published 1984.

Rubin, Gayle. 2002. "Studying Sexual Subcultures: Excavating the Ethnography of Gay Communities in Urban North America." In *Out in Theory: The Emergence of Lesbian and Gay Anthropology*, edited by Ellen Lewin and William Leap, 17–68. Urbana: University of Illinois Press.

Sedgwick, Eve Kosofsky. 1990. *Epistemology of the Closet*. Berkeley: University of California Press.

Sedgwick, Eve Kosofsky. 1993. *Tendencies*. Durham, NC: Duke University Press.

Seizer, Susan. 1995. "Paradoxes of Visibility in the Field: Rites of Queer Passage in Anthropology." *Public Culture* 8(I): 73–100.

Shange, Savannah. 2019. *Progressive Dystopia: Abolition, Antiblackness, and Schooling in San Francisco*. Durham, NC: Duke University Press.

Snorton, C. Riley. 2017. *Black on Both Sides: A Racial History of Trans Identity*. Minneapolis: University of Minnesota Press.

Sonenschein, David. 1966. "Homosexuality as a Subject of Anthropological Inquiry." *Anthropological Quarterly* 39(2): 73–82.

Towle, Evan B., and Lynn M. Morgan. 2002. "Romancing the Transgender Native: Rethinking the Use of the 'Third Gender' Concept." *GLQ: A Journal of Lesbian and Gay Studies* 8(4): 469–97.

Trouillot, Michel-Rolph. 2003. *Global Transformations: Anthropology and the Modern World*. New York: Palgrave Macmillan.

Tuck, Eve, and K. Wayne Yang. 2012. "Decolonization Is Not a Metaphor." *Decolonization: Indigeneity, Education and Society* 1(1): 1–40.

Valentine, David. 2007. *Imagining Transgender: An Ethnography of a Category*. Durham, NC: Duke University Press.

Valentine, David, and Riki Anne Wilchins. 1997. "One Percent on the Burn Chart: Gender, Genitals, and Hermaphrodites with Attitude." *Social Text* 52/53: 215–22.

Vance, Carole. 1991. "Anthropology Rediscovers Sexuality: A Theoretical Comment." *Social Science and Medicine* 33(8): 875–84.

Warner, Michael. 1993. *Fear of a Queer Planet: Queer Politics and Social Theory*. Minneapolis: University of Minnesota Press.

Weiss, Margot. 2016a. "Always After: Desiring Queerness, Desiring Anthropology." *Cultural Anthropology* 31(4): 627–38.

Weiss, Margot. 2016b. "Discipline and Desire: Feminist Politics, Queer Studies, and New Queer Anthropology." In *Mapping Feminist Anthropology in the Twenty-First Century*, edited by Ellen Lewin and Leni M. Silverstein, 168–88. New Brunswick, NJ: Rutgers University Press.

Weiss, Margot. 2020. "Intimate Encounters: Queer Entanglements in Ethnographic Fieldwork." *Anthropological Quarterly* 93(1): 1355–86.

Weiss, Margot. 2022. "Queer Theory from Elsewhere and the Im/Proper Objects of Queer Anthropology." *Feminist Anthropology* 3(2): 315–35.

Wekker, Gloria. 1993. "Mati-ism and Black Lesbianism: Two Idealtypical Expressions of Female Homosexuality in Black Communities of the Diaspora." *Journal of Homosexuality* 24(3–4): 145–58.

Westermarck, Edward. 1917. "Homosexual Love." In *The Origin and Development of Moral Ideas*. London: Macmillan.

Weston, Kath. 1993. "Lesbian/Gay Studies in the House of Anthropology." *Annual Review of Anthropology* 22: 339–67.

Weston, Kath. 1998. *Long Slow Burn: Sexuality and Social Science*. New York: Routledge.

Wiegman, Robyn. 2012. *Object Lessons*. Durham, NC: Duke University Press.

Wilson, Ara. 2019, July 31. "Queer Anthropology." *Cambridge Encyclopedia of Anthropology*. https://www.anthroencyclopedia.com/entry/queer-anthropology.

Part I

FOUNDATIONS

Queer Anthropology's Contested Genealogies

Jafari Sinclaire Allen

1

The Anthropology of "What Is Utterly Precious"

Black Feminist Habits of Mind and the Object (and Ends) of Anthropology

In his 1989 film *Tongues Untied*, Marlon Riggs renamed the "discipline" or project that he and other Black gay men, lesbians, trans, and bisexual cultural workers and intellectuals were engaged in as "anthropology . . . the unending search for what is utterly precious." In this intervention, I will propose some frameworks for ethnographic work drawn from this Black gay tradition of the long 1980s. While the larger work out of which this proposal emerges inaugurates a form that builds on and attempts to synthesize the Black feminist imperative to produce purposefully embodied narrative theory, the queer mandate to resist or subvert normativity, and the ethnographic warrant to poetically represent lived reality, here my aim is more constrained. Here we will *linger* at how purposefully embodied narrative theory innovated by Black lesbians provides models that can be appreciated as a form of critical (auto-) ethnography that not only grows out of the "three great points of departure" of the longer Black radical intellectual tradition of *description*, *correction*, and *prescription*, but also anticipates (and to some degree mitigates) some of the thorny epistemological, ethical, and aesthetic questions that anthropologists face and have critiqued since at least the early 1980s.[1]

These perennial issues are especially relevant for queer anthropologies and queer anthropologists. Aligned with streams of "native anthropology" (Jones 1970, 1995) and "decolonizing anthropology" (Harrison 1991, 2008) within the guild, the habits of mind and intellectual traditions highlighted here may be read to offer a redefinition and "rework(ing)" of how to conceive, carry out, analyze, and narrativize embodied social-cultural experience toward creating a useful human record and more humane futures—the bread and butter, or *ends*, of the enterprise of sociocultural anthropology. Still, this intervention should not be read as "what Black gay feminist intellectual traditions can do for (queer) anthropology."

The work highlighted here was not carried out in response to or with reference to the professional enterprise of anthropology. Likewise, it is not offered here to contribute to the by-now-exhausting and perhaps tragically enervating practice of trying to force engagement. This has been a formidable challenge since the 1980s. Anthropologists of many stripes—especially feminist, "decolonizing," "native," queer, Black, and other anthropologists of color—have already labored to save anthropology from itself. Instead, here we will take a cue from St. Clair Drake's "critical demeanor" (duCille 1994) in his 1990 "Further Reflections on Anthropology and the Black Experience." In that forward-looking essay, Professor Drake's self-critique extends the possibility that the author had overlooked some forebearers and underestimated the extent to which "Black scholars, journalists, speakers, etc." had used anthropological knowledge, "even though Black [scholars, et cetera,] were not extensive producers of such data" (Drake and Baber 1990, 1). Establishing the speculative stance I employ here, he calls for "collective effort" to create a future "careful and detailed study" (1). Drake does not specify that this collaborative study must take place within anthropology. Consider that he may be pointing outside of the disciplinary enclosure of anthropology, to a prospectively deterritorialized zone of Black Study ("anthropology and Black experience"), which acknowledges that anthropological knowledge, interpretation, production, and application must not be (and has never been) left to the professional guild of anthropology alone. The same is true for queer studies/LGBTQ studies.

But this is "not easy or quick, or pretty," as Pat Parker described Black (and) third world lesbian revolutionary work (2016). Necessarily also demonstrating the "permanent disruption" of this mode of work, I will describe how my recent ethnographic fieldwork troubled my ethical, methodological, and aesthetic commitments and ideals. In *There's a Disco Ball between Us: A Theory of Black Gay Life* (2022), I characterize this transnational fieldwork encounter as an ultimately salutary and perhaps unavoidable "Black gay mess." This prompted me to shift, or at least reimagine, my research modality from chiefly participant-observation to include sensing affect, haunting archives of "living and endangered documents" read alongside "the rigors of an inglorious present," and poring over and reconsidering secondary sources.[2] Thus, in this essay I insist on naming this mode of attention and intellectual work that I call *ethnographic sensibility as* Black gay feminist concepts. That is, *ethnographic sensibility, "a necessary theater,"* being a "relative," "first . . . knowing one another," "testaments, testimonies . . . and legacies," and "the unending search for what is utterly precious" are narrated as Black feminist and Black gay intellectual production on their own terms. These discourses do not seek validity through being forced into a disciplinary framework—rendered useful only if it contributes to (the further decolonization and transformation of) anthropology. Here I insist that you, now working in the wake of Black feminist and Black queer intellectual traditions (whether you knew it or not), engage and cite and grapple with them if you are serious about doing queer anthropology.

Beyond Critique

To be sure, anthropologists love a self-critique and an urgent call to "come to Jesus." This is not that. In 1992, Lisa Rofel organized an invited panel titled "Expanding the Boundaries: Anthropology and Cultural Critique," which focused on the work of Gloria Anzaldúa and Marlon Riggs, whom she correctly averred had helped us to rethink the intersections of gender, race/ethnicity, and sexuality, and, indeed, to rethink the entire concept of "culture." Ruth Behar said that "their writings and productions, as part of 'minority discourse' in the U.S., have provided us with the tools by which to critique anthropology and to move anthropology into a postcolonial, postmodern world."[3] With deep respect for Rofel's critical anthropological project and allyship, I write from a perspective in which Riggs's work constitutes the core, not the provocative edge/margin. This perspective refuses minoritization and cosmetic or additive "inclusion." What is offered here emerges from an intramural perspective and relationality, which is not necessarily invested in "expanding the boundaries of anthropology" (Behar 1993, 83). While this honors Faye Harrison's notion of and admirable commitment to "reworking anthropology" to meet the demands of the twenty-first century (for those who wish to continue to place their energies there), some of us have to regard the *work work work work work work* of the discipline as a distraction from the imperative to read, promote, and refine the sorts of "anthropologies" and ethnographic sensibilities that have always been a central part of the long Black intellectual tradition.

Riffing on Cathy J. Cohen's radical Black lesbian challenge to the queer movement issued in one of her early formative essays ("What Is This Movement Doing to My Politics?"), I have been exploring this critical intellectual and ethical question over the last several years: *What is this discipline doing to my Black gay habits of mind?* Today, I find myself equally as engaged in doing the ethnographic, methodological, critical, and pedagogical work as I am uninterested in the disciplinary enclosure in which it is currently entangled. And you cannot say you were not warned of Black scholars' overdue disinvestment from the professional discipline of anthropology. Aligned with Rofel's statement one year earlier, and resonant with the scholarly innovations and internal critiques of *the decolonizing generation* of Black diaspora anthropologists, Behar told you in 1993, "They (Black and Brown scholars and cultural critics) don't need our patronage anymore, thankfully. And they don't intend to become our native informants. Or do piece-work for us," she writes, after declaring "is it any wonder that the current multicultural movement is unfolding beyond the confines of academic anthropology?" (85). Here I recenter Black intellectual traditions as a corrective interdisciplinary norm. I will describe a few of the ways these traditions, as innovated by Black lesbian intellectuals artists and activists of the long 1980s, provide more workable *modes of attention* and *engagement* (you may read: *methodology*) and explanatory frameworks (theorization) and ethics (read also, *politics*) for what we now understand to be materially consequential representations of everyday life (you may read: *ethnography*). Rather than focus on seeing *the other*, this work departs from studied critical assessment of sociocultural "crosshairs"—by those caught in its murderous gaze and gauge.

Anthropology has pushed queer theory significantly, to provide not only empirical grounding and humanistic context of "over there," but, more fundamentally, to advance understanding of the inescapable social character of human beings (Boellstorff 2007, 18) beyond critique of Western canonical texts and cultural contexts available at an armchair's reach. Moreover, I agree with Sidney Mintz that anthropologists "uniquely argued on the basis of their ethnographic findings that commercial instincts were in fact not instincts at all; that war was not inevitable; that monogamy was not 'natural,' any more than is polygamy, or any other such socially created form for setting up housekeeping; and that human nature is at best a slippery term, not to be used too nonchalantly" (Mintz 2012, 53). He said, further, that "such observations held a mirror up to ourselves, made us wonder—perhaps even instilled a bit of doubt in our assessment of the world—all of it much to the good" (53). Notwithstanding the pesky "we" and "us" that Mintz employs, inferring that all of "us" employ ethnocentric hierarchies, I agree. Perhaps it is the very success of anthropology's singular intellectual project that also now calls us to create something different. Or, as Ryan Cecil Jobson has recently provoked, to *let it burn* (2020). I have "offer(ed) a friendly critical amendment," for example, to Tom Boellstorff's insightful discussion of the (dis)articulation of anthropology and queer studies in which he argued that an impasse had been reached in anthropology apropos of a proper relationship between sexuality (studies), race (studies), and gender (studies) (Allen 2016, 618). After all, while the term *impasse* connotes a relation of mutuality, or at least mutual recognition and engagement, "our" (this possessive personal pronoun emphatically distinct from Mintz's) relation to anthropology (read also: any academic discipline) is more properly expressed as one of compulsory mastery of a Eurocentric canon—which is now at least permanently in controversy and under indictment—up against broad and intransigent ignorance of Black intellectual traditions. Therefore, in this intervention I aim to move significantly beyond this impasse by privileging the Black intellectual tradition of radical Black lesbian feminists. (That is: try to understand *anthropology* beyond the academic discipline and profession of Anthropology.)

A Necessary Theater

To understand "anthropology (as) the unending search for what is utterly precious" is to say that the enterprise is personal and political—it is close. Precious and protracted (struggle) in which the written word is central. It reflects a larger engagement with the process of finding voice and "trying (one's) tongue" in the context of community, and the multivocal conversations that result. After all, Audre Lorde has already told us that "the quality of light by which we scrutinize our lives has direct bearing on the product which we live.... This is poetry as illumination... giving name to the nameless so that it can be thought" (1984a, 36–37). In his manifesto "Why I Write," Black gay poet, playwright, anthologist, and performer extraordinaire Assotto Saint assigns us, "like archeologists," to keep finely crafted fieldnotes that we "file and make available to the world" (1996, 3). These Black gay men were working within the aesthetic and ethical/political framework created by radical Black feminist lesbians and other women of color, whose understanding of themselves as third world women drove their intellectual, artistic, (and) political work. Here, Assotto issues a methodological mandate: a "necessary theater" composed of "testaments, testimonies... and legacies":

> I was cognizant of the wants and needs of our emerging community; my writings needed to serve its visibility and empowerment. Most revolutions—be they political, social, spiritual, or economic—are usually complemented by one in literature.... The best answer to the question of who we are resides in our experiences, from whence our strongest writings are derived. While we map out this new wilderness of our experiences, we must also bear witness. Like archaeologists, we have to file reports in the form of our finely crafted poems and plays, which we then make available to the world.... We must strive before it is too late to realize this creative wish: that the writings of our experiences serve as testaments to those who passed along this way, testimonies to our times, and legacies to future generations. (Saint 1996, 3)

Resonant with Manning Marable's tripartite characterization of the long Black intellectual tradition's three great points of departure (the mandate to create "descriptive," "corrective," and "prescriptive" intellectual work), Assotto Saint exhorts us to write our own experiences. He insists that these testimonies be finely wrought; inextricably connected to community visibility, empowerment, and revolution; and usable "testaments" for the future.

Emerging out of this intellectual tradition and Black gay habit of mind, therefore, the "necessary theater" *we* produce follows Hortense Spillers's insistence to attend to what she calls "first order naming" (2003, 168).

Spillers, of course, warned us of the consequences of Black women being rendered "beached whales . . . unvoiced, mis-seen, not doing, awaiting their verb" (153). Again, invoking the import of self-regard and writing of the self and her own community(ies), Professor Spillers notes that "their sexual experiences are depicted, but not often by them, and if and when by the subject herself, often in the guise of vocal music, often in the self-contained accent and sheer romance of the blues" (153). Note that this was first published in anthropologist Carole S. Vance's landmark collection *Pleasure and Danger: Exploring Female Sexuality* in 1984, which emerged from the Scholar and the Feminist IX conference, "Towards a Politics of Sexuality," held at Barnard College in 1982. Thus, this classic essay *reads* anthropology and at once contextualizes (without entering the morass of) the (white) feminist "porn wars" and sidesteps layers of (white) feminist disavowals, both raging at that time—laying groundwork for *something else*.

Today, in the spirits and in the wakes of poets, artists and dramatists, we not only argue for "clear" social-cultural depiction, but also defend "self-contained accent and sheer romance . . . by the subject herself," aesthetics as constitutive—indeed *essential*—parts of the contribution (Spillers 2003, 153). As Audre Lorde reminds us, this provides different "qualities of light" by which we examine and appreciate our various experiences, compounded situatedness, and histories.[4]

Intersectionality Is Vestibular to Queer Analysis

This work emerges from Black feminist thought, which is part of the long Black radical intellectual tradition. Consider its genealogies and intentions. Black women from various walks of life—many were students or well-educated and many had also been involved in civil rights, antiwar, Black Power, labor, abortion rights, antiviolence, and anti-forced-sterilization activism—came together to articulate their multiply constituted, "interlocking" positions at around the same time that the larger and overwhelmingly white middle-class, "second-wave" feminist movement began to swell with the recognition that *the personal is political*, also gleaned from the work and experiences of Black and other third world women. This occurred just ahead of English translations of French poststructuralist theory's enumeration of the diffuse discursive workings of power and alongside the start of international circulation of the Birmingham school of critical cultural studies, whose orientations to discursivity focused on contemporary material struggle. In anthropology, the crucial historical turn had just popped off as a corollary to Marxist or otherwise materialist reconsiderations and corrections of what had become a debilitating ahistoricism. Native, Marxist, "decolonizing," (and) third world anthropologists especially challenged the understanding of cultures studied as frozen in time of the anthropologist's arrival to an imagined discrete locality. This materialist orientation—related to anticolonial politics and movements around the world—is an important bedrock for the decolonizing calls and moves within anthropology at the dawn of the long 1980s.

As I attempt to elliptically re-narrate in *There's a Disco Ball Between Us*, whilst to say intersectionality is an embodied concept or politics is not to "limit" it to the bodies of Black women, the conceptual framework must not be invoked without referencing the particular Black women who invented it or indeed without what Jennifer Nash rightly refers to as "the fleshy materiality of Black women's bodies" (regardless of the circumstances of gender assignment at birth) (2019, 29). We must have it both ways because the reality works in at least both ways. And because you seem too easily to forget Black women. There would be no need for A. Lynne Bolles, Kimberlé Crenshaw, and Christen Smith, for example, to remind and insist that we #SayHerName and #CiteBlackWomen if this were not true. Consider the symmetry between those hashtags and logical relations. Perhaps having imbibed the surface, instrumental ways it is deployed in (the last weeks of) some college courses, folks often poorly or only symbolically perform the real meanings and constitutive politics of intersectionality and Black feminist knowledge production more broadly. In one short example of the complexity of the formulation, Crenshaw's (1989) notion of intersectionality is not only a metaphorical illustration of compounded subjectivities, experiences, or identity positions but more pointedly an expression of where Black women are structurally located: in the crosshairs. Shifting battlefields of the same war, Lorde said (2009). The Combahee River Collective statement holds, in different metaphorical language, that "we are actively committed to struggling against racial, sexual, heterosexual, and class oppression, and see as our particular task the development of *integrated* analysis and practice based upon the fact that the major systems of oppression are *interlocking*. . . ." They wrote that, ". . . as Black feminists and Lesbians[,] we know that we have a very definite revolutionary task to perform, and we are ready for the lifetime of work and struggle before us" (1983: 273). These frameworks are intimately related but not identical to earlier feminist theorization, such as Francis Beal's 1969 naming of the "double jeopardy" of Black women. It is more substantively about the compounding of specific forms of institutional political-economic harm.

These concepts complement, but are not identical to or mutually exclusive with, literary theorist Hortense Spillers's (2003) formulation of "interstices." The intersectional approach advanced by Crenshaw and others is more specifically about juridical structures that are rearticulated by groups and individuals for redress. This is most closely associated with the *prescriptive* impulse of the long Black intellectual tradition. Spillers's formulation of interstices is likewise spatially imagined. However, hers is a *corrective* framework observed via psychoanalytic and historicized phenomenological lenses. She offers structuring grammars and deep wells of consciousness out of which interactions emerge out of the "great (discursive) drama" in which *the Black woman* (yes, in this case discursively singular in her radical discontinuity) "became the principal point of passage between the human and the non-human world . . . therefore making Black . . . vestibular to culture" (2003, 155).

What is an ethnographer to do with this strong claim of vestibularity and this sturdy framework of sociocultural structuration? Spillers convincingly argues that "the Black woman" is central to the way the social is constituted and becomes "the principal point of passage between the human and the non-human world. . . . At this level of radical discontinuity in the 'great chain of being,' Black is vestibular to culture" (2003, 155). The stories I tell in *¡Venceremos?* (2011) highlight how discursive dramas, historical and everyday actions of citizens, family members, and police impact the bodies' minds and psyches of those in the active crosshairs. Recall, for example, dark-skinned Black and gay Octavio's bodily transformation as a drag queen (*transformista*) within heteronormative and putatively "mixed-race" Cuban culture. I have previously argued that to mark a woman as Black is to signify the kidnapped African woman whose laboring body was constituted as sexual chattel (along with all kidnapped Africans), antithetical to the image of chastity, modesty, and fragility putatively deserving of "respect" as the "weaker" or the "fairer" sex. She cannot therefore bring "honor." Here I follow anthropologist Angela Gilliam's assertion that "there was a critical difference between white and Black women as regards 'honor.' The Black woman had to earn honor through her comportment; the white woman would lose honor (which was assumed, a priori) by her behavior" (1991,

226). Octavio's story demonstrates at once that, for example, to be Black is to discursively fail to be whitened into mestizo eligibility; to be a Black woman troubles the systems of honor and personhood; and to be homosexual is to fail the test of Cuban manhood.[5] With severely limited opportunities to make any living at all, Octavio performed *as* Lili, a *mulata*, illustrating the intersections and highlighting the tight interstice in which he was *forced to choose* to operate. Intersectionality is vestibular to (quality) queer analysis. Without it, one cannot see the constitutive in-between spaces or flows of social traffic on which rigorous sociocultural analysis depends.

Still, as the ethnographic account suggests, Octavio's/Lili's agency/maneuverability contrasts with other Black (and) queer community members. Lesbians were effectively discursively *unseen* in that time and place. Discursively, therefore, one could find them "awaiting." Still, they were incontrovertibly known/visible to one another. Moreover, in some cases the lack of recognition could also be experienced as lessened surveillance: perhaps presenting to individuals a choice whether, when, and how to speak (*as* lesbians or women who have sex with women). As I have averred elsewhere—riffing off of Spillers's theme—Black gay intellectual traditions and habit of mind provide verbs that accent historically particular embodied *voicing* and *doing*—like lesbian, transgender, bisexual, gay, batty bwoy, masisi, bulldagger, Two-Spirited, maricón, same gender loving, buller, zami, mati working, dress-up girls, bois, butches, femme or butch queen, gender insurgent, marimacha, branché, homosexual, sexual minority, men, women, queer, et cetera. Of course, some eschew explicit naming, preferring to live their verbs, as, for example, simply am, is, are, been, being, be—or in some cases interrupt, invent, push, question, refuse, serve, or shade. Here is another privilege of ethnographic work, which insists on grounding in everyday social action: these folks were *living*— in practice/doing and being, not at all women-in-waiting.

Fieldwork and Archives: "First, We Must Know Each Other . . ."

Please allow me to invite you to engage the Black gay feminist habit of mind as a fieldwork ethic. Brackette Williams argues that in the case of ethnographic fieldwork "the identity of anthropologist as participant-observer could neither be constructed nor situated outside the double-edged, multifaceted question: 'who are you and what are you to me?'" This is key to ethically thinking through an encounter (1996, 84). Audre Lorde (1984a) offers a useful refinement of this perennial fieldwork conundrum by employing a different "quality of light." For example, following Lorde, my Black gay habit of understanding of difference as something to expect, honor, and explore had led me to understand that differences between myself and my research interlocutors "in the field" were not only inevitable but potentially generative, and that who we are to each other is *in relation*. That there is a *we* to be explored. Although elements of this are reflected, albeit in different ways, in activist anthropology, in both reparative and revindicationist streams of the Black intellectual tradition, and various forms of "engaged" scholarship, this more precisely emerges from a radical Black lesbian feminist politics of recognition and the dogged attempt to reconstruct and repair "home." This is also to say that radical Black Lesbian feminists have offered among the most cogent and powerful *prescriptive* intellectual-political work, following, and expanding the long Black radical tradition. For Audre Lorde, for example, this was not an altruistic position, one motivated only by heritable ascription (2009, 73).

In contrast, I worry that some of the well-meaning but too often oversimplified or instrumentally used pillars of the discipline of anthropology, like historical particularism and cultural relativism, are uncritically deployed as "incorrigible" theoretics that militate against more capacious and humane positions like Audre Lorde's "same war/same battlefield" formulation (2009). I worry that they lead us to focus only on discrete, out-of-context, or atomized historical specificities that can be viewed as having little to do with "us" and that can be studied at a distance/remove with something called "objectivity." Incorrigibility would insist that we understand macheted gay men in Jamaican, raped South African lesbians, slaughtered Black (and) Latinx trans women, dismembered Black gay men, exposed and neutralized bisexual politicians (and more) in the United States, and wrongly convicted queer Martiniquais in France, for example, as discrete occurrences to be understood only in particularized local contexts. In contrast, the Black radical intellectual tradition, in the hands of Black lesbian feminists like Audre Lorde, conceives of what she called the "borrowed sameness" of the strategies of empire (1984b, 26). One example she drew was between Black subjects in the Caribbean and the United States: "the tactics for quelling (any) conquered people. No courts, no charges, no legal process. Welfare, but no reparations" (1984b, 26).

To wit, the poet, mother, lesbian, Black socialist . . . derived her insights from on-the-ground observation while participating. There is a strong ethnographic sensibility in Lorde's work generally. Her incisive reports from Grenada and St. Croix, however, are especially pitched toward understanding a specific cultural context through documentation and description. The first time she traveled to Grenada, just eleven months after the triumph of the New Jewel Movement, Lorde tells us, "I came seeking 'home' for this was my mother's birthplace and she had always defined it so for me" (1984b, 21). The second time, she "came in mourning and fear. . . . [Grenada] had been savaged, invaded, its people maneuvered into saying thank you to their invaders" (1984b, 29). Connecting the 1983 US invasion of Grenada to the not-so-distant national memory of catastrophic defeat in Vietnam and racialized political unrest at home in the United States, she asks, "How better to wipe out the bitter memories of national defeat by Yellow people than with restoration of power in the eyes of the American public—the image of American Marines splashing through a little Black blood?" (1984b, 24). Note how she nimbly shifts geographies, calling out connections so often ignored or obscured by other observers: "In addition to being a demonstration to the Caribbean community of what will happen to any country that dares to assume responsibility for its own destiny, the invasion of Grenada also serves as a naked warning to thirty million African Americans. Watch your step. We did it to them down there and we will not hesitate to do it to you . . . the tactics for quelling a conquered people. No courts, no charges, no legal process. Welfare, but no reparations" (1984b, 26). Several years later, her detailed reportage of disaster in the aftermath of Hurricane Hugo's 1989 devastation of the "US territory" of St. Croix, Virgin Islands, is distinct in part because here she writes as a "local" (not a native), bearing up against the manmade effects of a so-called natural disaster (Lorde 1991).

On day three post-Hugo, Lorde's report is eerily akin to eyewitness accounts in the aftermaths of hurricanes Harvey, Irene, and Maria (in Barbuda, Puerto Rico, and throughout the Caribbean); and to Katrina, in a New Orleans in which defective levees broke, causing massive death and destruction in Black communities of the Lower Ninth Ward; and to 2010 post-earthquake and more recently postflood Haiti. There is more to say about how regarding one another via an ethic of intersubjectivity requires a willingness to *see* that both includes and extends beyond our own breached levees and lack of (electrical) power, no matter the terrains we inhabit. Lorde had held that as queer and Black people "self-preservation demands we involve ourselves actively in those policies and postures" (Lorde 2009, 73), with the understanding that the *self* to which she refers here is at once local and/but an intersubjective self, connected through history and materiality, as well as a deeper ethical bond with other Black and Brown folks living throughout the world:

> The battlefields shift: the war is the same. It stretches from the brothels of Southeast Asia to the blood-ridden alleys of Cape Town to the incinerated lesbians in Berlin to Michael Stewart's purloined eyes and grandmother Eleanor Bumpers, shot dead in the projects of New York. We are gays and lesbians of color at a time in [this] country's history when its domestic and international policies, as well as its posture toward those nations with which we share heritage, are so reactionary that self-preservation demands we involve ourselves actively in those policies and postures. (Lorde 2009, 73)

In 1970, at the leading edge of what we now understand as the decolonizing generation of anthropology, Delmos Jones offered that "a Black man in this century cannot avoid identifying with his people. I am an intrinsic part of the social situation that I am attempting to study. As part of the situation, I must also attempt to forge a solution" (1970, 255). In Cuba, I found that el pueblo was trying "to forge a solution." Still, Professor Jones was referring to fieldwork "at home." Audre Lorde offers the position of "(a) relative" (1984b, 29). In Grenada, she parsed her position this way: "I am a relative." Whilst "relative" can refer to "family," it can also mean merely "proximate." Relative can mean "to be compared," "in reference to," or "in relation" to something or someone else. I had learned a great deal being the object of curiosity and initial skepticism as a US citizen getting in people's business in Cuba during my first ethnographic experience. Suspicion of being a CIA agent goes with the territory. And people tend to watch closely. Still, the reality of a revolutionary society in deep socioeconomic crisis presented opportunities to prove or disprove suspicions. The relative strength of socialist political solidarity and Black diasporic cultural connection over animosities between the United States and Cuban states was regularly tested in small ways and large ones. Demonstrable fidelity—not to the Cuban state or project of socialism, necessarily, but to human kindness and Black (and) queer solidarity—was scrutinized daily as my respondents and friends looked for ways "to resolve the difficulties" of Cuba's Special Period in

Times of Peace. Below, please allow me to describe a more recent fieldwork reflection on a channel that may be regarded as less specifically "political," but which goes to demonstrate the complexities of "knowing one another."

Nicole says that her heart sank into her gut as the high iron gate of the Kitisuru Condominium slowly opened. The Askhari stared at her incredulously, as she prepared to leave the premises after midnight, on a Thursday night. She was unaccompanied, and by this time all of the other gatehouses in this upscale enclave of Nairobi had already shut their lights. Three other "inquisitive, meddling, gossipy" Askhari had begun to nod off, or have their own fun in the small guardpost near the gate—automatic guns slung on their backs and fabric wraps around their heads. Safe and comfortable indoors, Nicole's colleagues in the team of Canadian management consultants with whom she had undertaken this three-month assignment slept soundly, with no idea that she had left. Earlier, Nicole had generously tipped their usual driver, then dismissed him for the evening. His job was to arrange safaris and evenings out at the tonier restaurants and bars and to shuttle them from site to site in this bustling international city full of expatriates, returnees, and UN workers who pull in extra pay to work in this "troubled" capital of East Africa.

On one of those evenings out, she and her colleagues casually met Njeri, a young barrister. Only she and Nicole knew that their so-called chance meeting was anything but. It was the orchestrated result of a two-month internet conversation. Having been virtually introduced through friends of friends; these young women, who live their lesbian lives out of sight of employers, colleagues, and most family members, arranged the encounter in the most discreet way possible. For Nicole, regular quick trips from her home in Toronto, to Detroit or New York, also require quick changes of currency and fashion—from the Canadian to US dollar, and from the corporate togs she wore as "fashionable armor" to cashmere hoodies, low-slung jeans, and carefully collected snapbacks and diamond-stud earrings, punctuating her cultivated soft-butch style. For Njeri, moments of respite to live openly as a lesbian require even more complex international machinations. She takes infrequent "mental health" treks to Malindi or Lamu—off Kenya's coast, with friends from other East African countries, or even less frequently to London, where she went to graduate school and where she felt at once "sexually free and utterly invisible." In London, Njeri had been unable to fully express, in the flesh, the freedom she had there to walk hand-in-hand in Piccadilly with another Black woman; because smart, attractive, and "well-brought-up" Black women were the very small change of the British sexual economy. While one might assume that at home in Kenya, Njeri's class status would make her more sought-after, it also conditions vulnerabilities that make being open about her sexual desires impossible for her, she told me. Exposure would likely mean loss of her job and a debilitating erosion of the prestige that accords Njeri's family material privilege and protection. The daughter of working-class, small-island Caribbean people who migrated to Canada from the United Kingdom several years before she was born in the late 1970s, Nicole says that the presence of open Black lesbian and gay people in Toronto is no mean comfort when she is the only Black person, and one of only a few women professionals, working in her multinational firm. You will not find her hanging out on Queen Street or Bloor in Toronto's gay village. Nicole told me that she "refuse[s] to make [her]self a triple minority" and reports being "discreet" about a lot in her life, not just her sexual desires and orientation. So, Nicole and Njeri found each other in cyberspace, through friends of friends.

On this Thursday evening, Njeri had arranged a driver, who picked up Nicole at her huge iron gate. Just a click away, Nicole joined her for the starry velvet sky ride to a beautiful compound on just the other side of Kilimani. To be sure, this scene could have easily served as a cautionary tale. Perhaps a Lifetime (Television for Women!) melodrama advising "discreet" Canadian women traveling alone to stay cozily inside of their ample walk-in (and -out) closets. Of course, it is not: her story is like many others I have heard and experienced myself. Significant and intense, the scene is also by now ethnographically hackneyed, I am afraid. Nearly all of the descriptors—the moist air, the bass in the music and scent of jasmine in the air (or was it jacaranda?), the sway of the hips of the women assembled, and the heavy laughter of their temporary freedom—echo what I had seen and written about in Havana and likewise have witnessed in Kingston; Washington, DC; Paris; and a number of other sites. Re-narrativization is, after all, palimpsestic. It means at once re/over-writing stories, and/or writing into the record some of those who would have been mischaracterized or misread otherwise; but also, just as significantly, it means allowing others, whose fugitivity is intentional, to remain in the margins and shadows of the work. All of this requires the sojourner-witness, now also the confidant and would-be scribe, to re-think the narratives I have already co-constructed. "This could have been ten years ago in Havana," I told Nicole, referring to a scene I tried to recreate in ¡Venceremos?, which itself had reminded me so much of Lorde's biomythographic recollection of meeting Af-re-ke-te! (a snap after each syllable). Was I reading too much into this? Romanticizing too much? There is certainly a bit of *sodade*, the Brazilians or Cape Verdeans or Angolans might sing, or *nostalgia*, Cubans would say. There is an intense force of longing present in Nicole's recollection of her first trip to Nairobi a few years before—here, as we sit together taking tea in the courtyard of the Nairobi Fairmont Hotel, among white European and North American guests readying for safari, and Black African guests and locals conducting business. There is also, I am afraid, still a bit of "adventure" to the story as I recount it here: now thrice removed and retold with distance, as published ethnographic "data." Is this what Lorde meant by "if we win / *there is no telling*"? Does winning mean that writing our lives—*telling it*—is as uncertain and contingent and maybe as ephemeral as our other life-affirming pleasures?

This is an ethnographic conundrum, as well as another dimension of what a number of colleagues push us to carefully consider: How are we reading the archive? What can really be said, given its limits—and what *should* we say? Must ethnographic practice result in an *ethnographic monograph* or *thick description* of stories? What stories are important to tell? (How) *should we* represent them? To what end, and to whose or what purposes? Ethnographers—many of us as much secret-keepers as storytellers—consider and reconsider this often.

Toward Queertopias / Against "Global Gay"

Deb Amory writes to fellow members of SOLGA in 1992, "Given the meteoric rise to fame of gay and lesbian studies (at least the presses are foaming at the mouth for manuscripts; hiring committees seem to be another story), how do we respond when queer stuff becomes a faddish trend?" (1992, 8). This presentiment, suggested as the framework for a lunchtime discussion during that year's American Anthropological Association meeting, was also a provocative challenge. Amory asked colleagues to meditate on how to "let the natives speak for themselves" and asked "what happens when we are those natives—how do we make ourselves heard? How do we tell allies from opportunists in the scramble over knowledge/power? How do we all stay accountable?" These are, of course, issues of what Ann duCille has named "critical demeanor." One sturdy obstacle to the shifts she provokes here is a habit of mind that brackets "native," "local," or situated knowledges—which Black and third world feminisms and other forms of intersectional analysis claim all knowledge is, per force—not as legitimate knowledge per se, or theory, for example, but rather as "stories" or raw "data." Archives and subjects do in fact speak: both in "raw" terms and with refined techniques, idioms, habits of mind, and traditions that are not well understood by most scholars who simply "do not have the range" because of the profound (let's call it) *ethnocentrism* (which you may also read plainly as misogynoir, and/or racism, and/or queer/transphobia) of the academy and its "electoral politics of discipline" (Trouillot 1991).

The deterritorialized *in-between* space created by radical Black lesbian thinkers-artists-activists have created—among the most vital streams that have emerged from the longer Black intellectual tradition—has flourished on ground of constantly shifting ruptured solidarity and over roiling seas of claims of "gaps" or "aporia" in the literatures by those who had not bothered to pull up anchor from their own desiccated shores. Where does that put us now—more than a generation after scholars like Ann duCille, Barbara Christian, and Deb Amory in a different register had already warned of the marauders (those without the range, who'd rather steal than cite, learn, and respectfully interpret with an appropriate framework) who assemble at the gate of precious archives and living communities that have their own "hieroglyphic" canons and traditions? Should any knowledges be "protected"—for and from whom? Where does this place—and what does it require of those of us for whom these "texts" are *utterly precious*? I am reminded of my own need for constant awareness of appropriate "critical demeanor" as a US-born, cisgender, middle-class Black gay man of US and Anglophone Caribbean heritage, who currently works with (and "on") some folks who have dramatically less access and material resources than myself. Moreover, I am currently situated in the elite US academy, where I teach and work through the insights of (queer) Black and third world women scholars whose work is unassailable, but who faced consistent attempts at erasure, silencing, and (actual) dismissal by the academy, and in cases by their own communities (see Allen 2015). The stakes and debts are high and mounting, not only for our respondents and people we "work on," but for a growing measure of our colleagues too—discursively and in some cases materially. In my own work, for example, I do not claim the emergence of a new field within the discipline of anthropology, but rather situate my critical ethnography as a contribution to longer intellectual and political traditions that are largely unheralded, often unaccounted for, and uncited within the disciplinary economies and electoral politics of academe.

"I Am an Outlaw . . ."

Though not a comfortable one, I own the position I have chosen—not really an "insider/outsider" as Black anthropologists like to cast their positions, but really an outsider in (ruptured?) kinship or solidarity (Allen 2022). I learned this critical, corrective, and prescriptive intellectual stance from radical Black lesbian feminists. The work we reach toward takes up the call of a central figure of this assemblage, M. Jacqui Alexander, for "an erotic that is fully bodied and sexed, one that can take ample note of our many vulnerabilities" (2007, 156). Alexander's contribution has largely been in showing state efforts to constrain what she terms *erotic autonomy*, and the limits of integration or complicity with state and other institutional projects. Describing and theorizing what erotic autonomy *does* is left to those who follow. She revealed how vulnerabilities with respect to state power are intersectional, compounded, complex, and dynamic, (even) while living and traveling as a scholar. She famously writes, "I am an outlaw in my country of birth: a national; but not a citizen," at once local and transnational (Alexander 1994, 5). This Black/queer time-space must also become a fertile interstice for the constitution of new affinities and communities of support among gender and sexual "outlaws" across borders—including intellectual/scholarly ones. How to nurture the rhizomes of new affinities and communities of support across grounds and seas of difference? What would it mean for professional anthropologists (other than Black and/or queer and/or feminist scholars) to put their batty on the line—or "at risk" beyond ludic exhibitionism or otherwise performative display? (Allen 2015). *What becomes an outlaw most*?!

Notes

1   Manning Marable wrote that the Black intellectual tradition can be characterized by three great points of departure: "presenting the reality of Black life and experiences from the point of view of Black people themselves. . . . [T]he Black intellectual tradition at its best has always presumed the centrality of

Black life. . . . . It has attempted to challenge and to critique the racism and stereotypes that have been ever present in the mainstream discourse of white academic institutions. . . . Black scholars who have theorized from the Black experience have often proposed practical steps for the empowerment of Black people. In other words, there is a practical connection between scholarship and struggle, between social analysis and social transformation" (2000, 3).

2 This is chronicled more fully in my recent book, and this chapter draws from it to contribute this remixed distillation.

3 See Behar 1993.

4 Audre Lorde, of course, uniquely capacitates this "something else." This has many facets, including correction of the record addressed to the perpetrators. Her "The Master's Tools Will Never Dismantle the Master's House" (1984c) likewise "reads feminist theory and . . . the sex wars," as an anonymous reviewer noted in their encouragement to think about the connection between this essay and Spillers, I make this small point in an endnote to underscore, however, that, unlike my essay, Audre's address in "The Master's Tools" is decidedly not intramural. The read, or admonition (or presentiment), is specifically pitched to what she called out as "academic arrogance" of white feminist scholars. Audre's tact about the uses of the Master's House would have been different if she had been speaking directly to sisters (as she does in a number of other works).

5 Gilliam and Gilliam 1999; see also Allen 2011. Likewise heralded as the Cubana par excellence—representing this mixedness—the figure of the (assumed heterosexually available) mulata in Cuban literature and culture has already been well elaborated as a character with less honor than the white woman but more than the (putatively "nonhybrid") Black woman. She possesses a complex flexibility that should not, however, be read as freedom. The Black radical tradition offers a distinct view that corrects this and describes the actual experiences of women interpellated as Black, mulata, and various other non-white appellations. Consider, for example, that Cuban and Latin American cultures more broadly have been characterized by scholars as mixed/mestizo/ creole cultures and that notions of "race mixture" and "racial pluralism" have been celebrated.

References

Alexander, M. Jacqui. 1994. "Not Just (Any) Body Can Be a Citizen: The Politics of Law, Sexuality and Postcoloniality in Trinidad and Tobago and the Bahamas." *Feminist Review* 48(1): 5–23.

Alexander, M. Jacqui. 2007. "Danger and Desire: Crossings Are Never Undertaken All at Once or Once and for All." *Small Axe: A Caribbean Journal of Criticism* 11(3): 154–66.

Allen, Jafari Sinclaire. 2011. *¡Venceremos? The Erotics of Black Self-Making in Cuba*. Durham, NC: Duke University Press.

Allen, Jafari Sinclaire. 2015. "Erotics in Medias Res: Topping Caribbean Studies from the Bottom?" *Small Axe: A Caribbean Journal of Criticism* 19(1): 159–68.

Allen, Jafari Sinclaire. 2016. "One View from a Deterritorialized Realm: How Black/Queer Renarrativizes Anthropological Analysis." *Cultural Anthropology* 31: 617–26.

Allen, Jafari Sinclaire. 2022. *There's a Disco Ball between Us: A Theory of Black Gay Life*. Durham, NC: Duke University Press.

Amory, Deb. 1992. "Lunchtime Discussion: AAA Meeting News and Info." *Society of Lesbian and Gay Anthropologists Newsletter* 14: 8–11.

Beal, Frances M. 1969. *Black Women's Manifesto; Double Jeopardy: To Be Black and Female*. New York: Third World Women's Alliance, http://www.hartford-hwp.com/archives/45a/196.html.

Behar, Ruth. 1993. "Expanding the Boundaries of Anthropology: The Cultural Criticism of Gloria Anzaldúa and Marlon Riggs." *Visual Anthropology Review* 9: 83–91.

Boellstorff, Tom. 2007. "Queer Studies in the House of Anthropology." *Annual Review of Anthropology* 36: 17–35.

Cohen, Cathy J. 1999. "What Is This Movement Doing to My Politics?" *Social Text* 61 (Winter): 111–18.

Combahee River Collective. 1983. "Combahee River Collective Statement." In *Home Girls: A Black Feminist Anthology*, edited by Barbara Smith, 272–82. New York: Kitchen Table: Women of Color Press.

Crenshaw, Kimberlé. 1989. "Demarginalizing the Intersection of Race and Sex: A Black Feminist Critique of Antidiscrimination Doctrine, Feminist Theory and Antiracist Politics." *University of Chicago Legal Forum*, article 8.

Drake, St. Clair, and Willie L. Baber. 1990. "Further Reflections on Anthropology and the Black Experience." *Transforming Anthropology* 1: 1–14.

duCille, Ann. 1994. "The Occult of True Black Womanhood: Critical Demeanor and Black Feminist Studies." *Signs: A Journal of Women in Culture and Society* 19(3): 591–629.

Gilliam, Angela. 1991. "Women's Equality and National Liberation." In *Third World Women and the Politics of Feminism*, edited by Chandra Talpade Mohanty, Ann Russo, and Lourdes Torres, 215–36. Bloomington: Indiana University Press.

Gilliam, Angela, and Onik'a Gilliam. 1999. "Odyssey: Negotiating the Subjectivity of Mulata Identity in Brazil." *Latin American Perspectives* 26(3): 60–84.

Harrison, Faye V., ed. 1991. *Decolonizing Anthropology: Moving Further toward an Anthropology of Liberation*. Arlington, VA: Association of Black Anthropologists, American Anthropological Association.

Harrison, Faye. 2008. *Outsider Within: Reworking Anthropology in the Global Age*. Urbana: University of Illinois Press.

Jobson, Ryan Cecil. 2020. "The Case for Letting Anthropology Burn: Sociocultural Anthropology in 2019." *American Anthropologist* 122(2): 259–71.

Jones, Delmos. 1970. "Toward a Native Anthropology." *Human Organization* 29: 251–59.

Jones, Delmos, 1995. "Anthropology and the Oppressed: A Reflection on 'Native' Anthropology." *NAPA Bulletin* 16: 58–70.

Lorde, Audre. 1984a. "Poetry Is Not a Luxury." In *Sister Outsider: Essays and Speeches*, 36–39. Berkeley, CA: Crossing Press.

Lorde, Audre. 1984b. "Grenada Revisited: An Interim Report." *Black Scholar* 15(1): 21–29.

Lorde, Audre. 1984c. "The Master's Tools Will Never Dismantle the Master's House." In *Sister Outsider: Essays and Speeches*, 110–14. Berkeley, CA: Crossing Press.

Lorde, Audre. 1991. "Of Generators and Survival—Hugo Letter." *Callaloo: A Journal of African Diaspora Arts and Letters* 14(1): 72–82.

Lorde, Audre. 2009. "Turning the Beat Around: Lesbian Parenting 1986." In *I Am Your Sister: Collected and Unpublished Writings of Audre Lorde*, edited by Rudolph P. Byrd, Johnnetta Betsch Cole, and Beverly Guy-Sheftall, 73–79. New York: Oxford University Press. Originally published in 1987.

Marable, Manning. 2000. "Introduction: Black Studies and the Racial Mountain." In *Dispatches from the Ebony Tower: Intellectuals Confront the African American Experience*, edited by Manning Marable, 1–28. New York: Columbia University Press.

Mintz, Sidney. 2012. "Loveless in the Boondocks: Anthropology at Bay." In *Transforming Ethnographic Knowledge*, edited by Rebecca Hardin and Kamari Maxine Clarke, 51–72. Madison: University of Wisconsin Press.

Nash, Jennifer C. 2019. *Black Feminism Reimagined: After Intersectionality*. Durham, NC: Duke University Press.

Parker, Pat. 2016. "Revolution: It's Not Neat or Pretty, or Quick." In *The Complete Works of Pat Parker*, edited by Julie R. Enszer, 254–59. Dover, FL: Sinister Wisdom.

Riggs, Marlon, dir. 1989. *Tongues Untied*. California Newsreel.

Saint, Assotto, 1996. "Why I Write." In *Spells of a Voodoo Doll: The Poems, Fiction, Essays and Plays of Assotto Saint*, 3–8. New York: Masquerade.

Spillers, Hortense J. 2003. "Interstices: A Small Drama of Words." In *Black, White, and in Color: Essays on American Literature and Culture*, 152–75. Chicago: University of Chicago Press.

Trouillot, Michel-Rolph. 1991. "Anthropology and the Savage Slot: The Poetics and Politics of Otherness." In *Recapturing Anthropology: Working in the Present*, edited by Richard Fox, 18–44. Santa Fe, NM: School of American Research Press.

Vance, Carole S., editor. 1984. *Pleasure and Danger: Exploring Female Sexuality*. Boston: Routledge and Kegan Paul.

Williams, Brackette F. 1996. "Skinfolk, Not Kinfolk: Comparative Reflections on the Identity of Participant-Observation in Two Field Situations." In *Feminist Dilemmas in Fieldwork*, edited by Diane L. Wolf, 72–95. New York: Routledge.

Margot Weiss

2

Queer Theories from Somewhere

Situated Knowledges and Other Queer Empiricisms

Does Queer Theory + Ethnography = Queer Anthropology? This is the usual origin story: queer anthropology as the offspring of a union between humanities-based queer theory and anthropology's ethnographic purview. Or perhaps, rather than union, an affair—and a one-sided one at that. In the mid-1990s, the story goes, the relatively un- or undertheorized "gay and lesbian" anthropology was transformed by queer theory, as anthropologists flirted with innovative, groundbreaking work by scholars like Eve Kosofsky Sedgwick and Judith Butler. The resulting queer anthropology applied (queer) theory to (ethnographic) data, asking, "How does Butler's theory of gender performativity (or Jasbir Puar's homonationalism, or Lee Edelman's reproductive futurity) illuminate X local context?" As this story goes, queer anthropology is reducible to ethnographic context, generating no theory, and innovation goes only one way.[1]

This chapter tells a different story.[2] I explore how the hierarchical binary of *theory* and *data* positions ethnography as only data—local, particular, descriptive case study—and queer theory as unsituated, purportedly universal, available for any context because it is tied to none.[3] I consider how this binary has effaced both queer theory's own historical situatedness and other situated theory—including queer anthropology. Queer anthropology's contribution to multidisciplinary queer studies goes beyond "ethnographizing" it (offering a take on the so-called real world rather than a text) and even beyond "transnationalizing" it (attending to places outside its usual American purview) (Boellstorff 2007a, 3).[4] Instead, queer anthropology is the origin of several of queer theory's most celebrated critical innovations, including its foundational concern with antinormativity (via Gayle Rubin's [1993] "Thinking Sex," originally published in 1984) and gender (as) performativity (via Esther Newton's [1972] *Mother Camp*).[5]

But rather than end here, with a neat reversal of origins—Newton for Butler, Rubin for Sedgwick, anthropology on top—I follow queer of color scholars Kadji Amin (2020) and Michael Hames-García (2011), who argue that both canonical origin stories and attempts to rewrite them without grappling with their conditions of emergence will reproduce and consolidate their formative elisions. I consider how queer theory's disavowal of empiricism helps efface the situatedness of queer theory's knowledges and with that, shores up a queer theory that is white and American—even as it claims universal purview.[6] Writing in 2007, Tom Boellstorff highlights queer anthropology's "critical empiricism," which, while "not fetishizing 'data' nevertheless demands that theorizations be accountable to their subjects of study . . . the actual lives of persons embodied in specific historical, cultural, and material contexts" (2007b, 19). I double down on this call, considering how displacing situated theory and queer empiricism evades (queer) theory's accountability to both its subjects/sources and its historical context.

The legacies of the hierarchy of theory/data extend beyond anthropology: it is not only queer anthropology in the "data slot," but also scholars and interlocutors located outside Global North (primarily US) humanities departments. As Kenyan-based queer studies scholar Keguro Macharia puts it, the global travels of a deracinated queer theory not only produces African philosophers, theorists, and intellectuals as "illegible and uninteresting to mainstream queer studies" (2016, 186) but also positions "queer African voices and experiences . . . as 'data' or 'evidence,' not as modes of theory or as challenges to the conceptual assumptions that drive queer studies"

(185). In this dynamic, what is recognizably "queer" is what is legible to "the US thinkers we can care about" (186) and the United States remains centered as "the place to which information flows" (187; see also Mikdashi and Puar 2016).

With this in mind, I consider how reading empiricism back in to queer theory—centering empirical genealogies of situated queer theory by queer anthropologists; postcolonial theorists; and feminist and Black, Indigenous, and queer of color critics—might help dislodge the universalist aspirations that produce its unmarked white- and Americanness. How can we rethink the politics of knowledge production beyond insisting that queer anthropologists join the ranks of purportedly universal queer theory? How can we center our accountability not only to our interlocutors, but also to the effaced subjects and sources in our theory? These are the core questions that animate this chapter.

Queer Theory + Ethnography = Queer Anthropology?

Canonical origin stories of queer theory date it to 1990, the year of the conference organized on "queer theory" by Teresa de Lauretis (1991) and the publication of Butler's *Gender Trouble: Feminism and the Subversion of Identity* (1990) and Sedgwick's *Epistemology of the Closet* (1990). In 1991, Michael Warner's special section of *Social Text*, "Fear of a Queer Planet," was published (expanded as Warner 1993). Queer theory was anti-establishment and anti-identitarian—a challenge to the purportedly stable epistemologies of "gay and lesbian studies." Intellectually aligned with the political scene around AIDS activism, it built on (and queered) Michel Foucault's genealogical approach to sexuality and power, Jacques Derrida's deconstructive approach to textual play and signification, and Jacques Lacan's (and his feminist readers') rereading of sex and subjectivity.

And yet the first time a theorist sought to "queer" sex and power was not in 1990. That wasn't even the first use of "queer" (in this sense) in print: credit for that perhaps goes to Gloria Anzaldúa's (1983) "La Prieta." Genealogies are political. Hames-García argues that starting queer theory's canonical origin story in 1990 consolidates its whiteness by positioning prior Black and women of color feminism, queer of color critique, and postcolonial queer/gender theory (the work of, for instance, Barbara Smith, Audre Lorde, Joseph Beam) as derivative or peripheral, rather than preceding and formative. Hames-García (like Jafari Allen in this volume and in 2016) provides

QUEER THEORIES FROM SOMEWHERE   55

an "alternative genealogy . . . for thinking about sexuality outside the Eurocentric and colonial frameworks of queer theory" (2011, 21).

In queer anthropology, when we repeat queer theory's canonical origin story, we not only repeat its "Eurocentric and colonial frameworks," but also position queer theory as both prior and external to anthropology. Take, as one example of this frequently told story, Rosalind Morris's (1995) review of the "new anthropology of sex and gender," which promises to reveal the impact of queer performance theory *on* anthropology (567, 568)—even as her essay highlights innovative (and frequently prior) anthropological theorization from practice theory to Rubin's "sex/gender system" (1975) to Marilyn Strathern's rereading of gender.

This origin story also elides the multidisciplinary conversations that shaped early queer theory. For rather than solely a province of the humanities, the queer turn in the 1990s emerged across the humanities, arts, and humanistic social sciences, including anthropology. The multiple locations of theory in, for instance, *GLQ*'s 1994 special issue "InQueery/InTheory/ InDeed" (based on the 1994 North American Lesbian, Gay, and Bisexual Studies Conference at the University of Iowa) include anthropologists, literary critics, and performance and cultural studies scholars Lee Edelman, Kath Weston, Ann Cvetkovich, Peggy Phelan, Lawrence Cohen, Martin Manalansan, and Elspeth Probyn. These conversations also produced an early "transnational turn" (before its canonical "turn" in the mid-2000s), reflected in special issues (such as *positions*' 1994 "Circuits of Desire," *GLQ*'s 1997 "Queer Transexions of Race, Nation and Gender," and *GLQ*'s 1999 "Thinking Sexuality Transnationally") and conferences (such as CLAGS' "Queer Globalization" conference in 1998, published as Cruz-Malavé and Manalansan 2002) that featured insights from scholars in anthropology, area studies, art, cultural studies, English, ethnic studies, film, history, and postcolonial feminist studies.

Queer anthropology in the 1990s did not merely "apply" queer theory— it helped create it. Anthropologists like Martin Manalansan, Deborah Elliston, David Valentine, Elizabeth Povinelli, Lisa Rofel, and Gloria Wekker took up antifoundational postcolonial and transnational critiques of the categories "gay" and "lesbian" across cultures; advanced complex analyses of race, class, nation, gender, and diaspora; inaugurated reflexive explorations of queer and trans embodiment and erotics; and theorized the challenges of linguistic categorization as concepts, representations, and practices moved across borders (see the introduction to this volume for more of queer anthropology's history). Based as they are on empirical theorizations from somewhere, these queer theories critically interrogated US-based categories of sex and gender as they intersect with racialization, nation, colonialism, political economy, and globalization.

And yet, by the early 2000s, as queer studies became increasingly interested in the transnational, anthropology had seemingly dropped out of the conversation. For instance, in the field-defining 2005 special issue "What's Queer about Queer Studies Now?," editors David L. Eng, Jack Halberstam, and José Esteban Muñoz call for a theorization of queer's relationship to racialization, geopolitics, global capitalism, immigration, citizenship, and empire. They foreground crucial interventions in queer diaspora and queer of color critique, yet this work is seemingly disconnected from prior or ongoing work in queer anthropology.[7] Beyond the irony of ignoring the insights of queer anthropology while seeking a more transnational or global queer studies, early 2000s queer studies consolidates a view of anthropology as just "data"—and colonialist, voyeuristic, objectifying data at that. As Anjali Arondekar puts it, anthropology has been viewed in queer studies as "the *bête noire* of sexuality studies and a central trafficker in colonial models of culture" (2007, 339). Here, I do not displace or minimize anthropology's white supremacist and colonial epistemologies. Rather, I am interested in how projecting complicity with colonial ways of knowing onto anthropology (alone) enables an illusory political purity and erases the intellectual history of collaboration between scholars in multiple disciplines. It also, it bears mentioning, screens out decades of decolonizing scholarship by queer, feminist, Black, Indigenous, and other anthropologists of color.

Arondekar explores queer anthropology as a "consistent site of innovative queer scholarship" (2007, 339), its self-reflexive, situated theory a contrast to work in queer studies that advances historically thin understandings of "the materialities of colonialism and empire" (338). She critically examines the situated queer theory of Tom Boellstorff"'s "dubbing" as a critique of translation and globalization (2005), Gayatri Reddy's exploration of the "hyper (in)visibility" of *hijra* as exotic objects of difference (2005), and Ara Wilson's theorizations of the "intimate" economies of global capitalism (2004). We might add Martin Manalansan's reading of queer, diasporic language, play, and topography (2003); Elizabeth Povinelli's juxtaposition of the "autological" and the "genealogical" (2006); Gloria Wekker's innovative exploration of Afro-Surinamese gender/sexuality (2006); and, slightly later, Kale Bantigue Fajardo's "crosscurrents" as a critique of trans

QUEER THEORIES FROM SOMEWHERE   57

nation (2011), Jafari Allen's theorization of erotic subjectivity (2011), and Naisargi Dave's queer ethics (2012).[8] Rather than mere "data," this rich vein of queer anthropology challenges universal (Western) epistemologies of sex and gender by illuminating their culturally specific, historically produced intersections with race, (trans)nation, colonialism, class, religion, and gender.

Why, then, is this not the story we tell?

Situated Theories, Queer Empiricisms

One answer has to do with queer theory's anti-empiricism. Literary critic Heather Love's recent work considers how midcentury sociological theories of deviance were foundational to 1990s queer theory and yet are unrecognized—in the humanities, that is (Love 2021).[9] Love argues that this glaring omission is based both on the caricature of empirical/social science approaches as objectifying, naively positivist, and in league with state control, and on queer theory's aspirational identification with its own radical antidisciplinarity.[10] In this story, the social sciences are viewed as (only) sites of unsophisticated, violent complicity, allowing queer theory to imagine itself "beyond method and utterly undisciplined" (Love 2019, 30)—against "normal business in the academy," in Warner's phrase (1993, xxvi)—even as it frequently takes place in English departments using recognizable methods. The "refusal to locate ourselves," Love writes, is a disavowal in need of some critical reflexivity (2019, 30).

This intervention might sound familiar to those of us in queer anthropology. Back in 1998, Weston argued that social science is imagined as a latecomer to the queer studies party because what anthropology is asked to bring is data—the "facts" of "how the natives do it" (12). This voyeuristic fantasy of the anthropologist as "unskilled" collector or "documentarian"—"a purveyor of distilled data ready to be taken up into other people's theories and analyses" (12)—consolidates a data/theory, social sciences/humanities divide of academic labor. It also reproduces a fantasy of data as "raw," "pure content" awaiting discovery and collection like "driftwood on the beach," shorn of the (theoretical) epistemologies that produce it as such (21, see also Weston 1995). Weston links this salvage imagery to both the displacement of anthropological theory as theory and to the popular desire for anthropology's exotic/erotic depictions of Others.[11] The historical demand for anthropology to provide lavish, thickly described "data" about queer Others elsewhere shapes not only "ethnocartographic" epistemologies within the discipline (as Weston labeled this mapping project [1993, 341]), but also outside of it.[12] So if today we can reproduce, by rote, a critique of ethnocartography *within* queer anthropology (even as that project is nowhere near done), I see the extension of the ethnocartographic imagination in the fantasy that anthropologists have the data (about non-Western, non-white objects of study) while queer theorists have the theory—what might be made from that data, elsewhere, in the metropole.

Queer anthropologists, postcolonial theorists, feminist and queer of color critics, and Black, Indigenous, and other anthropologists of color have long charted a different approach to situated theory and queer empiricism not founded on (stolen) data about exotic Others. These epistemologies are resolutely partial and particularistic, and yet they scale up and outward to historical, economic, and structural connections, often disjunctive—including complex knowledge formulated outside the academy. Queer empiricism is "kinky," in Danilyn Rutherford's phrase: an "empiricism that admits that one never gets to the bottom of things" (2012, 465). Like Boellstorff's "critical empiricism" (2007b), these approaches deconstruct a static binary of theory versus data by producing situated theory that is accountable to emplaced locales, subjects, and contexts—a check on queer theory's fantasy of being nowhere and thus everywhere.

Reconsidering our origin stories in light of the fundamental problematic of theory/data reveals not only that queer theory's anti-empiricism locates anthropologists as "data-bearers" (Weston 1998, 23) but also that this anti-empiricism strips queer theoretical concepts of their historical and social particularity, rendering them purportedly universal, uniquely free to move without their situations of emergence. As Faye Harrison (2016) writes in the context of decolonizing anthropology, the fantasy of "theory" as free-floating and unmoored from location feeds the division of labor between disembodied, masculinist, white, Northern theory and data as the knowledge of situated Others, especially in the Global South. Harrison explores ex-centric theory from historically peripheralized locales (2016, 161) beyond the North Atlantic metropole, including theory from African and Indigenous intellectuals, from interlocutors, praxis-based theory, and theory in/of art and fiction. Underlining theory as a practice of situated knowledge, in line with decades of work by women of color and Black feminists, is critical to recenter queer theory's debt to situated knowledges—including those from anthropology.

To tell a new genealogy is to consider how queer theoretical insights are always situated, even when their empirical ground is disavowed. It is to consider how "different locations, archives, and histories" might "provincialize the United States" as the only source/site of queer theory (Mikdashi and Puar 2016, 218). And it is to underline theory's accountability to its subjects, sources, and historical contexts. As Gayle Rubin put it in a 1994 interview with Judith Butler, even as empirical work is "often treated as some kind of low-status, even stigmatized, activity that is inferior to 'theory,'" it remains the case that some "who are contemptuous of empirical research can be quite naive about the material used in their own 'theoretical' work. Often, data come in, as it were, by the back door" (1994, 92).

So let's stay with Rubin and Butler and jump back a bit further in our story, to two crucial concepts in early queer theory: antinormativity and gender performativity. I revisit these canonical figures and concepts with an emphasis on situated theorization to read queer empiricism back into queer theory. My aim in challenging queer theory's "naive" anti-empiricism is to dislodge the universalism that reproduces its unmarked white- and Americanness, and instead illuminate a genealogy of empirical, situated queer theory that includes, but goes beyond, queer anthropology.

"Thinking Sex": Sex, Power, and Queer Antinormativity

Gayle Rubin's "Thinking Sex: Notes for a Radical Theory of the Politics of Sexuality," first published in 1984, is a classic: it begins many a course in queer studies and opens *The Gay and Lesbian Studies Reader*, the first in queer studies (title notwithstanding). Its epochal opening line is "The time has come to think about sex" (1993, 3). Rubin unfolds a history of American and Western European morality crusades against homosexuals, sex workers, masturbators, and other "deviants" and "sexual outlaws." She focuses on how the state and social institutions "routinely intervene[]" in sexual behavior," producing "sexual stratification and erotic persecution" (18). Sex, she argues, "is a vector of oppression," operating through "identification, surveillance, apprehension, treatment, incarceration, and punishment" (18). It is, in a word, "political," "organized into systems of power, which reward and encourage some individuals and activities, while punishing and suppressing others" (34): the hetero, vanilla, married, and

Figure I. **The Sex Hierarchy: The Charmed Circle vs. the Outer Limits**

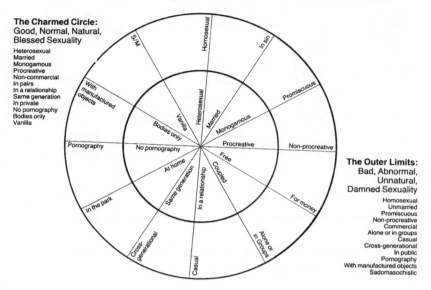

2.1   The Sex Hierarchy: The Charmed Circle vs. the Outer Limits (from *Deviations*, Gayle Rubin copyright 1984)

monogamous versus the homo, sex worker, sadomasochistic Others (13; see figures 2.1 and 2.2). And perhaps most critically, sex, she argues, is "autonomous" (34): "the system of sexual oppression cuts across other modes of social inequality, sorting out individuals and groups according to its own intrinsic dynamics. It is not reducible to, or understandable in terms of, class, race, ethnicity, or gender" (22).

It is difficult to exaggerate the impact of "Thinking Sex" on queer studies. Many consider it the field's inaugural text, as Heather Love put it at a conference in honor of the essay's twenty-fifth anniversary (2011, 10). Rubin demurs: "I was not trying to found a field," she says (Rubin and Butler 1994, 88); "lesbian and gay studies certainly didn't start with me, or at such a late date" (89). Rubin's own genealogy places "Thinking Sex" in the longer and underacknowledged history of gay liberation, homophile, mid-century deviance and urban sociological scholarship, much of it produced outside the academy before the translation of Foucault's *The History of Sexuality, Volume 1* into English in 1978 (Rubin 2002, 2023; see also Scott Morgensen's chapter in this volume). But it is the role played by both Rubin's

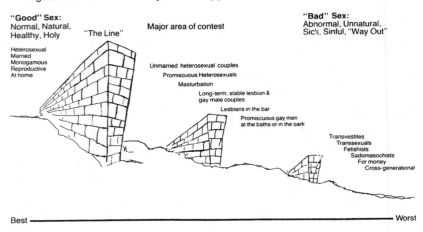

2.2 The Sex Hierarchy: The Struggle Over Where to Draw the Line (from *Deviations*, Gayle Rubin © 1984)

empiricism and her argument for sex as an autonomous vector of oppression that I consider here.

I don't think it is too much to say that, by treating sex as autonomous, Rubin enables the queer break with gay and lesbian studies—centralizing normativity (not identity). This line is taken up by Sedgwick's *Epistemology of the Closet*, as she teases out sexuality as a "master term" of modern Western identity, alongside yet distinct from gender, class, and race (1990, 11). It grounds Warner's reading of sexuality as a "field of power" and "primary category for social analysis" (1993, viii, xv), normalized and regulated through social institutions. The centrality of sexual normalization undergirds Warner's coinage of "heteronormativity," the "pervasive and often invisible" structuring function of "normal" sexuality (1991, 3).

"Thinking Sex" also expresses, presciently, the constitutive tension between an expansive (universalizing, in Sedgwick's language) and contractive (minoritizing) reading of "queer." Is queer about multiple forms of anti- or nonnormativity (defined "against the normal rather than the heterosexual," as Warner puts it [1993, xxvi]), or does it have special affinity to sexuality and/or heteronormativity?[13] Rubin characterizes her essay as "protoqueer" in its attention to coalitions of perverts (2011a, 40)—a line taken up in contemporary work on queer beyond homo/hetero dichotomies, in studies of sex work, porn, BDSM, and other non-LGBT queer practices and communities.

Rubin's empirical interest in the changing historical frames of sexual hierarchy, as shifting social norms and state recognition move the "line" between "good" and "bad" sex, helps show how some "sexual outsiders" move into the charmed circle and others remain punished or excluded. Forty years later, contemporary LGBT absorption in the state and structures of oppression shows the fruit of this approach: as in Lisa Duggan's (2002) work on "homonormativity" (the enfolding of some gay subjects into neoliberal US national culture) and Jasbir Puar's reading of "homonationalism" (how some white American gays and lesbians are celebrated and "folded into life," while Muslim/Arab Others are *queered* as "sexually pathological and deviant populations targeted for death" [2007, 24]). Rubin's insistence on sex as a historical locus of state surveillance and punishment is also borne out in new work on the state and its sexual panics and regulations.

So we might wish to correct the canonical origin story of queer theory and start not in 1990, but in 1984, giving Gayle Rubin, anthropologist, pride of place in establishing queer theory—perhaps especially its antinormative mode. And yet revisiting origin stories also means grappling with the critical legacies of the queer theory that follows from "Thinking Sex." Hames-García marks "Thinking Sex" as the origin of a "separatist" thread of queer theory that views sexuality "as distinct from gender, race, and class"—a narrative that depends on "the erasure or rejection of several decades" of intersectional work in feminist and queer of color and postcolonial critique (2011, 22). Similarly, Sharon Holland (2011) argues that, in addition to its salutatory effects, by centering a (white) history of sexuality and by using a gay:Black analogy to unfold sexual oppression, "Thinking Sex" consolidates the normative whiteness of queer theory's conceptions of sexuality, history, and power. Holland returns to Hortense Spillers's "Interstices: A Small Drama of Words," which, like "Thinking Sex," was also first printed in *Pleasure and Danger*, and asks what is missed when Rubin, and not Spillers, is considered the foundation of queer/sexuality studies.

These scholars argue that Rubin's extraordinarily generative emphasis on "an autonomous theory and politics specific to sexuality" (1993, 34) helped canonize the normative whiteness of queer theory by theorizing sexual marginality as an axis of difference autonomous from racialization (as well as class, gender, and disability). Consider Rubin alongside Cathy J. Cohen's (1997) analysis of Black "nonnormative heterosexualities." Like Rubin, Cohen also takes up coalitions of deviants seen as not "normal, moral, or worthy" (Cohen 1997, 442), the titular "punks, bulldaggers, and welfare queens." Both Cohen and Rubin are anti-identitarian, critiquing "simple dichotomies between heterosexual and everything 'queer'" as Cohen puts it (438); and both center those "outside of the dominant constructed norm of state-sanctioned white middle- and upper-class heterosexuality" (441). But while Rubin emphasizes the autonomy of sexual practice, Cohen's intervention into (white) queer studies and activism shows how norms around sexual practice are already raced and classed. Cohen's foundational work in queer of color critique frames sexual regulation as a practice of white supremacy: how "gender and sexual differences variegate racial formations," as Rod Ferguson describes the intervention of queer of color critique (2004, 3).

Simply acknowledging queer anthropology in queer theory's canonical origin story does not, then, redeem it.[14] But what queer anthropology *does* offer is an insistence on situated, empirical theory—a challenge to queer theory's universalism. For "Thinking Sex" is nothing if not keyed to a particular history; Rubin's situated theory and queer empiricism are marked on nearly every page by the exigencies of US feminism's sex politics during the ascendancy of the New Right in the late 1970s. As Rubin notes, wryly, "nothing dates scholarly literature more than references to current events . . ." "yet I feel strongly that we should use all the intellectual tools we possess to think about the present, so I live with the consequences" (2011b, 29).

And so, to highlight the legacies of Rubin's queer theory a decade before the canonical 1990s is also to suggest that we attend to the grounded nature of her theorization and read back in its queer empiricism. It is not often noted that many of the scholars in this brief account—Rubin, Cohen, Ferguson, Duggan—have social science backgrounds. And while "Thinking Sex," "Punks, Bulldaggers, and Welfare Queens," or *Aberrations in Black* are not typically described as empirical social science (not least because of their authors' vigorous critiques of their disciplines), I see in each a queer empiricism—a theoretical frame that illuminates particular forms of power (and not others), situated within particular intellectual, historical, and political contexts and moments (and not others). These are *theories*, not *a theory*. This kind of "humility about the imperfection of our formulations" (Rubin 2009, 371) is one way to resist the universalization that produces

64   MARGOT WEISS

work as *the* theory, and opens up queer theories from somewhere—situated, circumscribed, and accountable to their origins.

Gender Trouble: Performativity, Performance, Drag

In that same 1994 interview, Gayle Rubin reminisces about introducing Judith Butler to Foucault. It was 1979, and Rubin was presenting an early version of "Thinking Sex" at a conference in New York. "I think you were at one of these," she says to Butler, who replies, "Right. The first time I saw a copy of Michel Foucault's *The History of Sexuality*."

> GR Was I waving it around?
>
> JB Yes. You introduced it to me.
>
> GR I was really, just totally hot for that book.
>
> JB Yes, you made me hot for it too. (72)

The conversation certainly paid off. *Gender Trouble* (1990) is perhaps the most recognized text in queer theory: far surpassing *The History of Sexuality* in Google Scholar's citation count, it is taught, cited, translated, fanzined, memed, ridiculed, fawned over—because of its argument for gender as performative.

Gender, Butler writes, is "performatively constituted by the very 'expressions' that are said to be its results" (1990, 25). It is "the repeated stylization of the body" (33); a "doing, though not a doing by a subject who might be said to pre-exist the deed" (25). Butler's reading departs from (Derrida's reading of) J. L. Austin's theory of "performative" speech acts, in which saying something ("I now pronounce you husband and wife") *does* something (weds said couple). For anti-essentialist, poststructuralist feminist theory, gender performativity was a strong argument against the binary of sex/gender, as it located "sex" as an effect (rather than origin) of the stylized repetition of norms systematized through compulsory heterosexuality. Stable, fixed gender is thus an illusion, "a performative accomplishment" of compelled reiteration. And yet the citationality of gendered performativity opens up possibilities of resignification, of doing gender differently. As Butler asks: "which possibilities of doing gender repeat and displace through hyperbole, dissonance, internal confusion and proliferation, the very constructs by which they are mobilized?" (1990, 31).

As with "Thinking Sex," it would be hard to overstate the importance of this work for queer studies, including queer anthropology. Anthropologists immediately took up Butler's argument to consider gender norms and cultural intelligibility outside the United States: Jennifer Robertson among Takarasuka performers in Japan (1992), Rosalind Morris on Thai sex/sexualities (1994), and Don Kulick among *travesti* in Brazil (1998). Returning to its foundation in language theory, linguistic anthropologists challenged what Rudi Gaudio called Butler's "almost exclusive reliance on cultural evidence from the Euro-western world" to consider Hausa *'yan daudu* (Gaudio 1995, 124) or *hijras* in northern India (see Hall 2013 for a retrospective).

Our case for queer empiricism becomes doubly important, however, when we consider the infamous study of drag toward the end of *Gender Trouble*. "In imitating gender," Butler writes, "drag implicitly reveals the imitative structure of gender itself" (135). This insight into drag's illumination of gender performativity comes from Esther Newton's analysis in *Mother Camp: Female Impersonators in America*. Published in 1972 from Newton's 1968 dissertation, *Mother Camp* is based on ethnographic research with white Midwestern female impersonators in the 1960s; it is perhaps the first book-length ethnography in what-would-become queer anthropology (see Valentine 2018 for new reviews).

In 1988, Butler published "Performative Acts and Gender Constitution," an early take on performativity. In it, they note that they are drawing from "theatrical, anthropological, and philosophical discourses," including anthropological literature on kinship and Turnerian ritual as "social drama," Richard Schechner's work on the social distinctions between "on stage" and off (a nod to the 1980s formation of performance studies as the union of anthropology and theater studies—another displaced queer genealogy), and, finally, Newton, who appears in the following footnote: "In *Mother Camp* . . . anthropologist Esther Newton gives an urban ethnography of drag queens in which she suggests that all gender might be understood on the model of drag" (1988, 528).

Gender Trouble has more on Newton, crediting her with suggesting that "the structure of impersonation reveals one of the key fabricating mechanisms through which the social construction of gender takes place" (1990, 136–37). Butler writes, citing Newton, "at its most complex [drag]

66   MARGOT WEISS

is a double inversion that says, 'appearance is an illusion.' Drag says . . . 'my "outside" appearance is feminine, but my essence "inside" [the body] is masculine.' At the same time it symbolizes the opposite inversion; 'my appearance "outside" [my body, my gender] is masculine, but my essence "inside" [myself] is feminine'" (Butler 1990, 137; citing Newton 1972, 103). Here we can see how Newton's insight into drag's double inversion is at the center of Butler's reading of parody, imitation, and the subversion of sex/gender's own origin story.

So again, we might press queer theory's origin story back to 1972, to celebrate Newton as the originator of queer "performativity." This genealogical retelling does not displace what many have noted as the constitutive whiteness of both *Mother Camp* and *Gender Trouble*—indeed, it recenters whiteness in our queer genealogy. Yet, as with "Thinking Sex," this retelling does resurrect an absented queer empiricism, and with that, queer theory's accountability and its debt to the subjects of Newton's ethnographic work: the drag performers in the bars, clubs, and streets of Kansas City and Chicago (among other locales) who were her interlocutors.

Recentering grounded and situated queer theory might help us tell another genealogy, one that does not erase its sources or the context of its emergence. I am thinking of queer empirical theory that—like Newton's—explicitly grounds performativity in specific contexts of performance. For instance, performance studies scholar E. Patrick Johnson's (2001) "quare" critique of the whiteness of queer theory explores situated performances of Black queerness, grounding performativity in the materiality of raced, classed, and gendered embodiment (3, 10). Even as he refuses a binary between performativity and performance, Johnson emphasizes context, historical moment, audience, vernacular expression, and location. Sociologist Vivian Namaste's (1996) critique of Butler's effacement of trans lives also argues against decontextualized readings of performativity. The violence of representation, for Namaste, comes from queer theory's displacement of everyday practices and social worlds—the material realities that matter to trans people—when rendering trans subjects figures of gender or racial crossing (see also Horton and Edelman in this volume). Johnson and Namaste insist on queerly empirical approaches to queer theory: their call for accountability to their subjects grounded in the particular social contexts of their work. This is a situated queer theory that seeks to remain accountable to its subjects and sources—the drag queens, kinksters, and queers who are the "grounds" of queer theories, acknowledged or not.

QUEER THEORIES FROM SOMEWHERE   67

Queer Theories from Somewhere

In an important essay from 2016, Maya Mikdashi and Jasbir Puar argue that much of contemporary queer theory is, as they put it, "queer theory as American studies"—the United States the "arbiter and funnel for the legibility of theory elsewhere" (2016, 215, 216). This American-centeredness is disavowed, however, through a fantasy of queer theory as "unmarked and unencumbered by location," "geopolitically uninflected" (216). In this situation, "queer theory from elsewhere" can only be read as data: "the work of queer theorists in area studies (rarely read by queer theory as 'Queer Theory' and often relegated to 'sexuality studies') is understood as a 'case study' of specifics rather than an interruption of the canonical treatments" (216). Resonant with Macharia and penned two decades after Weston, the persistence of these elisions is one legacy of queer studies' origin story about where theory comes from, who writes it, and how it travels—and who is the object of that theory, the local case study, the data.

I have tried to tell a different story of queer theory, to show how—rather than emerging fully formed from the humanities in 1990—core theoretical interventions came from queer anthropology and other situated, queerly empirical theorizations. I have emphasized multidisciplinary conversations between scholars in a range of disciplines, including American studies, anthropology, Black studies, ethnic studies, feminist studies, history, performance studies, postcolonial studies, sociology, and, yes, English, to disrupt the story that queer theory is the purview of the humanities alone. I have sought not only to challenge the idea of anthropology/social science as "data"/particularity and queer theory/humanities as "theory"/universal, but to show how the latter elides its dependence on and derivation from the former—in ways that repeat the colonial relation between the periphery (Others in the Global South) and the center ("us" liberal subjects of modernity in the West/Global North). I have not, however, proffered queer anthropology as a panacea: instead, I have suggested queer anthropology might help us see the situatedness of all theory. This might help us tell a different story, a genealogy of kinky, queer empiricism calibrated to some theoretical horizons, some geopolitical locations—and not others: queer theories, not theory.

That genealogy might include recent transnational, transdisciplinary dialogues that show the value of queerly empirical epistemologies. For instance, Giancarlo Cornejo argues that it isn't possible to think critically about queer or *travestismo* in Peru, or for US-based queer studies scholars to "engage in a transnational dialogue with Latin American queer studies," while ignoring "the important tradition of queer ethnographies that has contributed and contributes to deprovincialize queer thinking" (2019, 458). There is new interest in critical area studies, often forged in conversations between anthropologists and literary critics (among others). For instance, Howard Chiang and Alvin Wong center China and the Sinophone world in a queer Asian regionalism that might move transnational queer studies beyond its "heavy reliance on the intersectional and diaspora models developed out of US-based ethnic studies" which, even when intended "to counter a Eurocentric version of gay and lesbian studies," "'still pivot on the first world'" (2016, 1645, citing Ara Wilson). Chiang and Wong turn to anthropology as part of a "transdisciplinary conversation" that might overcome "'the myth of (Western-derived) theoretical frameworks as general and universal and of local (non-Western) cultures as merely local and particular'" (1646, 1647, citing Martin et al.).

In Black queer and trans studies, the return to Spillers that Holland called for has disrupted queer theory's (white, US-centered) universalizations of foundational gendered categories of the human and opened up new multidisciplinary diasporic conversations. For instance, theorizations of the Black/queer Atlantic connect anthropologists, literary critics, poets, and artists, including Omise'eke Natasha Tinsley, Ana-Maurine Lara, Jafari Allen, Lyndon Gill, and Vanessa Agard-Jones (Tinsley 2008; Allen and Tinsley 2019). In African queer studies, a turn to African (rather than Euro-American) gender categories has also led to new theorizations, for instance, Ashley Currier and Thérèse Migraine-George's collaborations (e.g., 2016) and Kirk Fiereck, Neville Hoad, and Danai S. Mupotsa's recent examination of the "customary" in queer Africa (2020). This broad range of multidisciplinary queer work in Latin America, East Asia, the Black Atlantic, and Africa challenges queer theory's facile dismissal of the empirical as just data, stories, raw material—and insists, instead, on situated theory that is grounded in and accountable to particular histories and social worlds.

This chapter has reflected on the queer empiricisms and situated theorizations that precede, establish, interrupt, critique, and extend beyond the "around 1990s" canonical origin story of queer theory. My ode to other stories answers the call to "multiply [queer theory's] theoretical genealogies" by returning to its intellectual contexts and legacies (Amin 2020, 26). These legacies include the disavowal of the situatedness of all knowledges—a disavowal that comes from projecting specificity elsewhere while refusing self-reflexive accountability to sources, communities, and contexts. Queer anthropology also has multiple legacies: its foundational role in some of queer theory's most celebrated critical innovations, including antinormativity, gender performativity, and the transnational turn—but also its more ambivalent role disrupting some of queer's universalizing, ethnocartographic gaze on sexual/gendered Others while reproducing other forms of white and US (or Global North) categories of sex, gender, and sexuality. So if redemption is not my story arc, I end with that call to multiply the critical locations of our queer theory. As I see it, an important step in rethinking what counts as "theory" is to read what is written out of the story as "empirical." Doing so might help us move toward queer theories that build on the insights of anthropological, queer of color, and postcolonial feminist approaches to empiricism and accountability—and see all queer theories as particular, situated views from somewhere.

Notes

1 Two threads (of many) that disambiguate "anthropology" and "ethnography" include Ingold 2008, whose focus is on theory, method, and practice; and Gill 2018 and Jackson 2013, who both write against "ethnography" as a form of mastery/domination.

2 On the politics of origin stories, see Hemmings 2011.

3 For more on the relationship between data and theory as a problem of queer methodologies, see Boellstorff 2010. See also Weiss 2011.

4 I use *queer studies* to refer to the multidisciplinary field of study organized around *queer*—a field that includes anthropology, if in a minor key, and is in conversation with feminist, trans, Indigenous, critical race, Black, postcolonial, and diaspora studies—indeed, as formatively so. I use *queer theory* as the imperfect designation for what has come to be recognized as such: concepts and figures around which the field coheres. In this way, my use of *theory* is descriptive, not prescriptive: as we shall see, the very designation of theory against data is one of the main sites of trouble in the history I trace.

5 See Wiegman and Wilson 2015 for more on what they call queer theory's "normative antinormativity." My attention to anthropology should not be seen to negate other genealogies, including the feminist ethnomethodological work of the late 1970s.

6 My focus throughout is on the story of theory/data, not on the intent of particular authors (whose theory emerges from specific case studies and textual and filmic analysis). Nor am I arguing that theory must stay *only* with its context of emergence—indeed, anthropology's queerly promiscuous use of theory across contexts is one of the hallmarks of its comparative method. My point is that when we attribute situatedness only to ethnography and imagine queer theoretical concepts as uniquely portable, we efface the situatedness of queer theory's knowledge production.

7 To be clear, it is not that the special issue was anti-ethnographic; indeed, one (of the sixteen) contributors *is* an anthropologist, and other contributors ground their work in particular historical, social, and geopolitical contexts. But it is to say that the only explicit mention of "anthropology" in the introduction is negative, and none of the prior work by anthropologists, except Manalansan (as a contributor), is cited.

8 For a conceptual review of more recent theoretical scholarship in queer anthropology, see Weiss 2022.

9 Gayle Rubin in particular has long argued against the erasure of decades of empirical work on sexuality before the 1980s and 1990s. See especially Rubin 2002, 2023; Weston 1998.

10 See Wiegman 2012 for more on queer theory's radical aspirations; see also Weiss 2015.

11 See also Morris, who argues that the demand for anthropology to provide "testimonial examples of sex/gender systems less rigid or constraining than those of the postindustrial West" (1995, 579) for the consumption of liberal white, settler subjects has been active at least since Margaret Mead.

12 See Jackson 2013 for a critique of Geertzian "thick description" as a form of ethnographic mastery.

13 For crucial explorations of queer's normalizations in and beyond sexuality, see Eng and Puar 2020, Mikdashi and Puar 2016, Wiegman and Wilson 2015, and Cohen 1997. For an exploration of this dynamic in contemporary queer anthropology, see Weiss 2016, 2022.

14 In refusing to proffer anthropology as the solution to queer theory's effacements, I am thinking of Jobson's (2020) critique of the liberal "fix."

References

Allen, Jafari S. 2011. *¡Venceremos? The Erotics of Black Self-Making in Cuba*. Durham, NC: Duke University Press.

Allen, Jafari S. 2016. "One View from a Deterritorialized Realm: How Black/Queer Renarrativizes Anthropological Analysis." *Cultural Anthropology* 31(4): 617–26.

Allen, Jafari Sinclaire, and Omise'eke Natasha Tinsley. 2019. "After the Love: Remembering Black/Queer/Diaspora." *GLQ: A Journal of Lesbian and Gay Studies* 25(1): 107–12.

Amin, Kadji. 2020. "Genealogies of Queer Theory." In *The Cambridge Companion to Queer Studies*, 17–29. Cambridge: Cambridge University Press.

Anzaldúa, Gloria. 1983. "La Prieta." In *This Bridge Called My Back: Writings by Radical Women of Color*, edited by Cherríe Moraga and Gloria Anzaldúa, 198–209. New York: Kitchen Table Press.

Arondekar, Anjali. 2007. "The Voyage Out: Transacting Sex under Globalization." *Feminist Studies* 33(2): 337–49.

Boellstorff, Tom. 2005. *The Gay Archipelago: Sexuality and Nation in Indonesia*. Princeton, NJ: Princeton University Press.

Boellstorff, Tom. 2007a. *A Coincidence of Desires: Anthropology, Queer Studies, Indonesia*. Durham, NC: Duke University Press.

Boellstorff, Tom. 2007b. "Queer Studies in the House of Anthropology." *Annual Review of Anthropology* 36(1): 17–35.

Boellstorff, Tom. 2010. "Queer Techne." In *Queer Methods and Methodologies: Intersecting Queer Theories and Social Science Research*, edited by Kath Browne and Catherine J. Nash, 215–30. Farnham, UK: Ashgate.

Butler, Judith. 1988. "Performative Acts and Gender Constitution: An Essay in Phenomenology and Feminist Theory." *Theatre Journal* 40(4): 519–31.

Butler, Judith. 1990. *Gender Trouble: Feminism and the Subversion of Identity*. New York: Routledge.

Chiang, Howard, and Alvin K. Wong. 2016. "Queering the Transnational Turn: Regionalism and Queer Asias." *Gender, Place and Culture* 23(11): 1643–56.

Cohen, Cathy J. 1997. "Punks, Bulldaggers, and Welfare Queens: The Radical Potential of Queer Politics?" *GLQ: A Journal of Lesbian and Gay Studies* 3(4): 437–65.

Cornejo, Giancarlo. 2019. "*Travesti* Dreams Outside in the Ethnographic Machine." *GLQ: A Journal of Lesbian and Gay Studies* 25(3): 457–82.

Cruz-Malavé, Arnaldo, and Martin F. Manalansan IV. 2002. *Queer Globalizations: Citizenship and the Afterlife of Colonialism*. New York: New York University Press.

Currier, Ashley, and Therèse Migraine-George. 2016. "Queer Studies/African Studies: An (Im/)possible Transaction?" *GLQ: A Journal of Lesbian and Gay Studies* 22(2): 281–305.

Dave, Naisargi N. 2012. *Queer Activism in India: A Story in the Anthropology of Ethics*. Durham, NC: Duke University Press.

de Lauretis, Teresa. 1991. "Queer Theory: Lesbian and Gay Sexualities." *differences: A Journal of Feminist Cultural Studies* 3(2): iii–viii.

Duggan, Lisa. 2002. "The New Homonormativity: The Sexual Politics of Neoliberalism." In *Materializing Democracy: Toward a Revitalized Cultural Politics*, edited by Russ Castronovo and Dana D. Nelson, 175–94. Durham, NC: Duke University Press.

Eng, David L., Jack Halberstam, and José Esteban Muñoz. 2005. "Introduction: What's Queer about Queer Studies Now?" *Social Text* 23(3–4): 1–17.

Eng, David L., and Jasbir K. Puar. 2020. "Introduction: Left of Queer." *Social Text* 38(4): 1–24.

Fajardo, Kale Bantigue. 2011. *Filipino Crosscurrents: Oceanographies of Seafaring, Masculinities, and Globalization*. Minneapolis: University of Minnesota Press.

Ferguson, Roderick A. 2004. *Aberrations in Black: Toward a Queer of Color Critique*. Minneapolis: University of Minnesota Press.

Fiereck, Kirk, Neville Hoad, and Danai S. Mupotsa. 2020. "A Queering-to-Come." *GLQ: A Journal of Lesbian and Gay Studies* 26(3): 363–76.

Foucault, Michel. 1990. *The History of Sexuality: An Introduction*. Translated by R. Hurley. New York: Vintage.

Gaudio, Rudolph. 1995. "Unreal Women and the Men Who Love Them: Gay Gender Roles in Hausa Society." *Socialist Review* 95(2): 121–36.

Gill, Lyndon K. 2018. *Erotic Islands: Art and Activism in the Queer Caribbean*. Durham, NC: Duke University Press.

Hall, Kira. 2013. "'It's a Hijra!' Queer Linguistics Revisited." *Discourse and Society* 24(5): 634–42.

Hames-García, Michael. 2011. "Queer Theory Revisited." In *Gay Latino Studies: A Critical Reader*, edited by M. Hames-García and E. Javier Martinez, 19–45. Durham, NC: Duke University Press.

Harrison, Faye V. 2016. "Theorizing in Ex-centric Sites." *Anthropological Theory* 16(2–3): 160–76.

Hemmings, Clare. 2011. *Why Stories Matter: The Political Grammar of Feminist Theory*. Durham, NC: Duke University Press.

Holland, Sharon P. 2011. "The "'Beached Whale'." *GLQ: A Journal of Lesbian and Gay Studies* 17(1): 89–95.

Ingold, Tim. 2008. "Anthropology Is Not Ethnography." *Proceedings of the British Academy* 154: 69–92.

Jackson, John L., Jr. 2013. *Thin Description: Ethnography and the African Hebrew Israelites of Jerusalem*. Cambridge, MA: Harvard University Press.

Jobson, Ryan Cecil. 2020. "The Case for Letting Anthropology Burn: Sociocultural Anthropology in 2019." *American Anthropologist* 122(2): 259–71.

Johnson, E. Patrick. 2001. "'Quare' Studies, or (Almost) Everything I Know about Queer Studies I Learned from My Grandmother." *Text and Performance Quarterly* 21(1): 1–25.

Kulick, Don. 1998. *Travesti: Sex, Gender, and Culture among Brazilian Transgendered Prostitutes*. Chicago: University of Chicago Press.

Love, Heather. 2011. "Introduction: Rethinking Sex." *GLQ: A Journal of Lesbian and Gay Studies* 17(1): 1–14.

Love, Heather. 2019. "How the Other Half Thinks." In *Imagining Queer Methods*, edited by Amin Ghaziani and Matt Brim, 28–44. New York: New York University Press.

Love, Heather. 2021. *Underdogs: Social Deviance and Queer Theory*. Chicago: University of Chicago Press.

Macharia, Keguro. 2016. "On Being Area-Studied: A Litany of Complaint." *GLQ: A Journal of Lesbian and Gay Studies* 22 (2): 183–90.

Manalansan IV, Martin F. 2003. *Global Divas: Filipino Gay Men in the Diaspora*. Durham, NC: Duke University Press.

Mikdashi, Maya, and Jasbir K. Puar. 2016. "Queer Theory and Permanent War." *GLQ: A Journal of Lesbian and Gay Studies* 22(2): 215–22.

Morris, Rosalind C. 1994. "Three Sexes and Four Sexualities: Redressing the Discourses on Gender and Sexuality in Contemporary Thailand." *positions: east asian cultural critique* 2(1): 15–43.

Morris, Rosalind C. 1995. "All Made Up: Performance Theory and the New Anthropology of Sex and Gender." *Annual Review of Anthropology* 24: 567–92.

Namaste, Viviane. 1996. "Tragic Misreadings: Queer Theory's Erasure of Transgender Subjectivity." In *Queer Studies: A Lesbian, Gay, Bisexual, and Transgender Anthology*, edited by Brett Beemyn and Mickey Eliason, 183–203. New York: New York University Press.

Newton, Esther. 1972. *Mother Camp: Female Impersonators in America*. Chicago: University of Chicago Press.

Povinelli, Elizabeth A. 2006. *The Empire of Love: Toward a Theory of Intimacy, Genealogy, and Carnality*. Durham, NC: Duke University Press.

Puar, Jasbir K. 2007. *Terrorist Assemblages: Homonationalism in Queer Times*. Durham, NC: Duke University Press.

Reddy, Gayatri. 2005. *With Respect to Sex: Negotiating Hijra Identity in South India*. Chicago: University of Chicago Press.

Robertson, Jennifer. 1992. "The Politics of Androgyny in Japan: Sexuality and Subversion in the Theater and Beyond." *American Ethnologist* 19(3): 1–24.

Rubin, Gayle. 1975. "The Traffic in Women: Notes on the 'Political Economy' of Sex." In *Toward an Anthropology of Women*, edited by Rayna R. Reiter, 157–210. New York: Monthly Review Press.

Rubin, Gayle. 1993. "Thinking Sex: Notes for a Radical Theory of the Politics of Sexuality." In *The Lesbian and Gay Studies Reader*, edited by Henry Abelove, Michele Barale, and David Halperin, 3–44. New York: Routledge. Originally published 1984.

Rubin, Gayle. 2002. "Studying Sexual Subcultures: Excavating the Ethnography of Gay Communities in Urban North America." In *Out in Theory: The Emergence of Lesbian and Gay Anthropology*, edited by Ellen Lewin and William L. Leap, 17–67. Urbana: University of Illinois Press.

Rubin, Gayle. 2009. "A Little Humility." In *Gay Shame*, edited by David M. Halperin and Valerie Traub, 369–73. Chicago: University of Chicago Press.

Rubin, Gayle. 2011a. "Blood under the Bridge: Reflections on 'Thinking Sex.'" *GLQ: A Journal of Lesbian and Gay Studies* 17(1): 15–48.

Rubin, Gayle. 2011b. "Introduction: Sex, Gender, Politics." In *Deviations: A Gayle Rubin Reader*, 1–32. Durham, NC: Duke University Press.

Rubin, Gayle. 2023. "Geologies of Queer Studies: It's Déjà Vu All Over Again." In *Queer Then and Now: The David R. Kessler Lectures, 2002–2020*, edited by Debanuj DasGupta, Joseph Donica, and Margot Weiss, 33–48. New York: Feminist Press. Originally delivered as a lecture in 2003.

Rubin, Gayle, and Judith Butler. 1994. "Sexual Traffic." *differences: A Journal of Feminist Cultural Studies* 6(2–3): 62–99.

Rutherford, Danilyn. 2012. "Kinky Empiricism." *Cultural Anthropology* 27(3): 465–79.

Sedgwick, Eve Kosofsky. 1990. *Epistemology of the Closet*. Berkeley: University of California Press.

Tinsley, Omise'eke Natasha. 2008. "Black Atlantic, Queer Atlantic: Queer Imaginings of the Middle Passage." *GLQ: A Journal of Lesbian and Gay Studies* 14(2–3): 191–215.

Valentine, David. 2018. "Reviewing *Mother Camp* (Fifty Years Late)." *American Anthropologist* 120(4): 850–51.

Warner, Michael. 1991. "Introduction: Fear of a Queer Planet." *Social Text* 29: 3–17.

Warner, Michael. 1993. "Introduction." In *Fear of a Queer Planet: Queer Politics and Social Theory*. Minneapolis: University of Minnesota Press.

Weiss, Margot. 2011. "The Epistemology of Ethnography: Method in Queer Anthropology." *GLQ: A Journal of Lesbian and Gay Studies* 17(4): 649–64.

Weiss, Margot. 2015. "Queer Economic Justice: Desire, Critique, and the Practice of Knowledge." In *Global Justice and Desire: Queering Economy*, edited by Nikita Dhawan, Antke Engel, Christoph Holzhey, and Volker Woltersdorff, 79–95. New York: Routledge.

Weiss, Margot. 2016. "Always After: Desiring Queerness, Desiring Anthropology." *Cultural Anthropology* 31(4): 627–38.

Weiss, Margot. 2022. "Queer Theory from Elsewhere and the Im/Proper Objects of Queer Anthropology." *Feminist Anthropology* 3(2): 315–35.

Wekker, Gloria. 2006. *The Politics of Passion: Women's Sexual Culture in the Afro-Surinamese Diaspora*. New York: Columbia University Press.

Weston, Kath. 1993. "Lesbian/Gay Studies in the House of Anthropology." *Annual Review of Anthropology* 22: 339–67.

Weston, Kath. 1995. "Theory, Theory, Who's Got the Theory? Or, Why I'm Tired of That Tired Debate." *GLQ: A Journal of Lesbian and Gay Studies* 2(4): 347–49.

Weston, Kath. 1998. "The Bubble, the Burn, and the Simmer: Locating Sexuality in Social Science." In *Long Slow Burn: Sexuality and Social Science*, 1–28. New York: Routledge.

Wiegman, Robyn. 2012. *Object Lessons*. Durham, NC: Duke University Press.

Wiegman, Robyn, and Elizabeth A. Wilson, eds. 2015. "Queer Theory without Anti-normativity." *differences: A Journal of Feminist Cultural Studies* 26(1).

Wilson, Ara. 2004. *The Intimate Economies of Bangkok: Tomboys, Tycoons, and Avon Ladies in the Global City*. Berkeley: University of California Press.

Scott L. Morgensen

3

Intimate Methods

Reflections on Racial and Colonial Legacies within Sexual Social Science

Queer anthropology inherits the deeply entangled origins of social science and the analytical category "sexuality." Kath Weston argues that sexuality suffused social science throughout the twentieth century, spurring its theorization and its academic and social impacts (1998). As queer anthropology reckons with its diverse genealogies, official histories of sexual social science invite reevaluation in light of current stakes. I revisit them by inspiration of Lisa Lowe, who in *The Intimacies of Four Continents* (2015) situates sexual intimacy within the deeper intimacies of a world connected by five centuries of violently enforced interdependence. Lowe presents intimacy as a phenomenon for cultural study and as a means for encountering the relations that condition us and our knowing. I examine the linked inceptions of sexuality and social science by asking how they formed intimately with race and colonialism, generating legacies that queer anthropology continues to confront. I recall the sexual primitivism of colonial anthropology that inspired the project Weston termed "ethnocartography" (1993), before turning toward the complementarily intimate formation of the modernist ethnography of sexual minorities, as illustrated by the work of US psychologist Evelyn Hooker. As methodological precedents for what would become queer anthropology, both primitivist and modernist ethnography of sexuality (and specifically homosexuality) normalized whiteness among their authors and audiences when they obscured the intimacies that condition and inflect their formation.

Queer anthropologists today speak from genealogies that transcend disciplinary boundaries and trace to no single source. This volume and other works affirm that queer anthropology arises amid and articulates Black, Indigenous, and postcolonial genealogies of knowledge production, which exceed Western whiteness and defy its centrality (Allen 2016, 2022, this volume; Davis 2014; Fajardo 2011; Manalansan 2003; McGlotten et al., this volume; see also Allen and Jobson 2016). My reflections on the normalization of whiteness in social science consider how that process may be newly illuminated by an interdisciplinary theory of modernity. Lowe's analytic helps reveal how deeply encounters between ethnography and sexuality emerged within modern intimacies and reproduced their violences, even as such an analysis of historical sexual social science deepens our knowledge of the intimacies that conditioned it. A retrospective view can help clarify recurring patterns of silence and absence, so they might be better recognized within or displaced from the genealogies that inspire queer anthropologists today. I thus offer my comments in support of ongoing efforts in queer anthropology to queerly articulate modern intimacies and envision and practice their decolonial transformation.

I.

Within interdisciplinary scholarship bridging queer studies and Black, Indigenous, and postcolonial studies, we learn that race and colonialism condition the formation of the category "sexuality" and the sciences that have examined it. Scientific and other social investigations of sexuality became part of the racial formation of sexualized bodies under racial capitalism and colonial and imperial rule: in the Atlantic world produced by slavery (Sharpe 2010; Snorton 2017; Thomas 2007); as part of settler colonization in the Americas and Pacific (Kauanui 2018; Rifkin 2011; Tortorici

2018); amid imperialism and both franchise and settler colonization in Africa (Epprecht 2008; McClintock 1995; Tallie 2019) and Asia (Arondekar 2009; Stoler 2002); and in both local and translocal management of these projects' global interconnections (Shah 2012). US histories illustrate that science defined sexuality by distinguishing deviance from norms along the contours of white supremacy, such that racial and sexual ambiguity illuminated the color line (Somerville 2000), even as eugenics defined normality along the sexual boundaries of whiteness and its humanity (Carter 2006). Social science significantly contributed when it mapped deviance within racial geographies of anti-Blackness and nativism, codified homosexuality so as to fix racialized deviance within non-whiteness, or enclosed Indigenous sexuality as a national cultural inheritance of settler whiteness (Ferguson 2003; Morgensen 2011; Mumford 1997; Shah 2001; Terry 1999).

We learn from such studies that sexual social science arose by tracing the relations of modern intimacies. Scholars of colonial history have been served by Ann Stoler's feminist concern to interpret the sexual and gendered matrices of colonial and imperial rule as the "intimacies of empire" (Stoler 2002, 2006). Lisa Lowe (2015) further illuminates such relations when she theorizes intimacy arising amid the interdependencies of racial capitalism, colonialisms, and empire. Lowe argues that the liberal individual emerges as a subject of sexual intimacy even as modern intimacies propose and police racial and colonial boundaries for the human (2015, 18–19). As "the property of the possessive individual" (36), "liberal intimacy" directs desire, sexual and otherwise, toward an imagined freedom that obscures the unfreedoms that condition it, even as "emergent," alternative intimacies of collective struggle exceed modern violence and disturb its premises (19–21, 34). Following Lowe, studies of sexuality as a modern formation will seek not a unique intimacy, but a culmination of intimacies that condition a violently interconnected world. I sustain this meaning when I ask how social science encountered sexuality in the past and how queer anthropology might seek or interpret subjects of intimacy today.

Social scientists' long-standing commitments to attend to the sexual are illustrated by Kath Weston in *Long Slow Burn* (1998). Weston challenges official dismissals of sexuality as a topic of scientific study by illuminating "the forgotten legacy of sexuality" as a foundational focus of "social science as usual" (1998, 2, 6). Weston exhorts scholars to meet sexuality as a systemic process that conditions modernity and modern subjects, against any primitivist interest in sexuality that "fixates on what 'the X' *really* do in the privacy of the shack, the hut, or the boudoir" (25). Following Lowe's inspiration, Weston's archive presents a provocative catalogue of intimacies, one that illuminates the racial and colonial procedures that transfixed social science on the sexual and that set methods in motion that persist today. I take particular interest in the ways that intimately colonial narratives of primitive objects of mind formed contexts for scientists and their preferred audiences to propose and police a liberal individuality restricted to their own humanity.

Consider the writings of Bronislaw Malinowski, which, when addressing sexuality—even, as Weston argues, with "a certain distaste" (9)—made that category key to anthropology, even providing the field with an "early foray into interdisciplinarity" (21). Alongside works by Margaret Mead and Ruth Benedict, who first wrote on sexuality in the same era (Benedict 1934; Mead 1928, 1935), *The Sexual Life of Savages* (Malinowski 1929) advanced anthropology's sexual interests when it challenged the universality of the Oedipal complex, and so made what J. Kēhaulani Kauanui calls "savage sexualities" (2018) key to psychological and anthropological theories of modern sexuality (Weston 1998, 21–22).[1] Noting his methodological impact, Weston asks us "to read Malinowski for *how* he studies as well as *what* he studies" (22), a prompt I follow by asking how he illuminates the intimacies that conditioned early ethnography of sexuality.[2] Like so many of his contemporaries, Malinowski performed a colonial science with his ethnographic methods. For a Polish student at a UK university, sent to complete research in British-controlled Papua, colonial rule created a methodological context for negotiating intimacies through the use of ethnography (Asad 1973; Stocking 1991). Here, Lowe's analytic resonates with that of Johannes Fabian (1983) when Fabian portrays ethnography as the coeval interplay of anthropologists, their primitivist objects of mind, and the peoples whom they attempt to discursively colonize. Fabian reveals that anthropology's "denial of coevalness," which sets it in a time apart from its object, is colonial not only because it is racializing, but also because it obscures how ethnography already places its participants in present-tense relation (32–33). Anthropologists assigning primitivity to their subjects in order to deny that they live in the same time make a colonial kind of sense of the very intimacies that enable their encounter (35; see also Asad 1973, 11–12). While Fabian readily explains Malinowski's methods, Lowe's analytic further illuminates the intimacies ethnography then enters, which we witness obliquely in Malinowski's diaries (Malinowski 1989).

80   SCOTT L. MORGENSEN

In the diaries—written in Mailu (1914–15) and the Trobriand Islands (1917–18)—Malinowski recounts his fraught relations with the Papuan people who became his objects of research (Firth 1989; Geertz 1988; Stocking 1992). Racist language casually animates the diaries; anti-Black epithets in particular frame his daily interactions with his Indigenous hosts, who are periodically questioned about sexual topics, homosexuality included (Malinowski 1989, 235, 260, 276; see also 83). The author's violent speech increases when he appears vexed, vituperatively judging those around him or dismissing them from relationship. Such narratives also become spaces in which Malinowski recounts his own fraught sexual subjectivity. He expresses desire frequently for his fiancée (separated by work and war) and at least once toward himself (12–13). Yet his musings regularly recall women and young men of the communities where he lived, at times via fantasies of sexual conquest, other times with melancholic yearning for an erotic aesthetic that appears unreachable across chasms of difference (82–83, 255–56, 282). Malinowski's unceasing auto-analysis fervently interrogates his desire and failure to achieve civilizational sexuality, turning his aspirations toward liberal intimacy into a narrative context for projecting racializing hostility and fantasy onto Papuan people. Yet his very reflexivity sometimes forces to awareness that Papuans refuse his projections, or signal alternative framings of life that his text nevertheless cannot relate. The diaries' private attention to fraught relations thus offers a profound record of intimacies—not only for readers today but also originally for Malinowski—and so suggests that a return to colonial archives might reveal even more to the anthropology of sexuality than has already been made known.

Malinowski does not typically appear in genealogies of queer anthropology, but his references to sexuality became evidence for early syntheses of the anthropology of homosexuality that Weston examined as ethnocartography (1993). In the extractive, nondialogic mode of colonial ethnography, ethnocartography displaced racialized and colonized peoples from the audiences that its distortions meant to edify. Queer anthropology has reckoned with this formation's practice and effects.[3] Yet the field meets its ethnocartographic burden not only in the recurrence of objectification, but also whenever white, Western writers and audiences address one another through an ethnography of cultural "difference" that evades the intimacies conditioning perceptions of difference—the intimacies that already place differences in relationship. We need not be surprised to find, as Weston first noted long ago, that white settlers took up "the 'salvage anthropology' of

INTIMATE METHODS   81

indigenous homosexualities" to serve their sexual politics, only to produce and cite work that "remains largely insulated from important new theoretical work on postcolonial relations" (Weston 1993, 334). Colonial methods already condition ethnography to be read as an arbiter of human sexual truth. To sustain such authority and not consider its intimate formation would only signal that the ethnography of sexuality has not yet questioned its role in a colonial circuit, as purveyor of a "difference" its intended audiences desire to reconcile to their own aspirations to sexual modernity. Intimate analytics direct queer anthropology to examine such relations: no longer codifying a discrete sexual object, but rather answering the scope of modern relations that produce the sexual amid linked spaces and times. Just as such relations manifest through primitivism, they also inform the modernism that characterized the growth of an ethnography of sexual minorities about, and for the white West, to which I now turn.

II.

Even as "primitive" homosexuality became an object of mid-twentieth-century anthropology (cf. Ford and Beach 1951), modernist sexual science turned toward the ethnography of Western sexual minorities and their quests for recognition within the Western sexual self. Racial and colonial intimacies conditioned scientific efforts to define a minoritized relation to modern sexuality through the lens of whiteness. Early sex researchers and activists at times portrayed minoritized sexuality among white German, English, and US subjects via social accounts of sex, gender, or desire, but their interests in congenital and acquired syndromes largely remained within the frames of sexology and psychiatry.[4] In contrast, psychologist Evelyn Hooker was the first professional social scientist to take up ethnography as a method to document sexual minorities as sociocultural communities, making her a significant formative figure for the anthropology of homosexuality. Hooker focused her research on people recognized by the cisnormative term "homosexual men"; given that term's resonance with a folk category in formation at the time, I refer to her subjects as "gay men."

Hooker notably promoted ethnography as a corrective to pathologizing theories then dominant in psychiatry and psychology. Her methodological intervention rests in her modernist deployment of ethnography, which also enacts signal qualities of liberal intimacy. In the first publication from her research, after briefly citing Ford and Beach (1951) and ethnocartography to affirm human sexual variation, Hooker deploys ethnographic narrative alongside psychological case studies to portray her subjects as representative of the modern West and of a human sexual condition (Hooker 1956, 218, 220–22). Later stating that "my methods are essentially those of an ethnographer," Hooker relates that her project arose "quite accidentally in the course of normal processes of social interaction with a group of friends," who "made an urgent request that I conduct a scientific investigation" using them as core subjects (Hooker 1965, 91). Hooker states that when conducting interviews or participant observation, "my objective is to look at the homosexual world through the eyes of my research subjects, in the belief that it is the only way in which to know what is really going on, to look with the subject at his world as he knows it" (91).

When Hooker argues that the ties she formed were "not that of researcher to research subject but of friend to friend," she grounds her inquiry in a methodology of intimate relationship. Here Hooker reflects on the intimacies of liberal individuality, which Lowe references to "intimate friendship, close familiarity, closeness of observation or knowledge" (2015, 11). This definition complements Lowe's assertion that liberal individuality's claim on the interpersonal disguises the intimacies that subtend and exceed it. These "less visible," "residual," and "emergent" intimacies of "alliance, affinity, and society among variously colonized peoples beyond the metropolitan national center" confront the imperial, capitalist, colonial, and racial violences that condition the liberal individual and its distorted self-knowledge (12). In Hooker's work and its secondary accounts, we witness a method particularly attuned to liberal intimacy, as it collaboratively created ethnography of aspirants to liberal sexuality. Such a reading also illuminates her project's unknowing of the intimacies that conditioned it, as when it uplifts those close to her as subjects enfolded within a caring mode of research, while others remain under empirical and epistemic erasure by the theories and methods modeled here for social science.

Meeting the subjects toward whom Hooker showed care entails reading for what is explicit and implicit in accounts of their relations. Hooker's publications do not list her participants' identities or social locations by race or class (among other markers of difference), but we do know a great deal about the racial and economic conditions and formation of urban gay subcultures in Los Angeles, where Hooker's research was based, as well as in cities such as San Francisco, Chicago, and New York of which she attests some knowledge (Hooker 1956, 222). From the early to mid-twentieth century, the vice district contexts of urban sexual subcultures shifted, as migration and activism gathered newly identified homosexual minorities in cities small and large, within which some used wealth and whiteness to form more privatized networks or to seek acceptance within white cishet institutions (D'Emilio 1983; Ferguson 2019; Hanhardt 2013; Mumford 1997). These US social geographies conditioned the normative whiteness of homophile activism and its first group, the Mattachine Society, which formed in Los Angeles in 1950 (Hansen 2019; Peacock 2016) and thus set social contexts for Hooker's work.

The film *Changing Our Minds* (Harrison and Schmiechen 1991) portrays the inception of Hooker's research in her relationship with Sam From, "a former student" whom she met in her 1944 psychology course at UCLA and who, over years to come, became a close friend (Hooker 1965, 92; Minton 2002, 220). Noting that From "had a high school education. His father was a junk dealer," Hooker describes him at the time of their association as "a highly successful businessman" (Marcus 2009, 3; Hooker 1965, 92). From maintained ties with Hooker after his studies as part of his, and later his friends' and colleagues', efforts to encourage her to "conduct a scientific investigation of 'people like them.' By 'people like them,' they meant homosexuals who did not seek psychiatric help and who lead relatively stable, occupationally successful lives" (Hooker 1965, 92). Hooker accepted "their offer to supply unlimited numbers of research subjects and to provide entrée into homosexual circles and public gathering places" (92). After pausing the project in 1947, her return to research in 1953 with funding from the National Institute of Mental Health moved beyond From's friends to include "independent contacts with official homosexual organizations" such as the Mattachine Society (92). Hooker states that without Mattachine's assistance, "the project would not have been possible," as its members "persuaded their friends to become subjects" (19). After From died in a car accident in 1955, Hooker recommitted to advancing the project amid professional and political backlash against studies of homosexuality (Harrison and Schmiechen 1991). While Hooker portrays the project's founding cohorts with aspects of economically successful and "stable" life, *Changing Our Minds* attempts to visualize their social standing and relations. Recent interviews with an elderly Hooker are intercut with photos and film clips that project a remarkable whiteness onto midcentury LA and on the gay networks from which Hooker drew participants. Among images of unnamed subjects gathering

3.1   Evelyn Hooker and Christopher Isherwood seated in the backyard garden of Hooker's residence. Single screen capture from *Changing Our Minds, The Story of Dr. Evelyn Hooker* (New York: Frameline Distribution)

at private homes, clubs, and beaches in what appear to be white friendship networks, the film portrays Hooker and her husband socializing with gay men at their home, which also served as her research site due to danger that her subjects might be publicly exposed elsewhere. The film returns multiple times to show the Hookers sharing domestic time with author Christopher Isherwood, who had once rented a cottage on their property and who also contributed his ties within LA gay communities to Hooker's research as their friendship grew (Minton 2002, 225). (See figure 3.1.) James Harrison's script narrates Hooker's core subjects as representatively normal and human, but as impeded socially by a sexual stigma that they wished to transform.

Hooker reports that as her "research role became more clearly defined and separated from its social origin" among friends, her initial contacts helped her seek a broader sample of "the 'community,'" via "deliberate efforts to locate such representative members of its varying sectors as male prostitutes, bisexuals, bartenders and bar owners, adolescents, and the aged" (Hooker 1965, 92). In this characterization, scare quotes tentatively reference an expansive community, albeit one seemingly more diverse than

INTIMATE METHODS   85

her original contacts, who now appear more likely to be middle-aged gay men who know where to meet sex workers, bisexuals, or the figures behind bar culture but who do not represent them. In her initial demographic chart, Hooker indicates that her research sample used education to compare gay men to a control group of heterosexual men of similar achievement (Hooker 1957, 19). The thirty men skew toward educational advantage, with one-third having begun or completed a postsecondary degree (bachelor's to PhD) and only two not having graduated high school. This array recalls the policing of US education that has constricted primary through tertiary education access for Black, Indigenous, and racialized youth by means of criminalization, redlining, relocation, border control, and impoverishment (Gibbons 2018; Rooks 2020; So 2020). The apparent emergence of Hooker's research from relations with educationally advantaged, class-advancing white gay men thus reached toward the social margins, but from a grounding that remained unnamed even as it conditioned how the work advanced her core subjects' interests.

Once Hooker writes ethnographically, deracialized descriptions and race analogies perform whiteness as an unnamed norm of the people, spaces, culture, and status she defends from pathologization. In an early publication, Hooker attests that homosexual networks "may be very heterogeneous—and, in fact, I think they usually are—in terms of age, social class, occupation, and ethnic groups represented" (1956, 222). Yet, rather than documenting such evidence, her ethnographic stories introduce more exclusive networks. For instance, referencing her data, she posits that homosexuals share "certain common characteristics" in the form of two recurrent "topics of conversation." In the first—"the arts, particularly music, the theatre, graphic arts, and literature"—Hooker cites subjects invoking a "preoccupation with . . . standards of taste" or claiming ties to "a particular writer, painter, or composer . . . [who] may indeed be a member, or a friend of a member, of the group" (222). This first theme bridges with her second, "gossip and rumor," which she witnesses in her subjects' interests in "the homosexual community [as] an international one," as when visits to "London or Copenhagen" connect members to "distinguished members of the homosexual world, or 'homintern'" (222). These stories appear as evidence backing her earlier assertion that homosexuals may "constitute a considerable minority . . . in every large city of the world" (217). Here, a racially unmarked cultural class bridging the urban US and western Europe represents a sexual and social group with global reach, while portended ethnic and economic differences from this norm remain invisible among the subjects Hooker makes exemplary of the status and group she defends.

Hooker's ethnographic attention broadens somewhat in "Male Homosexuals and 'Their Worlds'" (1965), which acknowledges differentiation within LA gay communities, albeit again without their being brought under her ethnographic analysis. Hooker maps patterns of residence and bar establishments by noting their placement amid forms of social segregation and "surveillance by police"; yet she then states that this social geography "depends on multiple factors too complex for elaboration here" (95). She does establish that for gay bars, "as in residential areas, there is a clustering effect," which she locates near "beaches or other places of homosexual group recreation," "public entertainment districts . . . and areas of high tolerance and relative permissiveness toward other forms of deviant behavior" (95). Yet these spaces remain unmarked as products of the race and class restrictions of vice districts, redlining, and beach exclusions (Flamming 2006; Lvovsky 2021), or by the formation of "residential areas of the city with heavy concentrations of homosexuals . . . described by homosexuals as 'the swish Alps' or 'boys' town'" (Hooker 1965, 93) where we might not be surprised to find gay capital gentrifying formerly interracial, cross-class spaces (Hanhardt 2013; Orne 2019). While Hooker's 1965 essay introduces her remarkably nuanced ethnographic account of the gay bar as market, her original cultural analysis appears rather seamless when read against the stratifications and differences that her own research obliquely revealed, but that a commitment to predictively describe homosexual culture leaves unknown.

Hooker also takes a narrative turn familiar to homosexual emancipationists when she advances the representability of her subjects by comparing their sexuality to racialization, a move that Laurie Marhoefer reminds us narratively advances whiteness (2019). Racial analogy inflects all of Hooker's research, as it formed the first premise of her initial report's moral rejoinder to psychiatric pathologization. Hooker states, given that homosexuals gain shared experience by responding to "societal judgment," then as "member(s) of an out-group which is subject to extreme penalties . . . it would be strange indeed if all the traits due to victimization in minority groups were, in the homosexual, produced by inner dynamics of the personality" (1956, 219). She clinches her assertion of a social status for homosexuals with racial analogy, stating (and quoting G. W. Allport [1954]) that just

INTIMATE METHODS   87

as "'the racial frame of thought' is inescapable for the Negro, so that there is a haunting anxiety which he cannot escape . . . there can be no doubt, from interview data gathered from homosexuals, that this attitude characterizes a large number of them" (1956, 219). In this, possibly Hooker's only published reference to Black people, anti-Black racism sets a citable standard for discrimination: but as analogy, it locates sexual marginality exterior to racism, and race, thereby whitening the homosexuality to which Blackness is compared and erasing subjects of homosexuality and Blackness. While Hooker later surmises that "ethnic groups" must appear within homosexuality's heterogeneity, her original evidence portrays subjects absent any "ethnic" or "racial" marker (1956, 222). Her founding analogy, clinching homosexuals' minoritized status, illuminates the racial formation of her sample and of the logic that gathered it. Analogy might in fact reflect how Hooker's white subjects identified as minorities, via sexuality and *not* race, even as asserting a status analogous to racial minoritization trumps their whiteness and displaces it from view. We also might expect there to have been few Indigenous or racialized people in the white, class-advancing circles that gathered around Hooker, although lack of evidence in her reports does not mean none were there. Yet Hooker's silences nevertheless project whiteness onto "homosexuality" and all whom she uses the term to describe. Naming racism only as analogy thus doubly erases Black, Indigenous, and racialized sexual subjects, whether they were entirely absented from her study or found their experiences unremarked upon and inaccessible to its normatively white theorization.

I have presented Hooker's ethnographic model as instructive because of its significant and lasting influence within science and politics. Her initial publications quickly raised her profile in the United States as a public advocate for depathologization. Judd Marmor requested her contribution to his 1965 collection by stating, "You are the only one who holds the view that there is no inherent connection between homosexuality and [psycho]pathology" (Boxer and Carrier 1998, 4). Hooker recalls how her standing established her as a leader in scientific and legal debates of the late 1960s, as in her being solicited to chair the National Institute of Mental Health's task force on homosexuality (Hooker 1993, 452).[5] While the story is told elsewhere of "the Hooker Report," as the task force report came to be known (Hooker 1969), Boxer and Carrier explain that it "created so much controversy that publication of the final report was delayed by the Nixon administration. The report included policy recommendations for decriminalizing homosexuality . . . and for providing equal protection under the law to all homosexual persons. Because of the delay in its publication, one of the first homophile organizations for men published an early version of the now-famous report in the organization's magazine, *One Institute Quarterly*" (1998, 4).

Across two decades, Hooker's research synergized with gay rights activism by advocating depathologization. Hooker's distinctive contributions were to argue that psychiatric methods produced the pathology that they sought, and to present ethnography's attention to social and cultural integrity as psychiatry's moral and methodological counterpoint. Retrospectives of Hooker as the original ethnographer of sexual minorities recall her work as a model of ethical research, as it originated from friendships, activist collaborations, and advocacy (Boxer and Carrier 1998; Kimmel and Garnets 2003). Hooker inspired the ethnography of sexual minorities to reject objectification and to empower communities by linking science and activism in the defense of rights and the advancement of social justice.

Yet, a more intimate reading of Hooker's model of research reveals its entanglements with the modernist advancement of the liberal individual. Keeping in mind the intimacies shaping the midcentury United States— notably, national and global antiracist and decolonial movements for rights, sovereignty, and liberation—Hooker's work affirms Lowe's implication: the liberal individual arises into self-knowledge and civic recognition via the unknowing of subjugations and relations that condition it but remain unrecognizable. Hooker, of course, was not unique among scientists or advocates of her time in selecting US Americans as global representatives of a universal sexual minority status, or in normalizing whiteness and sidestepping its racial and colonial conditions. Yet her work remains notable, not just for its novel application of ethnography, but more so for the scientific and political impetus behind this methodological choice. Hooker presents ethnography as a tool of moral good, a method particularly amenable to sexual minority self-determination and advocacy for sexual freedom. At once, both Hooker and her historians recall the project's emergence from relationship, which affectively affirms that its achievements were rooted in and proliferated from intimacy. Hooker's legacy illustrates the compatibility of a relational, depathologizing, activist ethnography of sexuality with the advancement of liberal intimacy. Choosing ethnography in the spirit of sexual and social justice did not save Hooker or her collaborators from normalizing and reproducing whiteness; indeed, following her model, ethnography could readily produce it again.

III.

My chapter has examined two historical turns in sexual social science that made intimacies methodological. Read alongside one another, ethnocartography and the ethnography of modern sexual minorities illustrate that the racializing containment of sexual primitivity complements the deracialized advancement of sexual modernity. For Malinowski, as for other scholars of his era, primitive and modern sexuality were asserted relationally: attention to primitivity was never separate from efforts to clarify the boundaries of modern sex. Malinowski illustrated this in his ethnographic proximity to Black and Indigenous people whose sexual lives he posed as a challenge to modern sex, only to become an objectified subtext to more private appeals to sexual normality. Primitivism thus established ethnography within modern intimacies before Hooker shifted its focus, to portray US sexual subjects as an integral minority within modern sexuality. Arising from spaces of whiteness, Hooker's modernist ethnography turned science and politics toward sexual normalization, brushing past its evident intimacies with differences that remained unexamined. Yet whether absented or recurring as a deferred presence, relations with gendered and erotic possibilities among racialized and Indigenous peoples conditioned both accounts and their invocations of sexuality in Western logics of liberal individuality and freedom.

I reflected on intimacies in sexual social science in order to illuminate certain legacies queer anthropology inherits and their distinctions from where the field now heads. Queer anthropology is familiar with sexual primitivism, ethnocartography, and their mobilizations within Western sexual science and sexual politics. Yet though we might be quick to reject primitivism, it evinces intimacies that may reward further study in their own right, as well as in terms of primitivism's relation to the modernism that may supplant it. Hooker offers one case, in which liberal intimacy galvanized research that hastened depathologization, by ethnographically whitening sexual minority culture and presenting that as a global and universal sexual status. Read against histories of what Roderick Ferguson (2019) calls "one-dimensional queer" politics, Hooker's legacy offers a cautionary tale of the ethnography of sexual minorities producing multiple forms of complicit whiteness: relational whiteness, in friendships whose racial formation remained unexamined; epistemic whiteness, in the science and law through which they spoke and to which they appealed; and aspirational whiteness, by modeling white sexual humanity as a moral good while displacing the lives it excludes from presence or mind. I reckon with the ongoing life of such projects from my professional location in gender studies, whenever I field requests from white student applicants, professors, or publishers to mentor, codesign, or create an ethnography of LGBTQ+ communities and politics that presumes the querents' and their subjects' whiteness. Beyond affirming the persistence of what Allan Bérubé termed "gay whiteness" (2001), such efforts to recruit me—a tenured, academic, white queer anthropologist— seem to suggest more intimate methods. They imply that the legitimacy they seek for their subjects and agendas will flow from an institutional relation to ethnography that I, the white queer anthropologist, should be prepared to support. White queer anthropologists may not need a history lesson to know how to talk back to such requests, but I found that revisiting elder white ethnographers helped me better understand such recurrences of what Gloria Wekker calls "white innocence" (2016). Wekker, Bérubé, and Ferguson illustrate the many ways in which gay and queer whiteness promote love within bounds, solidarities that exclude, freedoms that obscure their own practices of violence. In this light, Hooker's legacy impels me to revisit claims on the ethnography of sexuality as a method of care, which analysis of intimacies may help us clarify. Care also may be practiced by answering white ethnographers of sexuality with a refusal to erase white supremacy as a condition and needed target of their ethnographic inquiry.

Queer anthropology grows today by attending to modernity's enduring structures and creative possibilities. The field already models the alternative, emergent intellectual heritages of Black queer anthropology, queer diaspora anthropology, and an array of decolonial genealogies that exceed Western scientific norms and displace them from the field's origins and directions (Allen 2011, this volume; Bailey 2013; Fajardo 2011; Gill 2018; Ochoa 2014; Spice, this volume). In this context I offered curiosity about queer anthropology's historic intimacies to invite interdisciplinary inquiry into their potential continued resonance and effects. As primitivist and modernist legacies of sexual social science recur, revisiting them may further reveal their power to reproduce the violences against which we work. Yet, as I understand it, Lowe's invitation to interpret intimacies leads us to relations, which means it brings our subjects and inquiry into closer relation. When confronting a legacy I wish not to repeat, an intimate analytic leads me not to remove it from knowledge, but to return to more deeply understand its formation, which queer anthropology can continue to do in light of where we are, distinctly, arriving.

Notes

1   Weston reminds us that this theory was informed originally by Freud's reading of primitivist anthropology (1998, 16).

2   Other examples within the anthropology of sexuality and gender include, in the US context, the legacies of Franz Boas, Ruth Benedict, and Margaret Mead, who may be read via their complex relations to the contributions of Zora Neale Hurston and Ella Cara Deloria, who as their students, research assistants, and colleagues produced distinctive genealogies of Black and Indigenous anthropology in which gender and the erotic figure significantly (Medicine 2001; Cotera 2008).

3   The scholarly and political effects of ethnocartography were first addressed to US anthropology by Two-Spirit / Indigenous LGBTQ scholars, community members, and activists. Their activism, which included engagement by the San Francisco organization Gay American Indians in and in relation to the 1992 American Anthropological Association meetings, informed the efforts of Sue-Ellen Jacobs to organize the 1993–94 Wenner-Gren conferences. There, Anguksuar Richard LaFortune, Beverley Little Thunder, and Clyde Hall, among other Indigenous contributors, named the romanticization and appropriation of indigeneity within gay and lesbian anthropology, and their contributions were published by Jacobs, Wesley Thomas, and Sabine Lang in *Two-Spirit People* (1997). Alongside Weston (1993) proposing the category of "ethnocartography" and its initial analysis, Deborah Elliston clarified the ethnocartographic burden of scholarship on Melanesia two years afterward (Elliston 1995). Legacies of ethnocartography continue to be diagnosed and displaced today within Indigenous anthropology and Indigenous community research on contemporary Two-Spirit / Indigiqueer identities, cultures, and politics (Davis 2014; Wesley 2015; Laing 2021).

4   In Germany, the Scientific Humanitarian Committee's collection of individual case studies, and commentaries on the social milieu and expression of subjects (Rosario 1997), can be compared to Jan Gay's community-based research within 1920s homosexual networks in New York City, London, Paris, and Berlin (Terry 1999, 275), which followed the committee's research model.

5   Hooker states, "I was called by Stanley Yolles, then director of NIMH [National Institute of Mental Health], asking me to come to Washington and 'tell him what we ought to be doing about homosexuality.' . . . I suggested that we needed a group of thoughtful people who were social scientists or were in law, religion, or psychiatry and who could bring their knowledge to bear on this question. The director replied that if I would give him a list, he would make the appointments for a 'blue ribbon task force'" (1993, 452).

References

Allen, Jafari. 2011. *¡Venceremos? The Erotics of Black Self-Making in Cuba*. Durham, NC: Duke University Press.

Allen, Jafari. 2016. "One View from a Deterritorialized Realm: How Black/Queer Renarrativizes Anthropological Analysis." *Cultural Anthropology* 31(4): 617–26.

Allen, Jafari. 2022. *There's a Disco Ball between Us: A Theory of Black Gay Life*. Durham, NC: Duke University Press.

Allen, Jafari, and Ryan Jobson. 2016. "The Decolonizing Generation: (Race and) Theory in Anthropology since the Eighties." *Cultural Anthropology* 57(2): 129–48.

Allport, G. W. 1954. *The Nature of Prejudice*. Cambridge, MA: Addison Wesley.

Arondekar, Anjali. 2009. *For the Record: On Sexuality and the Colonial Archive in India*. Durham, NC: Duke University Press.

Asad, Talal, ed. 1973. *Anthropology and the Colonial Project*. Atlantic Highlands, NJ: Humanities Press.

Bailey, Marlon. 2013. *Butch Queens Up in Pumps: Gender, Performance, and Ballroom Culture in Detroit*. Ann Arbor: University of Michigan Press.

Benedict, Ruth. 1934. *Patterns of Culture*. Boston: Houghton Mifflin.

Bérubé, Allan. 2001. "How Gay Stays White and What Kind of White It Stays." In *The Making and Unmaking of Whiteness*, edited by Birgit Brander Rasmussen et al., 234–65. Durham, NC: Duke University Press.

Boxer, Andrew M., and Joseph M. Carrier. 1998. "Evelyn Hooker." *Journal of Homosexuality* 36(1): 1–17.

Carter, Julian. 2006. *The Heart of Whiteness: Normal Sexuality and Race in America, 1880–1940*. Durham, NC: Duke University Press.

Cotera, Maria. 2008. *Native Speakers: Ella Cara Deloria, Zora Neale Hurston, Jovita González and the Poetics of Culture*. Austin: University of Texas Press.

Davis, Jenny. 2014. "More Than Just 'Gay Indians': Intersecting Articulations of Two-Spirit Gender, Sexuality, and Indigenousness." In *Queer Excursions: Retheorizing Binaries in Language, Gender, and Sexuality*, edited by Jenny Davis, Joshua Raclaw, and Lal Zimman, 62–80. Oxford: Oxford University Press.

D'Emilio, John. 1983. *Sexual Politics, Sexual Communities: The Making of a Homosexual Minority in the United States, 1940–1970*. Chicago: University of Chicago Press.

Elliston, Deborah. 1995. "Erotic Anthropology: 'Ritualized Homosexuality' in Melanesia and Beyond." *American Ethnologist* 22(4): 848–67.

Epprecht, Marc. 2008. *Heterosexual Africa? The History of an Idea from the Age of Exploration to the Age of AIDS*. Columbus: Ohio University Press.

Fabian, Johannes. 1983. *Time and the Other: How Anthropology Makes Its Object*. New York: Columbia University Press.

Fajardo, Kale. 2011. *Filipino Crosscurrents: Oceanographies of Seafaring, Masculinities, and Globalization*. Minneapolis: University of Minnesota Press.

Ferguson, Roderick. 2003. *Aberrations in Black: Towards a Queer of Color Critique*. Minneapolis: University of Minnesota Press.

Ferguson, Roderick. 2019. *One-Dimensional Queer*. Medford, MA: Polity Press.

Firth, Raymond. 1989. "Second Introduction 1988." In *A Diary in the Strict Sense of the Term*, by Bronislaw Malinowski, xxi–xxxi. London: Athlone Press.

Flamming, Douglas. 2006. *Bound for Freedom: Black Los Angeles in Jim Crow America*. Berkeley: University of California Press.

Ford, Clellan S., and Frank A. Beach. 1951. *Patterns of Sexual Behavior*. New York: Harper.

Geertz, Clifford. 1988. *Works and Lives: The Anthropologist as Author*. Stanford, CA: Stanford University Press.

Gibbons, Andrea. 2018. *City of Segregation: 100 Years of Struggle for Housing in Los Angeles*. New York: Verso.

Gill, Lyndon K. 2018. *Erotic Islands: Art and Activism in the Queer Caribbean*. Durham, NC: Duke University Press.

Hanhardt, Christina B. 2013. *Safe Space: Gay Neighborhood History and the Politics of Violence*. Durham, NC: Duke University Press.

Hansen, Will. 2019. "The Cold War and the Homophile, 1953–1963." *Australasian Journal of American Studies* 38(1): 79–96.

Harrison, James, writer, and Richard Schmiechen, dir. 1991. *Changing Our Minds, The Story of Dr. Evelyn Hooker*. New York: Frameline Distribution. 77 minutes.

Hooker, Evelyn. 1956. "A Preliminary Analysis of Group Behavior of Homosexuals." *Journal of Psychology* 42(2): 217–25.

Hooker, Evelyn. 1957. "The Adjustment of the Male Overt Homosexual." *Journal of Projective Techniques* 21(1): 18–31.

Hooker, Evelyn. 1965. "Male Homosexuals and Their 'Worlds.'" In *Sexual Inversion: The Multiple Roots of Homosexuality*, edited by Judd Marmor, 83–107. New York: Basic Books.

Hooker, Evelyn. 1969. "Task Force on Homosexuality. Final Report." Rockville, MD: National Institute of Mental Health (NMIH).

Hooker, Evelyn. 1993. "Reflections of a 40-Year Exploration: A Scientific View on Homosexuality." *American Psychologist* 48(4): 450–53.

Jacobs, Sue-Ellen, Wesley Thomas, and Sabine Lang. 1997. *Two-Spirit People: Native American Gender Identity, Sexuality, and Spirituality*. Urbana: University of Illinois Press.

Kauanui, J. Kēhaulani. 2018. *Paradoxes of Hawaiian Sovereignty: Land, Sex, and the Colonial Politics of State Nationalism*. Durham, NC: Duke University Press.

Kimmel, Douglas C., and Linda D. Garnets. 2003. *What a Light It Shed: The Life of Evelyn Hooker.* Psychological Perspectives on Lesbian, Gay, and Bisexual Experiences. New York: Columbia University Press.

Laing, Marie. 2021. *Urban Indigenous Youth Reframing Two-Spirit.* New York: Routledge.

Lowe, Lisa. 2015. *The Intimacies of Four Continents.* Durham, NC: Duke University Press.

Lvovsky, Anna. 2021. *Vice Patrol: Cops, Courts, and the Struggle over Urban Gay Life before Stonewall.* Chicago: University of Chicago Press.

Malinowski, Bronislaw. 1929. *The Sexual Life of Savages.* London: G. Routledge.

Malinowski, Bronislaw. 1989. *A Diary in the Strict Sense of the Term.* London: Athlone Press. Originally published 1967.

Manalansan, Martin F. 2003. *Global Divas: Filipino Gay Men in the Diaspora.* Durham, NC: Duke University Press.

Marcus, Eric. 2009. *Making Gay History: The Half-Century Fight for Lesbian and Gay Equal Rights.* New York: HarperCollins.

Marhoefer, Laurie. 2019. "Was the Homosexual Made White? Race, Empire, and Analogy in Gay and Trans Thought in Twentieth-Century Germany." *Gender and History* 31(1): 91–114.

McClintock, Anne. 1995. *Imperial Leather: Race, Gender and Sexuality in the Colonial Contest.* New York: Routledge.

McIntosh, Mary. 1968. "The Homosexual Role." *Social Problems* 16(2): 182–92.

Mead, Margaret. 1928. *Coming of Age in Samoa.* New York: Quill.

Mead, Margaret. 1935. *Sex and Temperament in Three Primitive Societies.* New York: William Morrow.

Medicine, Beatrice. 2001. *Learning to Be an Anthropologist and Remaining "Native": Selected Writings.* Urbana: University of Illinois Press.

Minton, Henry L. 2002. *Departing from Deviance: A History of Homosexual Rights and Emancipatory Science in America.* Chicago: University of Chicago Press.

Morgensen, Scott L. 2011. *Spaces between Us: Queer Settler Colonialism and Indigenous Decolonization.* Minneapolis: University of Minnesota Press.

Mumford, Kevin. 1997. *Inter/Zones: Black/White Sex Districts in Chicago and New York in the Early Twentieth Century.* New York: Columbia University Press.

Ochoa, Marcia. 2014. *Queen for a Day: Transformistas, Beauty Queens, and the Performance of Femininity in Venezuela.* Durham, NC: Duke University Press.

Orne, Jason. 2019. "Gayborhood Change: The Intertwined Sexual and Racial Character of Assimilation in Chicago's Boystown." In *Home and Community for Queer Men of Color: The Intersection of Race and Sexuality*, edited by C. Winter Han and Jesús Gregorio Smith, 85–106. New York: Lexington Books.

Peacock, Kent W. 2016. "Race, the Homosexual, and the Mattachine Society of Washington, 1961–1970." *Journal of the History of Sexuality* 25(2): 267–96.

Rifkin, Mark. 2011. *When Did Indians Become Straight? Kinship, the History of Sexuality, and Native Sovereignty*. Durham, NC: Duke University Press.

Rooks, Noiwe. 2020. *Cutting School: The Segrenomics of American Education*. New York: New Press.

Rosario, Vernon, ed. 1997. *Science and Homosexualities*. New York: Routledge.

Shah, Nayan. 2001. *Contagious Divides: Epidemics and Race in San Francisco's Chinatown*. Berkeley: University of California Press.

Shah, Nayan. 2012. *Stranger Intimacy: Contesting Race, Sexuality and the Law in the North American West*. Berkeley: University of California Press.

Sharpe, Christina. 2010. *Monstrous Intimacies: Making Post-slavery Subjects*. Durham, NC: Duke University Press.

Snorton, C. Riley. 2017. *Black on Both Sides: A Racial History of Trans Identity*. Minneapolis: University of Minnesota Press.

So, Richard Jean. 2020. *Redlining Culture: A Data History of Racial Inequality and Postwar Fiction*. New York: Columbia University Press.

Somerville, Siobhan. 2000. *Queering the Color Line: Race and the Invention of Homosexuality in American Culture*. Durham, NC: Duke University Press.

Stocking, George. 1991. *Colonial Situations: Essays on the Contextualization of Ethnographic Knowledge*. Madison: University of Wisconsin Press.

Stocking, George. 1992. "The Ethnographer's Magic: Fieldwork in British Anthropology from Tyler to Malinowski." In *The Ethnographer's Magic and Other Essays in the History of Anthropology*, 70–120. Madison: University of Wisconsin Press.

Stoler, Ann Laura. 2002. *Carnal Knowledge and Imperial Power: Race and the Intimate in Colonial Rule*. Berkeley: University of California Press.

Stoler, Ann Laura. 2006. *Haunted by Empire: Geographies of Intimacy in North American History*. Durham, NC: Duke University Press.

Tallie, T. J. 2019. *Queering Colonial Natal*. Minneapolis: University of Minnesota Press.

Terry, Jennifer. 1999. *American Obsession: Science, Medicine, and Homosexuality in Modern Society*. Chicago: University of Chicago Press.

Thomas, Greg. 2007. *The Sexual Demon of Colonial Power: Pan-African Embodiment and Erotic Schemes of Empire*. Bloomington: Indiana University Press.

Tortorici, Zeb. 2018. *Sins against Nature: Sex and the Archives in Colonial New Spain*. Durham, NC: Duke University Press.

Wekker, Gloria. 2016. *White Innocence: Paradoxes of Colonialism and Race*. Durham, NC: Duke University Press.

Wesley, Dana. 2015. "Reimagining 'Two-Spirit Community': Critically Centering Narratives of Urban Two-Spirit Youth." MA thesis, Queen's University.

Weston, Kath. 1993. "Lesbian/Gay Studies in the House of Anthropology." *Annual Review of Anthropology* 22: 339–67.

Weston, Kath. 1998. *Long Slow Burn: Sexuality and Social Science*. New York: Routledge.

Part II

REORIENTATIONS

Queering the Anthropological Canon

Lucinda Ramberg

4

Kinship and Kinmaking Otherwise

As a concept, kinship might seem tired, or even dead, to use David Schneider's (1984) formulation. To the contrary, this chapter argues, kinship remains vital to think and think with. Attending closely to the ways anthropological work on and through kinship has generated theorizations of sex, sexuality, and gender broadly, this chapter maps the liveliness of kinship across four areas: property and personhood; social death/social life; natures/cultures; and relatedness otherwise.

As a symbolic system and field of practice, kinship produces configurations of sexuality, gender, race, and power embodied by persons. This recognition is indebted to critical race, feminist, postcolonial, and queer interventions in the field of kinship studies, which, taken together, have moved the field away from exercises in description and classification of kin ties as facts on the ground and toward investigating relatedness as an open question. In between queer theory and anthropology, kinship has been reconceptualized as a technology for self and worldmaking as well as a normalizing and disciplinary regime. Kinship can fuck us by generating forms of queer exile and social death, but we too can fuck kinship by subverting its normalizing functions and corrupting the grids of intelligibility it mobilizes (Dahl 2014; Weiner and Young 2011). Queer folk have long been taking hold of kinship's tools and putting them to use in the fashioning of relations that promote queer thriving. As Kath Weston points out, anthropologists have not been the only ones to "subject the genealogical grid to new scrutiny" (1991, 34), queer folx have been constructing critical discourses of kinship for some time.

Postwar critiques of structural-functionalist analyses of culture challenged the assumption that kinship comprised a universal domain of human social organization undergirded by the biological facts of life. Kinship began to be reframed as a set of symbolic relations, an effect of human activity, and a field of power. Jane Collier and Sylvia Yanagisako (1987) argued that anthropological understandings of both kinship and gender were based on a folk conception of sexual reproduction. Cultural approaches to kinship drew the anthropological gaze to concrete practices and local articulations of the patterning and meaning of relationships and paved the way for new kinds of research. For instance, Carol Stack (1975) elaborated active and durable networks of exchange and mutual aid among African American urban kinfolk, thereby effectively contravening the racist representation of the Black family as pathological. Building on such innovations in the field, queer kinship studies pursue such questions as the following: What possibilities of life lie outside dominant kinmaking practices? What pleasures and what costs does exile from kinship entail? Which lives, forms of desire, modes of embodiment are enabled, and which are foreclosed through the grammar of kinship at work in a particular place and time?

Studies of kinship in a queer context have elaborated patterns of affiliation formed outside and against the law (Bailey 2013; Lewin 1993; Weston 1991). John Borneman (1997) has suggested that the presumed universal principles of descent and alliance produce exclusions and calls instead for the study of patterns of caring and being cared for. These works deny reproduction and marriage practices the centrality they have historically enjoyed in the study of kinship and critically engage the ways we think about relatedness. At the same time, variability in the house of kinship has functioned as a site of civilizational capture in which "we" have families and "they" have kinship (Carsten 2004, 15). Kinmaking otherwise is thus a troubled territory of both alternative affiliative possibility and exotic fixing. Before I elaborate the four areas mentioned above, I want to briefly note two dimensions of queer kinship studies that are shared across these areas.

The first is that kinmaking is understood within queer kinship studies as an activity or "tactic of everyday life" (Certeau 2011) through which humans and others (animals, deities, plants) form "networks of relations constituted by practices of obligation, support, and care with significant and beloved others" (Roebuck n.d., 6). While some scholars have emphasized the chosen character of queer kin relations (Weston 1991), others have illuminated the ways that conventions of kinmaking constrain which positions and relations can confer legibility and value on humans as subjects of kinship (Mariner 2019; Povinelli 2006; Ramberg 2014).

The second is that fascination with the sex lives of "others" has long animated and informed anthropological theorizing. Widely circulated European textual representations of Africa, the Americas, and the Indian subcontinent from the early modern period to the nineteenth century demonstrate the long-entangled histories and geopolitics of sexual and political forms and their investments in the form of the family. In "The Heterosexual Matrix as Imperial Effect," Vrushali Patil (2018) argues that agents of merchant capital, Christian missionization, and metropolitan science constructed non-European others for a European audience as sexually indiscreet and undifferentiated through figures of hermaphroditism, harlotry, polygamy, and sodomy. These early modern representations penned by travelers informed eighteenth-century evolutionary anthropology that performed concern for the treatment of women in so-called savage and barbaric societies while situating "companionate, monogamous, heterosexual marriage enfolding a private, domestic femininity and a public masculinity" as the civilized ground of social and political superiority (13). In short, from its inception as a field of study, anthropology has entangled sex and race in classificatory schemas of kinship as a civilizational discourse. To put the point another way, even when it does not take sex or kinship as its object of study, anthropology mobilizes theories of race/sex. Given this, the task of queer kinship studies is not only to denaturalize the white heterosexual matrix but also to dislodge it from its foundational position within the discipline.

Property and Personhood

Anthropologists have long understood kin relations to be entangled with material culture and regimes of property. In 1877, Lewis Henry Morgan linked the consolidation of the marital form around monogamy and paternity with the advent of private property. Drawing on these insights as they traveled through the work of Marx and Engels, but reading them against the grain, Gayle Rubin (1975) located the intertwined roots of the oppression of women and homosexuals in the organization of sex and gender through heterosexual marriage. The feminist materialist characterization of marriage as a property relation organizing gender and value in persons yields two key insights about kinship as a system of interrelated positions marked by gender and sexuality. The first speaks to the question of value: material transactions generate kin relations, kinship vests value in persons. To offer a simple example captured in the Chinese term for never-married women (*sheng nu*, or leftover women), within the heterosexual matrix a wife is a woman with added value. The second intervention points to questions of legibility and recognition; kinship mobilizes a grammar of legitimate persons and relations and therefore forms of exclusion as well as inclusion in human collectivities.

Speaking to the question of value, Gayle Rubin points out that as an exchange relation between men, marriage vests in men "rights in women that women do not have in themselves" (1975, 183). In this structuralist formulation one of the effects of marriage is gender as a hierarchical relation of binary complementarity. Marriage unevenly vests value in persons coded as gender. It also reproduces men and women as proper to each other even as they are differentially placed as transactors in and bearers of value. Further, it situates queer folk and the unmarried in general as improper subjects of kinship, belonging to no one.

Marxist feminist critiques of marriage as a property institution also drew attention to questions of class and economic inequity. Ideologies of family anchored around heterosexual marriage and nuclear families have been at the root of economic subordination in capitalist regimes. "The family," rather than being a "little world immune from the vulgar cash-nexus of modern society," could be seen as "a vigorous agency of class placement and an efficient mechanism for the creation and transmission of gender inequality," wrote lesbian feminist sociologists Michèle Barrett and Mary McIntosh (2015, 27–29). Advocates of same-sex marriage rights largely forgot this materialist history of marriage as an institution organizing property relations and personhood, focusing instead on the opportunities of positive recognition that access to the institution of marriage might provide.

Feminist historiographies of slavery offer rich instruction in the nexus between property and personhood. Hortense Spillers has taught us that histories of slavery delimit the possibilities of and for socially or legally recognizable kin relations. In "Mama's Baby, Papa's Maybe" (1987) she argues that the American grammar of kinship is haunted by the reproductive arrangements imposed by the system of chattel slavery. Property relations delimited possibilities of personhood and kinship. Enslaved African men found no access to social or legal recognition as fathers. Enslaved women found both their productive and reproductive labor channeled into the wealth of the white master; they could give birth but they could not properly mother their reproductive issue who belonged by law to their white slaver (Hartman 2016; Tinsley 2008; Snorton 2017; Vergès 2021). Critical race feminist accounts illuminate ways that "family ties"—relations deemed worthy of the designation "kinship"—are effects of social and material processes at least as much if not more than biological relatedness. How queer.

Recent work in queer anthropology has extended this thematic of the materiality of kinship in new directions. Engagements with Indigenous theories and worlds marks one direction. In Scott Morgensen's (2011) decolonial reading, settler colonialism is a structuring property relation that produces all natives as sexually deviant nonsovereign persons (see also Rifkin 2010). This reading situates the adoption of native cultures of gender and kinship otherwise as "our queer history" by nonnative queer counterculture collectives, such as the Radical Fairies, as a problem of sovereignty. Histories of land relations delimit the possibilities of queer affiliation for both native and nonnative queer folx. Drawing on life and fieldwork among Radical Fairies in the United States and aboriginal Australians, Elizabeth Povinelli (2006) has made similar arguments through the concepts of "genealogical society" and "autological subject" as twinned regimes of recognition characterizing late liberalism. In the words of Kim TallBear, "So marriage was yoked together with private property in settler coercions of Indigenous peoples. The breakup of Indigenous peoples' collectively held-lands into privately-held allotments controlled by men as heads-of-household enable the transfer of 'surplus' lands to the state and to mostly European or Euro-American settlers" (2018, 147–48).

Another queer pathway through questions of property and personhood has been marked by scholars bringing conventional heteropatriarchal familial arrangements and queer kinmaking together in one ethnographic frame. George Paul Meiu's ethnography of transactional economies of sex in contemporary Kenya follows young men styling themselves as "traditional" warriors or *morans* from beach towns, where they cultivate liaisons with European tourists, to their ancestral towns, where they contract marriages according to the expectations of their clan. In his analysis Meiu demonstrates the ways these two sexual economies flow into each other. One is sexually illicit, the other licit; both are governed by the logics of the gift and transactional relations. He writes, "But the underlying exchange value of ethnosexuality shaped, in myriad ways, women's attachments to their long-term partners and husbands, and to their families. With the commodification of moran ethnosexuality . . . money infused intimacy and affective attachments, while the logic of kinship and belonging shaped how money circulated in both intimate and public domains" (2017, 33). In her ethnography, Amy Brainer (2019) draws structural and processual models of kinship together in a single analytic framework and tracks the ways queer projects of self-making inform family of origin relations in Taiwan. She elaborates family change as a thoroughly gendered phenomenon negotiated by Taiwanese queers and their heterosexual kin through conceptions about and practices of filial duty, intergenerational care, domestic labor, and family care and resources. After the death of his father, one man, with the knowledge and support of his male life partner, gets married to and has children with a woman in order to reproduce the vitality of his mother's position in a patrilineal society. Taken together these works remind us that kin work is never not interested. Queer kinmaking, like all kinmaking, is a territory for the production and distribution of value and its investment in persons and relations.

Social Death / Social Life

As a grammar of legitimate positions, kinship generates exclusions as much as inclusions; it spells the terms of possible personhood and permissible relations. In *The Elementary Structures of Kinship* (1969), Claude Lévi-Strauss signaled the abjecting effects of kinship through the figure of the gaunt bachelor sitting apart from the family gathered around the fire to eat. His dependence on a female relative for the occasional meal illustrates the fact that, within Brazilian Indigenous communities, life itself was contingent on close kin ties. Lacking a connection to the reproductive function of conventional kinship, orphans and bachelors were precarious. Even as Lévi-Strauss notes the death-dealing potential of kinship, however, he naturalizes it by failing to envision life outside the elementary structures he universalized. Through a queer lens, the reproductive capacities of orphans, bachelors, and widows might be glimpsed, not to mention guncles and dyke aunties (Sedgwick 1993; Shange 2019).

But, first, let us linger a bit longer with death. John Borneman renders "marriage" and "death" as a single term—"marriage/death"—thereby insisting on the inextricability of the legitimation of certain kinds of persons and relations and the social death of others made to inhabit the constitutive outside. He writes, "Marriage is often associated with birth and life, but its relation to death, in the sense of exclusion, abjection, and closure, is frequently obscured if not altogether avoided" (1996, 228). At the height of the HIV/AIDS pandemic, Borneman called out the discipline of anthropology for failing to describe relatedness where reproductive heterosexuality replicated over time was not in evidence. Writing about A. R. Radcliffe-Brown's commentary on "unnatural" offenses ("incest, bestiality, in some societies homosexuality, and witchcraft"), Borneman notes that sex outside marriage has been placed outside the "social," as a matter of morality, perhaps, but not a constitutive element of human sociality in the way that sex–marriage is. Such failures discursively reproduce the social death that awaits those exiled from kinship, as critical race, feminist, and queer anthropologists have elaborated.

Feminist scholars such as Claudia Card (1996) and Lisa Duggan (2002) have argued that even same-sex marriages replicate normativity, if homonormativity. The pursuit of marriage as the means to make same-sex liaisons legible before the state and to procure needed social, economic, and legal rights may ameliorate the position of married same-sex couples but it further isolates and marginalizes those persons (polyamorous, single, throupled) or relations (friends, siblings, lovers but not domestic partners) who cannot or do not want to access their rights as citizens through the form of marriage. As a relationship to the state, marriage efficiently delivers forms of social and legal recognition and protection. It also regulates what kinds of persons and which kinds of relations are admissible to state-sanctioned forms of intimate partnership, as Judith Butler (2002) has pointed out. Given the ongoing force of civilizational discourse in which good reproductive, monogamous marital sex is parsed from bad nonreproductive and/or non-monogamous sex, we cannot be surprised that socially marginalized people continue to reach for and implicate themselves in a form that reproduces hierarchies of race, gender, class, and caste even as it confers legitimacy. A wife may be an abject form of social personhood in relation to a husband, but she is not socially dead in the way that a widow, a lesbian, or a prostitute is. A "husbian" has added value: somewhere there is a wife. Her relatedness radiates a vitality that the single lesbian is not seen to possess.

The insight that Borneman captured in the term *marriage/death* has been elaborated and complicated in recent queer scholarship attending to the regulating function of marriage in relation to conceptions of romance, family, and citizenship. Ashley Tellis (2014) has contended that marriage often constitutes the imagined horizon of queer relationships even as people enact a variety of affective and residential arrangements. Thinking alongside Tellis within an Indian archive of queer relatedness and politics, Nithin Manayath (2015) notes that proposals for same-sex marriage equality reproduce the couple as the proper center of a normative conjugal matrix, thereby erasing centuries-old forms of *hijra* desire, lineage, and house making. Drawing on queer of color critique, Priya Kandaswamy puts same-sex marriage rights advocacy efforts in the United States in conversation with histories of welfare reform in order to underline how marriage advocacy relies on and reproduces gendered and raced politics of respectability. She writes, "In seeking privileges that have historically been produced through black subjugation, same-sex marriage advocates accept and reinforce the operations of a stratified State Austerity and the Racial Politics of Same-Sex Marriage welfare state. In invoking the same language of marriage that has been used to deny welfare entitlements to single mothers and to demonize black women, advocates of gay marriage accept a very narrow and conservative vision of what sexual politics could be" (2008, 772).

Another way scholars have disturbed the presumptive kinlessness of singletons, those who are unmarried or child free, is by shedding a bright light on innovative patterns of affiliation, reproductive labor, and rituals of commitment that produce liveliness and thriving among queer folx. In his consideration of transnational adoption of "Asian" orphans by white gay couples in the United States, David Eng (2010) argues that adoptees perform reproductive labor: they make those who adopt them into parents. This reproductive labor, like so much reproductive labor, is racially stratified. Within such multicultural families, gay couples gain the coin of sexual respectability as parents while "Asian" adoptees are made to swap deracination for white family belonging. Focusing on house culture and performance worlds in Detroit, Marlon Bailey (2013) elaborates the distinct kin terms, gendered positions, and relations that generate networks of Black queer and trans* love and celebration among folx exiled from their families of origin. Keridwen Luis (2018) maps gift relations, collective domiciliation, and shared political feelings among almost exclusively white, often rural-dwelling landdykes. In urban Delhi, Naisargi Dave (2012) demonstrates the ways that shared political commitments among lesbian activists working to promote queer visibility and thriving constitute collaboratorative ethical worldmaking.

Building on the landmark scholarship of Carol Stack and Hortense Spillers, a new generation of feminist scholars has elaborated forms of Black creativity, vitality, and mortality in the afterlife of slavery. Because of the ways enslaved Africans were exiled from socially or legally sanctioned kinship and the reproductive labor of Black women was and is channeled into the production of white capital, the life-and-death stakes of Black love and kinmaking have been and remain high. Angela Davis situates the Black domestic under slavery as potentially generative of resistance and rebellion—a site of conscientization. Enslaved women, who also worked alongside men in the fields, experienced their reproductive labors as necessary to the survival of the community and, therefore, themselves as agents in the struggle for freedom (1981). By contrast, Ren Heintz frames the Black Atlantic as a queer diaspora, writing, "In New World slavery, kinship never even has a moment to hold" (2017, 242). Dána-Ain Davis (2019) demonstrates that race trumps class in precipitating adverse birth outcomes and offers an account of medical racism as experienced by professional Black women who have given birth prematurely. Her work attends to not only morbidity, but also vitality in celebrating the reproductive labor performed by midwives, doulas, and birth advocates addressing Black women's labor and delivery. Mignon Moore's (2008) research on Black lesbian stepfamilies suggests that, within such families, the value of Black women's reproductive labor overrides relative income or gendered scripts in determining degree of authority within the family. The American grammar of kinship produces forms of gendered, racial, and sexual exile and unevenly distributes death sentences and life chances. At the same time, within the space/time of exile, folx regenerate relatedness otherwise.

Natures/Cultures

In Lévi-Strauss's (1969) structuralist vision, the exchange of women between men constituted the threshold of civilization. As the means of crossing over from a state of nature, heteropatriarchal marriage was thus installed as the ground of culture and the boundary against humanity's natural savagery, or nature for Lévi-Strauss. This form of marriage assumed and asserted sexual dimorphism. Kinmaking is boundary work, Lévi-Strauss taught us. But even as he delivered what was to become a powerful analytic tool in the anthropology of gender, sex, and sexuality, he presumed neat boundaries between oppositional pairs: nature and culture; female and male; raw and cooked. In her effort to craft a cultural explanation of the nearly ubiquitous subordination of women, "Is Female to Male as Nature Is to Culture?," Sherry Ortner (1972) makes a similar maneuver. As she works to denaturalize the secondary status assigned to persons designated as women, she naturalizes sexual dimorphism and universalizes a hierarchized split between nature and culture.

Recent work has sought to upend these assumptions by exploring reproductive technologies, transgendered embodiment, and human/animal/ planetary relations as territories where natures/cultures are being reconfigured through human activity. Within this scholarship, natures/cultures are plural and boundary making is understood to be cultural activity. To put the point somewhat differently, the idea that nature and culture can be neatly distinguished from each other or that they exist in some oppositional relation to each other is itself an effect of the cultural work of boundary making. In light of such work, the distinction between so-called fictive and real kin collapses. For instance, Brigitte Fielder writes, "Black genealogies may not operate along merely biological lines. They include 'fictive' kin, aunties and uncles . . . othermothers, and play-cousins" as well as forms of racial mixture that displace and thus decenter whiteness as a biological relation (2020, 792). I want to explore three areas of research in particular that are pushing conversations through natures/cultures in novel directions. All draw on queer and feminist theory to trouble the idea that biological processes are ever free of social and cultural investment.

Anthropologists working on reproductive technologies have generated a rich literature that denaturalizes biological relatedness as a fact of nature. There are important feminist and queer interventions in this body of work that situates biology as both culture and politics otherwise, rather than neutral science. Research on artificial reproductive technologies broadly speaking has shed new light on longer histories of cultural investment in biological reproduction, such as the rhythm method, herbal fertility and abortifacient medicinals, child spacing, magic, and prayer. Research on IVF technologies in particular generated insights into the ways that extracting human eggs and sperm, fertilizing them in the lab, and reintroducing this supplemented material into the womb of would-be mothers keen to bear their own children produced new forms of commodification, gendered value, and relatedness. To cite but one example in this extensive literature, Charis Thompson (2005) developed the concept "ontological choreography" to capture the ways conservative scripts for gendered conduct within the lab and between parents worked alongside naturalized desire for children to stabilize biological relatedness as a fact of nature in cases of assisted reproduction.

Scholars working through gendered embodiment and relatedness have explored biological flows and forms as cultural materials. Thinking with hormones in Brazil, Emilia Sanabri tracks flows of sex hormones through the bodies of men, women, and *travesti*. Hormones materialize sex as a binary even as they participate in producing gender as a mailable and unstable object of investment. She writes, "The continuity between genital sex and the circulation of gender does not depend on the ineluctability of the facts of nature. Given the many biological and social elements that are required to make sex (and not just gender), efforts need to be constantly deployed to reassemble these with the consistency that makes us blind to the manufactured aspect of sex" (2016, 128). In "Lessons from a Starfish," Eva Hayward (2008) fashions a trans* ontology from starfish biology. Like starfish, trans* bodies regenerate themselves, turning cuts on the body into sites of becoming (see also Durban 2017).

Indigenous ontologies collapse settler bifurcations of nature from culture and emphasize human planetary relations as inextricably entangled. In "Critical Relationality: Queer, Indigenous, and Multispecies Belonging beyond Settler Sex and Nature," Kim TallBear and Angela Willey write, "Our ability to imagine nature and relationality differently are deeply enmeshed, and this imaginative work is vital to the re-worlding before us" (2019, 5).

Working with Indigenous and feminist methods, Max Liboiron (2021) situates plastic pollution as an ongoing colonialism that entangles fish, fisher folx, Indigenous communities, consumers, oceans, and bays in uneven relations to land and toxicity. New work on natures/cultures situates kinship as a technology of relatedness and confounds colonial and heteropatriarchal binaries such as male/female, hetero/homo, real/fictive, human/animal, and subject/object.

Variability/Relatedness Otherwise

Variations in socially sanctioned arrangements of gender, sexuality, reproduction, marital rites, and household labor and economy have long been elaborated by anthropologists through figures as diverse as Native North American Two Spirits, African female husbands, Brazilian *travestis*, Indian *devadasis* and *hijras*, Taiwanese *tongzhi*, urban US denizens of ball culture, and lesbian mothers (Amadiume 2015; Bailey 2013; Coleman and Chou 2013; Jacobs, Thomas, and Lang 1997; Kulik 1998; Lewin 1993; Ramberg 2014; Reddy 2010). Queer kinmaking practices innovate and extend possibilities of sexed and gendered personhood, drawing on kinship conventions and repurposing them toward queer and trans* thriving. Such practices open up possibilities of thinking kinship beyond ties through blood or the law as a creative practical labor of making and unmaking relations. Thinking with and through illegitimate relations is a queer move that locates critical possibilities in the sexual positions lying outside the kinship chart, denied legal or social legitimacy. Dwelling on such relations invites us to rethink what kinds of relations can count as kinship. Queer anthropology generates critical categories and methods for conceptions of kinship and theorizations of personhood and relatedness by moving beyond a categorical distinction between legitimate and illegitimate relations as the self-evident boundary between kin and kinlessness.

Within conventional kinship studies, the house, home, or space of the domestic has long been understood to organize and ground possibilities of belonging under the sign of kin (Carsten and Hugh-Jones 1995). Scholarship focusing on queer "housework" has contaminated the straight understandings of the domestic as a normalizing space. Cohabitation and shared holidays in their homes constitute two of the ways lesbians and gay men in San Francisco interviewed by Kath Weston (1991) work to consolidate their chosen families and displace biogenetic relations as the master term of kinship. Marlon Bailey's work on the historically sedimented house culture and ballroom scene in Detroit illuminates the ways Black LGBT folx invest affective, performative, and reproductive labor in their houses—composed of mothers, fathers, and children—making queer counterpublics, familial belonging, and intergenerational lineage (2013). Scholars working with *hijra* households in India have documented the ways these genealogical, propertied, religiously affiliated domestic units comprise queer families who can trace their ancestry into antiquity (Manayath 2015; Reddy 2010; Saria 2021). In *The Queerness of Home: Gender, Sexuality, and the Politics of Domesticity after World War II*, Stephen Vider (2021) traces how LGBTQ folx in the United States mobilized domestic space as a site of political and community formation in the decades after World War II.

If house cultures otherwise is one way scholars have elaborated forms of queer affiliation, another has been through investigation of shared subcultures as contexts for thick networks of belonging. In her work on the gay leathermen in 1980s San Francisco, Gayle Rubin (2011) outlines the ways that the shared sexual culture of kink generated other forms of mutual belonging expressed in attire, comportment, employment, neighborhood, and ritual. Focusing on the pansexual kink world of the early 2000s, Margot Weiss (2011) by contrast situates BDSM as ambivalent, as capable of reproducing hierarchies of race and gender as subverting them through nonreproductive sexual relations. Elizabeth Pérez (2016) opens up novel ways of approaching the study of both religious and queer belonging by focusing on the reproductive and ritualized labor of cooking for the gods shared among women and gay men practicing Lucumí (Santeria) in Chicago. In *Queer Freedom: Black Sovereignty*, Ana-Maurine Lara (2020) invites her readers to receive her work as a ceremony and *ofrenda* (offering) and to enter into shared "body-lands, water-memories, and altars-puntos" that make decolonial queer conviviality possible.

Kinship Otherwise

Queer approaches situate kinship as a disciplinary, creative, and enabling site of subject-, community-, and worldmaking. Kinship otherwise, whether inside or outside dominant familial forms, offers both risks *and* pleasures. Queer studies of kinship illuminate kinmaking as a social and material practice intimately intertwined with regimes of race, gender, and sexuality, rather than a biological given. To study kinship then means to investigate race, class, colonialism, gender, generation, reproduction, sexuality, and politics. In short, the study of relatedness goes to the heart of conceptual categories across anthropology and social theory more broadly. Within queer accounts, fundamental anthropological concepts—from lineage to nature/culture and social reproduction—are corrupted and exploded to accommodate life and death otherwise. If kinship is, as we might once have said, good to think, it also generates social and disciplinary worlds. Given the long history of and ongoingness of colonial logics imposed on and through kinship, it remains critical to push queer kinship studies beyond its taxonomic history. Let us embrace a lively anthropology of relatedness that denaturalizes the imperial and colonial white heterosexual logics of gender-race-family, and begin to see, and be, kin otherwise.

References

Amadiume, Ifi. 2015. *Male Daughters, Female Husbands: Gender and Sex in an African Society*. London: Zed Books.

Bailey, Marlon M. 2013. *Butch Queens Up in Pumps: Gender, Performance, and Ballroom Culture in Detroit*. Ann Arbor: University of Michigan Press.

Barrett, Michèle, and Mary McIntosh. 1982. *The Anti-social Family*. New York: Verso Trade. Originally published 1982.

Borneman, John. 1996. "Until Death Do Us Part: Marriage/Death in Anthropological Discourse." *American Ethnologist* 23(2): 215–35.

Borneman, John. 1997. "Caring and Being Cared for: Displacing Marriage, Kinship, Gender and Sexuality." *International Social Science Journal* 49(154): 573–84.

Brainer, Amy. 2019. *Queer Kinship and Family Change in Taiwan*. New Brunswick, NJ: Rutgers University Press.

Butler, Judith. 2002. "Is Kinship Always Already Heterosexual?" *differences: A Journal of Feminist Cultural Studies* 13(1): 14–45.

Card, Claudia. 1996. "Against Marriage and Motherhood." *Hypatia: A Journal of Feminist Philosophy* 11(3): 1–23.

Carsten, Janet. 2004. *After Kinship*. Cambridge: Cambridge University Press.

Carsten, Janet, and Stephen Hugh-Jones, eds. 1995. *About the House: Lévi-Strauss and Beyond*. Cambridge: Cambridge University Press.

Certeau, Michel de. 1980. *The Practice of Everyday Life*. 3rd ed. Translated by Steven F. Rendall. Berkeley: University of California Press.

Coleman, Edmond J., and Wah-Shan Chou. 2013. *Tongzhi: Politics of Same-Sex Eroticism in Chinese Societies*. New York: Routledge.

Collier, Jane Fishburne, and Sylvia Junko Yanagisako. 1987. *Gender and Kinship: Essays toward a Unified Analysis*. Stanford, CA: Stanford University Press.

Dahl, Ulrika. 2014. "Not Gay as in Happy, but Queer as in Fuck You." *lambda nordica* 19(3–4): 143–68.

Dave, Naisargi N. 2012. *Queer Activism in India*. Durham, NC: Duke University Press.

Davis, Angela. 1981. "Reflections on the Black Woman's Role in the Community of Slaves." *Black Scholar* 12(6): 2–15.

Davis, Dána-Ain. 2019. *Reproductive Injustice: Racism, Pregnancy, and Premature Birth*. New York: New York University Press.

Duggan, Lisa. 2002. "The New Homonormativity: The Sexual Politics of Neoliberalism." In *Materializing Democracy: Toward a Revitalized Cultural Politics*, edited by Donald E. Pease, Joan Dayan, and Richard R. Flores, 175–94. Durham, NC: Duke University Press.

Durban, Erin. 2017. "Postcolonial Disablement and/as Transition: Trans* Haitian Narratives of Breaking Open and Stitching Together." *TSQ:Transgender Studies Quarterly* 4(2): 195–207.

Eng, David L. 2010. *The Feeling of Kinship*. Durham, NC: Duke University Press.

Fielder, Brigitte. 2020. "Literary Genealogies and the Kinship of Black Modernity." *American Literary History* 32(4): 789–96.

Hartman, Saidiya. 2016. "The Belly of the World: A Note on Black Women's Labors." *Souls: A Critical Journal of Black Politics, Culture, and Society* 18(1): 166–73.

Hayward, Eva. 2008. "Lessons from a Starfish." In *Queering the Non/human*, edited by Noreen Giffney and Myra J. Hird, 249–63. Burlington, VT: Ashgate.

Heintz, Lauren. 2017. "The Crisis of Kinship: Queer Affiliations in the Sexual Economy of Slavery." *GLQ: A Journal of Lesbian and Gay Studies* 23(2): 221–46.

Jacobs, Sue-Ellen, Wesley Thomas, and Sabine Lang, eds. 1997. *Two-Spirit People: Native American Gender Identity, Sexuality, and Spirituality*. Urbana: University of Illinois Press.

Kandaswamy, Priya. 2008. "State Austerity and the Racial Politics of Same-sex Marriage in the US." *Sexualities* 11(6): 706–25.

Kulick, Don. 1998. *Travesti: Sex, Gender, and Culture among Brazilian Transgendered Prostitutes*. Chicago: University of Chicago Press.

Lara, Ana-Mauríne. 2020. *Queer Freedom: Black Sovereignty*. Albany: State University of New York Press.

Lévi-Strauss, Claude. 1969. *The Elementary Structures of Kinship*. Boston: Beacon Press.

Lewin, Ellen. 1993. *Lesbian Mothers: Accounts of Gender in American Culture*. Ithaca, NY: Cornell University Press.

Liboiron, Max. 2021. *Pollution Is Colonialism*. Durham, NC: Duke University Press.

Luis, Keridwen N. 2018. *Herlands: Exploring the Women's Land Movement in the United States*. Minneapolis: University of Minnesota Press.

Manayath, Nithin. 2015. "The Shameless Marriage: Thinking through Same-Sex Erotics and the Question of 'Gay Marriage' in India." In *Conjugality Unbound: Sexual Economies, State Regulation and the Marital Form in India*, edited by Srimati Basu and Lucinda Ramberg, 251–80. New Delhi: Women Unlimited Press.

Mariner, Kathryn A. 2019. "White Parents, Black Care: Entanglements of Race and Kinship in American Transracial Adoption." *American Anthropologist* 121(4): 845–56.

Meiu, George Paul. 2017. *Ethno-erotic Economies: Sexuality, Money, and Belonging in Kenya*. Chicago: University of Chicago Press.

Moore, Mignon R. 2008. "Gendered Power Relations among Women: A Study of Household Decision Making in Black, Lesbian Stepfamilies." *American Sociological Review* 73(2): 335–56.

Morgan, Lewis Henry. 1985 [1877]. *Ancient Society; Or, Researches in the Lines of Human Progress from Savagery to Civilization*. Reprint with a foreword by Elisabeth Tooker. Tucson: University of Arizona Press.

Morgensen, Scott Lauria. 2011. *Spaces between Us: Queer Settler Colonialism and Indigenous Decolonization*. Minneapolis: University of Minnesota Press.

Ortner, Sherry B. 1972. "Is Female to Male as Nature Is to Culture?" *Feminist Studies* 1(2): 5–31.

Patil, Vrushali. 2018. "The Heterosexual Matrix as Imperial Effect." *Sociological Theory* 36(1): 1–26.

Pérez, Elizabeth. 2016. *Religion in the Kitchen: Cooking, Talking, and the Making of Black Atlantic Traditions*. New York: New York University Press.

Povinelli, Elizabeth A. 2006. *The Empire of Love*. Durham, NC: Duke University Press.

Ramberg, Lucinda. 2014. *Given to the Goddess: South Indian Devadasis and the Sexuality of Religion*. Durham, NC: Duke University Press.

Reddy, Gayatri. 2010. *With Respect to Sex: Negotiating Hijra Identity in South India*. Chicago: University of Chicago Press.

Rifkin, Mark. 2010. *When Did Indians Become Straight? Kinship, the History of Sexuality, and Native Sovereignty*. Oxford: Oxford University Press.

Roebuck, Christopher. n.d. "Necessary Affiliations: A Dislodging Return of Kinship." Unpublished manuscript.

Rubin, Gayle. 1975. "The Traffic in Women: Notes on the 'Political Economy' of Sex." In *Toward an Anthropology of Women,* edited by Rayna R. Reiter, 157–210. New York: Monthly Review Press.

Rubin, Gayle. 2011. *Deviations: A Gayle Rubin Reader*. Durham, NC: Duke University Press.

Sanabria, Emilia. 2016. *Plastic Bodies: Sex Hormones and Menstrual Suppression in Brazil*. Durham, NC: Duke University Press.

Saria, Vaibhav. 2021. *Hijras, Lovers, Brothers: Surviving Sex and Poverty in Rural India*. New York: Fordham University Press.

Schneider, David Murray. 1984. *A Critique of the Study of Kinship*. Ann Arbor: University of Michigan Press.

Sedgwick, Eve Kosofsky. 1993. *Tendencies*. Durham, NC: Duke University Press.

Shange, Savannah. 2019. "Play Aunties and Dyke Bitches: Gender, Generation, and the Ethics of Black Queer Kinship." *Black Scholar* 49(1): 40–54.

Snorton, C. Riley. 2017. *Black on Both Sides: A Racial History of Trans Identity*. Minneapolis: University of Minnesota Press.

Spillers, Hortense J. 1987. "Mama's Baby, Papa's Maybe: An American Grammar Book." *Diacritics: A Review of Contemporary Criticism* 17(2): 64–81.

Stack, Carol B. 1975. *All Our Kin: Strategies for Survival in a Black Community*. New York: Basic Books.

TallBear, Kim. 2018. "Making Love and Relations beyond Settler Sex and Family." In *Making Kin Not Population*, edited by Donna Haraway and Adele Clark, 145–64. Baltimore: Paradigm Press.

TallBear, Kim, and Angela Willey. 2019. "Critical Relationality: Queer, Indigenous, and Multispecies Belonging beyond Settler Sex and Nature." *Imaginations: Journal of Cross-Cultural Image Studies* 10(1): 5–15.

Tellis, Ashley. 2014. "Multiple Ironies: Notes on Same Sex Marriage for South Asians at Home and Abroad." In *Marrying in South Asia: Shifting Concepts, Changing Practices in a Globalising World*, edited by R. Kaur and R. Palriwala, 333–50. Hyderabad: Orient Blackswan.

Thompson, Charis. 2005. *Making Parents: The Ontological Choreography of Reproductive Technologies*. Cambridge, MA: MIT Press.

Tinsley, Omise'eke Natasha. 2008. "Black Atlantic, Queer Atlantic: Queer Imaginings of the Middle Passage." *GLQ: A Journal of Lesbian and Gay Studies* 14(2–3): 191–215.

Vergès, Françoise. 2021. "Race, Gender, Colonialism, Racial Capitalism, and Black Women's Wombs." In *The Routledge Companion to Sexuality and Colonialism*, edited by Chelsea Schields and Dagmar Herzog, 159–68. New York: Routledge.

Vider, Stephen. 2021. *The Queerness of Home: Gender, Sexuality, and the Politics of Domesticity after World War II*. Chicago: University of Chicago Press.

Weiner, Joshua J., and Damon Young. 2011. "Queer Bonds." *GLQ: A Journal of Lesbian and Gay Studies* 17(2): 223–41.

Weiss, Margot. 2011. *Techniques of Pleasure: BDSM and the Circuits of Sexuality*. Durham, NC: Duke University Press.

Weston, Kath. 1991. *Families We Choose: Lesbians, Gays, Kinship*. New York: Columbia University Press.

Tom Boellstorff 5

Pronoun Trouble

Notes on Radical Gender Inclusion in English

Pronouns are giving us trouble.

English speakers face a dilemma: the current structure of our language is exclusionary with regard to gender. The personal pronouns **she** and **he** don't represent all the ways people see themselves. Having only these two options excludes trans persons, nonbinary persons, and others who don't identify as female or male. Language isn't just a set of labels to identify things: it shapes how we see the world and is a way of acting in the world. We must transform English to make it gender inclusive.

One solution has been preferred personal pronouns: someone explaining, verbally or in writing, that they use **she/they** pronouns, **he/him/ his** pronouns, and so on. This vast improvement has significant limitations. I will suggest that the more radically inclusive option is to eliminate preferred personal pronouns (including **she** and **he**) in favor of a non-gendered or "epicene" pronoun, for which the best option is **they**. (For clarity I'll use bold for pronouns when discussing them: for instance, "Joe saw **them** at the park.") The word "epicene" comes from a root meaning "common." An "epicene pronoun" doesn't mark gender: for instance, in English **you** isn't a feminine pronoun or a masculine pronoun; it's an epicene pronoun.

Allow me to clarify some points at the outset:

1   I refer to "notes" in my title because I employ several lists (like this one). As a rhetorical mode, I find numbered lists useful for preliminary analysis: while suggesting epicene **they** as the best way forward, I also discuss its drawbacks. Lists are often provisional memory devices—things to get at the store or pack for a journey. Lists resist closure: one can imagine adding something to a list, or crossing something off. Consider these lists of things to pack for our journey into pronominal possibility.

2   I speak of *radical* gender inclusion because the word "radical" originally referred to a root. I propose changing English structurally—at its "root"—not at the "leaves" of individual speakers. I'm inspired by social movements, from Black and Latinx to disability, that have changed language for everyone. Having individuals state preferences places the burden on the individual to account for their position in a system of subordination; it's also beholden to liberal capitalist notions of self-branding and free choice.

3   I look particularly to the history of feminist language activism. It's crucial that queer and trans movements continue to work in productive intersectional alliance with feminist movements, and not allow transexclusionary radical feminism (TERF) to damage this coalitional work. Despite its name, TERF isn't remotely "radical." It presumes rather than challenges a "root" assumption of patriarchy: that there are two distinct genders, female and male, rooted in a notion of biological sex presumed to be given, universal, and immutable. Building on the rich body of feminist scholarship on language and inclusion helps reveal the falsity of TERF as a radical framework. Indeed, my title references Butler's *Gender Trouble* (1990), which challenged essentialist feminisms (of which TERF, despite its misnomer, is a signal example), and which is also built on language theory (specifically, the work of Austin 1980 and others on performativity).

4   As is always the case, this analysis builds on personal history. I'm a queer scholar and activist with a background in anthropology and linguistics. I've conducted extensive research with queer Indonesians and draw some examples from the Indonesian language.[1]

5   One way this chapter comes from a queer perspective is that I propose reworking English from within. A key implication of "queer" is that cultural transformation rarely involves a total break from history or society. Instead, transformations of the status quo are messily connected to that status quo. Scholars of racial inclusion have long theorized these dynamics of immanent social change, including borderlands epistemology (Anzaldúa 1987) and double consciousness (Du Bois 1903). This is also a core insight of work in decolonial and postcolonial studies, which shows how these depend on "the reversal, not the disavowal, of many binaries that are central to colonialism" (Gupta 1998, 169). The notion of "queering" draws from Foucault's notion of reverse discourse (1987), but also from challenges to queernormative assumptions of oppositionality: "in the consolidation of queer 'studies' as an institutionalized project of antinormativity, queer critique has undergone its most sustained and confounding normalization" (Wiegman 2012, 205; see Boellstorff 2007b).

6   My analysis, specific to contemporary English, explores how English-language hegemony shapes political horizons of the radical. I do this through an anthropological perspective, but not the ethnographic approach for which anthropology is now best known. Another way this chapter comes from a queer perspective is that I employ a comparative analysis, which "was once anthropology's claim to distinction within the social sciences" (Strathern 1991, 8). Within colonial thought, comparison often played a justification role, used to claim white European superiority over other peoples, languages, and cultures. But this has long been critiqued (e.g., Boas 1940), and a major intervention of some early anthropology, including key ancestors of feminist anthropology, was to develop a critical comparison that reframed difference as selections from a rainbow of human possibility (Benedict 1934; Mead 1935). As I've noted elsewhere, "comparison is queer" in that it challenges conceptual norms of knowledge production founded in boundedness and proximity; additionally, queerness is comparative in that it "is an antifoundational concept that seems to belong nowhere and thus invites linkages across time and space" (Boellstorff 2007a, 183).

7   Indeed, comparison can work across time as well as space. Historical comparison served colonialism when claiming that some peoples, languages, or cultures were more evolved than others, but historical comparison can also denaturalize a taken-for-granted present. I engage in both interlinguistic comparison across the globe and intralinguistic comparison—showing

how pronouns in English have always been changing and can change again to achieve radical gender inclusion.

8   Linguistic inclusion doesn't automatically mean social inclusion: the fact that we use "humankind" instead of "mankind" doesn't mean sexism no longer exists. But language does shape thought—in a sense, it constitutes thought, shaping assumptions about the world and influencing how we act in everyday life.[2]

Personal Pronouns across Place and Time

Let's begin by noting how some aspects of personal pronouns are universal. All languages have first-person, second-person, and third-person pronouns (like **I**, **you**, and **she**). All languages distinguish between singular and plural pronouns (like **I** versus **we**). These universals don't always appear everywhere in a language. For example, English doesn't mark singular versus plural in the second-person pronoun: **you** is used to refer to one person or several.[3]

However, not all aspects of personal pronouns are universal. Here are some examples:

1   While all languages distinguish between singular and plural pronouns, some also have a "dual" pronoun for two people, so the plural pronoun refers to three or more. Dual personal pronouns aren't universal; English works fine without them.[4]

2   If I was at George's house with Asya and Kim, and I wanted all four of us to shop, I'd tell George "**we** should go to the store." If I wanted to shop with Asya and Kim but thought George should stay home, I'd also tell George "**we** should go to the store." In Indonesian, I'd use the inclusive pronoun **kita** in the first instance, but the exclusive pronoun **kami** in the second, because in that second case George is excluded from the **we**. Many languages have distinct "inclusive" and "exclusive" third-person plural pronouns, but they aren't universal; English works fine without them.

3   Some languages mark informal versus formal status on personal pronouns, like **tu/vous** in French or **du/Sie** in German. When talking to someone in such languages, you must indicate their social rank relative to yourself. In English, social status can be marked with words like "Sir" or "Madam," but it can also be avoided with **you**: if you met a celebrity you would say "nice to

meet **you**," the same pronoun as when telling a child "I love **you**." Status pronouns aren't universal; English works fine without them.[5]

We find differences across time as well. I mentioned that English doesn't mark plural with the second-person pronoun: **you** refers to one person or several. However, there used to be a distinction between **thou** and **you** as singular versus plural second-person pronouns. Through a historical process, **you** additionally became an honorific pronoun, and **thou** came to imply lower status: challenges to class hierarchy led to the loss of **thou** (save a few specialized uses). **You** replaced **thou** as the singular second-person pronoun while keeping its plural meaning: that's why we use a plural verb even when telling one person "**you** are late" (not "**you** is late"). And history continues: new second-person pronouns have emerged to compensate for the loss of the singular/plural distinction. Thus, in some English dialects **y'all** has become the second-person plural, with **you** becoming purely singular (Parker 2022).[6]

Gender and Pronouns

Now, let's apply this line of analysis to gender. *The crucial point is that gendered pronouns aren't universal*. This is absolutely pivotal for the question of radical gender inclusion. If something is linguistically universal, getting rid of it is likely impossible. It's hard to imagine a language without a first-person pronoun like **I**. But if some aspect of personal pronouns doesn't appear in some languages, that proves it's not obligatory for cognition and communication. In this regard **she/he** is like dual number, the inclusive/ exclusive distinction, or status marking. Gender pronouns aren't universal; many languages work fine without them.

To repeat: many languages already have no gendered pronouns; every pronoun is already epicene. For convenience I term these "epicene languages." For instance, in Indonesian **dia** refers to men, women, and trans persons. There's no equivalent to **she** or **he** at all. Other examples of epicene languages include Armenian, Bengali, Chinese, Finnish, Japanese, Korean, Ojibwe, Persian, and Turkish. Around 1.5 billion people speak epicene languages every day.[7]

I propose turning English into an epicene language. This would be the most radical gender inclusion: not personalized gender pronouns, but eliminating gender altogether. It's comparatively easy to do:

1   Contemporary English already marks gender only on pronouns. Some languages mark gender on nouns and adjectives (for instance, Spanish and French); a few even mark gender on verbs (for instance, the past tense in Russian). With regard to nouns, verbs, and adjectives, English is already epicene; all that remains is to extend this to pronouns.[8]

2   Furthermore, the only pronouns that need to change are the third-person singular pronoun series **she/her/hers/herself** and **he/him/his/himself**. We can term these "series" because we find the subject case (**she/he**), then variants for object case (**her/him**), possession (**hers/his**), and reflexivity (**herself/himself**). English pronouns are already epicene in the first person (**I/me/my/mine/myself; we/us/our/ours/ourselves**), second person (**you/your/yours/yourself/yourselves**), singular third person neuter (**it/its/itself**), and plural third person (**they/them/their/theirs/themselves**).[9]

3   We already have an epicene third-person pronoun: **they**. English speakers have been using epicene **they** since the 1300s—in everyday speech and in literature from Jane Austen to Shakespeare: "There's not a man I meet but doth salute me as if I were **their** well-acquainted friend." Every English speaker reading this chapter already uses epicene **they**, usually without realizing it and despite the discouragement of education systems, in utterances like "somebody left **their** coat in the room."[10] There's strong evidence that epicene **they** is already displacing sexist generic **he**, as well as phrases like "**she** or **he**." Some claim epicene **they** is incorrect because **they** is plural, but we have no trouble with **you** as both a singular and plural pronoun.

It's important to recognize how language shapes even deeply felt desires. Why don't we ever hear someone stating "my preferred pronouns are **I/you/he/him**?" As English speakers, the idea of personalized first-person or second-person gender pronouns never enters our consciousness, because those pronouns are already epicene. The ultimate way to avoid misgendering in English is to remove gender from third-person singular pronouns altogether.

Drawbacks of Personalized Gender Pronouns

I'm by no means the first to advocate turning English into a fully epicene language. The attack on epicene **they** as "bad English" began only around 1800. It was explicitly accompanied by male-centered advocacy for generic **he**: for instance, in the United Kingdom, an 1850 Act of Parliament legally mandated **he**. Calls for epicene **they** date back to at least the 1870s. Most significantly, a sustained feminist challenge began around 1970, emphasizing how generic **he** excluded women and often proposing epicene **they** as the best solution.[11]

Since 2000, the use of epicene **they** has been increasing in scholarly publications and everyday speech—even when the person mentioned has a known binary gender, as in "Professor Jones said **they** canceled the test." In 2019 the American Dialect Society voted epicene **they** "Word of the Decade"; that same year, the *Merriam-Webster Dictionary* recognized epicene **they**. Many contemporary queer, trans, and feminist scholars, activists, and allies have also called for epicene **they**.[12]

At present, we have a two-pronged movement for gender inclusion in English. Some use epicene **they**; others provide preferred personal pronouns when introducing themselves verbally or in print (for instance, an email signature line). Notably, such listings of personal pronouns only include third-person pronouns (never preferences for **I** or **you**). They usually include only two or three variants in a series (for instance, "**he/his**," but not "**he/him/his/himself**"). The listings sometimes combine pronoun options (for instance, "**she/they**") or include what are known as neopronouns (for instance, **em** or **ve**).[13]

From the perspective of gender inclusion, personalized gender pronouns are far better than **he** (because this encodes patriarchy) or phrases like "**she or he**" (because this encodes gender binarism). But there are drawbacks:

1   Personalized gender pronouns require stating one's preferences over and over again; they provide no help when referring to people we haven't met or for whom we haven't yet learned their preferences.

2   Personalized gender pronouns don't eliminate the possibility for misgendering that already exists with **she** and **he**. Indeed, they multiply the possibilities for misgendering, with well-documented negative consequences for self-esteem and belonging. *It can't be overemphasized that in English, these negative consequences of misgendering never occur when using first-person or second-person pronouns, because they're already epicene. In English, no trans or nonbinary person has ever experienced the trauma of misgendering with regard to the first-person pronoun I or the second-person pronoun you.* It's extremely important that we carefully consider the implications of this reality. What if it were the same for third-person pronouns?[14]

3   Insofar as the expectation is that, say, after meeting ten people in a meeting and learning their personalized gender pronouns, everyone at the meeting will thereafter consistently remember those pronouns, personalized gender pronouns are ableist. The idea one can remember so many personalized gender pronouns assumes a normative model of mental function. It's ableist in that it reframes cognitive difference as exclusionary intent.

4   Given the centrality of self-branding to contemporary capitalism, the idea that pronouns should be personalized places them within the oppressive system that produces gender exclusion in the first place. The whole point of pronouns is that they categorize: they group people together. An individualized pronoun becomes, in effect, a name.

5   If the solution to gender exclusion is personalization, why stop with third-person singular pronouns? Some languages mark gender on first- and second-person pronouns, or even on nouns, verbs, and adjectives.[15] Why hasn't there been a call for adding **I** or **you** to one's list of personal preferences, or the past tense for that matter? The reason is because it's only with third-person pronouns that gender exclusion still takes place in English. *Personalized third-person pronouns are an artifact of language structure.* The failure to realize this results in a failure to implement the structural solution to gender exclusion: eliminating **she** and **he** from the English language. Radical gender inclusion demands completing the historical transformation of English into an epicene language by eliminating, not increasing, the marking of gender.

6   Sustained activist attention to structural racism, structural sexism, structural heterosexism, and so on has been pivotal to social justice movements. The use of "structure" underscores how, for instance, racism isn't just the result of individual racist feelings. Instead, racism is the structural consequence of a system of social relationships embedded in power and history. Similarly, heterosexism isn't just the result of individual feelings of homophobia: it's the structural consequence of a system of social relationships that legitimates only some forms of desire. Eliminating racism and heterosexism requires structural change. Gender exclusion in language is also structural. *Eliminating it requires a structural move to gender inclusion*; namely, completing the transformation of English into an epicene language.[16]

From a truly radical perspective, personalized gender pronouns don't fundamentally challenge gender exclusion; in some respects, they further such exclusion.

Perils of Epicene English

While I advocate turning English into a fully epicene language, epicene **they** does have disadvantages. While outweighed by the advantages, it's important to consider them:

1   Epicene **they** requires both cisgendered persons and binary trans persons give up having their gender marked in English third-person singular pronouns. Giving up **she** and **he** might seem painful. But at one point **thou** was equally well known; over time it was eliminated without detriment. Furthermore, we already don't have gender marked in first-person and second-person pronouns, or in third-person plural pronouns: female- and male-identified persons use **I**, **you**, and **we** every day without feeling their gendered selves go unrepresented. Additionally, cisgendered persons and binary trans persons already use epicene **they** far more than they may realize, without any sense of self-effacement. I thus ask cisgendered allies to give up **she** and **he** in the name of radical gender inclusion. For binary trans persons, the issue of **she** and **he** in the context of struggles to assert gender is a real issue, but such persons already don't assert gender with **I**, **you**, or **we**. *The issue isn't linguistic self-expression, but where in language that self-expression takes place.*

2   Some persons (including but not limited to trans persons) feel a need to choose their pronouns. I'd ask such persons to consider how this need is shaped by language itself. Why is there no desire for personalized **you** or **I** pronouns? Furthermore, if we are truly committed to a decolonial approach, consider the English-centrism of this feeling. Were you speaking Indonesian or Turkish, you wouldn't feel a need to choose gendered personal pronouns, because such pronouns don't exist in those languages. Again, *the issue isn't linguistic self-expression, but where in language that self-expression takes place.*

3   With epicene **they**, we lose the linguistic social impact that comes from having people state their preferred pronouns. Even when there's little expectation our interlocutors will remember our preferred pronouns, the act of stating them indicates we support gender inclusion. In Peircean terms, the use of personalized gender pronouns in this manner (particularly combinations like **she/they**) is indexical, not symbolic. Like smoke indexes fire (rather than symbolizing or iconically representing fire), personalized gender pronouns index a speaker who supports gender inclusion. Such an effect is sometimes dismissed as virtue signaling, but it can be an important way to disrupt taken-for-granted norms. Once again, the issue isn't

that disrupting such "common sense" is unimportant. The issue is where in language that disruption takes place. Among the 1.5 billion speakers of epicene languages are many who work for radical gender inclusion in ways that don't involve pronouns. And in English-speaking contexts, we strive through language for inclusion across race, disability, sexuality, and other domains without doing so with pronouns.[17]

4   From a feminist perspective, a possible concern is that epicene **they** could become a new masculine generic pronoun, erasing the impact of generic **she**. However, generic **she** hasn't been inclusive for many persons (such as many queer women, Black women, and others historically excluded from full womanhood). As with the social impact of preferred pronouns, the social impact of generic **she** only exists because of gender marking on pronouns in the first place.

5   Epicene **they** might seem like assimilation, since there's no way to mark trans selfhood on epicene pronouns. The issue here is that if we're interested in eliminating structural oppression, then structural change is necessary. Structural change might seem like assimilation at first, because by definition it's change for everyone. But structural change isn't assimilation if the change is to something new—for instance, radical gender inclusion. It's crucial to distinguish assimilation from structural change.

6   **She** and **he** will still crop up in everyday speech. But slip-ups regularly occur, even with personalized gender pronouns. As noted earlier, it's ableist to expect no language errors or to assume such errors reveal gender exclusion. Language change is never all at once, and other languages teach us that it's possible to change gender pronouns. One example of this is Swedish, where since 2012 a new pronoun, **hen** (epicene **they**), is becoming increasingly accepted compared to the existing **she** (**hon**) and **he** (**han**).[18]

Conclusion: Toward a Queer Epicene

In this chapter I've begun a provisional argument for eliminating **she** and **he** from the English language and replacing those pronouns with epicene **they**. Except for **she** and **he** (and their variants), English is already an epicene language. Completing this process is the strongest move toward radical gender inclusion. Despite the work of patriarchal grammarians, epicene **they** has been widely used for hundreds of years: it's a feasible way to transform

English into an epicene language. The perils of epicene **they** are relatively minor and can be addressed.[19]

This is an anthropological argument, but it's not ethnographic (based on interviews with people using various pronouns, for instance). Rather, it is queerly comparative. There's a decolonial politics to comparison: too often, English speakers don't consider other languages. This is particularly ironic because in the United States and other English-speaking countries, many other languages are spoken. One way to challenge English's global dominance, a dominance rooted in colonialism, is learning from other languages—and we can learn from the fact that 1.5 billion people already speak epicene languages.

I've also worked to show how radical gender inclusion is specifically trans inclusion. I seek to repair queer anthropology's connections to feminist anthropology, which have been damaged by TERF and its demonstrably false claim to be "radical." My analysis thus not only links queer anthropology to queer linguistics (Motschenbacher 2011), but responds to the "persistent marginalization of feminism" within anthropology (Mahmud 2021)—to show the power of feminist structuralist arguments about "gender trouble."

As I noted at the outset, linguistic inclusion doesn't automatically mean social inclusion. But movements for linguistic inclusion correctly foreground the importance of language in cognition, culture, and power. I look forward to the day when **she** and **he** are like **thou**: archaic pronouns recognized in old texts, but no longer in common use. I see a time—let us call it a queer epicene—where obligatory gender marking is eliminated from English language, and structural transformation in our speech and thought contributes to a future of true inclusion. There is a path out of this pronoun trouble!

Notes

1 For examples of this work, see Boellstorff 2005, 2007a.

2 The question of how language influences thought is a long-standing domain of research (Sapir 1999).

3 My analysis focuses on personal pronouns; I will not discuss other pronouns like demonstratives (**this** bridge) or inanimate pronouns (for instance, using **it** to refer to a rock; for an extensive discussion of animacy, see Chen 2012).

4 A few languages have trial pronouns referring to three people, and/or paucal pronouns referring to "some" people (usually two to five).

5 A few languages (like Javanese) have more complex status marking on personal pronouns and/or mark status on verbs and nouns, so that there are status registers.

6 With regard to the history of **you** and the loss of **thou**, "the shift in language both resulted from and contributed to the shifting class structure. We can use pronouns to shift the gender structure, too" (Shlasko 2015, 5; see Silverstein 1985 for a detailed discussion). Another example of historical change is that Old English used to have a dual: **ič** (one person); **wit** (two people); **wē** (three or more people).

7 See Srinivasan 2020. It is most accurate to speak of "epicene **they**" rather than "singular **they**," because epicene **they** (like epicene **you**) is used for singular and plural. Some language families are predominantly or exclusively epicene, including Uralic and Austronesian languages. Thus Austronesian languages "rarely mark pronominal gender" (Blust 2013, 320); most (including Indonesian, Hawaiian, and Māori) are epicene. In modern Chinese, the pronouns for **he**, **she**, and **it** are written differently but pronounced the same when spoken in Mandarin and most other dialects.

8 As a result of these shifts, in contemporary English "'gender' is not a grammatical category, but a semantic one" (Balhorn 2004, 86). For more on the diachronic loss of gender in English, see Curzan 2003. See Silverstein for an extensive analysis of gender as not only a structural and pragmatic feature of language, but an "institutionalized expression of the tendency to metalevel apprehension of language as behavior and structure" (1985, 223).

9 The first-person and plural third-person series have five variants (not four, like the third-person series) due to distinct dependent/independent possessive pronouns (**"my** book" versus "the book is **mine"**). The singular third person neuter has three variants due to identical nominative and accusative variants, and the lack of an independent possessive variant. The second-person series has five variants due to distinct reflexive singular/plural pronouns (**yourself/ yourselves**). I will not discuss "grammatical gender" (i.e., "noun classes," like masculine, feminine, and neuter German nouns).

10 There is evidence of epicene **they** from Middle English in the 1300s (Curzan 2003); the Shakespeare quote is from the *Comedy of Errors* (Baron 2020, 228). Other historical discussions regarding epicene **they** include Baranowski 2002 and Wheeler 2019. Balhorn notes "overwhelming evidence, both anecdotal and statistical, of the ubiquity of generic **they** in Modern English speech and writing and the existence of this structure for hundreds of years," finding an increase in **they** from 9 percent in the sixteenth century to 45 percent in the twentieth century (2004, 80). This was noted in the 1970s and 1980s (e.g., Bodine 1975, 130; Green 1977; Jochnowitz 1982; Miller and Swift 1976).

PRONOUN TROUBLE 127

11 For more on historical attacks on epicene **they**, see Bodine 1975, 130, 136. For more on the Act of Parliament see Baron 1981, 84. For further discussion of the role of prescriptive grammarians and public policy in supporting generic **he** against epicene **they**, see Zuber and Reed 1993.

12 See American Dialect Society 2020 for the announcement of *they* as "Word of the Decade." There are "indications that **they**, already the most common gender-neutral pronoun, is now the nonbinary pronoun of choice" (Baron 2020, 213). Given the common use of epicene **they**, what might seem its "sudden resurgence" is better characterized as a "restoration" (Balhorn 2009, 393; see Noll, Lowry, and Bryant 2018).

It is well recognized that "it was not until 1970s and 1980s feminist interventions that **he** as an epicene pronoun became more broadly associated with sexist language" (Noll, Lowry, and Bryant 2018, 1058). These interventions emphasized the psychological impact of generic **he** with regard to everything from job applications to education, as well as its inconsistency: "the male in Lionel Tiger's *Men in Groups* excludes the female in Phyllis Chesler's *Women and Madness*, while the male in Thomas Paine's *Rights of Man* is supposed to encompass the female of Mary Wollstonecraft's *Vindication of the Rights of Woman*" (Martnya 1980, 483; see also Abbott 1984; Khosroshahi 1989; MacKay and Fulkerson 1979; Newman 1992; Stanley 1978). For contemporary work on generic **he** and sexist discourse, see Gastil 1990; McConnell-Ginet 2006; Miller and James 2009; and Silveira 1980.

The ubiquity of epicene **they** has long been noted (MacKay 1980). In terms of its contemporary expansion, one study found epicene **they** used almost fifteen times as often in scholarly articles in 2019 compared to 2010 (Yakut, Genç, and Bada 2021); for other discussions, see Stormbom 2020 and also LaScotte 2016, who found 68 percent of study participants already using epicene **they**. For a discussion of the rise in acceptability of epicene **they** even when someone's "binary gender is known to both speaker and hearer," see Bjorkman 2017, 2. Examples of contemporary calls for epicene **they** (often noting its inclusion of nonbinary and trans persons) include Balhorn 2009, Bradley 2020, Bradley et al. 2019, Brown 2020, Hernandez 2020, Noor 2020, Paterson 2014, and Shlasko 2015.

13 Neopronouns have a long history: **em** was first proposed in 1841; **ve**, in 1864. For more on the history of neopronouns, see Baron 1981, 86–87; and Baron 2020, 272–75.

14 Discussions of the negative consequences of misgendering include Matsuno 2019 and McLemore 2015.

15 Languages with gendered first-person pronouns include Thai; languages with gendered second-person pronouns include Minangkabau. See Siewierska 2013.

16 There is strong comparative evidence that "personal pronouns are particularly susceptible to modification in response to social and ideological change" (Bodine 1975, 130).

17 For introductions to indexicality see Lee 1997 and Parmentier 1994.

18 For a discussion of **hen** (borrowed from Finnish, which, like all members of the Uralic language family, is epicene), see Gustafsson Sendén, Bäck, and Lindqvist 2015.

19 Personalized gender pronouns and epicene **they** need not be antagonistic options in the struggle for gender inclusion: they can be mutually reinforcing. There is evidence that personalized gender pronouns increase the likelihood of using epicene **they** (Arnold, Mayo, and Dong 2021).

References

Abbott, Gerry. 1984. "Unisex 'They.'" *ELT Journal* 38(1): 45–48.

American Dialect Society. 2020, January 3. "2019 Word of the Year Is '(My) Pronouns,' Word of the Decade Is Singular 'They.'" *American Dialect Society*. https://www.americandialect.org/2019-word-of-the-year-is-my-pronouns-word-of-the-decade-is-singular-they.

Anzaldúa, Gloria. 1987. *Borderlands / La Frontera*. San Francisco: Spinsters/Aunt Lute.

Arnold, Jennifer E., Heather C. Mayo, and Lisa Dong. 2021, May 4. "My Pronouns Are They/Them: Talking about Pronouns Changes How Pronouns Are Understood." *Psychonomic Bulletin and Review*. https://doi.org/10.3758/s13423-021-01905-0.

Austin, J. L. 1980. *How to Do Things with Words*. Oxford: Oxford University Press.

Balhorn, Mark. 2004. "The Rise of Epicene *They.*" *Journal of English Linguistics* 32(2): 79–104.

Balhorn, Mark. 2009. "The Epicene Pronoun in Contemporary Newspaper Prose." *American Speech* 84(4): 391–413.

Baranowski, Maciej. 2002. "Current Usage of the Epicene Pronoun in Written English." *Journal of Sociolinguistics* 6(3): 378–97.

Baron, Dennis E. 1981. "The Epicene Pronoun: The Word That Failed." *American Speech* 56(2): 83–97.

Baron, Dennis E. 2020. *What's Your Pronoun? Beyond He and She*. New York: Liveright.

Benedict, Ruth. 1934. *Patterns of Culture*. New York: Mentor Books.

Bjorkman, Bronwyn M. 2017. "Singular *They* and the Syntactic Representation of Gender in English." *Glossa: A Journal of General Linguistics* 2(1): 80, 1–13.

Blust, Robert. 2013. *The Austronesian Languages*. Canberra: Australian National University.

Boas, Franz. 1940. "The Limitations of the Comparative Method of Anthropology." In *Race, Language, and Culture*, 270–80. Chicago: University of Chicago Press. Originally published 1896.

Bodine, Ann. 1975. "Androcentrism in Prescriptive Grammar: Singular 'They,' Sex-Indefinite 'He,' and 'He or She.'" *Language in Society* 4(2): 129–46.

Boellstorff, Tom. 2005. *The Gay Archipelago: Sexuality and Nation in Indonesia*. Princeton, NJ: Princeton University Press.

Boellstorff, Tom. 2007a. *A Coincidence of Desires: Anthropology, Queer Studies, Indonesia*. Durham, NC: Duke University Press.

Boellstorff, Tom. 2007b. "When Marriage Falls: Queer Coincidences in Straight Time." *GLQ: A Journal of Gay and Lesbian Studies* 13(2/3): 227–48.

Bradley, Evan D. 2020. "The Influence of Linguistic and Social Attitudes on Grammaticality Judgments of Singular 'They.'" *Language and Communication* 78: 101272.

Bradley, Evan D., Julia Salkind, Ally Moore, and Sofi Teitsort. 2019. "Singular 'They' and Novel Pronouns: Gender-Neutral, Nonbinary, or Both?" *Proceedings of the Linguistic Society of America* 4(36): 1–7.

Brown, Heidi K. 2020. "Get with the Pronoun." *Legal Communications and Rhetoric: JALWD* 17: 61–102.

Butler, Judith. 1990. *Gender Trouble: Feminism and the Subversion of Identity*. New York: Routledge.

Chen, Mel Y. 2012. *Animacies: Biopolitics, Racial Mattering, and Queer Affect*. Durham, NC: Duke University Press.

Curzan, Anne. 2003. *Gender Shifts in the History of English*. Cambridge: Cambridge University Press.

Du Bois, W. E. B. 1903. *The Souls of Black Folk: Essays and Sketches*. Chicago: A. C. McClurg.

Foucault, Michel. 1978. *The History of Sexuality, Volume 1: An Introduction*. Translated by Robert Hurley. New York: Vintage.

Gastil, John. 1990. "Generic Pronouns and Sexist Language: The Oxymoronic Character of Masculine Generics." *Sex Roles* 23(11/12): 629–43.

Green, William H. 1977. "Singular Pronouns and Sexual Politics." *College Composition and Communication* 28(2): 150–53.

Gupta, Akhil. 1998. *Postcolonial Developments: Agriculture in the Making of Modern India*. Durham, NC: Duke University Press.

Gustafsson Sendén, Marie, Emma A. Bäck, and Anna Lindqvist. 2015. "Introducing a Gender-Neutral Pronoun in a Natural Gender Language: The Influence of Time on Attitudes and Behavior." *Frontiers in Psychology* 6: 1–12.

Hernandez, Ellis E. 2020. "Pronouns, Prescriptivism, and Prejudice: Attitudes toward the Singular 'They,' Prescriptive Grammar, and Nonbinary Transgender People." MA thesis, Department of English, Purdue University.

Jochnowitz, George. 1982. "Everybody Likes Pizza, Doesn't He or She?" *American Speech* 57(3): 198–203.

Khosroshahi, Fatemeh. 1989. "Penguins Don't Care, but Women Do: A Social Identity Analysis of a Whorfian Problem." *Language in Society* 18(4): 505–25.

LaScotte, Darren K. 2016. "Singular They: An Empirical Study of Generic Pronoun Use." *American Speech* 91(1): 62–80.

Lee, Benjamin. 1997. *Talking Heads: Language, Metalanguage, and the Semiotics of Subjectivity*. Durham, NC: Duke University Press.

MacKay, Donald G. 1980. "On the Goals, Principles, and Procedures for Prescriptive Grammar: Singular They." *Language in Society* 9(3): 349–67.

MacKay, Donald G., and David C. Fulkerson. 1979. "On the Comprehension and Production of Pronouns." *Journal of Verbal Learning and Verbal Behavior* 18: 661–73.

Mahmud, Lilith. 2021. "Feminism in the House of Anthropology." *Annual Review of Anthropology* 50: 21.1–17.

Martyna, Wendy. 1980. "Beyond the 'He/Man' Approach: The Case for Nonsexist Language." *Signs: A Journal of Women in Culture and Society* 5(3): 482–93.

Matsuno, Emmie. 2019. "Nonbinary-Affirming Psychological Interventions." *Cognitive and Behavioral Practice* 26(4): 617–28.

McConnell-Ginet, Sally. 2006. "The Origins of Sexist Language in Discourse." *Annals of the New York Academy of Sciences* 433(1): 123–35.

McLemore, Kevin A. 2015. "Experiences with Misgendering: Identity Misclassification of Transgender Spectrum Individuals." *Self and Identity* 14(1): 51–74.

Mead, Margaret. 1935. *Sex and Temperament in Three Primitive Societies*. New York: Penguin.

Miller, Casey, and Kate Swift. 1976. *Words and Women*. Garden City, NY: Anchor/Doubleday.

Miller, Megan M., and Lori E. James. 2009. "Is the Generic Pronoun He Still Comprehended as Excluding Women?" *American Journal of Psychology* 122(4): 483–96.

Motschenbacher, Heiko. 2011. "Taking Queer Linguistics Further: Sociolinguistics and Critical Heteronormativity." *International Journal of the Sociology of Language* 212: 149–79.

Newman, Michael. 1992. "Pronominal Disagreements: The Stubborn Problem of Singular Epicene Antecedents." *Language in Society* 21(3): 447–75.

Noll, Jane, Mark Lowry, and Judith Bryant. 2018. "Changes over Time in the Comprehension of He and They as Epicene Pronouns." *Journal of Psycholinguistic Research* 47(5): 1057–68.

Noor, Poppy. 2020, January 14. "So Your Friend Came Out as Non-binary: Here's How to Use Pronouns They/Them." *Guardian*. https://www.theguardian.com/world/2020/jan/14/janelle-monae-non-binary-pronouns-they-them.

Parker, David B. 2022. "'Y'all,' That Most Southern of Southernisms, Is Going Mainstream—and It's about Time." *Conversation*. https://theconversation.com/yall-that-most-southern-of-southernisms-is-going-mainstream-and-its-about-time-193265.

Parmentier, Richard J. 1994. *Signs in Society: Studies in Semiotic Anthropology*. Bloomington: Indiana University Press.

Paterson, Laura Louise. 2014. *British Pronoun Use, Prescription, and Processing: Linguistic and Social Influences Affecting "They" and "He."* New York: Palgrave Macmillan.

Sapir, Edward. 1999. "The Unconscious Patterning of Behavior in Society." In *The Collected Words of Edward Sapir, Vol. 3*, edited by Regna Darnell and Judith T. Irvine, 155–72. New York: Mouton de Gruyter. Originally published 1928.

Shlasko, Davey. 2015, February 3. "How Using 'They' as a Singular Pronoun Can Change the World." *Feministing*. http://feministing.com/2015/02/03/how-using-they-as-a-singular-pronoun-can-change-the-world/.

Siewierska, Anna. 2013. "Gender Distinctions in Independent Personal Pronouns." In *The World Atlas of Language Structures Online*, edited by Matthew S. Dryer and Martin Haspelmath. http://wals.info/chapter/44.

Silveira, Jeanette. 1980. "Generic Masculine Words and Thinking." *Women's Studies International Quarterly* 3: 165–78.

Silverstein, Michael. 1985. "Language and the Culture of Gender: At the Intersection of Structure, Usage, and Ideology." In *Semiotic Mediation: Sociocultural and Psychological Perspectives*, edited by Elizabeth Mertz and Richard J. Parmentier, 219–59. Orlando, FL: Academic Press.

Srinivasan, Amia. 2020. "He, She, One, They, Ho, Hus, Hum, Ita." *London Review of Books* 42(13). https://www.lrb.co.uk/the-paper/v42/n13/amia-srinivasan/he-she-one-they-ho-hus-hum-ita.

Stanley, Julia. 1978. "Sexist Grammar." *College English* 39(7): 800–11.

Stormbom, Charlotte. 2020. "Gendering in Open Access Research Articles: The Role of Epicene Pronouns." *English for Specific Purposes* 60: 193–204.

Strathern, Marilyn. 1991. *Partial Connections*. Lanham, MD: Rowman and Littlefield.

Wheeler, Andre. 2019, September 18. "Merriam-Webster Dictionary Adds 'They' as Nonbinary Pronoun." *Guardian*. https://www.theguardian.com/science/2019/sep/17/merriam-webster-they-nonbinary-pronoun.

Wiegman, Robyn. 2012. *Object Lessons*. Durham, NC: Duke University Press.

Yakut, Ilyas, Bilal Genç, and Erdogan Bada. 2021. "Epicene Pronoun Usage in the Social Sciences: The Case of Research Articles." *Journal of English for Academic Purposes* 52(April): 101–5.

Zuber, Sharon, and Ann M. Reed. 1993. "The Politics of Grammar Handbooks: Generic *He* and Singular *They*." *College English* 55(5): 515–30.

Brian A. Horton

6

Stylization in the Flesh

Queer Anthropology and Performance

Setting the Stage

The word *performance* often conjures images of the stage or of art that elicits emotion out of an audience. It references metaphors of theatricality and spectacularized embodiments, and it raises questions of truth and falsity, authentic and inauthentic. In its most intimate registers, performance might also point to the small things we do with our bodies each day. A sequin here. A limp wrist there. The warm embrace of a binder encasing our raw and tender flesh. Performance can be the microscopic ways people etch alternative social meanings onto and also through their bodies. It is perhaps a means of becoming less governed (Foucault 1997). Or it might be "a promiscuous lover," capacious and abundant, but also wayward, faithfully belonging to no one (Madison 2010). And as, Soyini Madison's use of the word "promiscuous" suggests, our most intimate and personal acts never fully belong to us. Where performance might name acts of embodiment or acts of self-presentation, those actions are social insofar as they repeat (faithfully and unfaithfully) the repertoire of actions that preceded them. What we do, how we act, is open for observation, interpretation, and meaning making—the core domains of cultural anthropology.

For scholars in queer studies (including queer anthropology), performance has been an animating concept for understanding how broad categories like gender and sexuality are contingent, porous, and hegemonically arbitrary; they are frequently structured through the uneasy relationships between action and socially inscribed meanings placed upon our actions, without our consent. And if queer is about a kind of relationship of alienation to social structures, or an umbrella term to name how some bodies and lives are outcaste, then performance has been a useful analytic for articulating how some lives and bodies are constituted as other. The theatrical, spectacular, and improvised ways that dissident genders and sexualities are constituted through bodily actions have been well documented across works in queer studies and anthropology (see Morris 1995). Figures like the *travesti* (Kulick 1998), *hijra* (Nanda 1998), and the drag queen (Newton 1972; Butler 1990) have become central characters in scholarly dramas about the discursive limits of identity categories. But rather than settle for the disruptive work that some queer bodies might do for theory or for structures like identity, this chapter also considers how scholarship might stage queer figures differently. Instead of seeing the value of queer figures in the ways that their acts and embodiments undermine broad categories like gender and sexuality, I consider how performance might help map the routes people might take to cope with, thrive in, and at times resignify the terms of their alienation.

In this chapter, I do not set out to make complete sense of performance, its status as a proper disciplinary object, or even to fully articulate its complicated conceptual kinship chart. Rather, this chapter explores the thresholds between queer anthropology and performance studies as openings to consider the debates around performativity as a discursive framework—a repetition of stylized acts that might congeal over time (Butler 1990)—and performance as materially grounded in the flesh and words of everyday life (Johnson 2001). Scholars in anthropology, linguistics, folklore studies, theater and drama studies, and performance studies have understood performance as the following: aesthetic practices whose repetitions can structure individual and collective identities across time and space (Kapchan 1995); "doing something or something done" (Taylor 2016); dramatic cultural events that emanate underlying cultural meanings through collective rituals (Turner 1975); or "all the activity of a given participant on a given occasion which serves to influence in any way any of the other participants" (Goffman 1959, 8). These disparate definitions pivot around the different ways that stylized individual and collective presentations might translate into broader social effects: concretized social meanings, the coalescing of social bonds, or playing with norms. In the following sections, I take an expansive approach to performance, relying on Joshua Chambers-Letson's (2013) definition of performance as "embodied acts of self-presentation." Defining it so expansively also enables me to "think of a wide range of presentational and communicative behaviors as performance" (2013, 6). This broad definition helps situate how queer anthropology and performance studies can attend to queer bodies not only as spectacularizing or dramatizing structures and categories, but also as eking out modes of endurance in spite of the failures of categories, discourses, and structures to attend to queer complexity.

If performance is the stylized and embodied ways that people present themselves, then "performances operate as vital acts of transfer, transmitting social knowledge, memory, and a sense of identity through reiterated actions" (Taylor 2016, 25). This transmission has more commonly been understood as "performativity," after Judith Butler (1990): the discursive meanings codified through consistent repetition of certain acts. *Performance* and *performativity* are conceptually intertwined within anthropology and performance studies. Both are key to thinking about how aestheticized modes of self-presentation have material and discursive effects. *Performance* and *performativity* have also been crucial concepts for thinking about how gender and sexuality—particularly nonnormative gender and sexuality—are rendered through different modes of self-presentation. Where the initial impetus behind anthropological engagements with *performance* was to unsettle the primacy of text (e.g., Bauman 1975) and to consider the modes of communication and the broader cultural contexts within which communication occurred (e.g., Gumperz and Hymes 1972), *performance* and *performativity* in studies of gender and sexuality have aimed to unsettle the presumed universality of the subject at the center of feminist, gay and lesbian, and subsequently queer and trans studies.

STYLIZATION IN THE FLESH   135

Performance and Performativity

Judith Butler's *Gender Trouble* (1990) implores its readers to think about the techniques and processes through which identities are made and potentially unmade. Rather than taking the sign *woman* as coherent, stable, and essential, Butler aims to show how gender is a corporeal style, a consistent repetition of acts that produces gendered meaning. The effect of some performances being understood as natural or real is what Butler calls *performativity*. At the heart of their theory is not the individual performance, but the structures of authority that reinforce some performances as real and others as fake. Thus, patterns of repetition must be disrupted or transgressed with new or unconventional performances to shake up the ways identities are naturalized. Specifically, Butler lauds transgressive performances, such as drag, that disrupt normative gender. "*In imitating gender, drag implicitly reveals the imitative structure of gender itself—as well as its contingency*" (Butler 1990, 175, emphasis Butler's). By focusing on the power of drag to parody gender's arbitrary structure, drag artists—for Butler—are the paradigmatic example of how gender can be troubled. Drag represents not merely a defining feature of Butler's argument, but a key symbol of gender's synthetic qualities (see Butler 1993). But this subversion is not without challenges. Drag performance also raises distinct questions around the relationships between drag and camp (see Newton 1972), the subversive power of parody (e.g., Robertson 1998), and whether drag (especially as female impersonation) is a critique of gender norms *or* its reification (e.g., Newton 1993; Frye 1983; see Morris 1995 for an extensive analysis of these debates).

Esther Newton's pathbreaking *Mother Camp: Female Impersonators in America* is perhaps *the* key ethnographic specter in *Gender Trouble*'s engagement with drag. In her ethnography of drag queens, Newton highlights how female impersonators manipulate their appearances to perform as women and in so doing demonstrate the lack of coherence between gender's supposed internal truth and external reality. Butler's (1990) insistence that drag "reveals the imitative structure of gender itself" relies on Newton's point that gender as an outside representation can be manipulated, adopted, and performed. Newton's accounts of female impersonators and the mutability of gender/sex systems also form the basis for future ethnographic studies of gender performance (e.g., Kulick 1998; Robertson 1998). With Butler, Newton's work also points to how gender performances might deconstruct the presumed essential gender/sex binary through parody, or behaviors that aesthetically exaggerate gender to demonstrate that, far from natural, it is a construct. Marjorie Garber highlights this subversive power of cross-dressing as the "category crisis." In her study of cross-dressing, Garber argues that the power of cross-dressing is that it is "a space of possibility structuring and confounding culture" (1992, 17). Performance, especially when it exaggerates gender, can throw into crisis the stability of seemingly natural constructs like *woman* and *man*. This confounding of culture is marked by attending to the ways that peoples' bodies and their choices with what to do with their bodies can have profound effects on the meanings of gender and its larger cultural life in a given place and time. Thus, what might seem like frivolity or camp—from wearing a wig and lashes, to dramatized performances and behavior—might carry the potential to unseat normative conceptions of gender.

Parody in Passing: The Question of Gender "Transgression"

The attention to and search for meaning through the body has been one of the key ways that queer anthropologists have taken up Butler's analysis of *performativity*. For instance, studies outside of US contexts, such as Kalissa Alexeyeff's (2000, 2008) research on drag in the Cook Islands, consider how queer performances of drag and cross-dressing might identify breaks between local cross-dressing habits of *laelae* ("feminized masculinity") and global drag. While *laelae* operate within a framework of gender and sex that is capacious and holds a multiplicity of meanings and possibilities for gender and sexual embodiment, Alexeyeff notes that *laelae* are not necessarily synonymous with Western constructions like drag and transgender. Instead, performances of cross-dressing might accent category crises between local and Western understandings of gender (2008, 109). Cross-dressing in this context is not merely a means of playing with the contours of gender and its meanings: it is also "performative commentary on the tension between global and local forms of sexual and gender identity and, ultimately, the relationship between individual and community, personal desires, and public conventions" (2008, 109). Alexeyeff demonstrates that some drag performances might be transgressive not just because they disrupt gender, but also because they disrupt culturally specific boundaries between local and global.

At times, performances may be subversive because they center the desires of the performers, above the need to dramatically transgress gender norms. For instance, Don Kulick's (1998) research with *travesti* in Brazil suggests that gender's performative substance lies in how *travesti* use their body parts, not just their citations of the gender binary. For instance, masculinity among *travesti* is understood by being a top (*activo*), creating a gender binary between "men" and "not men." Kulick's attention to the binary of active and passive (or top and bottom) demonstrates that *performance* might help us attend to the meanings made of gender—as with Butler, not by simply relying on flesh as a mirror of inner truth, but instead showing how ideas of masculinity and femininity are wrapped up in how bodies are used (rather than what bodies are made of). *Travesti* can sit between a near-flawless mimesis of womanhood as well as a fabulous exaggeration and parody of it. Moving between transgressions of binary gender and its reification, *travesti* in Kulick's ethnography signal the multiplicities of idioms for performing gendered embodiment in ways that might fuse together subversion, parody, and mimesis. But *travesti* also evince an indifference to passing as women or to disrupting the gender binary. Their exaggerations and playful mimesis of womanhood signal perhaps alternate frameworks and paradigms of gender that are rooted in their pleasure as practitioners of gender and not in their desires to reframe gender's broader cultural meanings. And perhaps this melding together of parts, desire, and indifference is itself a mode of transgressing gender binaries.

The centrality of transgression to the concept of performativity is perhaps most clearly articulated in debates about gender-nonconforming performances, passing, and parody. As Jennifer Robertson argues in her study of the all-female Takarazuka Revue in Japan, cross-dressing must mobilize "serious parody" for it to do the work of unsettling the gender binary (1998, 38). Robertson sees drag that is not exaggerated but mere passing as the movement from one side of the gender binary to the other, rather than the work of throwing gender into crisis. Robertson's argument is notable for two reasons. First, it highlights a key tension in trans studies between passing and gender transgression. Robertson's suspicion about the power of passing sublimates trans desires into a broader politics of gender disruption. One of the overarching critiques of Butler's *performativity* has been its gloss of transgender as transgressive, the "syllogism transgender = gender performativity = queer = subversive" (Prosser 1998, 33). For some, Butler's theorizations of performativity render the transgender figure exceptional in

138   BRIAN A. HORTON

queer studies, valuable insofar as they can be transgressive. In queer studies, passing can be chided for not being radical or revolutionary for queer and trans politics (e.g., Stone 1994), a critique that misses the strategic ways trans folks choose their own relationships with trans embodiment. As Black trans studies scholar C. Riley Snorton argues, passing and misrecognition might actually become occasions for a gender-nonconforming person's disassociation and disidentification with normative gender (Snorton 2009, 88). Put differently, rather than critique trans persons who might pass or wallow in the failures of being misrecognized, passing might be an opportunity for individual refusals and disidentifications (see Muñoz 1999) with dominant interpolations of identity.

In Contra Robertson's critique of Takarazuka passing, Snorton reminds us that performances of gender must center the feelings of the performer—and not just the audience. Snorton demonstrates that there is an inner psychic aspect to performativity and its failures (such as misrecognition), an aspect that might allow individuals to reassert their identities in moments where they do not pass. Eric Plemons (2017) accents this point about people centering their own desires in his study of facial feminization and passing. In his explorations of trans women who seek gender affirmative care, Plemons suggests that surgery is the material effect of performative models of sex and gender integrated into trans care (10). The desire for particular modes of recognition—realness and passing—compels patients to get surgery but also gives shape to the meanings of surgery. Plemons's approach to *performativity* reverses the flow of performance to performativity to think instead about how *performativity* touches the skin to imbue it with specifically codified meanings that can be cited, re-created, and literally embodied.

The second issue raised by Robertson's delineation between passing and parody is that scholarship dealing with gender performance and subversion has heavily relied on the bodies of gender outcasts to nourish theoretical desires for antinormativity—without grappling with the material stakes of the very bodies being theorized. As Vivian Namaste writes, "Transvestites and transsexuals function as rhetorical figures within cultural texts; terms wherein the voices, struggles, and joys of real transgendered people in the everyday are noticeably absent" (2000, 16). Butler's theory of *performativity* foregrounds the means of subjection—or the processes by which some bodies are made subjects—rather than the primacy of the subjects themselves. In Butler's framework, performativity and its concomitant meanings can be shifted in the moments when repetitions fail and expose an underlying tension. However, this approach to *performance* and *performativity* stages performance as (politically) useful only insofar as it can disrupt broader chains of signification and meaning. Thus, "performance remains performativity's weak sister—a kind of incidental tremor in a system that depends on live repetition for its upkeep" (Pollock 2007, 243).

These debates and concerns about the politics of performance raise critical questions for queer anthropology after Butler. *Gender Trouble* not only inaugurated a new wave of feminist scholarship that centered on deconstructing essential ideas of gender, particularly in anthropology (see Visweswaran 1997), but also gave way to queer theory and ethnographic scholarship centered on queer and trans disruptions of normativity, or what Margot Weiss (2016) glosses as "transgression and the new normal" (631). By demonstrating that the performance of normative cis womanhood stands in a necessary relationship to heterosexuality, Butler's work highlighted the heterosexual matrix at the heart of conversations around gender: when we talk about gender (particularly womanhood), we are also always talking about a heterosexuality and a subject presumed to be straight. While queer theory has endeavored to find alternatives to the rigid frames of identity, queer of color and Black feminist scholars have noted the challenges of abandoning identity. Far from desiring identity in purely representational terms, scholars have challenged the "subjectless critique" implicit in some queer theorizing (Johnson 2001; Cohen 1997). At times, the postidentity scholarly practice of queer scholarship evades clearly delineated objects and subjects as reference points for theorizing. This practice can also presume that we all mean the same things or are referencing the same bodies when speaking about queerness. Like the problems of feminism and the sign *woman* that *Gender Trouble* responds to, queer theory runs the risk of presuming the universal ontological status of the subject on whose behalf it intervenes.

Put otherwise, queer theory's excitement for the drag artist and their potentially subversive power onstage can obfuscate the question of her life offstage: How is she getting home? Does she even have one? And is it safe? What I might call the "race for transgression" risks obscuring material conditions: the worlds people navigate off of queer theory's stage. Namaste names a crucial problem for queer scholarship informed by Butler and the broader interventions of queer theory: that the material conditions of queer lives are at times elided in the use of queer bodies to settle intellectual debates.

Namaste's critique is also relevant for anthropology and the ways early anthropologists cannibalized queer and trans life in the service of ameliorating the political conditions of Western (mostly white) LGBTQ+ subjects. As Rosalind Morris wrote in her review of performativity in anthropology, "much of the new anthropology of gender seeks its Barbins" (Morris 1995, 570) in culturally specific figures like the *xanith* (Wikan 1977, 1982), *laelae* (Alexeyeff 2008), *hijra* (Nanda 1998), *kathoey* (Morris 1994), and *berdache* (Morgensen 2011) as well as concepts like "third gender" (Herdt 1993). However, as Morgensen (2011) warns, scholars must be critical of investment in sexuality and gender if only to fulfill Western anthropology's desires to find cross-cultural evidence of queer and trans practices (see also Weston 1993 on "ethnocartography"). I link the story of these cross-cultural figures to the story of the drag performer in *Gender Trouble*. As V. V. Chaudhry (2019) reminds us, the invocation of trans figures as valuable for their disruptive potentiality runs the risk of producing a marginalization through reduction to being "name and idea alone" (47). Rather than seeing performance as merely that which reveals the master codes of social grammars of gender and sexuality, one that is keyed to celebrating gender transgression, how might queer anthropologists engage with the materiality of performance?

Staying with the Flesh

In his "riff" on Butler's notion of "gender trouble," performance studies scholar E. Patrick Johnson highlights queer theory's "race problem," particularly performativity theory's erosion of the self, agency, and the materiality of the body (2001, 5). As Johnson asks, "What is the utility of queer theory on the front lines, in the trenches, on the street, or any place where the racialized and sexualized body is beaten, starved, fired, cursed—indeed, where the body is the site of trauma?" (4). Johnson's response to queer theory via Butler is two-pronged. On the one hand, queer theory has not taken into account the materiality of its subjects. On the other, it has not seriously engaged with the contributions of working-class folks and queers of color. He suggests, via Cathy Cohen (1997), that the refusals of identity, agency, and community ties in queer theory miss the ways queers of color make strategic choices that are about staying with trouble to survive. Deploying the playful term "quare studies," Johnson proposes a scholarly move that engages with the flesh of the queer of color subjects that queer theory seeks to deconstruct. He labels his project a "theory in the flesh," from Cherríe Moraga and Gloria Anzaldúa (1983, 23). Johnson's theory in the flesh demands scholars attend to individual performances (of stylized self-presentations) not for the sake of an identity construction that is out there, but as "performance of self for the self" (2001, 11).

Johnson's use of the word "flesh" hearkens back to Hortense Spillers's (1987) distinction between *body* and *flesh*. Spillers notes, writing of Black women in the afterlives of enslavement, that "before the 'body' there is 'flesh,' that zero degree of social conceptualization that does not escape concealment under the brush of discourse or the reflexes of iconography" (1987, 67). Building on Spillers's work by bringing it into conversation with Foucault and Agamben, Alexander Weheliye (2014) posits that "if the body represents legal personhood qua self-possession, then the flesh designates those dimensions of human life cleaved by the working together of depravation and deprivation" (2014, 39). Weheliye, via Spillers, warns that we cannot take for granted the body before the law or presume that its repetitions and citations will produce the same disruptive power equally. Theories of performativity both center the body and rely on juridical metaphors (e.g., citation and representation) to help demonstrate how repetitions and their meanings take on authoritative meaning. But, returning to Johnson, what might performativity mean for those subjects who have only ever been regarded as *flesh*? Johnson's compelling argument for thinking with *performance* rather than *performativity* builds on the central problem outlined by Spillers's differentiation between *body* and *flesh*: materiality cannot be ignored because for some of us, it is all we have. Queer of color folks, and Black women in particular, may never reach the ideal tropes of womanhood or queerness that circulate within performativity's emphasis on terms like *queer* and *gender*, even in their counterhegemonic registers (Shange 2019). Instead, *performance* may name the provisional and contingent ways that people deploy their flesh in the service of survival.

As Savannah Shange (2019) brilliantly demonstrates through her ethnography of Black gender in a public school, the "coordinates of our outsideness, are still mapped onto the logics and languages of normative gender" (21). In thinking with a lesbian stud's citation of the phallus ("you want the dick though!," 41), Shange theorizes how gender-nonconforming bodies are never fully outside of the coordinates of their subjection, but creatively work within and through them, occasionally reasserting dominant language even as they attempt to subvert it. *Performance* and *performativity* play together, much like *flesh* and *body* are interwoven into symbolic orders of meaning.

Christen Smith (2016) elucidates this point in her ethnography of police violence in Brazil, arguing that Blackness is produced through the violence done to Black bodies. Smith's exploration of racial performativity through police violence, hearkens back to Spillers's hieroglyphics of the flesh. Traces of dehumanizing behavior do not necessarily produce a subject or body before the law, a subject that follows performativity's model of subjection. Instead, as Smith illustrates, "violence against the Black body is a boundary-making performance" (14), such that any attention to *performativity* ought to be so that we can "recorporealize [B]lackness" (13): to think not in abstraction but *with* the fleshy ways Black people are made and unmade in performance. Smith's move is akin to Gregory Mitchell's (2016) explorations of "commissioned performances" of racialized male sex workers (*garotos*). Among local Brazilian male sex workers trying to satiate the sexual (and racial) appetites of consumers from the Global North, the *garoto*'s flesh ensconces the trace of the tourist's particular sexual appetites and fantasies. Between their flesh and the tourist's desires, *garotos* stage racial and erotic performances of masculinity that are precariously enacted yet do not congeal. These performances are not primarily about self-definition or meaning-making, but about labor and compensation, about indulging a fantasy to make ends meet.

Performance as a means of endurance and survival can also speak to the production of specific kinds of cultural citizenship. Martin Manalansan (2003) deploys *performance* as a key way of understanding not just the fraughtness of frameworks like *gender* and *homosexuality*. He also uses performances like *biyuti* and *drama* to name practices of self-fashioning and the culturally specific ways that Filipino gay men navigate the "exigencies of everyday life" (2003, 15). *Performance*, in Manalansan's assessment, helps shift the terms of Filipino gay men's lives from narrow conversations on identity and "coming out" to a broader engagement with the everyday ways that they manage being precarious immigrants of color in the United States. Similarly, Carlos Decena (2011) examines the performative work of silence or what he names "tacit subjectivity" (19). Thinking with the implied subject of a sentence in Spanish—the grammatical construct that presumes the speaker of a sentence without the use of a pronoun—Decena suggests that Dominican gay and bisexual men's silence regarding their sexuality (by not talking about it) is an implied mode of naming their own subjectivity. As Decena illustrates, queer performance need not always be spectacular or pure pageantry. Sometimes it can be the tender ways that people hold onto language, leaving room for silence to do the talking. Like Manalansan and his Filipino gay interlocutors, Decena highlights the nuanced ways that performances of queer subjectivity might be fugitively enacted beyond dominant gazes of cis, white gay men as well as coproduced alongside multiple kinship networks.

Style as Evidence and Ephemera

Performance demands that we think about the material practices of queer bodies: what bodies do, how they are perceived, and how they are staged. It also names the ways people turn their bodies into sites of art, beauty, and pageantry through particular modes of stylization. And while self-stylization as excess, pageantry, and aestheticized performance might be critiqued as a narrow identitarian project of self-disciplining or callow consumerist fantasy, what I describe below are not simply acts of consumption or being excessive for excess's sake. Many of the minoritarian subjects described in newer scholarship are queer and trans of color folks for whom daring to inhabit space on their own terms and in their own aestheticized ways comes at immense risk of injury and violence. As Madison Moore's (2018) work on fabulousness reminds us, the work of being fabulous is not just about consuming capital or putting on excessive clothes, but about creating beauty in spite of duress and violence—specifically about how Black, queer, trans, and other subjects at the margins use their bodies to play with risk.

Running through the disparate definitions of performance that this chapter has offered are words like *aesthetic/aestheticized* and *style/stylized*. Although the questions of embodiment and performance that I have discussed have been central to queer anthropology's engagement with the constructed and culturally situated ways that people experience gender and sexuality, further engagement with performance as excessive aesthetics (e.g., Moore 2018; Hernandez 2020; Horton 2020), nightlife (e.g., Khubchandani 2020; Adeyemi, Khubchandani, and Rivera-Servera 2021; Rodríguez 2014) and as beauty and pageantry (Jarrin 2017; Bailey 2013; Ochoa

2014) could be productive ways to push queer anthropology's explorations of performance even further, beyond the ways that courtrooms and clinics reify some performances of gender and sexuality and not other.

One of the challenges of anthropology has been to capture the drama of everyday life and to bring the messy worlds of our interlocutors into the semipositivist capture of ethnographic writing. In a field that stresses forms of evidence that can be accurately captured and represented on the page, *queerness* highlights a problem of evidence: how to bring the drama of the everyday into ethnographic writing. Afterall, *queerness* is not just the identities that people narrate or live out in the open. It is also ephemeral: hidden in gestures, turns of phrases, playful glances, or other difficult-to-perceive modes of expression. Ethnographically, this challenges disciplinary norms that demand clear connections, neat stories, and evidentiary proof for scholars to be taken seriously. Minoritarian scholarship that centers questions of gender, sexuality, and race has often lacked "historical grounding and conceptual staying power" because its archives are disparate and often housed not in specific places, but in the bodies of minor subjects themselves (Muñoz 1996, 7).

In "Ephemera as Evidence: Introductory Notes to Queer Acts," José Esteban Muñoz (1996) demonstrates that queer scholarship is often challenged as not being "rigorous" because it does not conform to prevailing institutional or disciplinary structures. But rather than running toward rigor, Muñoz eschews it, arguing that *queerness* often stands in a necessary relation to ephemerality. Performance as ephemera names a kind of "anti-rigor" that is "interested in following traces, glimmers, residues, and specks of things" (10). Recent scholarship in queer anthropology has taken up these flows and residues via explorations of topics such as affect (e.g., Dave 2012), the imperceptible bonds between human and nonhuman animals (Govindrajan 2018), and the concept metaphor of sand as queerness (Agard-Jones 2012). Martin Manalansan's explorations of mess demonstrate how a hoarder house's chaotic archive of stuff "embodies the fleeting, nomadic, messy, and elusive experiences and processes of self-making" (2014, 105). Like Muñoz, Manalansan invites us to sit with ephemera, not to come to an organized sense of meaning but to consider how people eke out space for their own magnificence within worlds making concerted efforts to erase them.

Beyond the stuff of a messy archive, ephemera might also be the highly stylized gestures queer and trans subjects deploy in defiance of bodily prohibitions. In *Sexual Futures, Queer Gestures, and Other Latina Longings,*

Juana María Rodríguez (2014) invites her readers to play in the din and the dark of our own fantasies. Rodríguez powerfully demonstrates how gestures enable us to act out our fantasies and desire, but also to be touched and touch others, to find modes of kinship and community in a precarious present. Similarly, in his analysis of a New York club-scene fixture, Muñoz deftly describes how Kevin Aviance's graceful gestures allow his Blackness, his queerness, and his femininity to spill into the predominantly white and masculine spaces of gay nightlife. Aviance's gestures are "vast storehouses of queer history and futurity" that "matter more than many traditional modes of evidencing lives and politics" (Muñoz 2009, 81).

Gestures on a dance floor might also be ways for queer of color subjects to enact reparative relations with embodiment. In *Ishtyle: Accenting Gay Indian Nightlife* (2020), Kareem Khubchandani traces Bollywood, diva, and queer gestures as three interrelated modes of dance that gay Indian men channel in the packed, sweaty dance floors of gay Indian parties and clubs, emulating Bollywood screen goddesses like Sridevi and Madhuri Dixit. These high femme, stylized movements are not only about what Khubchandani glosses as "diva worship" (2020, 150). Instead, these bodily movements are first and foremost social dances that allow gay men disciplined into acting like "men" and racialized as undesirable in gay nightlife in the West to perform femininity, queerness, and Brownness as well as "a sharing of subaltern affects, bound simultaneously to pleasure and shame" (2016, 83). For Khubchandani and other queer ethnographers, performance allows practitioners to return to the scenes of childhood traumas and moments when their bodies might have been disciplined for being too femme, too hairy, too Indian, and to refuse disciplining through letting loose on the dance floor. These different stylizations are bodily performances that vulnerable and excluded interlocutors rely on to make meanings for themselves. They are also fabulous stylizations of the body that demand anthropologists pay attention to the fleeting nature of performance and devise strategies of witnessing that eschew (straight) academic conventions.

Performance Once More, with a Difference

A promiscuous concept deserves a promiscuous end. Until now, I have convinced you that performance is a stylized mode of self-presentation. In Judith Butler and their contemporaries' works, *performance* was taken up for its effects (*performativity*): for what it could do to denaturalize identity. I have also suggested that performance's value is perhaps in the ways it can enable those who have never been recognized or represented to "play with the world" (Manalansan 2003, 144) through their bodies, aesthetics, and gesture. While performance is stylized repetition, gesture, aesthetic excess, and modes of resisting dominance, performance's most valuable quality for anthropology is that it is also the "stylistically marked expressions of otherness" (Kapchan 1995, 479). To be clear, performance then is not a call for us to find more "others." Rather, it is a demand to attend to the ways self-stylization is also part of a repertoire of embodied critique; a form of daily negotiation with worlds built on reducing some people to their flesh. This stylization in the flesh is at once a call to attend to materiality as well as to engage with minor practices of endurance and creativity routed through the ways that selves maneuver the contingencies of the world.

While style and otherness are perhaps queer bedfellows, seemingly celebratory of the other as mere aesthetic, to hold these terms together is to also hold open the possibilities of the flesh, that those in the most vulnerable and precarious of positions are capable of magnificence. In my own scholarship with queer and trans people looking for public sex, touch, and intimacy in Bombay, I call stylized expressions, such as playful sexual gestures in crowded publics or wearing fashionable excess in spite of sartorial policing, *shimmers*: ephemeral moments of possibility and potential that nourish queer and trans demands for life in the face of death, violence, and erasure (Horton n.d.). If performance can help us grapple with the disjuncture between what people say, what people do, and the categories they are slotted into, then it is an invitation not only to think about subversions of categories or the failures of discourse, but also to examine the materially grounded ways that people use their bodies in the service of living otherwise. Performance not just for what it does to critique discourse, but also for what it might teach us about how to endure the limits placed on us. To think of performance as an expression of otherness that is routed through style is, perhaps, to attend to the creative, coded, and intimate ways people eke out life amid precarious and uncertain times. And for anthropology, rather than reduce our interlocutors to the sum of their trauma, performance is a vibrant reminder to get out of the text, to disrupt the disciplinary conventions around evidence, and to bring the full complexities of our interlocutors' worlds—in all their beauty, ugliness, and mess—into as sharp a relief as possible. It is to stylize flesh, not to deny the processes of othering, but rather to deny that othering diminishes the capacities of even the most vulnerable of subjects to fashion a response.

References

Adeyemi, Kemi, Kareem Khubchandani, and Ramón H. Rivera-Servera. 2021. *Queer Nightlife.* Ann Arbor: University of Michigan Press.

Agard-Jones, Vanessa. 2012. "What the Sands Remember." *GLQ : A Journal of Lesbian and Gay Studies* 18(2–3): 325–46.

Alexeyeff, Kalissa. 2000. "Dragging Drag: The Performance of Gender and Sexuality in the Cook Islands." *Australian Journal of Anthropology* 11(3): 297–307.

Alexeyeff, Kalissa. 2008. *Dancing from the Heart: Movement, Gender, and Sociality in the Cook Islands.* Honolulu: University of Hawai'i Press.

Bailey, Marlon M. 2013. *Butch Queens Up in Pumps: Gender, Performance, and Ballroom Culture in Detroit.* Ann Arbor: University of Michigan Press.

Bauman, Richard. 1975. "Verbal Art as Performance." *American Anthropologist* 77(2): 290–311.

Butler, Judith. 1990. *Gender Trouble: Feminism and the Subversion of Identity.* New York: Routledge.

Butler, Judith. 1993. *Bodies That Matter: On the Discursive Limits of "Sex."* New York: Routledge.

Chambers-Letson, Joshua. 2013. *A Race So Different: Performance and Law in Asian America.* Durham, NC: Duke University Press.

Chaudhry, V. V. 2019. "Centering the 'Evil Twin': Rethinking Transgender in Queer Theory." *GLQ: A Journal of Lesbian and Gay Studies* 25(1): 45–50.

Cohen, Cathy. 1997. "Punks, Bulldaggers, and Welfare Queens: The Radical Potential of Queer Politics?" *GLQ: A Journal of Lesbian and Gay Studies* 3(4): 437–65.

Dave, Naisargi. 2012. *Queer Activism in India: A Story in the Anthropology of Ethics.* Durham, NC: Duke University Press.

Decena, Carlos. 2011. *Tacit Subjects: Belonging and Same-Sex Desire among Dominican Immigrant Men.* Durham, NC: Duke University Press.

Foucault, Michel. 1997. "What Is Critique?" In *The Politics of Truth,* edited by Sylvère Lotringer, 41–83. Los Angeles: Semiotext(e).

Frye, Marilyn. 1983. *The Politics of Reality: Essays in Feminist Theory.* Berkeley, CA: Crossing Press.

Garber, Marjorie. 1992. *Vested Interests: Cross-Dressing and Cultural Anxiety.* New York: Routledge.

Goffman, Erving. 1959. *The Presentation of Self in Everyday Life.* New York: Anchor Books.

Govindrajan, Radhika. 2018. *Animal Intimacies: Interspecies Relatedness in India's Central Himalayas*. Chicago: University of Chicago Press.

Gumperz, John, and Dell Hymes, eds. 1972. *Directions in Sociolinguistics: The Ethnography of Communication*. New York: Holt, Rinehart, and Winston.

Herdt, Gilbert, ed. 1993. *Third Sex, Third Gender: Beyond Sexual Dimorphism in Culture and History*. New York: Zone Books.

Hernandez, Jillian. 2020. *Aesthetics of Excess: The Art and Politics of Black and Latina Embodiment*. Durham: Duke University Press.

Horton, Brian A. 2020. "Fashioning Fabulation: Dress, Gesture, and the Queer Aesthetics of Mumbai Pride." *South Asia: Journal of South Asian Studies* 43(2): 294–307.

Horton, Brian A. n.d. "Shimmers of the Fabulous: Public Sex and Intimate Touch in Queer and Trans Bombay." Manuscript in progress.

Jarrin, Alvaro. 2017. *The Biopolitics of Beauty: Cosmetic Citizenship and Affective Capital in Brazil*. Berkeley: University of California Press.

Johnson, E. Patrick. 2001. "'Quare' Studies or (Almost) Everything I Know about Queer Studies I Learned from My Grandmother." *Text and Performance Quarterly* 21: 1–25.

Kapchan, Deborah A. 1995. "Performance." *Journal of American Folklore* 108(430): 479–508.

Khubchandani, Kareem. 2016. "Snakes on the Dance Floor: Bollywood, Gesture, and Gender." *Velvet Light Trap* 77: 69–85.

Khubchandani, Kareem. 2020. *Ishtyle: Accenting Gay Indian Nightlife*. Ann Arbor: University of Michigan Press.

Kulick, Don. 1998. *Travesti: Sex, Gender, and Culture among Brazilian Transgendered Prostitutes*. Chicago: University of Chicago Press.

Madison, Soyini D. 2010. "Performance Is a Lover." *International Review of Qualitative Research* 3(2): 199–201.

Manalansan, Martin. 2003. *Global Divas: Filipino Gay Men in the Diaspora*. Durham, NC: Duke University Press.

Manalansan, Martin. 2014. "The 'Stuff' of Archives: Mess, Migration, and Queer Lives." *Radical History Review* 20: 94–170.

Mitchell, Gregory. 2016. *Tourist Attractions: Performing Race and Masculinity in Brazil's Sexual Economy*. Chicago: University of Chicago Press.

Moore, Madison. 2018. *Fabulous: The Rise of the Beautiful Eccentric*. New Haven, CT: Yale University Press.

Moraga, Cherríe, and Gloria Anzaldúa, eds. 1983. *This Bridge Called My Back: Writings by Radical Women of Color*. New York: Kitchen Table.

Morgensen, Scott. 2011. *Spaces between Us: Queer Settler Colonialism and Indigenous Decolonization*. Minneapolis: University of Minnesota Press.

Morris, Rosalind. 1994. "Three Sexes and Four Sexualities: Redressing the Discourses of Gender and Sexuality in Contemporary Thailand." *positions: east asian cultural critique* 2(1): 15–43.

Morris, Rosalind. 1995. "All Made Up: Performance Theory and the New Anthropology of Sex and Gender." *Annual Review of Anthropology* 24: 567–92.

Muñoz, José Esteban. 1996. "Ephemera as Evidence: Introductory Notes to Queer Acts." *Women and Performance* 8(2): 5–16.

Muñoz, José Esteban. 1999. *Disidentifications: Queers of Color and the Performance of Politics*. Minneapolis: University of Minnesota Press.

Muñoz, José Esteban. 2009. *Cruising Utopia: The Then and There of Queer Futurity*. Durham, NC: Duke University Press.

Namaste, Vivian K. 2000. *Invisible Lives: The Erasure of Transsexual and Transgendered People*. Chicago: University of Chicago Press.

Nanda, Serena. 1998. *Neither Man nor Woman: The Hijras of India*. Belmont, CA: Wadsworth.

Newton, Esther. 1972. *Mother Camp: Female Impersonators in America*. Chicago: University of Chicago Press.

Newton, Esther. 1993. *Cherry Grove, Fire Island: Sixty Years in America's First Gay and Lesbian Town*. Boston: Beacon.

Ochoa, Marcia. 2014. *Queen for a Day: Transformistas, Beauty Queens, and the Performance of Femininity in Venezuela*. Durham, NC: Duke University Press.

Plemons, Eric. 2017. *The Look of a Woman: Facial Feminization Surgery and the Aims of Trans-Medicine*. Durham, NC: Duke University Press.

Pollock, Della. 2007. "The Performative I." *Cultural Studies ↔ Critical Methodologies* 7(3): 239–55.

Prosser, Jay. 1998. *Second Skins: The Body Narratives of Transsexuality*. New York: Columbia University Press.

Robertson, Jennifer. 1998. *Takarazuka: Sexual Politics and Popular Culture in Modern Japan*. Berkeley: University of California Press.

Rodríguez, Juana María. 2014. *Sexual Futures, Queer Gestures, and Other Latina Longings*. New York: New York University Press.

Shange, Savannah. 2019. "Play Aunties and Dyke Bitches: Gender, Generation, and the Ethics of Black Queer Kinship." *Black Scholar* 49(1): 40–54.

Smith, Christen A. 2016. *Afro-Paradise: Blackness, Violence and Performance in Brazil*. Urbana: University of Illinois Press.

Snorton, C. Riley. 2009. "'A New Hope': The Psychic Life of Passing." *Hypatia: A Journal of Feminist Philosophy* 24(3): 77–92.

Spillers, Hortense. 1987. "Mama's Baby, Papa's Maybe: An American Grammar Book." *Diacritics: A Review of Contemporary Criticism* 17(2): 64–81.

Stone, Sandy. 1994. "The Empire Strikes Back: A Posttransexual Manifesto." *Camera Obscura* 29: 150–76.

Taylor, Diana. 2016. *Performance*. Durham, NC: Duke University Press.

Turner, Victor. 1975. *Dramas, Fields, and Metaphors: Symbolic Action in Human Society*. Ithaca, NY: Cornell University Press.

Visweswaran, Kamala. 1997. "Histories of Feminist Ethnography." *Annual Review of Anthropology* 26: 591–621.

Weheliye, Alexander G. 2014. *Habeus Viscus: Racializing Assemblages, Biopolitics, and Black Feminist Theories of the Human*. Durham, NC: Duke University Press.

Weiss, Margot. 2016. "Always After: Desiring Queerness, Desiring Anthropology." *Cultural Anthropology* 31(4): 627–38.

Weston, Kath, 1993. "Lesbian/Gay Studies in the House of Anthropology." *Annual Review of Anthropology* 22: 339–67.

Wikan, Unni. 1977. "Man Becomes Woman: Transsexualism in Oman as a Key to Gender Roles." *Man* 12: 304–19.

Wikan, Unni. 1982. *Behind the Veil in Arabia: Women in Oman*. Chicago: University of Chicago Press.

Ara Wilson   **7**

Worldly Power and Local Alterity

Transnational Queer Anthropology

Cultural Orders

After a half of a century of globalization, where is sexual alterity? What makes sexual cultures queerly different?

Since the 1990s, queer anthropology has described sexuality and gender in relation to a transnational scale (Weston 1993). If queer anthropology marks a departure from lesbian and gay anthropology (itself a departure from conventional anthropological accounts of sex/gender variance), the "transnational turn" in anthropology also marks its own departure from established twentieth-century anthropological frameworks. The transnational approach replaces a classic anthropological view of insular societies with emphasis on scales beyond the local. Transnational queer anthropology situates queer being in relation to forces beyond local culture. Both queer and transnational orientations begin with critiques of conventional ways of explaining difference.[1]

The mandate of anthropological knowledge has been to organize differences across human societies. Anthropology declared itself the expert on alterity—on Others to the West, that is, to urbanized northwestern Europe and its settler societies. Through studying Indigenous populations and non-Western peoples, anthropology developed its fundamental toolkit: fieldwork, participant observation, the culture concept, the ethnographic monograph, a comparative lens, and cultural relativism. Sex served the discipline well in its formation.

Works by Margaret Mead and other now-forgotten authors offered up striking examples of cultural alterity around matters of sexuality and gender. Such diversity provided a perfect field for demonstrating a revised, modern discipline predicated on intellectual relativism. Norms around intimate life varied, anthropologists told us, not because their societies were more or less evolved, but because the very nature of culture was to vary. The culture concept, predicated on alterity, undercut presumptions that Western compulsory heterosexuality or binary gender schemes expressed a universal human nature. Ethnographies showed, at least to some extent, that sex was socially organized.

The culture theory of canonical twentieth-century American anthropology became its most famous contribution to general discourse for a reason. The culture concept was powerful and generative. It offered a highly effective way of conceptualizing the world's cultural differences. Context-sensitive comparisons led to far-reaching, enduring ideas about kinship, socialization, social structure, and functions served by institutions. Now old-fashioned, anthropological interpretations of alterity influenced other critical theories of culture, including queer theory (Boellstorff 2007; Weston 1993). And yet these critical theories also led anthropologists to abandon the canonical culture concept that forged the field.

Transnational queer anthropology rests on critiques of "the fiction of culture as discrete, object-like phenomena occupying discrete spaces," as Akhil Gupta and James Ferguson put it (1992). Margaret Steedly argues that views of culture as a total system were motivated by the "desire for order, coherence, and stability" (1999, 441). The "fiction of culture" deflected attention away from encompassing forces that impinged on local cultures, notably colonialism; it also neglected the way culture acts as ideology to reinforce inequality. Critical anthropological approaches rejected the model of objectlike cultures and turned their attention to energylike power.

WORLDLY POWER AND LOCAL ALTERITY   153

This switch is more complicated than it sounds. Transnational queer anthropology still wrestles with the implications of ethnographic analysis following on the critique of the concept of local cultures. What and where is alterity? Transnational queer ethnographies sift through multiscalar influences on queer worlds and track the changing geographic referents to identity. That is to say, transnational queer anthropology grapples as much with accounting for space as it does for sex. Its prose aims to counter, rather than perpetuate, the representational forms of global power—the Eurocentric, Orientalist, racializing, or colonial views that have dominated portraits of the Others to the West.

Transnational Power

Transnational clearly refers to the crossing of nations.[2] In English, transnational is distinguished from the literal meaning of international, meaning relations *between* or *among* distinct countries.[3] From the 1970s on, circulations of people, goods, culture, and capital across national borders intensified. This development was named globalization, although for anthropologists that word became tainted by being used to champion global markets. The processes behind the term were nonetheless real, affecting national governments, the environment, and certainly the queer lives that anthropologists studied. The movement from studies of bounded communities to niches in global cities; from villagers to migrants; from traditions to novel assemblages repurposing foreign elements involves rethinking the idea that cultural identity was rooted in particular territory. It requires analyzing, not assuming, the relation of cultural practices and identifications to space.

Transnational anthropology takes a critical view of the powers that choreograph global flows. As an analytical lens, this transnational orientation emerged from radical thought—from Marxist traditions, decolonizing movements in the Global South, and, in the United States, from the structural critiques of civil rights, Black Power, and immigrant labor movements.[4] These theories explained how colonialism, imperialism, global capitalism, or New World chattel slavery continued to affect people into their intimate lives.

Since 9/11, leading currents of queer studies have emphasized geopolitical arrangements as crucial for queer analysis (Massad 2007; Puar 2017). These are overarching, even global, systems of power associated with white supremacy, Islamophobia, the neoliberal juncture of economic and political policies, and US or Western hegemony in general. Critique of these transnational Western-based forces is the defining feature of transnational queer studies and is at least the backdrop, if not the object of study, for ethnographers working in a queer transnational frame.

This priority for this transnational critique is not global forms of homophobia or heteronormativity: often, in fact, the domains of power in question are not defined in an immediate way by sexuality or gender. The starting point is the understanding that liberal modernity (e.g., human rights), Enlightenment Humanism, and allied modes of knowledge (e.g., mainstream anthropology) have contributed to the West's oppression of its Others. Destructive violence and racist suppression are not exceptions to liberalism, in this view, but reside at the heart of white Western liberal modernity—including in its do-good versions of LGBT rights.

Jasbir Puar's *Terrorist Assemblages* offers the articulation that has influenced queer anthropological discussion. Puar argues that gay and lesbian efforts to claim fuller membership in the United States, Europe, or Israel do so by perpetuating the exclusion of those who are not the normative members of the dominant society, especially along the axes of race, ethnicity, and nationality, and particularly of Muslims. Building from the concept of homonormativity (Duggan 2002), Puar names this dynamic *homonationalism*: ways that countries that allow some set of LGBT rights assimilate some queer people into mainstream society at the expense of less respectable queers, and racial and Muslim Others, who remain excluded from full membership in society.

This critique of mainstream advances that seem progressive resonates with anthropologist Elizabeth Povinelli's argument that multicultural neoliberal welfare states judge forms of intimate relationships as worthy or unworthy of social inclusion (Povinelli 2006). In some countries, like Australia or the United States, some forms of queer intimacy are now included in the fold. Governments have used their relatively liberal LGBT protections, or cities promoted as LGBT-friendly tourist sites, as a smokescreen for more egregious state violence, a tactic known as pinkwashing.

In liberal eyes, LGBT rights offer a yardstick to evaluate the democratic conditions of countries or even the legitimacy of a state. Measures that evaluate non-European, non-US governments as less advanced draw critiques for arguably perpetuating racist discourse about a society's place in the evolution from barbarism to civilization. Similarly, charges that "traditional cultures" present obstacles to progress in achieving better conditions for

LGBT lives likewise echo representations of societies as savage, backward. White supremacist ideologies held that non-white, non-Western peoples were incapable of self-governance (as were women) and rationalized colonialism, chattel slavery, and other ways of disenfranchising these Others.

Transnational queer anthropology incorporates these analyses of LGBT rights in a number of situations. This perspective makes the most sense for countries where some kinds of LGBT identities have been normalized with some forms of protections, such as Western settler colonial societies (Morgensen 2011; Povinelli 2006). Ethnographers deconstruct discourses about lesbians, gays, and trans existence that portray non-White, non-Western, and especially Muslim peoples as illiberal and unmodern (Shakhsari 2013, see also Shakhsari in this volume).

In the post–Cold War era, the UN-NGO arena and humanitarianism became a powerful conduit for spreading concepts, money, and agendas around the world. Anthropologists have argued that international projects concerning HIV/AIDS or LGBT rights impose a Western identity logic—as with terms like "sexual orientation," "gay," or "trans woman"—on vastly different communities, which frame desire and identity in utterly divergent ways (Dutta and Roy 2014).

A particularly complicated juncture is LGBT asylum, when people make asylum cases on the basis of being at risk for their sex/gender identity in their home country. These people must make their identities legible as being LGBT as understood by the receiving countries. (How do you prove that you're gay? Requirements for evidence can be startlingly graphic [Zengin 2016].) LGBT categories may not be how sex/gender-nonconforming asylum seekers enunciate their lives in more local terms. Their cases also rest on portraying their home society as dangerously homophobic or transphobic to them (a portrayal often validated by expert testimony from queer anthropologists). Rationales for queer asylum rest on understandings of non-Western societies as conservative places defined by illiberal traditions. (See Sima Shakhsari's chapter in this volume.)

Global Gays

In a series of articles in the 1990s, Dennis Altman argued that "gay" was becoming a globalized identity displayed in gay male cultures in metro areas around the world: gay bars in Rio, Bangkok, or Cape Town feel like those in

Sydney or Berlin. Altman did not attribute this development to the unfolding of universal sexual identities; he saw gay culture as a construction. Instead, Altman argues that this sexual culture spread along channels established by global capital flows (Altman 1996). Global gay male culture reflected global capitalist modernity.

Transnational queer anthropologists objected to Altman's representation of gay life in the Global South as derivative extensions of Western gay culture. Anthropologists argued that, even in major international gay tourist zones, gay cultures are heterogeneous. They explained that there was a complex vernacular queer life that emerged from local life and that remained tied to traditions, behind the scenes of clubs and saunas that elite gay tourists saw (e.g., Boellstorff 2005; Manalansan 2003). Even Grindr takes on particular styles in particular societies (Dasgupta 2019).

Ethnographies of sex/gender variance especially in the non-West are motivated by investments in challenging one form or another of Western hegemony. The focus has been nonheterosexual relations and gender variance, but with an emphasis on alterity that reveals limits to Western categories of identities (lesbian, gay, homosexual). Many authors argue that Western categorization are incommensurable with non-Western dissidence to heteropatriarchal or gender norms (Jarrín 2016; Currier and Migraine-George 2018; Dutta and Roy 2014).

For example, Gloria Wekker's ethnography (2006) explains that, in Suriname, women having sex with women is conceptualized as an activity, *mati* work. This Surinamese category differs from the notion of an entrenched sexual orientation underlying a lesbian or bisexual identity. Many of these women also have sexual relations with men. Even when categories derive from Western words, as in East and Southeast Asia, terms like *les*, lesbi, *la-la* from lesbian (Engebretsen 2013; Newton 2016) or *tom, tomboi, T* from tomboy (Fajardo 2011; Sinnott 2004; Wieringa, Blackwood, and Bhaiya 2007) have become embedded within vernacular languages. People's embodied identities and their intimate relations are contoured by kinship relations, state policies, and cultural conceptions of sexuality and gender.

If we were to arrange queer ethnographies by geographic area, one of the largest sets would concern trans female identities in South Asia, such as the *hijra (khwaja sira* in Urdu) (Hossain 2018; Khan 2016) or *kothi* in India (Boyce 2007). Queer ethnographies argue that these variant terms are not simple synonyms with trans women: not just the word itself, but its underlying logic. The very conceptualization of an identity in relation to gender is not everywhere the same. What Carole Vance says of sexuality applies as well to gender variance: "Cultures provide widely different categories, schema, and labels for framing sexual and affective experiences" (1991, 878). According to Dutta and Roy (2014), the homegrown categories for such feminine people do not rest on binaries between cis and trans. *Hijras'* shared sensibilities are bound up with spiritual commitments that are not captured by secular NGO transgender discourse.

Queer Cartographies

The transnational frame also complicates a straightforward sense of distinct local societies grounded in particular territories. Transnational queer anthropology has questioned conventional categories for thinking about the location of queer life—its geographic, territorial, and scalar dimensions. In this exploration, queer anthropologists have made the national scale a problem to explore rather than a conventional boundary for research. Ethnographies of countries constituted by islands, such as the Philippines and Indonesia, have used this insular feature in analyses that consider the nature of the nation for queer life. In *The Gay Archipelago*, Tom Boellstorff queered the nation of Indonesia. Boellstorff argued that queer Indonesians—chiefly *gay* (men) or *waria* (trans women)—shared a culture that crossed the various island's ethnic groups. Gay and trans communities created a truly national argot (Boellstorff 2005). Benjamin Hegarty (2018) also identifies a national scope of Indonesian queer life in models of femininity that *waria* across islands laboriously strive to realize. These projects situate queer life on the national scale of Indonesia, but in a way that reflectively approaches nation and locality.

The Philippines offers another archipelago formation through which to think about queer national identities. Emmanuel David (2018) found that Filipina contestants in trans beauty pageants embraced specific island identities more than identification with the nation. In Southeast Asia then, queers articulate with the archipelago differently, forging a cross-island queer culture in Indonesia while decentering the national umbrella, at least in trans performance, in the Philippines. Working with island geography is one example of how queer anthropologists reflect on the constitution of the nation and, more generally, on identity formed in relation to territory.

Trans women's performances offer rich events for interpreting the construction of queer identities with reference to location. In Venezuela, Marcia

Ochoa (2014) explored how both trans women contestants (*transformistas*) and the "misses" (cis women) constructed femininity in the context of national investments with beauty pageants (in research conducted before the post-2015 crisis).

As David's use of archipelago suggests, the Philippines have a deep island orientation, with a history of skilled seafaring. Kale Fajardo's research focused on modern maritime transportation. Fajardo considered the vagaries of masculinity—including the anthropologist's own—of Filipinos at sea, in relation to gendered national identifications of seafaring (Fajardo 2011).

Filipinx migrants in the United States are part of an established diaspora. Diasporas have offered a significant frame for transnational queer studies in general: as an alternative to nationally based studies that explore identities that cross national borders. In the United States, Martin Manalansan (2003) found Filipina trans women closely tracked trans culture, such as a fast-changing trans argot, in the Philippines. This look to queer culture in the homeland reverses that pervasive assumption that non-Western queers copy mainstream (white) US LGBT culture.

Queer Regionalism

Knowledge about the non-West reflects geopolitical patterns. "The power disparities within the academy . . . have rendered the global North the production site of theoretical knowledge," Julie Moreau and T. J. Tallie say, "and often relegated the global South to a source of data" (2019, 51). They find this global division of intellectual labor replicated in the ways that queer theory defines theory.

Attentive to the geopolitics of representations, transnational queer anthropology explores ways to avoid recentering the Euro-United States as the constant reference point for queer life elsewhere. At the same time, attention to transnational forces demands more than illustrating discrete local sex/gender variance. One proposed way to navigate these poles is to situate queer life within regions of the Global South, a queer regionalism. Regions involve flows across nations within them, including the flows of capital and political influence (Wilson 2006). For example, on the South Asian subcontinent, most queer research has centered on India (itself a vast expanse of diverse cultures). Adnan Hossain (2018) argues that taking a regional perspective will illuminate broader cultural contours of *hijra*.

With Spanish as a lingua franca and common political trajectories, Latin America operates as a region for queer/trans worlds there. Queer networks follow trails of migration to link people in Latin America to the north. Researchers are also developing a hemispheric outlook on the Americas, a cross-border blending of Latin American with Latinx queer and trans culture (Rizki 2019). This course is laid out in a special issue of *TSQ*, "Trans Studies en las Américas." A hemispheric orientation builds on Chicana feminism's valuable demarcation of the borderlands while also extending beyond the fraught US border (Anzaldúa 1987). Patterns of Latin American political dynamics help to connect studies across national cultures: Argentina, Chile, and other countries represent postdictatorship regimes, while Indigenous communities share similar positions vis-à-vis Latino settler societies. These contexts have included insurgent queer activism, such as for identity markers for *travesti* and trans women (Rizki 2019; Pimentel and Segura 2018).

Queer writing on countries in sub-Saharan Africa likewise often embraces a regional perspective (Hoad 2007; Spronk and Nyak 2021) that recognizes "African modes of blending, bending, and breaking gender boundaries" (Nyanzi 2014, 66). Moving from studies of discrete nations to the regional scale promotes "theorizing African gender and sexual diversity in a continental, pan-African, or transnational-comparative context" (Currier and Migraine-George 2018, 613). The construct of Africa as region is less debated in African queer studies than is the salience of "queer" (e.g., Moreau and Tallie 2019; Nyanzi 2014). Black queer anthropology also often takes up a diasporic frame (Currier and Migraine-George 2018), which recasts the Black Atlantic through a queer perspective (Allen and Tinsley 2019). Work on the Caribbean shows how queer subjects draw on, and create, diasporic Black cultures to inhabit with hope and joy (e.g., Agard-Jones 2012; Allen 2011; Gill 2018), approaches that intentionally insert attention to pleasure in queer analysis.

The space of Asia is less unified culturally or politically, or through a lingua franca other than English. Recognizing that Asia is a construct, scholars still argue for a regional perspective on queer life, by considering how queer life results from dynamics of flows within Asia (Hossain 2018; Sinnott 2010; Wilson 2006). Dredge Käng's work on the influence of K-Pop outside of Korea exemplifies such an intra-Asian approach. In one example, Käng shows that gay men and toms in Thailand draw on K-pop boy-band style as inspiration for their masculine self-presentation (Käng 2014).

Postsocialist Queer

Perhaps the major transformation to the geopolitical order of the later twentieth century was the collapse of actually existing communist economies. This process radically changed political, economic, and cultural realities for citizens in countries transitioning away from government planning of production and controls on consumption. In a wide-sweeping work, Lisa Rofel (2007) argues that post-Mao, post-socialist China (still governed by the Communist Party) has created a culture oriented to desire, a context in which queer desires became part of a new national sensibility.

Rofel's work points to the significant context of postsocialism for changing conditions for sexual cultures and erotic politics. Queer research on the former Soviet Union and its satellites, particularly Eastern Europe, identifies a common landscape for queer life. The post-Soviet era has seen the rise of LGBTQ-identified cultures facing reactionary authoritarian rule and rejuvenated Eastern Orthodox or Catholic religiosity, both of which have empowered reactionary homophobic agendas (e.g., Shirinian 2018). The geographic orientations of this region are less familiar to the ordinal references upon which queer studies relies. The USSR was the Second World, with deep engagements in the Third World. If a European or North American who supported the USSR was called "pro-Eastern," today Russia and Eastern Europe continue to see themselves as an East to Western Europe's West. The end of the Soviet Union also ended material support for countries in the Global South, a consequential change that explains why Noelle Stout (2014) delineates the context for her study of queer transactional sex as "post-Soviet Cuba."

The best-known postsocialist settings are China and the former USSR and its satellites. Anthropologists broaden the scope of reflection on postsocialism with knowledge about less well-known formerly planned economies in a state socialist vein, such as Vietnam (Newton 2016) or Nicaragua (Babb 2003; Howe 2013). The erosion of socialist policies in much of the Global South connects with the rise of neoliberal policies and the end of the Cold War. It also signals the end of the Non-Aligned Movement, also known as the Bandung era (the name of the Indonesian city that hosted the 1955 Asian-African Conference), which envisioned solidarity across the Third World to counteract the interference of First or Second Worlds. Queer anthropology has yet to collect accounts of this transnational context into a comparative conversation about postsocialist sites for queer living. Bringing queer research on these spaces together would also generate a queer vantage point on the great geopolitical transformation of the past several decades.

Cultural Transnationalism

Writing in the 1990s about the anthropology of Southeast Asia, Steedly asked, "As anthropologists turn their attention to processes of domination . . . can the concepts of culture areas or of local cultures retain their analytical salience?" (Steedly 1999, 432). The transnational scale presents an amalgam of governmental, economic, and discursive normative power that shapes people, places, and relationships. Does this global amalgam constitute a kind of culture? Do the various vocabularies to describe imperial Western knowledges—ideology, discourses, disciplines—describe culturelike attributes? I would argue there are more continuities with twentieth-century versions of culture than queer scholarship allows.

Steedly's review essay offers another way to relate culture to the scale of transnational power. She argues that "the desire for order, coherence, and stability" that the culture concept gratified has now been "displaced upward," from a local bounded society to the national level of the state (1999, 441). The pre–World War II concept of culture was characterized by an emphasis on structure and systematicity, which often sounds more all-encompassing and totalizing than discontinuous, even contradictory "shreds and patches." Is the desire for systematicity now sought globally? The structural nature and regulatory authority formerly found in culture, and then in the state, now finds itself in transnational forces: above all, global capitalism, global liberal projects, and the United States or the West. Queer critiques of transnational powers present these forces as cohesive, orderly forms, with little internal contradiction, the way culture once was a standardized whole.

Transnational queer *studies* may bring more of the culture concept to describing global power than does transnational queer anthropology. Anthropology invites a nuanced study of the ways non-Western regional and local worlds differ from Western forms (Moreau and Tallie 2019; Ramberg 2014). Attention to situated realities orients the ethnographer to modes of power from outside the West, such as the regulatory capacities of the Chinese state (Engebretsen 2013) or the influence of transnational religions (Golomski 2020; Savci 2020). Exclusively focusing on US-Europe hegemony risks again making the West the engine of queer history for queers in the Global South. To decenter the West, transnational queer anthropology attends to power elsewhere.

Ethnographies describe varying modalities of powers that manifest in everyday queer lives. A rich body of work points to queer experiences of family pressures (e.g., Savci 2020), national homophobic panics (Meiu 2020), or repressive state laws (Dave 2012; Dehesa 2010). While recognizing ideological deployments of LGBT rights, anthropologists also find people in the Global South making use of LGBT categories (Dave 2012; Saleh 2020) rather than excluding them as too Westernized to identify authentic local subjects (Massad 2007). The people we group under the label of *queer* also engage NGO vocabularies about sexuality in West Africa (Nguyen 2010), India (Dutta and Roy 2014), and Turkey (Saleh 2020). LGBT vocabularies originating in the United States do not necessarily supplant local terminology but can also expand people's repertoires of self-making. Much queer critique finds NGOs in the Global South associated with hegemonic liberal or security agendas (Mitchell 2016; Shakhsari, this volume). NGOs are also variegated social sites. Complicating this association, research on specific NGOs finds that many small NGOs do not serve that ideological function or that, even when they do, such transnationally inflected sites can be generative spaces for queer lives, particularly when queer spaces were otherwise limited (Biruk 2020; Nguyen 2010; Saleh 2020; Wilson 2010).

Of Queers and Cultures

Research on queer lives involves a different temporality than that of the twentieth-century culture concept: few queer people can lay claim to inheritances from some queer antiquity. (Those that do—like the *hijra*—are noteworthy for such a genealogical sensibility.) In *The Wretched of the Earth*, Frantz Fanon presented a view of culture in a dramatically changing context. He was not interested in preserving timeless tradition. Living culture is to be found in people's unfolding, hard-scrabble modes of living: "we must join them in that fluctuating movement which they are just giving a shape to." To understand their lives means going "to this zone of occult instability where the people dwell," he said (Fanon 1963, 227).

More than a few queer dwellings could be described as zones of occult instability. Martin Manalansan has proposed valuing mess and messiness to make sense of queer culture, in his case, "the un-HGTV dwellings of several undocumented queer households" (2014, 94). Twentieth-century anthropological accounts of culture as pastiche or bricolage, as "shreds and patches," may well suit queer cultures formed in relation to multiscalar flows.

Queer of color critique brings an affirming approach to studying the lives of Black, Native, and non-white queers, as exemplified by the influential work of performance scholar José Muñoz. There is significant overlap between writing identified as queer of color critique, queer Black and Latinx studies, and the work of transnational queer anthropologists of color. They each see queers of color reworking cultures into resources for living—including sometimes its heteronormative forms or homophobic religions. Portraits of queer culture in the African diaspora also manifest through the senses (Allen and Tinsley 2019). This writing stresses creativity, world-making, and joy in resistance to intersectional oppression (Gill 2018; Lara 2020). The stuff that crowds the undocumented queer household, for Manalansan, "embodies the fleeting, nomadic, messy, and elusive experiences and processes of self-making" (2014, 105).

Queer thought needs alterity. Chronicling the operations of power on and through culture, transnational queer ethnographers locate the queer Other to global, Western, and non-Western hegemonic orders. Transnational queer anthropology authorizes differences that body forth queer living otherwise.

Notes

1   I use the term *queer* in keeping with much of queer anthropology's two-fold usage, which is defined by the object of study's relation to (often Western) norms and by critical analytical orientations (Weiss 2016). At the same time, I understand that using the term *queer* in discussions of people who do not themselves use it perpetuates the problem of Western analytical imposition on the non-West, a problem I do not resolve in this chapter.

2   *Transnational* has encapsulated different concepts, which are traced in detail by the historian Pierre-Yves Saunier (2009). Saunier says that anthropology and cultural studies shaped the sense of transnationalism now present in much critical scholarship: that is the sense I describe here.

3   For example, the United Nations exists institutionally as an *international* assemblage of sovereign countries. UN agencies and nongovernmental agencies operate *across* national boundaries, forming a *transnational* realm of global civil society or global humanitarian networks.

4 In twentieth-century anthropology, Marxist approaches offered important models for transnational analyses of non-Western societies before the transnational turn (e.g., Gough 1968).

References

Agard-Jones, Vanessa. 2012. "What the Sands Remember." *GLQ: A Journal of Lesbian and Gay Studies* 18(2–3): 325–46.

Allen, Jafari S. 2011. *¡Venceremos? The Erotics of Black Self-Making in Cuba*. Durham, NC: Duke University Press.

Allen, Jafari Sinclaire, and Omise'eke Natasha Tinsley. 2019. "After the Love: Remembering Black/Queer/Diaspora." *GLQ: A Journal of Lesbian and Gay Studies* 25(1): 107–12.

Altman, Dennis. "Rupture or Continuity? The Internationalization of Gay Identities." *Social Text* 48 (1996): 77–94.

Anzaldúa, Gloria. 1987. *Borderlands: The New Mestiza = La Frontera*. Spinsters/Aunt Lute, San Francisco.

Babb, Florence E. 2003. "Out in Nicaragua: Local and Transnational Desires after the Revolution." *Cultural Anthropology* 18(3): 304–28.

Biruk, Cal (Crystal). 2020. "'Fake Gays' in Queer Africa: NGOs, Metrics, and Modes of (Queer Theory)." *GLQ: A Journal of Lesbian and Gay Studies* 26(3): 477–502.

Blackwood, Evelyn. 2010. *Falling into the Lesbi World: Desire and Difference in Indonesia*. Honolulu: University of Hawai'i Press.

Blackwood, Evelyn, and Mark Johnson. 2012. "Queer Asian Subjects: Transgressive Sexualities and Heteronormative Meanings." *Asian Studies Review* 36(4): 441–51.

Boellstorff, Tom. 2005. *The Gay Archipelago: Sexuality and the Nation in Indonesia*. Princeton, NJ: Princeton University Press.

Boellstorff, Tom. 2007. "Queer Studies in the House of Anthropology." *Annual Review of Anthropology* 36: 17–35.

Boyce, Paul. 2007. "'Conceiving Kothis': Men Who Have Sex with Men in India and the Cultural Subject of HIV Prevention." *Medical Anthropology* 26(2): 175–203.

Currier, Ashley, and Thérèse Migraine-George. 2018. "The Incommensurability of the 'Transnational' in Queer African Studies." *College Literature* 45(4): 613–22.

Dasgupta, Rohit K. 2019. "'Keep It Classy': Grindr, Facebook and Enclaves of Queer Privilege in India." In *The Routledge Companion to Media and Class*, edited by Erika Polson, Lynn Schofield Clark, and Radhika Gajjala, 90–98. London: Routledge.

Dave, Naisargi N. 2012. *Queer Activism in India: A Story in the Anthropology of Ethics*. Durham, NC: Duke University Press.

David, Emanuel. 2018. "Transgender Archipelagos." *TSQ: Transgender Studies Quarterly* 5(3): 332–54.

Dehesa, Rafael. 2010. *Queering the Public Sphere in Mexico and Brazil: Sexual Rights Movements in Emerging Democracies*. Durham, NC: Duke University Press.

Duggan, Lisa. 2002. "The New Homonormativity: The Sexual Politics of Neoliberalism." In *Materializing Democracy: Toward a Revitalized Cultural Politics*, edited by Donald E. Pease, Joan Dayan, and Richard R. Flores, 175–94. Durham, NC: Duke University Press.

Dutta, Aniruddha, and Raina Roy. 2014. "Decolonizing Transgender in India: Some Reflections." *TSQ: Transgender Studies Quarterly* 1(3): 320–37.

Engebretsen, Elisabeth L. 2013. *Queer Women in Urban China: An Ethnography*. London: Routledge.

Fajardo, Kale Bantigue. 2011. *Filipino Crosscurrents: Oceanographies of Seafaring, Masculinities, and Globalization*. Minneapolis: University of Minnesota Press.

Fanon, Frantz. 1963. *The Wretched of the Earth*. Trans. Constance Farrington. New York: Grove Press.

Gill, Lyndon K. 2018. *Erotic Islands: Art and Activism in the Queer Caribbean*. Durham, NC: Duke University Press.

Golomski, Casey. 2020. "Countermythologies: Queering Lives in a Southern African Gay and Lesbian Pentecostal Church." *Transforming Anthropology* 28(2): 156–69.

Gough, Kathleen. 1968. "New Proposals for Anthropologists." *Current Anthropology* 9(5): Part 1, 403–35.

Gupta, Akhil, and James Ferguson. 1992. "Beyond 'Culture': Space, Identity, and the Politics of Difference." *Cultural Anthropology* 7(1): 6–23.

Hegarty, Benjamin. 2018. "Under the Lights, onto the Stage: Becoming Waria through National Glamour in New Order Indonesia." *TSQ: Transgender Studies Quarterly* 5(3): 355–77.

Hoad, Neville Wallace. 2007. *African Intimacies: Race, Homosexuality, and Globalization*. Minneapolis: University of Minnesota Press.

Hossain, Adnan. 2018. "De-Indianizing Hijra: Intra-regional Effacements and Inequities in South Asian Queer Space." *TSQ: Transgender Studies Quarterly* 5(3): 321–31.

Howe, Cymene. 2013. *Intimate Activism: The Struggle for Sexual Rights in Postrevolutionary Nicaragua*. Durham, NC: Duke University Press, 2013

Jarrín, Alvaro. 2016. "Untranslatable Subjects: Travesti Access to Public Health Care in Brazil." *TSQ: Transgender Studies Quarterly* 3(3–4): 357–75.

Käng, Dredge Byung'chu. 2014. "Idols of Development: Transnational Transgender Performance in Thai K-Pop Cover Dance." *TSQ: Transgender Studies Quarterly* 1(4): 559–71.

Khan, Shahnaz. 2016. "What Is in a Name? Khwaja Sara, Hijra and Eunuchs in Pakistan." *Indian Journal of Gender Studies* 23.2: 218–42.

Lara, Ana-Maurine. 2020. *Queer Freedom: Black Sovereignty*. Albany: State University of New York Press.

Manalansan, Martin F., IV. 2003. *Global Divas: Filipino Gay Men in the Diaspora*. Durham, NC: Duke University Press.

Manalansan, Martin F., IV. 2014. "The 'Stuff' of Archives: Mess, Migration, and Queer Lives." *Radical History Review* 120: 94–107.

Massad, Joseph. 2007. *Desiring Arabs*. Chicago: University of Chicago Press.

Meiu, George Paul. 2020. "Underlayers of Citizenship: Queer Objects, Intimate Exposures, and the Rescue Rush in Kenya." *Cultural Anthropology* 35(4): 575–601.

Mitchell, Gregory. 2016. "Evangelical Ecstasy Meets Feminist Fury: Sex Trafficking, Moral Panics, and Homonationalism during Global Sporting Events." *GLQ: A Journal of Lesbian and Gay Studies* 22(3): 325–57.

Morgensen, Scott Lauria. 2011. *Spaces between Us: Queer Settler Colonialism and Indigenous Decolonization*. Minneapolis: University of Minnesota Press.

Moreau, Julie, and T. J. Tallie. 2019. "Queer African Studies and Directions in Methodology." In *Routledge Handbook of Queer African Studies*, edited by Sybille N. Nyeck, 49–60. New York: Routledge.

Newton, Natalie. 2016. "Contingent Invisibility: Space, Community, and Invisibility for Les in Saigon." *GLQ: A Journal of Lesbian and Gay Studies* 22(1): 109–36.

Nguyen, Vinh-Kim. 2010. *The Republic of Therapy: Triage and Sovereignty in West Africa's Time of AIDS*. Durham, NC: Duke University Press.

Nyanzi, Stella. 2014. "Queering Queer Africa." In *Reclaiming Afrikan: Queer Perspectives on Sexual and Gender Identities*, edited by Zethu Matebeni, 61–66. Athlone: Modjaji Books.

Ochoa, Marcia. 2014. *Queen for a Day: Transformistas, Beauty Queens, and the Performance of Femininity in Venezuela*. Durham, NC: Duke University Press.

Pimentel, Alejandra Wundram and Mónica Leonardo Segura. 2018. "Paradoxes of Visibility: The Proposed Guatemalan Gender Identity Law." *TSQ: Transgender Studies Quarterly* 5 (1): 83–99.

Povinelli, Elizabeth A. 2006. *The Empire of Love: Toward a Theory of Intimacy, Genealogy, and Carnality*. Durham, NC: Duke University Press.

Puar, Jasbir K. 2007. *Terrorist Assemblages: Homonationalism in Queer Times*. Durham, NC: Duke University Press.

Ramberg, Lucinda. 2014. *Given to the Goddess: South Indian Devadasis and the Sexuality of Religion*. Durham, NC: Duke University Press.

Rizki, Cole. 2019. "Latin/x American Trans Studies: Toward a Travesti-Trans Analytic." *TSQ: Transgender Studies Quarterly* 6(2): 145–55.

Rofel, Lisa. 2007. *Desiring China: Experiments in Neoliberalism, Sexuality, and Public Culture*. Durham, NC: Duke University Press.

Saleh, Fadi. 2020. "Transgender as a Humanitarian Category: The Case of Syrian Queer and Gender-Variant Refugees in Turkey." *TSQ: Transgender Studies Quarterly* 7(1): 37–55.

Saunier, Pierre-Yves. 2009. "Transnational." In *The Palgrave Dictionary of Transnational History*, edited by Akira Iriye and Pierre-Yves Saunier, 1047–55. Basingstoke, UK: Palgrave Macmillan.

Savci, Evren. 2020. *Queer in Translation: Sexual Politics under Neoliberal Islam*. Durham, NC: Duke University Press.

Shakhsari, Sima. 2013. "Transnational Governmentality and the Politics of Life and Death." *International Journal of Middle East Studies* 45.2: 340–42.

Shirinian, Tamar. 2018. "The Nation-Family: Intimate Encounters and Genealogical Perversion in Armenia." *American Ethnologist* 45(1): 48–59.

Sinnott, Megan. 2004. *Toms and Dees: Transgender Identity and Female Same-Sex Relationships in Thailand*. Honolulu: University of Hawai'i Press.

Sinnott, Megan. 2010. "Borders, Diaspora and Regional Connections: Trends in Asian 'Queer' Studies." *Journal of Asian Studies* 69(1): 17–31.

Spronk, Rachel, and S. N. Nyeck. 2021. "Frontiers and Pioneers in (the Study of) Queer Experiences in Africa Introduction." *Africa: International Journal of the Africa Institute* 91(3): 388–97.

Steedly, Mary Margaret. 1999. "The State of Culture Theory in the Anthropology of Southeast Asia." *Annual Review of Anthropology* 28.1 (1999): 431–54.

Stout, Noelle M. 2014. *After Love: Queer Intimacy and Erotic Economies in Post-Soviet Cuba*. Durham, NC: Duke University Press, 2014.

Vance, Carole S. 1991. "Anthropology Rediscovers Sexuality: A Theoretical Comment." *Social Science and Medicine* 33(8): 875–84.

Weiss, Margot. 2016. "Discipline and Desire: Feminist Politics, Queer Studies, and New Queer Anthropology." In *Mapping Feminist Anthropology in the Twenty-First Century*, edited by Ellen Lewin and Leni M. Silverstein, 168–87. New Brunswick, NJ: Rutgers University Press.

Wekker, Gloria. 2006. *The Politics of Passion: Women's Sexual Culture in the Afro-Surinamese Diaspora*. New York: Columbia University Press.

Weston, Kath. 1993. "Lesbian/Gay Studies in the House of Anthropology." *Annual Review of Anthropology* 22(1): 339–67.

Wieringa, Saskia, Evelyn Blackwood, and Abha Bhaiya, eds. 2007. *Women's Sexualities and Masculinities in a Globalizing Asia*. New York: Springer.

Wilson, Ara. 2006. "Queering Asia." *Intersections: Gender, History and Culture in the Asian Context* 14(3). http://intersections.anu.edu.au/issue14/wilson.html.

Wilson, Ara. 2010. "NGOs as Erotic Sites." In *Development, Sexual Rights and Global Governance*, edited by Amy Lind, 86–98. New York: Routledge, 2010.

Zengin, Aslı. 2016. "Violent Intimacies: Tactile State Power, Sex/Gender Transgression, and the Politics of Touch in Contemporary Turkey." *Journal of Middle East Women's Studies* 12(2): 225–45.

Sima Shakhsari 8

Queer States

Geopolitics and Queer Anthropology

Queer seems to sustain an uncomfortable, if not adversarial relationship to the state. Queer's desire for antinormativity, outlawness, subversion, and fluidity often stands against the state's normalizing and/or disciplinary techniques, its laws, its identity-based categorizations for rights distribution (and, by extension, management of the population), and its heteronormative systems of kinship. As many scholars have argued in the context of the United States, different relationships to the state have divided queer/LGBT activism and scholarship for decades.[1] In particular, since the 1980s, with the acceleration of neoliberal policies, assimilationist agendas have focused their energies on demanding protections from the state through antidiscrimination laws and marriage equality.[2] In North America and much of Western Europe, the division between nonnormative approaches to queerness (refusal to marry or join the military, etc.) and the liberal assimilationist LGBTQ/queer-as-identity approaches (visibility, state recognition, and protection) is, to great extent, a reflection of their relationship to the state and, its correlate, civil society.

Given that inclusion of queers and their protections by the state have come to stand for the progressive nature of the civil(ized) society, it is important to understand how the modern state lays claim on civilization and progress through its expansion and constriction of the notion of civil society—which at this juncture in Europe and North America includes queer and trans nongovernmental organizations (NGOs) and advocacy groups. The emergence of NGOs (including LGBTQ ones) in the Global South and the social media presence of groups have increased the currency of civil society. Projects of democratization enshrine queer civil society institutions as indices of progress in the race toward liberal democracy. The measure of the progress of a state has become contingent on its openness to the flourishment of civil society organizations, especially LGBT organizations. Even as "sexual deviance" was a barring criterion for queer immigration in the United States until the 1990s, after the so-called war on terror "LGBT rights are human rights" became the mantra of US liberatory projects that made foreign aid contingent on the LGBT rights records of "third world" states.

By the 1980s, mainstream LGBT organizations in the United States increasingly succumbed to the logic of neoliberalism, wherein civil society, seemingly free of the morals of the nuclear family, was organized according to the needs of the market. After the 1989 events in Eastern Europe, "democratization" impulse articulated through the notion of color revolutions gave civil society a new currency. In post-1989 Eastern Europe (which among other things was to free itself of the "soviet-style" homophobia), civil society came to be valorized as the road to democracy. The Reagan-Thatcher neoliberal agendas to "roll back" the state along with the postsocialist "democratization" wave culminated in the universalization of civil society as the fad of national and transnational politics, which was reflected in the proliferation of "international" gay and lesbian NGOs such as International Gay and Lesbian Association (ILGA) and the International Gay and Lesbian Human Right Commission (IGLHRC), among others. It is by no accident that IGLHRC (now called Outright), an organization which was founded in San Francisco in 1990, initially focused most of its activities on civil society and the violation of LGBT rights in the post-Soviet states.[3]

Whether civil society is seen as a gateway to democracy, as a leftist response against neoliberalism (through the formation of nonstate associations) or as the consolidation of new social movements, civil society is often imagined in a vertical and oppositional position in relation to the state. In *The Birth of Biopolitics*, Foucault takes issue with the "inflationary" critique of the state, which in his words entails the assumption of "the intrinsic power of the state in relation to its object-target, civil society" (2010, 187). Rather than the vertical and oppositional relationship between the state and civil society, a Foucauldian approach would pay attention to how government encompasses not only political structures or the management of states, but also the way in which the "conduct of individuals or of groups might be directed" in civil society. In other words, the governmentalization of the state (rather than the statization of government) involves the regulation and management of populations through the language of rights and the rhetoric of natural liberties to generate a self-organizing and self-regulating civil society. The government of populations is not necessarily achieved through the direct imposition of law, but via calculation techniques and programs that may very well be implemented by nonstate agents that participate in the art of governmentality to regulate the conduct of the individuals.[4] As such, civil society, including queer organizations and NGOs, is an integral part of the art of governmentality, of which the state is only one element. The unsettling of the vertical relationship between state and civil society also enables analyses that demystify the state as a homogeneously oppressive force having monopoly over violence.

While Foucault's analysis of power complicates the assumptions of the verticality of power (state → civil society), he was concerned neither with the operations of power outside of the Euro-American context, nor with the multiplicity of states and their uneven power relations in the transnational arena. However, unlike the United Nations' logic of a "family of nations" being represented by their states in the international arena, not all states hold the same level of power in a transnational context. Neither do they all follow the normative operations and philosophies of the idealized liberal state. Despite the myth of the sovereignty of the nation-states (upon which international treaties are based), colonial and imperial relations of power continue to sustain gross inequalities, albeit under the guise of decolonization and independence. The concept of "international civil society" and the looming "threats" to its security continue to be deployed by the United States (and the UN) to discipline and dominate states that deviate from the norms of liberal democracy and global capitalism. As elements of transnational governmentality, assimilationist LGBT rights organizations are often complicit with neoliberal agendas and geopolitical interests of the US empire.

Anthropology—particularly postcolonial anthropology—because of its interest in multiple and uneven operations of power within globally stratified systems, provides one lens to rethink both state and civil society. In this chapter, by thinking beyond sexual identities and rights, and without assuming queer to be inherently and necessarily antinormative, I focus on the Iranian state and take up questions of queer geopolitics, transnational refugee regimes, and the politics of rights/rightlessness, to suggest a queer anthropological approach that explores the state as a contradictory and transnational assemblage of multilayered institutions, people, and practices that unevenly map the geopolitics of sex and sexuality.[5]

Queer States

While the "queering" trend might give the impression that the term *queer states* seeks to excavate queerness in otherwise heteronormative structures of the state, we might consider states that are punished or demonized for their "dirty" human rights records and perversions as queer states. *Failed states*, a common phrase in political discourse, refers to states that are unable to provide public services (thanks to neoliberal policies, wars, and sanctions), lose authority over their citizens (thanks to US military interventions), and fail to participate in the "international community" (by violating human rights that are defined by the arbitrators of rights and its violations). The deployment of this phrase sums up the normalization of liberal democracies and the exclusion of states that do not fit the tenets of liberal democracy and global capitalism. If failure is a queer art (to borrow from Halberstam 2011), then one could consider "failed states" to be queer states—those that refuse to abide by the norms of liberal secular statehood or are excluded from the "family of nations" for being outlaws, "terrorists," and threats to the "international community." As I will discuss, sanctions and wars become disciplinary measures to straighten the unruly illiberal (queered) states such as the Iranian state. In the context of the United States, important scholarship such as Margot Canaday's *Straight State*, Eithne Luibhéid's *Entry Denied*, or Siobhan Somerville's *Queering the Color Line*, among other works, demonstrate the heteronormalization of the US citizenry through state laws and policies. My use of the term *queer state* is neither to juxtapose it with the "straight states"—those invested in upholding heteronormativity (arguably, all modern states)—nor does it suggest that queer states are necessary queer-friendly. By going beyond the binary of straight/queer (to follow Cathy Cohen's rearticulation of queer in 1997) and tracing queerness in shared exclusions (of the racially queered, to borrow from Puar), I consider queer states (such as the Iranian state) to be those which are excluded from the realm of normal statehood (i.e., liberal/secular) and often deemed to be sexually perverse. This move to uncouple queerdom from the liberal state is to draw the attention of anthropology—and queer anthropology in particular—to geopolitical deployments of sexuality in the transnational context, wherein "illiberal states" such as Iran are demonized and deemed as violators of LGBTQI rights.

The discursive production of Iran as sexually perverse is exemplified in Karim Sadjadpour's "The Ayatollah under the Bed(sheets)."[6] In this *Foreign Policy* article that resembles a national character studies account, Sadjadpour claims that to understand "what makes Tehran tick [is] the regime's curious fixation on sex."[7] According to Sadjadpour, "The outwardly chaste nature of Khomeinist political culture has perverted normal sexual behavior, creating peculiar curiosities—and proclivities—among Iranian officialdom." Sadjadpour characterizes the "traditional" Islamic sexuality as one that is guilty of bestiality, sodomy, pedophilia, and polygamy, which he juxtaposes to a heteronormative modern sexuality. To regime-change enthusiasts (which include not only diasporic opposition groups and individuals such as Sadjadpour, but the "liberating states"), having sex in the private sphere and talking about sex (of the acceptable and sanitized form) are characterized as signs of a "sexual revolution" in defiance of the "theocratic regime." Interestingly, while the Iranian "regime" is deemed as perverse/queer, heteronormative (and more recently homonormative) sex becomes a revolutionary act to defy the Iranian "theocracy." What the regime-change enthusiasts uncritically call "Iran's regime," however, is a fragmented and dynamic formation that, at times, relies on civil society for its disciplinary and regulatory work and is always characterized by contradiction and internal conflict. In fact, as I have argued elsewhere (Shakhsari 2020b), the fissures within the postrevolutionary Iranian state have *enabled* spaces in which contestation and reform have become possible.[8] Seemingly sex-positive claims of "liberating states" that show excitement about "sexual revolutions" and "LGBT rights" in Iran reach their limits when one notes the underlying heteronormativity of liberation/democratization

QUEER STATES   173

projects. A comical and embarrassing instance of this hypocrisy surfaced when the US Department of State, which hires private companies such as Anonymizer to provide free antifiltering proxies to Iranian internet users (to facilitate US propaganda operations in Iran under the cloak of "Internet freedom") blocked certain words to prevent moral perversions. Ironically, in the beginning of its "Internet freedom" projects in Iran, the US-sponsored proxies filtered the word "ass" to discourage Iranians from surfing gay-porn sites. Subsequently, all words that contained the letters "a-s-s," including the "American Embassy," were filtered.

Of course, not all illiberal states pose a threat to the security of the "international community" and the market. Even as the fantasy of secularism dominates the idealized standards of liberal statehood, neither seemingly secular states are completely secular, nor are "religious" states purely religious.[9] And even as states such as India ("the greatest democracy in the world") or Israel ("the only democracy in the Middle East") are organized around religion and terrorize their internal racialized others (let alone Palestinians in the occupied territories or Kashmiris), they seem to be exempt from indictments of theocracy, authoritarianism, and terrorism. While the state of Israel instrumentalizes queers to pinkwash its settler colonial violence, Saudi Arabia, with one of the most conservative religiously driven state laws in the Middle East, seems to be an exception to the disciplinary actions taken by the United States against "homophobic and transphobic theocracies."[10] Queered states, such as the Islamic of Republic of Iran, on the other hand, are deemed as "authoritarian theocracies" subjected to sanctions for defying the universalized norms of statehood and in the name of threatening "international security."[11] This is by no means to exonerate the Iranian state, nor is it to claim that queer Iranians do not face discrimination and violence. In fact, the Iranian state is not an exception in its biopolitical management of the population according to the heteronormative ideals of citizenship. Yet, as Scott Long (2009) has argued, the exaggerated accounts of exceptional violence are predicated on misrecognition and assumptions of universal sexual identities and geopolitical deployments of LGBTQ rights. This is what Kath Weston in her seminal article "Lesbian/Gay Studies in the House of Anthropology" identified as the problem of ethnocartography, where "by setting out in advance to look for sexuality, the anthropologist cannot help but reify the object of (ethnographic) desire" (1993, 347). While queer anthropology has been more conscious of the universalist approaches to sexualities "elsewhere," sexual identity (in its Euro-American iteration) remains the defining element of queer anthropology, political science, and international human rights discourse.[12]

Queer Geopolitics

Assuming necessary antagonistic or assimilationist relationships between queer and state requires a clear definition of both queer and the state—a task that runs the risk of reductionist simplification, given that queer has been a contested field of signification and a productive site of ontological interrogations. While the proliferation of scholarship in queer theory has culminated in a range of methodological approaches (from queer theory as a study of sexual identities to challenges to normativity, and "queering" as methodology), critical engagement with women of color feminisms, transnational feminism, postcolonial theory, and decoloniality have shifted the conversation from a seemingly anti-identitarian focus to theorizing queer beyond whiteness as queer's default modus operandi. However, as Anjali Arondekar and Geeta Patel (2016) point out, queer theory's engagement with geopolitics remains limited. They write, "With a few exceptions, the citational underpinnings that provide the theoretical conduit for such explorations were and continue to be resolutely contemporary and drawn primarily from the United States; that is, geopolitics provides the exemplars, but rarely the epistemologies" (152). Of course, in the past couple of decades the analysis of homonationalism (Puar 2007) has extended the concept of homonormativity (Duggan 2002) to pay attention to the geopolitical investments of the empire in queer liberalism's utility in the justification of neocolonial projects in North America, Europe, and Israel. However, geopolitics remains the "un-queer" topic that stays out of queer scholarship for the most part. As Maya Mikdashi and Jasbir Puar in their critique of queer studies argue, an ostensibly area-less queer studies has become the turf of American studies—"an invisibilized area studies formation from which all other area studies are derived and defined" (2016, 216). While there are several transnational queer anthropological studies outside of North America and Europe, with a few exceptions queer studies does not critically engage with geopolitics.[13] The seemingly transnational queer scholarship, even when it is the anthropology of "elsewhere," ultimately recenters Euro-American epistemologies of queerness by queering the "elsewhere" or adding queer to "elsewhere." Mikdashi and Puar aptly point out that "the work of queer theorists in area studies (rarely read by queer theory as 'Queer Theory' and often relegated to 'sexuality studies') is understood as a 'case study' of specifics rather than an interruption of the canonical treatments of the area studies field at large" (216).

While anthropology is not as US-centered as American studies, and even as postcolonial anthropology has challenged this discipline's colonial legacies, the critique pointed at area studies might resonate with much of the queer anthropology of the third world, wherein Euro-American understandings of queerness and state underpin the analyses of queerness, sexualities, and genders. Queer theory and ethnographies that are unintelligible to canonical Euro-American queer theory are deemed un-queer and heteronormative, if not atavistic. For example, when a colleague suggested a text by a Middle Eastern scholar in response to my social media call for texts to be taught in a graduate seminar titled "Queer Geopolitics," another fellow anthropologist and a queer theory scholar whose research is on sexuality in a location outside of the United States objected that the said text was good but needed to be "queered." In such queer territorial entitlements, while it is not clear what the criterion for a properly queer text is, it is often expected that the object of study center transgressions or injuries that center sex, gender, and sexuality, especially in their overdetermined Euro-American articulations. But as Mikdashi and Puar ask (220–21), "Does queer theory (still) require a sexual or gendered body or a sexual or gendered injury—particularly if part of the project of homonationalism is to produce and stabilize transnational, imperial, and settler colonial forms of sexual and gendered injury? . . . Should we remain wedded to queer theory's general obsession and commitment to the sexualized human form to recognizable 'queer sexualities,' given that the war on terror has thus far killed at least 1.3 million people (a conservative estimate) in Iraq, Afghanistan, and Pakistan alone?"

Rather than focusing on US-centered approaches to the state and queer, a critical queer anthropology of state that is not divorced from geopolitics and moves beyond the Euro-American epistemological traditions has the potential to challenge the abstraction of "state," the normalization of power relationships in colonial, settler colonial, and imperial contexts, *and* an American-centric reading of "queer" and sex/sexuality. As Rahul Rao (2020) has rightly argued, in the postcolony, homosexuality has either been written off as "Western" or claimed as native and precolonial (and thus homophobia becomes a colonial export to the postcolony). Rao convincingly argues that the contingency of transnational aid on the LGBT rights record of "underdeveloped" states not only works to reify universal definitions of homo-

176 SIMA SHAKHSARI

sexuality and homophobia, but also points to the logic of progress and the "foundational grammar of the state" that deem some nation-states civilized (read gay friendly) and others "underdeveloped/backward" (i.e., homophobic). Rao's research in Uganda shows how the shrinking state (a neoliberal condition for aid) opens room for conservative Christian NGOs that fill the gap left by the disappearance of state services. The moral anxieties and the fear of the loss of Ugandan family values give rise to homophobia, as homosexuality comes to stand for the demise of the Ugandan culture. Informed by Puar's homonationalism, Rao suggests homocapitalism as the rehabilitation of capitalism through gender and sexuality, wherein some queers are folded into capitalism and others are disavowed and illegible to the "foundational grammar of the state."[14]

To make geopolitics a central axis of analysis not only helps us understand the complex relationships between multiple states and local and transnational civil society organizations (which in the transnational context includes queer human rights organizations, queer NGOs, and queer diasporas), but also the uneven power relationships between multiple states. In a time when transnational aid and development projects are contingent on the LGBT friendliness of the "third world" recipients of aid, and when some states are designated as violators of LGBT rights while the liberal states become purported protectors of LGBT individuals and communities, centering geopolitics in the queer analysis of state and more ethnographic attention to these dynamics are necessary.

Queer Refugees of a Queered State

One of the areas that the state is seen as having monopoly over violence is the "refugee crisis." Even as the United Nations High Commissioner on Refugees (UNHCR) considers the "refugee problem" to be resulting from states violating the rights of their citizens or states failing to protect their citizens' safety, ethnographic work among refugees highlights the fact that multiple elements besides the state contribute not only to the production of refugees, but also to the disposability of refugee lives under the "protection" of refugee regimes. In the past few years, I have focused my research on the inconsistencies in refugee regimes, wherein Iranian queer and transgender refugee applicants in Turkey who are waiting for their cases to be processed by the UNHCR, the Turkish state, and the "third country of asylum" are denied rights while seemingly living under the protection of rights as stateless people.[15] Many queer and trans refugees in Turkey live under dire conditions without an income or the right to work.[16] Since 2010, Turkey has seen a significant surge in the number of non-Syrian asylum seekers, which has caused a backlog in the cases and extremely slow refugee recognition and resettlement processes. While before 2010 the refugee recognition and resettlement process for most Iranian queer and trans asylum seekers took anywhere from one and a half to three years, at the time of the writing of this essay some Iranian queer and trans refugee applicants have been waiting for as long as nine years because of the UNHCR's backlog and the immigration restrictions in the third countries of asylum such as the United States and Canada.

The dominant refugee discourse emphasizes state persecution of "LGBTI" people and the medical torture of trans Iranians, while completely ignoring the role of the sanctions in producing refugees. In an interview with a UNHCR officer, I was told that the post-2010 backlog in the non-Syrian refugee cases in Turkey was mainly due to the increase in the number of Afghan refugees who left Iran (home to almost three million Afghans), after the Obama administration's tightening of the sanctions on Iran (5,000 in 2009 in comparison to 50,000 in 2013).[17] While millions of Afghan refugees left Afghanistan for Pakistan and Iran (and in smaller numbers to India, the United States, and Europe) during the rise of Taliban and the US occupation of Afghanistan in the 1980s into the first decade of the new millennium, a significant number of Afghan refugee applicants in Turkey after 2010 were those who left Iran (and not Afghanistan). The "second migration" of Afghan refugees, some of whom had lived in Iran for decades, was due to the harsh economic conditions, cuts in state subsidies, and the rising xenophobia in Iran. While the United States has consistently imposed sanctions on Iran since the Iranian Revolution in 1979, the Obama administration imposed the harshest sanctions in the history of the US sanctions on Iran. Obama's sanctions exerted excruciating economic pressure on the Iranian population, jeopardized Iranian lives by causing rampant air pollution resulting from domestic oil-refining technologies, and cut access to life-saving medicine. Even though Obama lifted some (and not all) sanctions in 2015, Trump's reversal of the "Iran Deal" in 2018 and the imposition of "maximum pressure," which continue under the Biden administration, have further devastated the Iranian economy. Under the pressure of the economic sanctions and austerity measures, when many Iranians have had to take more than one job to make ends meet, scarcity and competition for jobs and resources have led to the scapegoating of the most vulnerable segments of the Iranian population, which include working-class queer and trans Iranians and Afghan refugees in Iran. Although not comparable to the number of Afghans who left Iran, the number of working-class queer and trans refugee applicants leaving Iran also increased after 2010. With the increasing competition for jobs under the weight of inflation and cuts in subsidies—such as the cuts in subsidies for gender affirmation surgeries—many working-class trans and queer Iranians have had no choice but to leave Iran.[18]

While state violence and the state's failure to protect its citizens are the most important criteria for refugee recognition, the violence of the refugee regimes, neoliberal privatization of refugee sponsorship, and the underlying racist and transphobic assumptions of the refugee regimes are erased in the civilizational narratives of refugee rescue. Elsewhere, I have detailed how Sohrab (a trans man), Minoo (his wife), and their tween son were stuck in Turkey for nine years, waiting to be resettled in Canada while experiencing hardship.[19] Highlighting the transphobic, economic, xenophobic, and sexist violence that this family (and other queer and trans refugee applicants) faced while waiting indefinitely in Turkey, I have argued that refugee regimes deny queer and trans refugees their basic rights, in the name of human rights. This paradox is congruent with refugee regimes' lack of concern for refugee lives and its preoccupation with the authenticity of refugee claims, which are expected to vilify the Iran state and the "homophobic Iranian culture," and reify Eurocentric sexual and gender identities.[20] In Sohrab and his family's case, the assumptions of deception attached to Sohrab's body as a trans man and the gendered "risk of terrorism" attached to the body of his son, as he grew from a tween to a young cis heterosexual Iranian man while waiting in Turkey, show how the refugee rights regimes expose refugees to forms of violence that exceed the violence of the Iranian state.

To make matters worse, Canada's closure of borders to non-Syrian refugees during the Syrian refugee crisis (which forced Sohrab and his family to request an administrative change for the "third country of asylum" from Canada to the United States), and the subsequent US Muslim ban (which banned Sohrab and his family from resettling in the United States), subjected this refugee family to further violence through indefinite waiting in Turkey without the right to work and without access to healthcare—a form of violence that Elif Sari's ethnographic work convincingly highlights (2020a, 2020b). After nine years of waiting, Sohrab and his family were able to resettle in Canada through private sponsorship and after raising

$40,000 CAD, donated by individual Canadian citizens, who—despite their good intentions—were moved by images and narratives of third world misery and white-savior narratives of refugee rescue in the fundraising campaign. Sohrab and his family are among the "lucky" refugees whose image of a couple with a child garnered the sympathy of a few Canadian donors. Many queer and transgender refugees, who are single and come from working-class backgrounds are engaged in sex work, are not neurotypical, or have physical disabilities—and are therefore undesirable for private sponsorship—continue to wait in Turkey without any hope for resettlement. Despite the dire conditions within which working-class queer and transgender refugee applicants—who stand outside of the norms of citizenship as refugees and queer/trans—live, the everyday violence they face under the "protection of refugee rights" is almost never mentioned in refugee narratives that solely focus on the state's monopoly over violence. By obsessively fixating on state violence while erasing the violence to which the NGOs, the UN, human rights organizations, embassies of the "third country of asylum," and the privatization of refugee resettlement subject the refugees, state-focused ethnographic studies exert their own epistemic violence by banking on stories of refugee victimhood and rescue.

It is irrefutable that, like many other states, the Iranian state as a modern biopolitical state uses its medical, psychological, and legal apparatus to produce an optimal form of "normal" life while excluding or disposing its racialized or queer others. As Afsaneh Najmabadi (2013) has argued, despite its subsidies for gender-affirming surgeries, the Iranian state's medical, legal, religious, and psychological apparatus remains invested in the binary of gender and wishes to exclude trans people from full citizenship. However, the Iranian state's normalization of trans people, wherein passing as cis becomes the measure of "success," is not exceptional. Neither is the Iranian state—from its medical and psychological establishments to its legal and religious apparatus—uniformly or exceptionally transphobic or trans-friendly. To demonize Iran as exceptionally transphobic erases the nuances and multiplicities in the Iranian society and state, while assuming a top-down operation of power, wherein trans activists and individuals appear only as victims of a perceived monolithic and repressive Islamic state. Najmabadi's archival and ethnographic work shows how the Iranian trans people have multiple and uneven relationships to different elements of the state. While Najmabadi does not engage with geopolitics, her work on state-subsidized gender affirmation surgeries reveals how different fragments of the state may have contradictory approaches to queerness/trans-ness that make assuming a uniform and generalized hostile position from the state toward queerness to be simplistic. Equally important is the fact that not all Iranian queers (whether they identify as gay, lesbian, trans, *hamjensgarā*, or not) approach the state through the framework of rights. Najmabadi's research shows that, unlike the middle-class Iranian women's rights activists, Iranian trans activists (especially working-class trans activists) have found the rights framework to be unhelpful and instead have focused their energies on receiving services and subsidies from the state through the deployment of needs. As Najmabadi has rightly argued (2013), trans activists have had a significant and active role in negotiating and contesting legal, religious, and medical discourses and practices regarding transgender people in Iran. Also, many key actors in contestations to anti-trans laws and practices are a part of the fragmented and stratified state. To reduce the multiplicity of positions, behaviors, and attitudes to a single narrative of repression and torture is not only inaccurate, but a violent erasure of the long history of Iranian trans activism. Equally important is to pay attention to the fact that the violence that queer and trans Iranians face is not reducible to a simplistic and universalized rhetoric of homophobia or transphobia. As I have argued, the economic violence resulting from the US sanctions has devastated the most vulnerable segments of the Iranian population.

Queer Anthropology of the State

If a queer anthropology of the state is to unsettle fixed and already-existing Euro-American notions of queer and state, it must go beyond comparative approaches to laws and policies toward LGBTQ individuals, where LGBTQ identities in different locations are assumed to be either copies or modular forms of those existing in North America or Europe. Rather than studying LGBTQI rights and state policies in X country with the predetermined agenda of exposing the exploitative and vertical relationship between the state and queer, a queer anthropology of the state can start from understanding how queerness might constitute the state and how the state might participate in the production of queerness beyond purportedly universal LGBTQ "rights." Some scholars of the state and sexuality outside of the Euro-American context are already doing this. For instance, Jyoti Puri's *Sexual States* explores the regulation of sexuality in India as necessary to the existence of the state, Ghassan Moussavi's *Disruptive Situations* documents daily queer survival strategies in Beirut while challenging orientalist representations of the Arab world, and Aslı Zengin's "Violent Intimacies" analyzes trans people's relationship to everyday state violence in Istanbul.

But what is equally important is to engage with the state not as *sui generis*, but in relationship to geopolitics and embedded in transnational governmentality. Some scholars have explored how territoriality and sovereignty have been reconfigured by a range of events that include colonialism and settler colonialism, immigrant and refugee movements, the "global war on terror," securitization, imperialist queer "liberation" projects, and the proliferation of NGOs. Paul Amar's work in Egypt and Brazil (2013) on the role of sexuality in the rise of the "security state," J. Kēhaulani Kauanui's work on the heteropatriarchal colonial legacies in discourses of Hawaiian sovereignty and the US domestic laws (2018), Lisa Rofel's work on the production of "desiring subjects" in postsocialist China and the state's changing relationship to its citizens and to the transnational world (2007), Jasbir Puar's work on the "war on terror," homonationalism, and her critique of US-centered queer theory, trans studies, and disability studies (2007, 2017), Jodi Byrd's work on the relationship between the settler state and the US colonial and imperial histories (2011), and Elizabeth Povinelli's work on the relationship of life and non-life and Indigenous Australian understandings of power that challenge the settler state (2016) are examples of the scholarship that engages with geopolitics. The queer anthropology of state can benefit from more ethnographic studies that contribute to this scholarship.

By highlighting uneven geopolitical relationships, the queer anthropology of state can challenge comparative models wherein "liberal democratic" states become the yardstick against which other states are measured for their queer rights. Not only is the queer anthropology of state capable of challenging mainstream studies of the state that ignore sexuality by relegating it to the private sphere, but it can also help us understand queerness beyond sexuality, sexuality beyond queerness, and the state beyond its assumed vertical relationship to civil society. Rather than naturalizing liberal democracy as the ideal state form, delimiting the study of the state to the realm of rights and visibility, or ignoring colonial, imperial, and settler state relations of power, queer anthropology can draw on Indigenous and local knowledges to understand the state as a fragmented and contingent assemblage in an uneven field of power relations. Doing so entails abandoning attachments to predetermined understandings of state and queerness and showing the mutually constitutive production of the queer state and the state of queerness.

Notes

1   See Brown 2003; Hanhardt 2013; and Weiss 2016, among others.

2   During the first half of the twentieth century in the United States and some parts of Europe, a "welfare state" was established in which the state intervened in the economy and promised to provide high levels of employment, social security, and economic growth. After the 1970s, however, a neoliberal form of governing social and economic life emerged. Unlike welfarism, where the interventionist state seeks to guarantee mechanisms of social security, neoliberalism highlights the inefficiencies of state-regulated economy and emphasizes the market. However, neoliberalism does not require the withering of the state, as much as it reorganizes its political rationalities according to neoliberal technologies of government, often in the realm of civil society.

3   Before establishing IGLHRC in the United States, Julie Dorf, the executive director/founder of IGLHRC, assumed herself the role of advocacy for LGBT civil society organizations in the Soviet Union. Joseph Massad's *Desiring Arabs* includes a critique of IGLHRC as a part of the "gay international."

4   Foucault defines governmentality as "the ensemble formed by the institutions, procedures, analyses and reflections, the calculations and tactics that allow the exercise of this very specific albeit complex form of power, which has as its target population, as its principal form of knowledge political economy, and as its essential technical means apparatus of security" (2007, 108).

5   For a few critiques/reviews of queer anthropology, see Weston 1993; Allen 2016; Manalansan 2016; Morgensen 2011, 2016; and Weiss 2016, 2022.

6   Sadjadpour 2012.

7   The post–World War II national character studies aimed to understand the characteristics of the enemy. Ruth Benedict, in whose honor an American Anthropology Association queer anthropology prize is named, was among the anthropologists who produced cultural determinist accounts of the Japanese people.

8   As I revise this article, almost two years after writing it, ongoing protests three months after the death of Mahsa Jina Amini continue. The Iranian state, under the control of the conservative factions, has imprisoned many reformists. The death of hundreds of protesters by the Iranian state and parastate forces, the outrage from some state personalities and millions of Iranians to the unlawful executions of four imprisoned protesters, and the increased securitization of

the state on one hand, and the looming threat of a NATO/US war, fueled by the segments of the Iranian diaspora who are a part of the transnational Iranian civil society on the other, further complicates the binaries of a unified state versus a unified civil society.

9   Examples of the critique of the secular/religious binary include scholarship by Moallem 2005; Mahmood 2005; and Asad 2003.

10 For literature on pinkwashing, see Chavez and Shafie 2019; Kuntsman and Stein 2015; Haritaworn et al. 2014; Mikdashi 2011; and Mikdashi and Puar 2016, among others.

11 The sanctions are seemingly imposed on the Iranian state for its potential to produce nuclear weapons. Iran does not own any nuclear weapons. Israel, on the other hand, has an estimated ninety nuclear missiles but has not signed the Non-proliferation Treaty.

12 Also see Weiss 2016 on queer anthropology.

13 This includes some of the anthropological studies in East Asia, Latin America, Middle East, and Africa.

14 While Rao distinguishes homocapitalism from homonationalism, Puar's definition of homonationalism considers global capitalism as an integral part of the assemblage that she has called homonationalism.

15 For other ethnographic work on queer and trans refugees, see Murray 2015; Sari 2020a, 2020b; Saleh 2020; Lewis 2014; and Allouche 2017, among others.

16 For a detailed account of the living conditions of queer and trans refugee applicants in Turkey, see Shakhsari 2014.

17 UNHCR, "Islamic Republic of Iran," https://www.unhcr.org/en-us/islamic -republic-of-iran.html, accessed August 23, 2021.

18 For the health, economic, environmental, and social effects of the sanctions and the way that sanctions subject the Iranian population to slow death, see Shakhsari 2020b.

19 See Shakhsari 2023.

20 See Shakhsari 2020a.

References

Allen, Jafari Sinclaire. 2016. "One View from a Deterritorialized Realm: How Black/ Queer Renarrativizes Anthropological Analysis." *Cultural Anthropology* 31(4): 617–26.

Allouche, Sabiha. 2017. "(Dis)-intersecting Intersectionality in the Time of Queer Syrian-Refugee-ness in Lebanon." *Kohl: A Journal for Body and Gender Research* 3(1). https://kohljournal.press/dis-intersecting-intersectionality.

Amar, Paul. 2013. *The Security Archipelago: Human-Security States, Sexuality Politics, and the End of Neoliberalism.* Durham, NC: Duke University Press.

Arondekar, Anjali, and Geeta Patel. 2016. "Area Impossible: Notes toward an Introduction." *GLQ: A Journal of Lesbian and Gay Studies* 22(2): 151–71.

Asad, Talal. 2003. *Formations of the Secular: Christianity, Islam, Modernity.* Stanford, CA: Stanford University Press.

Brown, Wendy. 2003. "Neo-liberalism and the End of Liberal Democracy." *Theory and Event* 7(1). doi:10.1353/tae.2003.0020.

Byrd, Jodi A. 2011. *The Transit of Empire: Indigenous Critiques of Colonialism.* Minneapolis: University of Minnesota Press.

Canaday, Margot. 2009. *The Straight State: Sexuality and Citizenship in Twentieth-Century America.* Princeton, NJ: Princeton University Press.

Chavez, Karma, and Ghadir Shafie. 2019. "Pinkwashing and the Boycott, Divestment, and Sanctions Campaign." *Journal of Civil and Human Rights* 5: 32–48.

Cohen, Cathy J. 1997. "Punks, Bulldaggers, and Welfare Queens: The Radical Potential of Queer Politics?" *GLQ: A Journal of Lesbian and Gay Studies* 3(4): 437–65.

Duggan, Lisa. 2002. "The New Homonormativity: The Sexual Politics of Neoliberalism." In *Materializing Democracy: Toward a Revitalized Cultural Politics*, edited by Russ Castronovo and Dana D. Nelson, 175–94. Durham NC: Duke University Press.

Foucault, Michel. 2007. *Security, Territory, Population: Lectures at the Collège De France 1977–1978.* Edited by Michel Senellart. Translated by Graham Burchell. London: Picador.

Foucault, Michel. 2010. *The Birth of Biopolitics: Lectures at the Collège De France 1978–1979.* Edited by Michel Senellart. Translated by Graham Burchell. London: Picador.

Halberstam, Jack. 2011. *The Queer Art of Failure.* Durham, NC: Duke University Press.

Hanhardt, Christina. 2013. *Safe Space: Gay Neighborhood History and the Politics of Violence.* Durham, NC: Duke University Press.

Haritaworn, Jin, Adi Kuntsman, and Silvia Posocco, eds. 2014. *Queer Necropolitics.* Routledge: Abingdon.

Kauanui, Kēhaulani J. 2018. *Paradoxes of Hawaiian Sovereignty: Land, Sex, and the Colonial Politics of State Nationalism.* Durham, NC: Duke University Press.

Kuntsman, Adi, and Rebecca Stein. 2015. *Digital Militarism: Israel's Occupation in the Social Media Age.* Stanford, CA: Stanford University Press.

Lewis, Rachel. A. 2014. "Gay? Prove It: The Politics of Queer Anti-deportation Activism." *Sexualities* 17(8): 958–75.

Long, Scott. 2009. "Unbearable Witness: How Western Activists (Mis)recognize Sexuality in Iran." *Contemporary Politics* 15(1): 119–36.

Luibhéid, Eithne. 2002. *Entry Denied: Controlling Sexuality at the Border*. Minnesota: University of Minnesota Press.

Mahmood, Saba. 2015. *Politics of Piety: The Islamic Revival and the Feminist Subject*. Princeton, NJ: Princeton University Press.

Manalansan, Martin F., IV. 2016. "Queer Anthropology: An Introduction." *Cultural Anthropology* 31(4): 595–97.

Massad, Joseph A. 2008. *Desiring Arabs*. Chicago: University of Chicago Press.

Mikdashi, Maya. 2011. "Gay Rights as Human Rights: Pinkwashing Homonationalism." *Jadaliyya*. https://www.jadaliyya.com/Details/24855.

Mikdashi, Maya, and Jasbir Puar. 2016. "Queer Theory and Permanent War." *GLQ: A Journal of Lesbian and Gay Studies* 22(2): 215–22.

Moallem, Minoo. 2005. *Between Warrior Brother and Veiled Sister: Islamic Fundamentalism and the Politics of Patriarchy in Iran*. Berkeley: University of California Press.

Morgensen, Scott. 2011. *Spaces between Us: Queer Settler Colonialism and Indigenous Decolonization*. Minneapolis: University of Minnesota Press.

Morgensen, Scott L. 2016. "Encountering Indeterminacy: Colonial Contexts and Queer Imagining." *Cultural Anthropology* 31(4): 607–16.

Moussavi, Ghassan. 2020. *Disruptive Situations: Fractal Orientalism and Queer Strategies in Beirut*. Philadelphia: Temple University Press.

Murray, David. 2015. *Real Queer? Sexual Orientation and Gender Identity Refugees in the Canadian Refugee Apparatus*. London: Rowman and Littlefield.

Najmabadi, Afsaneh. 2013. *Professing Selves: Transsexuality and Same-Sex Desire in Contemporary Iran*. Durham, NC: Duke University Press.

Povinelli, Elizabeth. 2016. *Geontologies: A Requiem for Late Liberalism*. Durham, NC: Duke University Press.

Puar, Jasbir. 2007. *Terrorist Assemblages: Homonationalism in Queer Times*. Durham, NC: Duke University Press.

Puar, Jasbir K. 2017. *The Right to Maim: Debility, Capacity, Disability*. Durham, NC: Duke University Press.

Puri, Jyoti. 2016. *Sexual States: Governance and the Struggle against the Antisodomy Law in India's Present*. Durham, NC: Duke University Press.

Rao, Rahul. 2020. *Out of Time: The Queer Politics of Postcoloniality*. Oxford University Press.

Rofel, Lisa. 2007. *Desiring China: Experiments in Neoliberalism, Sexuality, and Public Culture*. Durham, NC: Duke University Press.

Sadjadpour, Karim. 2012. "The Ayatollah under the Bed(sheets)." *Foreign Policy*, April 23, 2012. https://foreignpolicy.com/2012/04/23/the-ayatollah-under-the-bedsheets/.

Saleh, Fouad. 2020. "Queer/Humanitarian Visibility: The Emergence of the Figure of the Suffering Syrian Gay Refugee." *Middle East Critique* 29(1): 47–67.

Sari, Elif. 2020a. "Lesbian Refugees in Transit: The Making of Authenticity and Legitimacy in Turkey." *Journal of Lesbian Studies* 24(2): 140–58.

Sari, Elif. 2020b. "Waiting in Transit: The Sexuality of (Im)Mobility and Iranian LGBTQ Refugees in Turkey," PhD Dissertation. Cornell University.

Shakhsari, Sima. 2014. "The Queer Time of Death: Temporality, Geopolitics, and Refugee Rights." *Sexualities* 17(8): 998–1015.

Shakhsari, Sima. 2020a. "Displacing Queer Refugee Epistemologies: Dreams of Trespass, Queer Kinship, and Politics of Miseration." *Arab Studies Journal* 28(2): 108–33.

Shakhsari, Sima. 2020b. *Politics of Rightful Killing, Civil Society, Gender, and Sexuality in Weblogistan*. Durham, NC: Duke University Press.

Shakhsari, Sima. 2023. "What Counts as Violence? Transgender Refugees, Torture, and Sanction." In *The Cunning of Gender Violence: Feminism and Geopolitics*, edited by Lila Abu-Lughod, Rema Hammami, and Nadera Shalhoub-Kevorkian: 361–90. Durham, NC: Duke University Press.

Somerville, Siobhan. 2000. *Queering the Color Line: Race and the Invention of Homosexuality in American Culture*. Durham, NC: Duke University Press.

Weiss, Margot. 2016. "Always After: Desiring Queerness, Desiring Anthropology." *Cultural Anthropology* 31 (4): 627–38.

Weiss, Margot. 2022. "Queer Theory from Elsewhere and the Im/Proper Objects of Queer Anthropology" *Feminist Anthropology* 3(2): 315–35.

Weston, Kath. 1993. "Lesbian/Gay Studies in the House of Anthropology." In *Annual Review of Anthropology* 22: 339–67.

Zengin, Aslı. 2016. "Violent Intimacies: Tactile State Power, Sex/Gender Transgression, and the Politics of Touch in Contemporary Turkey." *Journal of Middle East Women's Studies* 12 (2): 225–45.

Part III

DEPARTURES

Reworlding Queer Anthropology

Shaka McGlotten and Lyndon Gill,
Marshall Green, Nikki Lane, and Kwame Otu

9

Black Queer Anthropology Roundtable

Speculations on Activating Ethnographic
Practice in and for Community

This roundtable, edited for clarity, took place on June 18, 2021. I proposed the
roundtable format in lieu of authoring a chapter on my own; it felt important that this be a collective endeavor that emphasized the always relational
energies that go into producing ethnographic scholarship, or a field. It
was a table big enough to stretch across various locales: New York, California, Massachusetts, and Texas, as well as Germany, Ghana, and Tobago.
Indeed, while Black queer anthropology coheres around key themes and
analytics—in its genealogical antecedents (Allen, this volume) and embrace
of the erotic, Spirit, misterios (Lara 2020; Shange, this volume)—it is also
an assemblage in process, connection as praxis. It is an abolitionist practice
of Black study: we "study without an end, plan without a pause, rebel without a policy, conserve without a patrimony" (Moten and Harney 2013, 67).
Black study is about thinking and being together. The neoliberal academy writ
large, though, or even subfields writ small, can inhibit that belonging together,

whether through formal administrative policies or through in/formal circuits of social pressure tied to the politics of respectability, keenly felt by each of us.

As an assemblage in process, cohered by spiritful exchanges yet resistant to closures (theoretical, political, otherwise) the conversation was live. Our Zoom call became a brief refuge where we could experiment with being vulnerable or voicing wishful refusals (see Manalansan, this volume). We tried to retain that spirit even as we edited the text. Some of the liveness we rendered opaque to readers. Our story truths displayed our furies, pleasures, joys. Some of these were just for us and so we have BLACKDACTED portions of text, recognizing that the exposure of Black queer feels makes us vulnerable to white voyeurism and institutional retaliation. We sometimes need the cover of Black opacities to make space for emergence, for somethings that won't bend to the hegemony of the transparent (Glissant 1997; Blas 2018; McGlotten 2016).

Our feels and thoughts, which is to say our study, assembled around a few key themes: ethnography, art, and activism; the abolitionist potentials in their coming together; the dislocation of Black queer anthropologists in the academy and the discipline; the complex sociality of ethnographic practice, relationality, and community accountability; and the need for another/Black queer nonuniversity, spaces for study, and the recharging of resiliencies.

In addition to the work we have cited, we have also included suggested further reading in Black/queer anthropology in our bibliography. This noncomprehensive list features work from within and without anthropology that we have found especially inspiring, including some of our own accomplishments of which we are particularly proud.

Shaka McGlotten

SHAKA MCGLOTTEN Okay, welcome doctors. To start: one thing that really struck me is that everyone here has a practice, everyone is a maker, and people came to anthropology through these different paths. There is a long history of Black and queer art, activism, and nonacademic scholarship combined with practice. Anthropologists like Katherine Dunham, Zora Neale Hurston, and cultural workers like Marlon Riggs or Audre Lorde all come to mind. How do you understand those more creative practices in relation to your ethnographic practice?

NIKKI LANE I can't say that I currently have a sustained public-facing creative practice. I do some work outside of academia, but ultimately, it's my ethnographic work that makes it easier to connect with people who are outside of academia. I found ethnography to be a really rich site to bridge those gaps between academia and "the real world." People get things in important ways when you tell them a story about *this* specific place-time you've gone to, talk with them about the experiences you had in that place. Ethnography lends a unique insight into a different way of being or understanding or seeing the world. They get it in a way that, if you enter into conversations strictly from the perspective of theory, it can really alienate people who don't understand that vocabulary. So I found my ethnographic work to be crucial—integral—to the work that I do outside of academia and a really amazing way to bridge the gap between the academy and those not situated there.

KWAME OTU I'm thinking about how ethnography became the vista through which I accessed activism. Ethnography in Ghana, and working with queer communities, in particular, somehow became the gateway into an activist world. Engaging Ghanaian activists in the Ghanaian queer movement allowed me to rethink ethnographic method. I became quite attached to the idea and practice of activist ethnography. I have always had a complicated position with ethnography and activism. It's hard to even determine where my ethnography ends and where my activist commitments begin because, on the one hand, I know ethnography exposed me to this whole new world of activism. And on the other hand, I feel that my ethnography has become activist work, especially in the Ghanaian context.

SHAKA Could you say a little bit more about where ethnography ends and activism begins? Activism takes many forms, but one is the way you might establish your voice, establish a presence in some kind of space. And for me, ethnographic praxis is fundamentally oriented around attunement. It's listening, it's becoming as receptive as possible to whatever is happening.

KWAME I think that's the difficulty; it's hard to draw the line between where activism starts and where ethnography ends. You're talking about attunement, and I think in a way activism is quite about that, right? It invites us to be sensitive, or it activates our senses, if you will, to certain social situations. In my ethnography, there is already an activation of the senses to certain things, to certain realities—it might actually already be activist. There may not be any line whatsoever between ethnography and activism. Of course, there are professional or other designations that distinguish activism from ethnography, but in my mind having worked with NGOs in Ghana and with people who are deeply rooted in grassroots queer politics and environmental politics, I'm beginning to see the ways in which I managed to enter those worlds was because of ethnographic practice. Because like you said ethnography somehow attunes us, it massages our senses to context, and it may be that the distinction between activism and ethnography becomes very thin.

LYNDON GILL I wrote a little bit in the conclusion of my book *Erotic Islands* (2018) about my distaste for the term *ethnography* insofar as its practice has been historically connected to a particular kind of surveillance for purposes of domination. This does not mean that I do not deeply value participant observation as a method; following John Jackson's lead in *Thin Description* (2013), I just try to decouple the two, though I recognize that there's this relationship between them that gets taken for granted. I am not interested in writing/mapping/exposing the intricacies of a race/people/culture for consumption or domination by folks not of those groups. To my mind, *that* is still the (now unspoken) intention of ethnography inherent in its etymology. Still, it's great that we bring activism into the picture because there's a through line there between the activist and the anthropologist, I think.

Shaka, when you talk about Katie Stewart's (2007) work and pedagogy and what it means to be in an open/receptive space it sounds so similar to Kwame saying that anthropology and activism and perhaps activist anthropology is a kind of consciousness and openness to what is happening in the world. That's also the place where artistry comes from; that's the place where the best activism comes from; and that's where anthropology is at its best. The organizer who's reading the room, who's attentive to community, who's open to suggestions, is a lot like the anthropologist or the artist who is in a zone of suggestion open to other human beings, but also to spirit entities. These are the moments when the ancestors are trying to say something through you. That is the space when we're at our most powerful, when we're attuned in that way.

So, I do found-object installation work and I write poetry. I do these things because they feed my intellectual and spiritual self more than most scholarly academic texts. In fact, it's the texts written by anthropologists who are also reading literature, making visual art, or writing poetry that speak to me the most. "Ethnographic" stories land most beautifully and delicately when they are written by someone who's invested in the artistry of writing or another kind of artform like constructing objects. When I get frustrated while writing, I have these things I want to paint, things I want to glue together; they may or may not become something, but let me hammer a nail into something and just that act opens a passage to another kind of knowing. It makes my body feel different and then I can think differently. It helps me get out of being in my head all the time. The artistry is what sustains me and also what makes the work more interesting. Not just mine, but the work that I love by visionary artist-anthropologists like Gina Ulysse (2002, 2006, 2008, 2010, 2015), who is living and thinking fully in her art practice. And that's why her work hums to me—because it is an artist who is writing it!

MARSHALL GREEN First off, thank you all for inviting me to be a part of this conversation! I often feel there is no disciplinary home space for me ("disciplinary home space"? Sounds like prison . . .). I am comfortable now having relinquished all desires for the illusion of a disciplinary home that's good to us! In fact, I relinquish my allegiance to all of "the disciplines"! This is not to say I'm antidiscipline as discipline, for the writer, artist, scholar, lover, is essential. Particularly for those of us who are storytellers, practice and play must be the heart of our discipline. It is in these moments of practice and play that we stumble upon that *new sound*; it is the zone where we might touch that *something else to be*. As my teacher Ruthie Wilson Gilmore has argued, "abolition is practice!"

So what does practice have to do with ethnography? EVERYTHING! Ethnography is a method that asks us to not simply write down our meticulous observations, all that THICK description to help the world get to know "the other" (which is usually me and people like me). Ethnography is about relationship-building and that requires practice.

Many discussed the relationship between their work and their activism as Black queer people. I am a founding member of BYP100 (Black Youth Project), an organization that follows in the order of the Black Radical Tradition while also expanding our commonsense notions of what the Black Radical Tradition is and can be, by centering Black queer healing (Green et al. 2018; Green and Taylor 2018). What often gets forgotten in the heat of white supremacy and anti-Blackness is that Black people who want freedom don't really want to fight, we want to win, so that we can finally REST! And I believe in that rest we will find healing.

SHAKA I want to make stuff that activates. And it is a struggle to find a genre and objects, too, because right now I'm at a moment where I don't want to have *a thing*. I'm looking for the genre that can accommodate an object that isn't singular.

Nikki, you got your summer school, your Instagram videos. You were the first person I met—we met in 2017 at AAA [the American Anthropological Association conference]—who had what seemed like a successful alt-academic thing going on. First of all, you were alive—

NIKKI —which a lot of academics—

SHAKA —are just very tired, and you were alive. I was like, why are you still alive, and you're like, well, "I don't have a full-time job." And then you're like, "I don't want one." Oh, it was like a miracle to hear that. I admire you, Nikki, as someone who has constructed themself as a public intellectual out there like, "Hey, world, I will meet you here." How did you get to that?

NIKKI I think I entered into the academy not wanting to be in the academy. I never wanted that for myself anyway, but when I got to the stage where it was time to apply for jobs, I got caught up in the academy's discourse: "You're almost done. Great! Now, you're supposed to get a job in the academy. Apply to all these places and pray you don't end up in the middle of nowhere." I got kind of wrapped up in that, along with a lot of us, you know. But I remembered at some point—around the time when it seemed that, despite a book, despite the years of teaching, despite having carved out a niche in the field, I wasn't going to land on the tenure track—that I never entered a PhD program so that I could go into academia anyway. I entered it because I wanted to write, I wanted to read, I wanted to think, I wanted to teach—those were the things that I wanted to do. I didn't necessarily need it to be connected to an institution to do that.

It's funny because now I do have this tenure-track academic gig in Atlanta, which gave me the ability to move closer to family, gave me a full-time gig, gave me great colleagues, and an academic home—it's great, I get to be rich auntie now—but—

[WE CLAP AND SNAP]

Thank you! But I will say this: [BLACKDACTED] even with this good job, I *still* think academia might be trying to kill us. And I mean that in the worst way possible. I think they may be trying to kill our creativity, I think they're trying to kill our spirit. I think they're trying to erase us, I think they're trying to stamp our queerness out, and I want to remove myself from that [BLACKDACTED]. Teaching at a PWI [predominately white institution] was the most hostile experience of my adult working life. I feel PTSD around it. So, for me this academic thing was really just a *part* of what I wanted to do, so I'm doing it, but I'm still always thinking about how I plan to get out of it. Being in the public is one way to do that. My public intellectual work is centered around engaging projects that I believe in, engaging in places where I know I can be a change agent, where I feel like I can change or shape the experiences of at least one or two people, you know [BLACKDACTED]. But it's a dance and it's complicated.

MARSHALL So, along the lines of what Nikki was saying, the reason that I even went to get a PhD was because I had a professor in undergrad saying to me, "You know, this is a job you can have, and you won't be rich but you'll never be poor again" and, for me, as a person who came from a working-class background, that is what appealed to me about this profession. It seemed really safe and secure, like a place where I could be and create and not be a starving artist, right? The longer I've been in the academy, the more I don't think it's worth it. I don't think the security is worth what we're naming and talking about and that's the institution, the academy's ability to discipline, to crush our creative spirit and our ability to just be in relationship, in right relationship with other people. And that's one of the reasons—to go back to your question about ethnography and creativity—that ethnography appealed to me.

The way I came to anthropology was through visual anthropology specifically; I did the master's program in visual anthropology at USC [University of Southern California] while completing my PhD in American studies. I was twenty-five, and I was stressed out in my own gender journey, still figuring out who my people were. I used my master's project, which later became the short film *It Gets Messy in Here* (2011), to build relationships with other gender-nonconforming Black and Brown folk. Here we are ten years later, and I realize just how much has changed and stayed the same. At a recent screening, a student said, "It's so interesting that no one identified as nonbinary, because that's the language I'd assume . . ." I had to remind everyone that nonbinary was not part of our vocabulary ten years ago! And still we find ourselves in boxes. Sometimes we are also the ones who've set the trap! My dissertation was interested in Black LGBT space and place in South

Central LA post HIV/AIDS. While this future book/four-hundred-plus-page dissertation is important, it will never circulate in the same way *It Gets Messy in Here* can. There are many ways that a thirty-minute film about gender identity is more accessible than a four-hundred-page manuscript. They are both important kinds of work and have the ability to move different ways and move people in different ways.

In order to be a good ethnographer, you have to know how to interact and relate to other human beings. I think a lot of us in the academy don't have that skill set, and we don't know how to relate to each other. We're very awkward and there's nothing wrong with being awkward! But there's something about ethnography that actually wants us to practice being in relationship with other people, and I think that is one key to creativity—relationship. The ability to think, wander, dream, build, write, and more with other people requires a creative praxis. Another reason why ethnography is so appealing to me, and I always say this to students: ethnography is essentially "a deep hanging out" and what a wonderful job it is to hang out—that should be everyone's job. By hanging out, talking, and just being with people you get to know others AND yourself better. That's wonderful! I started my graduate studies in an English PhD program, and the main method in that field is gossip, I mean, close reading. I can't with that lesson—close reading—because I'm not relating to another person. Words are powerful and they can guide and even save, but it's not like being able to touch someone or someone looking you directly in your eyes and saying, "Hey, you misrepresented me!" There's a greater need for accountability in ethnography because of its liveliness and the fact that what WE do in "the field" is not always separate from what WE do at home. We have to seriously consider the real-life material ramifications of our bodies and work as ethnographers who are also activists, organizers, and artists, who want a world that is not anti-us.

LYNDON Marshall, I completely agree with your point, but I would expand the reach of that awkwardness a little further. I think a lot of folks go into anthropology in particular because we spent a lot of time watching people. And who spends the most time watching people? People who are not included or feel excluded or don't know how to socialize in particular ways early on. So, I think a lot of anthropologists are actually, ironically enough, really socially awkward. We use "ethnography" or participant observation as a way to smooth over some of those social anxieties that everyone feels, but we now have a motivation to find our way around it. I think that the discipline forces us out of that comfort zone, to push past that awkwardness and make something of it. And that's really instructive; we're forced to grow in conversation, in community with folks, with living people who can hold you accountable and that's a transformative experience. I don't want to idealize or fetishize fieldwork at all; being in the field—I've been stuck in the field for two years!—can be hellish. It can be hellish trying to figure out those social dynamics—there's a way that we are forced to negotiate all of those dynamics; the same dynamics that we have with the uncle you don't like and the auntie who—even worse—perpetuated violence against you. You are in relationship (or not) with them and trying to figure out how to manage that.

Not to be confused with family or even difficult friendships though, the academy can be so traumatic in no small part because it is a corporation, but unlike most actual multinational corporations, it tries to pretend as though it's something else. Once the scrim of that lie gets ripped away, that's, I think, where the trauma is. I think it's not seeing these institutions for what they are, them intentionally not presenting themselves as what they are, even as they are becoming, like M. Jacqui Alexander (2005) reminds us, increasingly more corporate and further removed from any kind of above-the-fray ivory tower ideology (though one wonders where the ivory came from in the first place?)—that makes for a really weird disconnect. That's gaslighting on an institutional scale! It's telling you it's doing everything for the good of society and humanity, but it's absolutely working in the service of the bottom line and it's a corporation, which we are seeing even more clearly now thanks to COVID-19.

And the university is certainly more concerned about its bottom line than it is about us. So, when academics say, "*We* are hiring in *my* department"; well, that's a problem. It doesn't belong to us. We need to be careful with the idea of "we" here because that kind of identification with an institution that was not built for us makes the trauma we experience in those spaces cut even deeper. Because you start to feel, even subconsciously, like this university or this department is "my family." We can start to think our colleagues, often because of the ways we associate with one another, are our friends. And often we're hanging out like cousins. Then all of a sudden, they seem to flip and they do something that is in the interests of the institution or their own careers and not at all in your best interest. And we feel so hurt by that. But many of these folks were never your friends and they certainly aren't your family. They were always colleagues. We just have a hard time recognizing that. I think staff at any institution understand that very well, but we get it twisted as academics and start to hang out with only other academics in "our" departments. We're in these confined circles so often. So when people we have not been seeing clearly or who have not been seeing us clearly do something that seems really fucked up and corporate to us, we're stunned by the trauma of that and left wondering: "Whoa, whoa, where did that come from?" But these institutions are set up to aggressively protect their own interests and to reward behaviors that also protect those interests no matter how violent.

We have to push hard to be able to do something else, to move in the opposite direction of so much institutional violence. And that will always be a struggle for those of us who are determined to live differently, more humanely, even in the belly of the academy. Some days I don't have the wherewithal for that kind of struggle, which is why we need larger intellectual, emotional, and artistic communities than the academy could ever provide. This is where our strength has always come from. And this is not to say that we do not also struggle with those communities too. I struggle with my own family nearly daily, but with love. What I am not going to do is struggle on my own against institutions and colleagues like they are my family. My actual family—given and chosen—is more than enough. We can figure out together how these institutions can be better, can be less abusive, but we don't have to make family to do that.

SHAKA I like this idea that gaslighting would be inherent to any definition of an institution. I've certainly experienced that at Purchase, where I'm very fortunate to have almost universally good colleagues. But I do these activisms for the institution, and it's like, "thank you," but then it's also "don't, don't do that, but thank you, but why are you making us look a kind of way"? I mean, I'm talking to you from the college, from [BLACKDACTED].

Nikki, you had this line in a previous conversation that struck me— you said "everything was so rich" when you were studying at the Center for African Studies in Cape Town. I've had experiences like that too in my intellectual and creative life, and I think that's what I want to cultivate now. And that means that I cannot sacrifice my body for this institution, I can't let them be slurping my marrow while reassuring me, "Look, we're making progress. Look, we're hiring." Look, there are three tenured black faculty in the entire School of Liberal Arts and Sciences. Against this scarcity, you say "everything was so rich"—like what does it mean to cultivate that? In the past, I would focus on how to make it rich for my students, and now I'm like how do I make it rich, as in fertile? How to make it rich as in, if I laid down, I'm nourished, I'm fed and not depleted, you know. I don't want to take a calcium supplement.

NIKKI I think we're still working through this, Shaka. And I think us having this conversation is so important because I feel like probably each of us has networks in which we have these conversations one-on-one, but I feel like it's so powerful to have this conversation together, you know? We have to keep thinking about what it means to do this work, and I feel like sometimes we're not doing it from within anthropology departments.[1] I want to think about what it means for us to build something to provide this kind of rich experience for others who want to do this work with us and be in relationship with us. I want to keep thinking about that because I have been connected to things that I felt really enriched by, and I want all of us to be there, and I'm also like "what if we built some of these things ourselves?"

SHAKA You know that's going to be key. What if we built something like a Black Panther Party for Academic Self-Defense?

NIKKI What would it mean for us to get together every summer, bring some students who want to come through with us and, just get full off just being around each other for a couple of weeks and maybe we don't do shit, maybe we don't talk about a damn thing that's academic and we just like replenish and strategize, you know what I mean? I want more of that. Sometimes these things will show up as papers or works of art, but I'm like, they don't have to, you know? How can we get more creative? I want to steal the staples, à la Harney and Moten's Black study (2013). I want us to get creative with each other and be really generous with each other. But that's how you create the rich site—that's spoiled for richness—is through that generosity.

MARSHALL Nikki, I agree we gotta build these things ourselves and, for me, I spent a lot of my life doing organizing work, mostly political education, and before that I was sort of holidaying, sort of healing and tending to the transformative justice branch of BYP100. And that work is what brings me life, but I think that what I've learned is that everywhere I go, every university that I've been in, I always bring in BYP100 people to teach change, to teach "what is transformative justice," "what is enthusiastic consent," and so, for me, part of my work in the academy is shifting who gets to be the teacher and who gets to be seen as the person who holds knowledge. I always think that it's a miracle that I ended up in this position because I really don't like school, and nobody in my family made it to this level in terms of education. It means a lot to me and it doesn't mean a lot to me. The reason why it means so much to me is because of the resources that I have access to that I'm able to share with other people who may not have that same access. So for me too the university is never going to house us in this way that we are together right now, and the way that this conversation is sort of medicine, right, and we get to hear each other—it makes me feel less alienated and less alone in Williamstown, where I am very alone. But this kind of collaborative work, which is both work and like healing right, this is not going to be respected by our institutions. [BLACKDACTED]

I continue to push back against that, because I think one of the things that we can do, and that we are doing, is working with each other, talking to each other, collaborating like this, and I think that makes us stronger, and it makes us more fierce. But the other thing I wanted to say is that we have examples of people who are doing these alternative kinds of schools and spaces where it's like connecting to ancestors. I think about Sangodare and Alexis Pauline Gumbs in Durham, I think about my friend Prentis Hemphill is working on the Embodiment Institute.[2] So I agree with you, Lyndon, that yes, ethnography is colonial with all these things that are really messed up. I think one thing that is really cool about ethnography is that it asks us to be embodied, to sit with somebody, and so I don't know how many fields actually ask you to think about your own body with that kind of awareness.

SHAKA Thank you, Marshall. Kwame, this might be something that you might be interested in talking about because your research can do that kind of classic work of making legible, visible, and thereby legitimizing a social movement. Of course, there are complexities—like all the critiques of transnational human rights—but we'll set that aside and just say, look, doing this work and getting it published will make a difference in material ways to people, right? I wonder if you have a perspective on that because I think you and Lyndon, of all us, are most engaged in research in other parts of the diaspora outside of the United States.

KWAME I like how you are thinking about diaspora, but before I respond to that, I want to speak to pedagogy. We have a saying back home, which goes like this: "knowledge is not in the head of one." And that has always driven me to think about how I open my students up to other forms of knowledge, so, for example, COVID has revolutionized my ability to invite scholars from the continent to join the class, to come and speak to the students, rather than have them merely read a text about, you know, social movements in Ghana. I really want to encourage my students to think differently about how they ingest knowledge. There is something about truth production in anthropology, especially by white anthropologists, that is about a certain detachment from the truth—white anthropologists (and maybe some anthropologists of color too) often somehow convey this idea that they are producing truth, but are also detached from the truth. But what if we begin to embed ourselves in those truths, right, and not fall victim to claims to objectivism?

And that is one of the things that I, as someone who's from the continent (but who has lived in the United States for thirteen years now, so when I go back to Ghana, people see me as a diasporic Ghanaian), bristle against. In African studies, there are Africanists and there are scholars of African descent. What does that mean to our field and how do we challenge these provincialisms that continue to mar how we think about our fields? What kinds of generative conversations and interactions can be yielded when we refuse to submit to being an Africanist *or* a scholar from the continent? So one thing I've gravitated toward since COVID is to try to dismantle these categories. I bring in a lot of scholars from the continent to just have conversations with students and with my colleagues. But when I go back to the kinds of intellectual cultures that are actually being cultivated, I feel there's still a detachment. This is one of the things I've done at UVA [University of Virginia], I take Black students with me every year just so they can be in a place with Black people and experience what it's like to be there as a diasporic subject in Ghana, like what does it mean to be in a space like that, what does that do to you, how is that part of the intellectual journey you are undertaking? I'm not sure I answered your question, Shaka, but you know these are the kinds of things I'm trying to do in practice, activating them to worlds that they'd probably not have any touch with, worlds they have only read about, so they begin to live in these worlds rather than just read about them.

SHAKA Thank you. Lyndon, I'm going to give you some last words, activating worlds—you want to activate my world?

LYNDON To activate someone's world?! That's a lot of pressure, Shaka, I know it takes a lot to activate your world!

But what to say? I think about going back to this idea of building our own institutions, building meta institutions together, collectively imagining other models and not having to start from scratch to do it. Black lesbian feminists have taught us, pan-Africanists have taught us what it means to blur some of those boundaries between thinking about ourselves, as you know, African American subjects, Black subjects in America, versus Black subjects in other places. And what is it to connect ourselves back to the continent, culturally, socially. And so, to understand it as part of one world; that is diaspora as a concept and it is instructive for us to be able to think about how can we, as Black academics, Black queer academics, Black queer anthropologists, build relationship to each other in a world that's determined to reify borders, be they national, institutional or disciplinary, or genealogies mapped to set us apart. A relentless defiance of this kind of difference idolatry was one of the commandments Audre Lorde devoted her life to teaching us. So the African diaspora is actually a beautiful metaphor. That's a beautiful model that was forged under far more duress than we are experiencing now for the most part (though, of course, chattel slavery still persists and many of us are wearing its evidence right now). Stories that sustain the African diaspora are our sustenance, and the place that we can go for models on how this thing can work, on how to deal with difficult family issues, on how to think while gardening. How might that shift to thinking with the land help you to be able to sustain your thought and root your ideas in a different way?

Participant observation can be so instructive because it shows us really important lessons from the very people we're in conversation with about how they sustain themselves and how they build community institutions, how they organize, how they make art, how they love, how they pray. I think we too often get stuck in the same models and they're largely, you know, white heterosexual male models of operating and the academy disciplines us into behaving in these ways. It's beautiful for Shaka to say "let's just come together and talk; it doesn't have to be a panel"! It's great for us to invite each other and pay people to visit our classes, but also can we just have a conversation and build with each other? But one of the major barriers that we will have to face are the academics, even fellow Black queer anthropologists, who are completely committed to the *we* of the university and that familiar way of operating that may be killing them, but they are happily in these codependent, often abusive relationships with these institutions. Still, I have faith that we can imagine other ways to be with each other. Black queer anthropology is an institution that we can build that doesn't have to be housed in any particular space, but is rather all about us going back to

Marshall's point about being in right relationship to each other. Let's be playful. Let's be patient. Let's be open; it is going to require more artists than bureaucrats to build these Black queer meta-institutions.

SHAKA That is so beautiful and such a great way to end, and it really makes me think that maybe there is a bigger project down the road that isn't about some kind of output but is about coming together and just hanging out and having fun and listening and learning. Some kind of like capacitation activation, a capacity retreat.

NIKKI Dead ass before we get off this call, can we just agree to do this next month sometime and put our heads together to figure out, like, what we're gonna do, you know, like why don't we just figure it out?

SHAKA Agreed. It was such a pleasure to get to see all of your beautiful faces and, yeah, the Black Capacity Institute or something, that's what we need, right? We'll work on that.

Notes

1 None of us have full-time appointments in anthropology departments.

2 See https://www.sangodare.com/, https://www.theembodimentinstitute.org /, and https://www.alexispauline.com.

References

Alexander, M. Jacqui. 2005. *Pedagogies of Crossing: Meditations on Feminism, Sexual Politics, Memory, and the Sacred*. Durham, NC: Duke University Press.

Allen, Jafari S. 2011. *¡Venceremos? The Erotics of Black Self-Making in Cuba*. Durham, NC: Duke University Press.

Allen, Jafari S., ed. 2012. "Black Queer Diaspora." *GLQ: A Journal of Lesbian and Gay Studies* 18 (2–3): 1–220.

Allen, Jafari S. 2022. *There's a Disco Ball between Us: A Theory of Black Gay Life*. Durham, NC: Duke University Press.

Blas, Zach. 2018. "Informatic Opacity." In *Posthuman Glossary*, edited by Rosi Braidotti and Maria Hlavajova, 198. New York: Bloomsbury Academic.

Chinyere, Ukpokolo. 2016. *Being and Becoming: Gender, Culture and Shifting Identity in Sub-Saharan Africa*. Denver: Spears Media Press.

Cox, Aimee, Daná-Ain Davis, and Shaka McGlotten, eds. 2012. "Black Queer Anthropology." *Transforming Anthropology* 20(1): 1–102.

Gill, Lyndon K. 2012a. "Chatting Back an Epidemic: Caribbean Gay Men, HIV/AIDS, and the Uses of Erotic Subjectivity." *GLQ: A Journal of Lesbian and Gay Studies* 18(2–3): 277–95.

Gill, Lyndon K. 2012b. "Situating Black, Situating Queer: Black Queer Diaspora Studies and the Art of Embodied Listening." *Transforming Anthropology* 20(1): 32–44.

Gill, Lyndon K. 2014. "In the Realm of Our Lorde: Eros and the Poet Philosopher." *Feminist Studies* 40(1): 169–89.

Gill, Lyndon K. 2018. *Erotic Islands: Art and Activism in the Queer Caribbean*. Durham, NC: Duke University Press.

Glissant, Édouard. 1997. *Poetics of Relation*. Ann Arbor: University of Michigan Press.

Green, Kai M. (Marshall) 2011. *It Gets Messy in Here*. Documentary. http://drkaimgreen.com/kai-m-green-films.

Green, Kai M. (Marshall). 2016. "Troubling the Waters: Mobilizing a Trans* Analytic." In *No Tea, No Shade: New Writings in Black Queer Studies*, 65–82. Durham, NC: Duke University Press.

Green, Kai M. (Marshall), and Marquis Bey. 2017. "Where Black Feminist Thought and Trans* Feminism Meet: A Conversation." *Souls: A Critical Journal of Black Politics, Culture, and Society* 19(4): 438–54.

Green, Kai M. (Marshall), and Treva Ellison. 2014. "Tranifest." *TSQ: Transgender Studies Quarterly* 1(1–2): 222–25.

Green, Kai M. (Marshall), and Je Naé Taylor. 2018. "27 Interventional Healing and Accountability—BYP100 Healing and Safety Council." Healing Justice Podcast. Accessed September 6, 2021. https://healingjustice.podbean.com/e/27-interventional-healing-accountability-byp100-healing-safety-council-je-nae-taylor-kai-green/.

Green, Kai M. (Marshall), Je Naé Taylor, Pascale Ifé Williams, and Christopher Roberts. 2018. "#BlackHealingMatters in the Time of #BlackLivesMatter." *Biography* 41(4): 909–41.

Hartman, Saidiya. 2019. *Wayward Lives, Beautiful Experiments: Intimate Histories of Riotous Black Girls, Troublesome Women, and Queer Radicals*. New York: W. W. Norton.

Jackson, John L. 2013. *Thin Description: Ethnography and the African Hebrew Israelites of Jerusalem*. Cambridge, MA: Harvard University Press.

Jobson, Ryan Cecil. 2020. "The Case for Letting Anthropology Burn: Sociocultural Anthropology in 2019." *American Anthropologist* 122(2): 259–71.

Johnson, E. Patrick. 2001. "'Quare' Studies, or (Almost) Everything I Know about Queer Studies I Learned from My Grandmother." *Text and Performance Quarterly* 21(1): 1–25.

Lane, Nikki. 2011. "Black Women Queering the Mic: Missy Elliott Disturbing the Boundaries of Racialized Sexuality and Gender." *Journal of Homosexuality* 58(6–7): 775–92.

Lane, Nikki. 2018. "Narratives of Affect: Language and Feeling in Black Queer Space." *Journal of Language and Sexuality* 7(1): 55–76.

Lane, Nikki. 2019. "The Ethnography of Ratchet: Studying Language Practices of the Black (Queer) Middle-Class." In *The Black Queer Work of Ratchet: Race, Gender, Sexuality, and the (Anti)Politics of Respectability*, edited by Nikki Lane, 1–34. Cham: Springer International Publishing.

Lara, Ana-Maurine. 2020. *Queer Freedom: Black Sovereignty*. Albany: State University of New York Press.

Lorde, Audre. 2020. *Sister Outsider: Essays and Speeches*. New York: Penguin.

McGlotten, Shaka. 2013. *Virtual Intimacies: Media, Affect, and Queer Sociality*. Albany: State University of New York Press.

McGlotten, Shaka. 2016. "Black Data." In *No Tea, No Shade: New Queer of Color Critique*, edited by E. Patrick Johnson, 262–86. Durham, NC: Duke University Press.

McGlotten, Shaka, and Daná-Ain Davis, eds. 2012. *Black Genders and Sexualities*. New York: Palgrave.

Moten, Fred, and Stefano Harney. 2013. *The Undercommons: Fugitive Planning and Black Study*. New York: Minor Compositions.

Otu, Kwame Edwin. 2017. "LGBT Human Rights Expeditions in Homophobic Safaris: Racialized Neoliberalism and Post-traumatic White Disorder in the BBC's *The World's Worst Place to Be Gay*." *Critical Ethnic Studies* 3(2): 126–50.

Otu, Kwame Edwin. 2021a. "Decolonizing Freedom through Voodoo: Queer World-making in a Ghanaian Music Video." *QED: A Journal in GLBTQ Worldmaking* 8(1): 154–60.

Otu, Kwame Edwin. 2021b. "Heteroerotic Failure and 'Afro-Queer Futurity' in Mohamed Camara's Dakan." *Journal of African Cultural Studies* 33(1): 10–25.

Phillips, Rasheedah, ed. 2015. *Black Quantum Futurism: Theory and Practice*. Vol. 1. Philadelphia: House of Future Sciences Books / AfroFuturist Affair.

Shange, Savannah. 2019. *Progressive Dystopia: Abolition, Antiblackness, and Schooling in San Francisco*. Durham, NC: Duke University Press.

Sharpe, Christina. 2016. *In the Wake: On Blackness and Being*. Durham, NC: Duke University Press.

Spillers, Hortense J. 1987. "Mama's Baby, Papa's Maybe: An American Grammar Book." *Diacritics: A Review of Contemporary Criticism* 17(2): 65–81.

Stewart, Kathleen. 2007. *Ordinary Affects*. Durham, NC: Duke University Press.

Ulysse, Gina Athena. 2002. "Conquering Duppies in Kingston: Miss Tiny and Me, Fieldwork Conflicts, and Being Loved and Rescued." *Anthropology and Humanism* 27(1): 10–26.

Ulysse, Gina Athena. 2006. "Papa, Patriarchy, and Power: Snapshots of a Good Haitian Girl, Feminism, and Dyasporic Dreams." *Journal of Haitian Studies* 12(1): 24–47.

Ulysse, Gina Athena. 2008. *Downtown Ladies*. Chicago: University of Chicago Press.

Ulysse, Gina Athena. 2010. "Little Gina's Rememory #2: An Soudin (in Secret)." *Feminist Studies* 36(1): 174–79.

Ulysse, Gina Athena. 2015. *Why Haiti Needs New Narratives: A Post-quake Chronicle*. Middletown, CT: Wesleyan University Press.

Wekker, Gloria. 2006. *The Politics of Passion: Women's Sexual Culture in the Afro-Surinamese Diaspora*. New York: Columbia University Press.

Elijah Adiv Edelman

10

The Subject of Trans Lives and Vitalities

Queer and Trans Anthropological Object-Making

Trans is not a simple term or concept—either in anthropology *or* in today's transnational geopolitical and NGO landscape. Both *trans* and *LGBT* have increasingly been employed internationally as umbrella terms intended to be inclusive of gender or sexual identities and practices that deviate from cultural standards. Yet anthropological research on gender and sexual practices has established that regionally specific identities are themselves not static categories (e.g., Blackwood 1998 in Indonesia; Gaudio 2011 in northern Nigeria; Namaste 2011 in Canada; Sinnott 2004 in Thailand; and Weiss 2011 in the United States). Moreover, ethnographic work that has focused directly on the use of *trans* as an umbrella referent continue to warn of the dangers in doing so (as discussed in Boellstorff et al. 2014; Edelman 2020; Stryker and Aizura 2013; Towle and Morgan 2002; Valentine 2007). Finally, internationally and regionally focused community-produced reports show that LGBT-oriented projects often fail to capture discontinuities in lived experience, resulting in the erasure of profound structural inequities.

In this chapter, I disrupt a static notion of *trans* as object in anthropology *and* global NGOs, and argue instead for participatory, activist, or coalitional-based research models that center lived experience at the intersections of gender, race, class, and community. I begin by tracing a brief history of the myriad uses of *trans* in trans anthropology to show how queer (and trans) anthropology has challenged the singularity of a universal trans, even as "queer" and "LGBT" frameworks in LGB-dominated political organizations proffer a single-issue approach to trans rights out of step with the actual priorities of trans and gendered expansive people. I offer an alternative model, "trans vitalities," which emphasizes trans needs and lived experiences as the basis of knowledge—rather than holding out trans as an object (of study, or of transnational NGO articulations like "the trans community"). Trans vitalities challenges the international metrics that define and measure "quality of life" and instead takes up trans life-*making*. Writing against trans object-making and toward trans life-making, I center the relations of accountability that are obscured in research *on* trans and the trans community. A trans vitalities approach might offer a way to rethink trans object-making in anthropology—as in process, unfinished, messy, and, most of all, in coalition with trans and gender-expansive people as subjects of their own lives.

What Is Trans Life?

At the global level, there exists no single unifying category of trans or transgender experience or identity that could be understood as simply and accurately reflecting the immense diversity of gender expressions within and across nation-states. Gender-marginalized identities and practices—often housed within the umbrella terms *transgender* or *trans*—are perhaps best understood as referring to a shared experience of deviating from regionally valued or established categories of gender normativity. Increasingly these categories are understood as occupying a place within a binary wherein one's gender identity and gender expression are to be aligned with the gender assigned at birth or early in life. This lack of a single shared identity has, however, not preempted attempts at a globalized definition for gender identity and expression and, importantly, measurable implications for gender transgression (see also Shakhsari's chapter in this volume).

At the level of international governance, the Yogyakarta Principles—a set of guidelines emerging out of a 2005 international convening of gender and sexual minority activists, academics, and legal scholars—reflect a list of mutually experienced and identifiable human rights concerns based on sexuality and gender identity. This document defines gender identity as "each person's deeply felt internal and individual experience of gender, which may or may not correspond with the sex assigned at birth, including the personal sense of the body (which may involve, if freely chosen, modification of bodily appearance or function by medical, surgical or other means) and other expressions of gender, including dress, speech and mannerisms" (2007, 6). Importantly, there exists no global legal code that would compel nation-states or local jurisdictions to integrate or uphold any of the definitions or recommendations outlined in the Yogyakarta Principles. Instead, these documents have functioned to provide a shared set of goals or common discourses that can then be integrated into local laws and policies by invested stakeholders and social actors. However, given the scale with which these reports are to be applied, the language of these suggestions reflects a fundamental flaw in how primarily North Atlantic, Eurocentric, and Anglophone-based institutions have understood sexuality and gender identity at the global scale. These recommendations overwhelmingly privilege an understanding of sexual and gender minority rights or needs as located within the domain of domesticity and marriage. Moreover, the call for an increased reliance on the criminal justice system to address systemic inequities encourages policies and practices that function to harm—rather than support—trans and gender-marginalized communities.

The study of trans and gender-liminal identities and practices has relied on interdisciplinary research but also, notably, emerged from a focus on sexuality or queer studies. Importantly, cross-cultural anthropological and social science research have directly problematized identity categories such as "lesbian," "gay," "bisexual," and "transgender" as they are applied to populations for whom these are not salient identities or categories of practice (Boellstorff et al. 2014; Stryker 2017; Stryker and Aizura 2013; Towle and Morgan 2002). Moreover, a great deal of attention has been paid to distinguishing how the study of sexuality differs in cross-cultural contexts (Boellstorff 2007; Hines 2006; Davidson 2007) and might differ from the study of specifically "trans" populations (Denny 2013; Serano 2016).

Queer and trans-focused anthropological research spans the subdisciplines of cultural, archaeological, linguistic, physical, and forensic anthropology.

Anthropological studies on gender and sexuality reflect critical differences in how sexuality and gender are, themselves, understood and experienced. For instance, Evelyn Blackwood (1998) notes how gender and desire among West Sumatran "women" differ from models used in the West. Similarly, Witchayanee Ocha and Barbara Earth (2013) focus on the ways in which gender models used in the North Atlantic contexts to frame trans experience do not necessarily work in the context of Thai sex workers. Randy Conner and David Sparks (2014), Aniruddha Dutta and Raina Roy (2014), Faris Khan (2016), and Susan Stryker (2012) identify how the notion of "transsexuality" emerges as a distinct form of Western Anglophone discourse.

Regionally focused ethnographic work on trans and gender-minority communities (such as Gaudio 2011 in Northern Nigeria; Sinnott 2004 in Thailand; Najmabadi 2013 in Iran; and Namaste 2011 in Canada) reflects the relationships of individuals to institutions such as marriage or policing as far more complex, and culturally specific, than as suggested by the United Nations Human Rights Council Report (UNHRC) recommendations.[1] This is perhaps most potently exemplified in trans research across Muslim-majority countries and practices across modern Islam. For instance, Afsaneh Najmabadi's work in Iran, as a nation-state that both partially subsidizes gender-confirming procedures and supports trans autonomy, directly critiques approaching trans as either a static subject position or experience. This directly undermines sweeping claims made by entities such as the UNHRC that these are spaces and places marked consistent and ubiquitous anti-LGBT social and legal practices (Najmabadi 2013). Furthermore, ethnographic work conducted among trans communities within the United States (such as Bolin 1988; Valentine 2007) also reflect discontinuities of lived experience among trans-identifying persons, resulting in an impoverished discussion of the relationships of gender transgression with religion, class, race, ethnicity, linguistic practices, and other cultural traditions. Overall, the picture that emerges from trans anthropology is of a nonunified, cross-cutting "trans" who refuses any singular definition.

LGB-Guided Trans Lives

Scholars and activists working on both sexuality and gender liminality within and across nation-states have noted that the "LGBT framework" has functioned to privilege subjectivities and desires that align with those valued in North Atlantic and Anglophone contexts (on sexuality, see Blackwood and Wieringa 1999; Jacobs et al. 1997; Lewin and Leap 2002; on gender liminality, see Driskill 2011; Johnson 2016; Kuntsman et al. 2014). For example, in many North Atlantic contexts social and legal frameworks may place importance on documentation that reflects one is married. Marriage in many other contexts, as well as the significance, importance, or even existence of documentation of marriage, may either not be a priority or even a goal for gender or sexual minorities.

In contrast to this single issue, the vast majority of research and reports on trans and gender liminal rights regionally, nationally, and internationally articulate a broad definition of trans rights. The issues of fundamental human rights, social justice, anti-violence, or maltreatment constitute a large segment of research and discussion in trans studies. Dean Spade (2015) and Paisley Currah and Lisa Jean Moore (2009) provide both a historical and contemporary analysis for broad trans political work. Similarly, reports such as by Elijah Adiv Edelman and colleagues (2015) provide a focused outcome for trans public anthropological work. Scholarship related to more theoretical discussions on trans rights includes Sally Hines and Ana Cristina Santos (2018) in the United Kingdom and Portugal; Susana Peña (2010) in the Miami-Cuban diaspora, and Louise Vincent and B Camminga (2009) in postapartheid South Africa. For instance, in Saffo Papantonopoulou's (2014) trans autoethnographic work in occupied Palestine, the reader is provided direct insight into the material and felt sensations of "the absent Palestinian" in Western theorizations of trans rights. Pinkwashing, Israeli, and Western-subsidized propaganda that champions Israel for their LGBT rights while demonizing occupied Palestine and Palestinians as inherently anti-queer functions as a distraction and justification for Israeli apartheid (Papantonopoulou 2014, 279). In this context, Papantonopoulou does not question notions of trans rights but rather considers how powerful nation-states, the Global North, and ideologies emerging out of Western academic traditions predetermine and delimit which trans persons get recognized for having what trans rights.

Ultimately, these studies reflect that trans rights tend to refer to documentation that reflects one's identity; access to medical care (state-subsidized or private); freedom from violence or exclusion from family and community life; increased access to education, employment training, and affordable housing; decriminalization of gender transgression; "survival crimes"; labor viewed as sex work; and gray or informal economic work.

Trans rights also include attention to state-sanctioned violence—including persecution, torture, and killings by both state and nonstate actors—and state-sanctioned or complicit tolerance of cruel and unusual punishment in state or privately maintained facilities. Access to health care, including access to gender-affirming care *and* general health care, and HIV/AIDS treatment and prevention (Poteat et al. 2015; Winter et al. 2016) are also dominant needs and rights expressed across different cultural landscapes.

The "LGBT rights" model, understood as primarily an issue of recognition, has had a well-documented deleterious effect on the rights and empowerment of trans persons across multiple cultural contexts. Crucially, the "State of Trans Organizing" report, the largest survey of global trans organizations yet conducted (Howe et al. 2017), also reflects that autonomous organizations led by members of local gender-minority communities were also far more likely to attend to and address the needs of those most marginalized. Specifically, trans rights organizations that were not housed within a larger LGBT organization reported their constituencies as including "low-income people (53.6%), sex workers (30.1%), ethnic minorities (27.4%), and people living with HIV/AIDS (24.7%). Smaller numbers also worked directly with migrants and refugees (14.3%), people with disabilities (12.0%), people involved in the criminal justice system (11.9%), [and] intersex people (7.0%)" (2017, 19).

In the North Atlantic context, the subjugation of gender-liminal subjects in lesbian and gay spaces emerged alongside the increased focus on a politics of respectability. Historically, gender-nonconforming, gender-transgressing, and trans-identifying persons—often locating themselves within sexual marginal communities—were a central part of sexually liminal community formation. In the late 1980s and 1990s, the push to include the "T" in the various LGB acronyms describing gender-variant and sexually diverse communities emerged simultaneously with larger structural critiques of gay and lesbian rights and feminist projects. While at one time these projects relied on a politics of difference to succeed, the inherent exclusivity of the politics failed to meet the goals of the members (Califia 1997). As exclusion and a politics of difference shifted to include queer of color critiques and responded to third wave feminisms, the addition of a T to LGB functioned to express the *inclusivity* of the movement (Green 2004). The way these post-identity politics maintain the aforementioned exclusion should be understood as "both illegitimate and politically problematic—coupled with the assumption that any exclusion is equivalent to any other kind of exclusion"

(Park 2002, 754). As a result, "difference" was collapsed so as to avoid the anxieties of addressing complicated structural exclusionary practices. Many formerly LGB organizations began to "add the T" to their organizational name and mission statement (Devor and Matte 2004, 180; Minter 2000). Ultimately, the inclusion of the T, along with Indigenous forms of gender transgression (such as Two Spirit) and other distinct categories of identity and expression would fulfill only the appearance of inclusion rather than evidence of an engaged and sustained commitment to trans, intersex, and Indigenous gender identities, or their rights.

Conceptualizing Trans Vitalities: What Constitutes Trans Quality of Life-Making?

Just as trans does not exist as a singular category, neither does trans quality of life. In order to address the complexity of trans life and advance the needs of trans people, researchers must deprioritize their own interests or evaluations when considering quality of life metrics and instead follow the lead of trans subjects and what counts as meaningful or quality trans lived experience. I call this approach to centering trans life-*making* "trans vitalities."

Rather than appealing to discourses of "success" or "struggle," trans vitalities calls for a rethinking of how researchers and policymakers approach the quality of trans lives. A framework of trans vitalities requires that we always keep in our analytic that these discourses also prioritize accumulation of capital, social and material, above life. Trans-specific research holds trans as the object of study; frameworks of trans vitalities recognize trans as a subject position populated by subjects. What this means, logistically, is that projects that seek to attend to trans communities of practice must integrate and support ways of doing and being that go beyond existing categories or set notions of perceived impacts of gender transgression. Agencies and laws seeking to aid the imagined trans community must integrate the bodies and practices that mainstream LGB civil rights groups abandon.

Drawing on my own recent analysis of trans coalitional work in Washington, DC, I illustrate some of the components of this approach in what follows, showing how frameworks of trans vitalities—models that foreground the knowledge of trans persons—are divergent, overlapping, contradictory, and necessarily messy.

Coalitional over Community-Based Research: A Washington, DC, Case Study

As a case study exemplifying the dangers of focusing on the trans community, I focus in this section on two overlapping research projects on trans coalitional work of which I was the lead researcher in Washington, DC: (1) a series of community roundtables and mapmaking conducted among trans-identifying persons in Washington, DC, and (2) the design and implementation of a large-scale DC-focused trans community needs assessment (DCTNA) survey. Taking David Valentine's critique of the concept of transgender as holding a static meaning at the benefit to those that are believed to know best, I call for an even further smudging of this category. I argue here for replacing the concept of trans *community* with trans *coalition*. The notion of community allows us to hypersimplify the messiness of life and group individuals into artificial categories within which we think they fit. A coalition is, in contrast and by design, constituted intentionally by individuals who share an investment. The intentionality of a trans coalition highlights that being trans around other trans people does not necessarily create community—it only reflects proximity. Rather, a trans coalition is constituted by various social and political actors who may share a trans identity but not a lived experience.

In early 2010, members of the DCTC, including myself, began what would become a three-stage process to produce the largest US city-based, trans-specific community-produced trans needs assessment project. Within this needs assessment project, I functioned as a grant writer and fundraiser, co-organizer and data analyst. The project was deployed to ascertain and document the issues with which trans spectrum persons in DC were concerned. During each roundtable we—typically myself and another co-facilitator—requested participants draw a map of a "trans DC" from their perspectives. Following the mapmaking activity, participants discussed their maps, addressing what they drew and, in some cases, explaining in great detail why they included what they included. At the close of each session, participants were asked to identify the issues or concerns they believed to be of importance when describing the needs of trans spectrum persons living in DC.

Importantly, the data collected during the roundtable discussions and mapmaking activity reflect that trans lived experience cannot be captured through just interviews or a survey. Rather, as the two maps exemplify, there is no singular "trans DC." As seen in the map in figure 10.1, Brett, a white and trans masculine–identifying Washingtonian, depicts the trans population in Washington, DC, as being diffuse, literally dotting the land-scapes of the city alongside greater concentrations of what they refer to as "all others." There is no single or easily identifiable location in which one could see "trans community." As seen in figure 10.2, Cameron, a Black and trans feminine–identifying Washingtonian, depicts a version of Washington, DC, that is packed tight with life. The images we see reflect the complexity of life; to be trans is not the totality of one's self.

This kind of mapping moves away from normative cartographic meth-ods of geographic information systems and objective scientific means and instead utilizes conceptualizations of space and place with which to visual-ize the city as lived. The act of map production encourages participants to consider how they fit in within the city, both physically and metaphorically. Additionally, we utilized this notion of "radical cartography" as a means to "actively promote social change" with the resulting research (Bhagat and Mogel 2007, 13).

The themes included in maps and mentioned in discussions referred to areas and experiences of the city that were connected to circulations of friendship, support, affirmation, and struggle, often as contrasts to the vio-lence of other elements of the city. In many of these contexts, such as the significant representation of sex work(er) strolls, a lack of access to sustain-able employment, and the historical pathologization of feminine bodies of color coalesced to criminalize bodies viewed as out of place. Importantly, even for those occupying social and political positions relatively supported by the nation-state, the impact of sex work, whether as one's form of em-ployment, the source of the criminalization, or as a productive ground form which to organize politically, emerged as a core organizing principle. Radi-cal cartography thus showed, ethnographically, trans DC as a live coalition rather than singular trans "community."

In response to a consistently articulated desire during the roundtables for a larger DC-based trans-focused activist project, we also chose to im-plement a large-scale needs assessment in the form of a survey. We based the language of the DC Trans Needs Assessment (DCTNA) on issues raised during the roundtables, as well as those in nationally used LGBT-specific surveys, such as the joint 2011 survey produced by the National Center for Transgender Equality and the National Gay and Lesbian Task Force, as well as federal census questions and community-produced surveys used in local

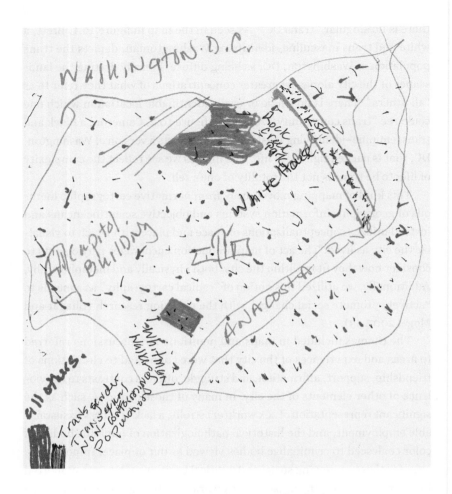

10.1 Brett's map of Washington, DC. (Property of author)

needs assessment projects, such as the 2007 Virginia Transgender Health Initiative Study and the 2000 Washington Transgender Needs Assessment Survey. After two rounds of internal testing, the survey in both English and Spanish was released in both electronic and paper form in May 2012 and was closed in May 2013. Upon closing, 624 surveys were completed, with a total of 521 surveys qualifying for inclusion in the data analysis. In November 2015 we released *Access Denied*, a 104-page executive summary examining the survey data.

The results from the DCTNA reflected a large cross-section of what trans might "look like" and provided data that we now had documented in

10.2 Cameron's map of Washington, DC (Property of author)

a form more readily acknowledged as valid by policymakers, researchers, and other direct service providers. Approximately 63 percent of survey respondents identified as trans or gender-nonconforming and were assigned male at birth, and approximately 37 percent identified as trans or gender-nonconforming and assigned female at birth. The racial demographic breakdown for the survey was approximately 59 percent respondents of color and 41 percent white respondents. Over 46 percent of respondents reported earning less than $10,000 a year, compared to only 11 percent of Washington, DC, residents as a whole. Trans persons of color, particularly trans women of color, reported the greatest economic hardships among those we surveyed, with 57 percent making less than $10,000 a year. Twenty-five percent of Black participants and 70 percent of Latinx participants reported similar hardships. Seventy-one percent of trans masculine persons reported attaining a higher education degree, compared to only 29 percent of trans feminine individuals. Yet, as useful as these data might be, I want to stress that the community-produced maps collected in the first phase of this project elucidate lived experience in ways that metrics collected from the survey cannot. And so while I use data here, I do so while simultaneously critiquing the use of big data to measure a livable life (see also Manalansan's chapter in this volume).

Indeed, were one to analyze the data collected in this survey in the absence of the roundtable discussions and mapmaking activity, it would appear that, with few exceptions, the trans persons that participated in this survey have a dismal "quality of life." Variables such as yearly income and HIV status are factors that researchers and academics latch on to as a means of measuring "life's quality" and providing evidence that all is not equal. This is a point that cannot be emphasized enough: *the metrics that are used to define quality of life are the same metrics used to define suffering*. And yet, as ethnographers, we know that lived experience is not measurable by rates of poverty alone, nor is having class mobility evidence of living a good life. We cannot ignore the materiality of how resources are allocated according to need or how lacking housing, sustainable income, or medical resources is a quality-of-life issue. But we need to approach data such as those collected in the DCTNA in the context of community-produced maps. This reframing suggests that life is not measured by just income or health but, rather, is marked by cartographies of where one experiences belonging and where one accesses care and support.

A framework of trans vitalities foregrounds structures of power when approaching the variability of trans experiences. This foregrounding must include a persistent commitment in acknowledging that we do not exist outside of prevailing discourses of what is—or is not—valuable trans life. As demonstrated in my own DCTNA project, these discourses can prevent, rather than facilitate, explorations of livable life when metrics reduce livability to set categories. Instead, the fuller trans vitalities approach insists that we must start by considering all life as valuable. This approach is critical if we are to address why we continue to bear witness to an ongoing passive disavowal of suffering and death as it applies to bodies that have been marked as disposable. A framework of trans vitalities requires we take ownership in our roles in enabling that disposability. This ownership of power forces an intentionally disturbing recognition that we directly facilitate who may live and who may die. Trans vitalities offers a framework that values the messiness of lived experience as well as calling attention to the slippery ethics of research and LGBT activism. We create the very conditions that cultivate a kind of salvage resilience—celebrating trans persons who perform what it is we want to see—until they don't.

A Future for Anthropology: Applying Trans Vitalities

I offer this lesson in the complexities of a public, coalitional trans anthropological approach in order to rethink trans object-making in both academic research and LGBT rights activism. A trans vitalities approach builds on the insights of prior trans (and queer) anthropology that has shown us that *trans* is not a stable or universal concept, but rather must be animated by the local, specific, cultural, messy parameters of trans lives as they are lived in particular cartographies around the world. And yet that ethnographic project of particularization, too, is a project of capture, of trans object-making.

Academia, anthropology, and even queer and trans research cannot be plucked from their historical legacies of white supremacy, misogyny, anti-immigrant, and procapitalist approaches. As such, the ways in which a framework of trans vitalities unsettles how trans subjects are researched is one that also unsettles how we constitute and enact the discipline of anthropology. As ethnographers capturing and reducing the essence of life into text, we are the ones who distill subjects into objects that we then present as our subjects of study. Anthropology functions (now as it has historically) as much to question as it does to populate the notion of what might constitute the Other. This process further delimits legitimacy, illegality, and, ultimately, the erasure of vulnerable life from our work. The same formations of neoliberal self-making that are lauded across our own lives equally taint our ethnographic research and in the ways in which we author the objects of our work. Often, we reflect on the cohesion of identity as a means to characterize experience. This is perhaps a core flaw inherent to all academic research.

However, in doing so, we willfully ignore the radical possibilities of embracing and celebrating the variabilities of lived experience as promised by both prevailing discourses in anthropology as well as social justice movements.

Trans vitalities is not simply a refusal or disavowal of projects of normalization or the commodifiability of "trans rights" but rather a vigilance against the violent homogenization of the heterogeneity of trans lived experience in queer and trans activism *and* anthropological research. Applying a framework of trans vitalities to anthropological and ethnographic work, regardless of topical focus, requires that we radically shift how we measure quality of life. Time, space, bodies, and action are all variables that cannot be overlooked or merged to fit scalable "rights frameworks." Within a framework of trans vitalities, the failure is with the measurement; it is not with the bodies or subjects who fail to reify and produce the proper citizen-subject. Rather the researcher, the academic, the social service worker, and the LGBT rights organization are the entities that have sustained systems of inequity. The boundaries that differentiate good from bad are often based on the desire to discipline and manage the bodies and subjects under consideration. Programs, organizations, and even trans research that focus on trans and gender-liminal persons may, in truth, be less invested in rethinking their own approaches that mold life into valued forms than in questioning how one provides real support. This requires the recognition that the notion of expertise on life is itself a mechanism of power and control: there can be no experts when we must continuously question our own interpretations of life.

Ultimately, trans lives are not preexisting objects worth writing about; rather, we must acknowledge that we write trans lives into being as subjects of our ethnography, analysis, or research. This concern is extendable to how we might envision trans anthropology as articulating with queer anthropology. As explored in this chapter, and as echoed across this entire volume, we cannot approach the term "trans" as having a stable referent. Moreover, as the chapters in this volume also make clear, the concept of "queerness" itself does not and should not hold a stable referent. This overlap—the erasure produced by applying the concepts of "queer" or "trans" to the subjects we are making into our objects—is the fracture point where queer anthropology and trans anthropology might do something else. This is where we can and should hold accountable those who produce research and provide services, trainings, or programming on queer, trans, or LGBT issues, asking who benefits from this work? This is not a means of identifying lapses in what topical foci or communities of practice on which we have yet to publish but, rather, is one of the first of many steps to clarify power, labor, and outcomes for trans lives within and beyond anthropology.

Here I echo João Biehl and Peter Locke's call for anthropologists to "resist synthetic closure and totalizing explanation and to keep our focus on the interrelatedness and unfinishedness of all human life—indeed of all life and of the planet itself—in the face of precarity and the unknown" (2017, 11). As a discipline and as social actors invested in sustaining work that is focused on the human experience as experienced by humans, this cannot be simply upended. I propose that our entry point into unfinishing queer and trans anthropological work is to look not at where we find meaning but at the discontinuities, deviations, and messiness that confuse our data. Meaning is made in the mistakes; we owe it to our discipline, our subjects, and ourselves as ethnographers to bring into our analytic fold the wonderous and beautifully productive inevitabilities of fucking up.

Note

1   See the United Nations Human Rights Council Report (UNHRC) 2015 report, "Discrimination and Violence against Individuals Based on their Sexual Orientation and Gender Identity," which provides recommendations for changing regional and national laws toward practices that ameliorate and attend to the rights of gender identity and gender-marginalized communities.

References

Bhagat, Alexis, and Lize Mogel. 2007. *An Atlas of Radical Cartography*. Los Angeles: Journal of Aesthetics and Protest Press.

Biehl, João, and Peter Locke, eds. 2017. *Unfinished: The Anthropology of Becoming*. Durham, NC: Duke University Press.

Blackwood, Evelyn. 1998. "Tombois in West Sumatra: Constructing Masculinity and Erotic Desire." *Cultural Anthropology* 13(4): 491–521.

Blackwood, Evelyn, and Saskia Wieringa, eds. 1999. *Female Desires: Same-Sex Relations and Transgender Practices across Cultures*. New York: Columbia University Press.

Boellstorff, Tom, 2007. "Queer Studies in the House of Anthropology." *Annual Review of Anthropology* 36(1):17–35.

Boellstorff, Tom, Mauro Cabral, Micha Cárdenas, Trystan Cotten, Eric A. Stanley, Kalaniopua Young, and Aren Z. Aizura. 2014. "Decolonizing Transgender: A Roundtable Discussion." *TSQ: Transgender Studies Quarterly* 1(3): 419–39.

Bolin, Anne. 1988. *In Search of Eve: Transsexual Rites of Passage*. Westport, CT: Bergin and Garvey.

Califia, Pat. 1997. *Sex Changes: The Politics of Transgenderism*. Jersey City, NJ: Cleis Press.

Conner, Randy P. Lundschien, and David Sparks. 2014. *Queering Creole Spiritual Traditions: Lesbian, Gay, Bisexual, and Transgender Participation in African-Inspired Traditions in the Americas*. New York: Routledge.

Currah, Paisley, and Lisa Jean Moore. 2006. "'We Won't Know Who You Are': Contesting Sex Designations in New York City Birth Certificates." *Hypatia: A Journal of Feminist Philosophy* 24(3): 113–35.

Davidson, Megan. 2007. "Seeking Refuge under the Umbrella: Inclusion, Exclusion, and Organizing within the Category Transgender." *Sexuality Research and Social Policy* 4(4): 60.

Denny, Dallas. 2013. *Current Concepts in Transgender Identity*. New York: Routledge.

Devor, Aaron H., and Nicholas Matte. 2004. "ONE Inc. and Reed Erickson: The Uneasy Collaboration of Gay and Trans Activism, 1964–2003." *GLQ: A Journal of Lesbian and Gay Studies* 10(2): 179–209.

Driskill, Qwo-Li, ed. 2011. *Queer Indigenous Studies: Critical Interventions in Theory, Politics, and Literature*. Tucson: University of Arizona Press.

Dutta, Aniruddha, and Raina Roy. 2014. "Decolonizing Transgender in India: Some Reflections." *TSQ: Transgender Studies Quarterly* 1(3): 320–37.

Edelman, Elijah Adiv. 2020. *Trans Vitalities: Mapping Ethnographies of Trans Social and Political Coalitions*. New York: Routledge.

Edelman, Elijah Adiv, with Ruby Corado, Elena Lumby, Robert Gills, Jona Elwell, Jason Terry, and Jady Emperador Dyer. 2015. *Access Denied: Washington, DC Trans Needs Assessment Report*. Washington, DC: DC Trans Coalition.

Gaudio, Rudolf P. 2011. *Allah Made Us: Sexual Outlaws in an Islamic African City*. Hoboken, NJ: John Wiley and Sons.

Green, Jamison. 2004. *Becoming a Visible Man*. Nashville, TN: Vanderbilt University Press.

Hines, Sally. 2006. "What's the Difference? Bringing Particularity to Queer Studies of Transgender." *Journal of Gender Studies* 15(1): 49–66.

Hines, Sally, and Ana Cristina Santos. 2018. "Trans* Policy, Politics and Research: The UK and Portugal." *Critical Social Policy* 38(1): 35–56.

Howe, Erin, Somjen Frazer, Melissa Dumont, and Gitta Zomorodi. 2017. "The State of Trans Organizing (2nd Edition): Understanding the Needs and Priorities of a Growing but Under-Resourced Movement." New York: American Jewish World

Service, Astraea Lesbian Foundation for Justice, and Global Action for Trans Equality.

Jacobs, Sue-Ellen, Wesley Thomas, and Sabine Lang, eds. 1997. *Two-Spirit People: Native American Gender Identity, Sexuality, and Spirituality*. Urbana: University of Illinois Press.

Johnson, E. Patrick, ed. 2016. *No Tea, No Shade: New Writings in Black Queer Studies*. Durham, NC: Duke University Press.

Khan, Faris A. 2016. "Khwaja Sira Activism: The Politics of Gender Ambiguity in Pakistan." *TSQ: Transgender Studies Quarterly* 3(1–2): 158–64.

Kuntsman, Adi, Jin Haritaworn, and Silvia Posocco, eds. 2014. *Queer Necropolitics*. New York: Routledge.

Lewin, Ellen, and William L. Leap, eds. 2002. *Out in Theory: The Emergence of Lesbian and Gay Anthropology*. Urbana: University of Illinois Press.

Minter, Shannon. 2000. "Do Transsexuals Dream of Gay Rights—Getting Real about Transgender Inclusion in the Gay Rights Movement." *New York Law School Journal of Human Rights* 17: 589.

Najmabadi, Afsaneh. 2013. *Professing Selves: Transsexuality and Same-Sex Desire in Contemporary Iran*. Durham, NC: Duke University Press.

Namaste, Viviane K. 2011. *Sex Change, Social Change: Reflections on Identity, Institutions, and Imperialism*. Ontario: Canadian Scholars' Press.

Ocha, Witchayanee, and Barbara Earth. 2013. "Identity Diversification among Transgender Sex Workers in Thailand's Sex Tourism Industry." *Sexualities* 16(1–2): 195–216.

Office of the United Nations High Commissioner for Human Rights. 2015. Discrimination and Violence against Individuals Based on Their Sexual Orientation and Gender Identity. Office of the United Nations High Commissioner for Human Rights.

Papantonopoulou, Saffo. 2014. "'Even a Freak Like You Would Be Safe in Tel Aviv': Transgender Subjects, Wounded Attachments, and the Zionist Economy of Gratitude." *Women's Studies Quarterly* 42(1/2): 278–93.

Park, Pauline. 2002. "GenderPAC, the Transgender Rights Movement and the Perils of a Post-Identity Politics Paradigm." *Georgetown Journal of Gender and the Law* 4: 747–65.

Peña, Susana. 2010. "Gender and Sexuality in Latina/o Miami: Documenting Latina Transsexual Activists." *Gender and History* 22(3): 755–72.

Poteat, Tonia, Andrea L. Wirtz, Anita Radix, Annick Borquez, Alfonso Silva-Santisteban, Madeline B. Deutsch, Sharful Islam Khan, Sam Winter, and Don Operario. 2015. "HIV Risk and Preventive Interventions in Transgender Women Sex Workers." *Lancet* 385(9964): 274–86.

Serano, Julia. 2016. *Whipping Girl: A Transsexual Woman on Sexism and the Scapegoating of Femininity*. New York: Seal Press.

Sinnott, Megan. 2004. *Toms and Dees: Transgender Identity and Female Same-Sex Relationships in Thailand*. Honolulu: University of Hawai'i Press.

Spade, Dean. 2015. *Normal Life: Administrative Violence, Critical Trans Politics and the Limits of Law*. Durham, NC: Duke University Press.

Stryker, Susan. 2012. "De/Colonizing Transgender Studies of China." In *Transgender China*. New York: Palgrave Macmillan.

Stryker, Susan. 2017. *Transgender History: The Roots of Today's Revolution*. New York: Seal Press.

Stryker, Susan, and Aren Z. Aizura, eds. 2013. *Transgender Studies Reader 2*. New York: Routledge.

Towle, Evan B., and Lynn Marie Morgan. 2002. "Romancing the Transgender Native: Rethinking the Use of the 'Third Gender' Concept." *GLQ: A Journal of Lesbian and Gay Studies* 8(4): 469–97.

Valentine, David. 2007. *Imagining Transgender: An Ethnography of a Category*. Durham, NC: Duke University Press.

Vincent, Louise, and B Camminga. 2009. "Putting the 'T' into South African Human Rights: Transsexuality in the Post-apartheid Order." *Sexualities* 12(6): 678–700.

Weiss, Margot. 2011. "The Epistemology of Ethnography: Method in Queer Anthropology." *GLQ: A Journal of Lesbian and Gay Studies* 17(4): 649–64.

Winter, Sam, Milton Diamond, Jamison Green, Dan Karasic, Terry Reed, Stephen Whittle, and Kevan Wylie. 2016. "Transgender People: Health at the Margins of Society." *Lancet* 388(10042): 390–400.

Yogyakarta Principles. 2007. The Application of International Human Rights Law in Relation to Sexual Orientation and Gender Identity. www.yogyakartaprinciples .org/principles_en .pdf (accessed September 5th, 2023).

Erin L. Durban

11

Doing It Together

A Queer Case for Cripping Ethnography

COLLECTIVE LIBERATION: No body or mind can be left behind—only moving together can we accomplish the revolution we require.

Sins Invalid

Queer anthropology has yet to contend in a substantial way with disability, ableism, and crip critique. The field has developed in a way that makes "disability" seem tangential, rather than intrinsic. This historical accident is especially curious considering that the pathologized category of "homosexuality" and the HIV/AIDS epidemic have shaped the work of multiple generations of queer scholars, including queer anthropologists. Whereas queer anthropology has been on the cutting edge of contributions to what is now interdisciplinary queer studies, scholars trained in English literature and humanities disciplines have been the ones on the forefront of articulating the relationships between gender, sexuality, race, nation, and disability in crip theory (McRuer 2006), critical disability studies (CDS; Minich 2016), and crip of color critique (J. Kim 2017).[1]

Queer scholars and activists have shown the compatibilities between queer and crip analytics, with shared investigations of normativities, pathologies, and the limitations of identity politics. While we might claim Ruth Benedict, Michel Foucault, Gloria Anzaldúa, and Audre Lorde as progenitors theorizing the intersections between these contemporary analytics, "queer, crip" theory was officially inaugurated in the early twenty-first century with publications like Eli Clare's *Exile and Pride: Disability, Queerness, and Liberation* (1999), Robert McRuer's *Crip Theory: Cultural Signs of Queerness and Disability* (2006), and Alison Kafer's *Feminist, Queer, Crip* (2013).[2] Elizabeth Freeman's theorization of "chrononormativity" (2010) might be included, alongside Kafer (2013) on "crip time."[3] Queer, crip theory approaches "queer" and "crip" as necessary contestations and provocations, and it cross-pollinates the intersectional and transnational insights of feminist, queer, and trans* theories and theories about dis/ability. Queer, crip theory critically affirms the value of queer and crip lives and futures and is integrally connected to progressive social movements. Despite its potential for activist scholarship in queer anthropology, contributions to queer, crip anthropology are primarily emanating from interdisciplinary activist scholarship and disability anthropology.[4]

My goal here is to make a queer argument for cripping ethnography. I do this by engaging crip theory and arguing that we must shift how we conceive of anthropological methods: away from the white, colonial model of fieldwork that maintains ableist anthropology and toward accessible methods that open up spaces for disabled anthropologists. Given our training and—for so many of us—bodyminds with the inclinations, skills, and other capacities it takes to excel in an ableist academy, the simplest (and normative) path toward building a queer, crip anthropology would be for queer anthropological scholarship to more fully engage crip theory, CDS, and crip of color critique. Engaging the theory generated by crip activists is important. But it is only the beginning—and is not the more radical epistemological transformation of cripping ethnography.

The challenge I take up here on the way to cripping ethnography is to dismantle and reconstruct the methodologies of our work—where ableism reproduces itself. Ableism is broader than discrimination against disabled people. As Qwo Li Driskill argues, "Ableism is colonial. It is employed to maintain an ideal body of a white supremacist imagination . . . heterosexual, male, white, Christian, non-disabled, and well muscled. It is an ideal with a long and troubling history inseparable from racism, genocide, misogyny, and eugenics" (Levins Morales et al. 2012, 84). If queer anthropologists commit to countering the ableism of anthropology, we must go beyond acquiring new objects or learning new analytics. A true queer/crip ethnography means radically changing *how* we do our work on the way toward a decolonial, antiracist, anticapitalist, feminist, and anti-ableist and otherwise liberatory anthropology.

Bringing a queer eye to the methodologies of queer anthropology, we can notice that our methods are not always as antinormative as one might hope. They adhere to the norms of sociocultural anthropological research in that a single anthropologist—though often queer/trans*—is solely responsible for all parts of knowledge production. Collaborators might be more common in sociocultural anthropology, including dynamic duos who are heterosexually married. But alas, although queer anthropologists might like to party and create anthologies together, in research we usually *do it alone* in our various fields.[5] Should we want queer disabled anthropologists in the mix, should we want to counter the effects of ableism as it is bound up with colonialism, racism, capitalism, xenophobia, and heteropatriarchy, then *we have to be more promiscuous and start doing it together*.

Crip Engagements in Queer Anthropology

As a first step, queer anthropologists might familiarize themselves with crip theory, CDS (which includes disability anthropology), and crip of color critique. Unlike the anthropology of disability, or even disability studies broadly, these fields move away from the objectification of disability and disabled people toward crip critique. With commitments to intersectional and transnational analyses that articulate the connections between ableism, colonialism, imperialism, racism, and militarism, crip critique opens up ways to think through disablement and disability beyond narrow legal definitions. These fields importantly begin with and center the work of feminist, women and femme, queer and trans*, and BIPOC disabled scholars, including the theorizing of activists and cultural workers who are nonacademics, academic-adjacent, or have academic appointments but write for audiences outside the academy like Patricia (Patty) Berne, Lydia X. Z.

Brown, Eli Clare, Qwo-Li Driskill, Nomy Lamm, Talila "TL" Lewis, Aurora Levins Morales, Stacey Milbern, Mia Mingus, Leroy F. Moore Jr., Leah Lakshmi Piepzna-Samarasinha, Alice Wong, and so many more that the names could fill this entire chapter.[6]

The possibilities are endless in terms of the connections queer anthropologists can make were we to fully engage these fields. Critical inquiries prompted by this expansive literature include (among many others) the debilitating violences of anti-Black racism (Gossett and Hayward 2020; Schalk 2018; Pickens 2019), slavery (Boster 2012; Barclay 2021), and colonialism and imperialism (Burch 2021; Erevelles 2011; Puar 2017); critical crip approaches to care work (Piepzna-Samarasinha 2018); the contradictory politics of cure (Clare 2017; E. Kim 2017); how dis/ability shapes categories of the human and nonhuman (Chen 2012; Taylor 2017); and the detrimental impacts of institutionalization and incarceration (Ben-Moshe 2020; Burch 2021; Clare 2017; Fritsch et al. 2022). What would anthropologists interested in the queer politics of medical "access" contribute to discussions of cure and institutionalization? How might the vast literature on care work in anthropology be challenged by notions that center queer mutuality and interdependence—or those that begin with eugenics? How would the theory generated by intersectional crip activism provide new insights to our scholarship about queer social movements? By engaging crip critique, queer anthropology would necessarily shift from studying disability, illness, and madness (as objects)—as it has "homosexuality" and HIV/AIDS—to substantially engaging and generating crip theory.

In this chapter, I conjure "queer, crip anthropology" as a necessary field of scholarship that brings together queer, crip critique with anthropological and nearby ethnographic scholarship. This nascent field might include queer anthropologist Don Kulick's collaboration with Jens Rydström on *Loneliness and Its Opposite: Sex, Disability, and the Ethics of Engagement* (2015), a book that combines historical and anthropological approaches to sexuality and disability in Sweden and Denmark. Tom Boellstorff, another established queer anthropologist and contributor to this volume, has also taken up the topic of disability in a variety of publications (e.g., 2020). But while queer engagements inform the path of his inquiries, this scholarship primarily cites disability anthropology and crip theory rather than queer theory. Queer, crip *entanglements* become more apparent in ethnographic scholarship by interdisciplinary scholars whose training is not primarily in anthropology—including S. Lochlann Jain (2013), Kelly Fritsch, and

Carly Thomsen (2021). These entanglements seem particularly important to a new generation of scholars in disability anthropology like Salih Can Açiksöz (2020), Sara M. Acevedo (2021), Cassandra Hartblay (2020), and Zoë H. Wool (2021). Karen Nakamura—whose books have been about sign languages, deaf social movements, and psychiatric disabilities in Japan (2006, 2013)—is likewise exploring these connections. Nakamura's yet-to-be-published research analyzes the construction of transgender subjectivity through disability in the category of gender identity disability (GID) articulated by activists in transgender social movements in Japan.

My initial contribution to this field of queer, crip anthropology came out of relatively traditional ethnographic fieldwork (with a single researcher using their own hypermobility to navigate informants' immobilities), before that was no longer possible for my bodymind. Unlike the book that came out of this fieldwork (Durban 2022), the article "Postcolonial Disablement and/as Transition: Trans* Haitian Narratives of Breaking Open and Stitching Together" (2017) explicitly engaged crip theory as queer, crip anthropology. By engaging crip theory and disability studies, I was able to ask different kinds of questions and make connections that were not possible when I followed narrowly conceived queer studies threads. In the article, I argue that the 7.0 earthquake on January 12, 2010, is the most prominent transition in Haitian transgender lives because of the ways that it altered bodies and social relations. I frame the earthquake as an instance of "postcolonial disablement"—the resulting damage to buildings and human bodies is directly related to Haiti's underdevelopment stemming from European colonialism and US imperialism. I elaborate this argument in the context of one self-identified transgender woman's life herstory and concentrate on the effects of breaking open (the shifts in gender embodiment and social life that have taken place in Haiti alongside the earth's tectonic movements) and stitching together (transgender Haitian strategies of imperfect reparation and survival).

That article took up disability studies in its intersections with trans* studies, both of which Jasbir K. Puar rightly assessed as "suffer[ing] from a domination of whiteness and contend[ing] with the normativization of the acceptable and recognizable subject" (2017, 42). Making a critical, intersectional break with these interdisciplinary fields, Puar draws on McRuer's (2006) conceptualization of compulsory ablebodiedness and queer/disabled existence and Clare's anticure writings (2013, 2017) that trouble medical intervention as the solution to "fix" transgender bodies. In this theorization of "becoming trans, becoming disabled," Puar proliferates the possibilities of trans* becoming beyond predetermined trajectories and calcified relationships in the white, liberal imagination. This opened space to think through the life events of "Kelly": specifically, how the earthquake resulted in Kelly's masculinization as she endured extreme injury and reparative surgeries. As Kelly relayed to me, "Of all the people who survived, I was the one who was most broken." Her situation raised the question: What happens for trans* people when injuries (or in other situations, chronic illnesses) and medical treatments have trans-ing effects that impact their embodied experiences of gender?

Building on this research, I began a second book project based on field-work in Haiti, focused on the imperial debris of plastic (inspired in part by the scholarship of Vanessa Agard-Jones on colonialism and toxicities in the Anthropocene). I was intrigued by the plastic work of the Atis Rezistans sculptors living in Port-au-Prince (http://www.atis-rezistans.com), who critique Americans and Europeans who use Haiti as a dumping ground for used items, plastics, and toxic waste. Atis Rezistans has convened the Ghetto Biennale International Arts Festival in their neighborhood since 2009—I had participated three times as an artist and researcher. The sculptures of Atis Rezistans contrast with the work of foreign artists at the biennale who imitate the "junk" aesthetic but whose underlying ideas replicate those of white environmentalisms: containment and purification, which resonate with eugenics. These foreign art projects miss the Black environmentalism and spiritual work of Atis Rezistans that incorporates plastic into representations of humans and spirits, ones who are cared for and tended to by the artists. My project, tentatively entitled "Queer Haitian Ecologies: The Trash Church and (Other) Plastic Bodies," explored how, rather than exalting a "pure" human body, Atis Rezistans represents value in Black bodies of the majority poor—"polluted," "toxic," "disabled," and "queered" (unnatural) bodies—as they are transformed by environmental racism, while working to create more livable futures.

I was excited by the ways engaging CDS, which again centers analysis of colonialism, racial capitalism, and heteropatriarchy, enabled me to begin to analyze how plastics unevenly help and hinder human life and alter the chemical makeup of human bodies. Mel Y. Chen's interest in "the marriage of bodies and chemicals" (2012, 1) and theorization of animacies that brings together disability, sexuality, race, and species is foundational to this approach. Amid the now-proliferating trans* studies scholarship on toxicities, Eva Hayward's scholarship (Ah-King and Hayward 2013; Hayward 2014) specifically reflects CDS sensibilities and takes up plastic animacy. Hayward argues that the "danger" of human intimacy with plastic is so often linked with "sex changes" (such as disruption of endocrine function, enlarged male breasts, early onset puberty in females, and inability to reproduce), so she implores queer scholars to lean into the sex panic and take up our interconnection with plastic molecules and other anthropologically and racially marked "nonhuman" estrogens as the basis for a new trans politics. Likewise, my plastics project takes up environmental illness (Alaimo 2010) and environmental injury (Cohen Ettinger et al. 2019) as the basis for solidarity politics in the Anthropocene—explicitly centering intersectional approaches to dis/ability in interdisciplinary inquiries about toxicity.

But grounding ethnography in disability means attending to the conditions and institutions in which our scholarship is produced. To my own neat narratives about research, then, I necessarily insert notes about the slowdowns, interruptions, foreclosures, and disappointments of working on crip time. Hayward's unpublished scholarship about plastics, for instance, has greatly shaped my own. However, I am not yet able to cite this work— and many other works in progress—because of ableist norms in academic publishing. For anyone who has ever mounted a tirade against the tyrannies of academic publishing, try adding madness, disability, and a chronic illness (or two!) into the mix.[7] Anti-ableist citation practices might need to go beyond standard publications, blogs, or even audio or video recordings, to include crip brilliance on social media and thick descriptions of conversations and interactions where this essential scholarly work is happening. For myself, I am not sure whether continuing research in Haiti is possible, even without pandemic conditions. Between the heightened insecurity that impacts the well-being and mobility of Haitians and the intensification of my chronic illnesses, the trajectory of my own research is . . . well, a giant question mark. As excited as I am about the potential of my "Queer Haitian Ecologies" project, I am also aware that—if we take the lessons of this work and the activism behind it seriously—we need to find creative ways to *crip* ethnographic practice in ways that do not only enable the most privileged among us. We need to counter the effects of ableism and (neo)eugenics in the university by opening up more spaces for disabled scholars who are not only white, middle-class, US citizens, nontransgender, or heterosexual.

Queer anthropology has yet to really consider the capacities of different bodyminds, especially the fact that mad, chronically ill, and other disabled scholars have all the usual challenges of nondisabled scholars in terms of academic knowledge production as well as a variety of diminished and fluctuating capacities that are difficult to acknowledge, let alone "accommodate," in the academy. Those who have faced debilitating illnesses and our elders who are aging into disability might be thinking about this predicament now for the first time. However, the queer disabled scholars of younger generations congregate in disability anthropology, which is relatively more attentive to these issues, and conduct the bulk of the access work for the American Anthropological Association (AAA). Queer anthropology is leaving these disabled scholars behind and our institutional practices risk reproducing missteps in anthropology and other disciplines that support scholarship *about* disability primarily by nondisabled scholars, rather than crip-centered critique. Thus there are ableist dangers in incorporating crip theory if we do not also address the multiple ways that disabled scholars have been shut out, erased, marginalized, devalued, disregarded (or given no thought at all), and deemed unworthy in our scholarly practices. Contending with these exclusions requires that we reimagine how to do the work.

Cripping Ethnography

How do we create models for ethnography from the recognition that disabled researchers and a greater diversity of bodyminds (Price 2015; Schalk 2018) are beneficial and necessary to decolonial, feminist, and queer anthropological knowledge production? I arrived at this question as a white, queer, disabled activist scholar who has been writing about ableism and anthropology and wants to move beyond critique toward new possibilities—and also as an embodied researcher who has faced challenges of the ableist academy. Before doing so, however, some work is required to outline the challenges of creating collective access in anthropology.

The usual concern about chronically ill and disabled anthropologists is how to "accommodate" us in an ableist discipline. In "Anthropology and Ableism" (2021), I instead focus on the underlying ableist mandates of fieldwork. I make a series of related claims to support the argument that ableism is inherent to anthropology's disciplinary formations, including that (1) the normate[8] anthropologist has a "nondisabled" bodymind and uses their own hypermobilities to navigate informants' immobilities; (2) the continuation of fieldwork practices from the colonial model of anthropology naturalizes able bodyminds, and, without intervention, will continue to reproduce an ableist anthropology; (3) the turn toward multisited fieldwork and therefore increased mobility has compounded the ableist pressures normative to the discipline; and (4) once disability became a proper and distinguishable object for anthropology, a line was solidified between "anthropologist" and "the disabled," thereby making *disabled anthropologist* a seeming conceptual impossibility.

Given these structures, as well as active discrimination against disabled scholars, it is no wonder that there are so few chronically ill and disabled anthropologists—in queer anthropology or elsewhere. Certainly, I have a personal stake in changing how we think about the place of disabled and chronically ill people in (queer) anthropology, but the implications of doing so are much broader: the majority of people with chronic illnesses, disabilities, or who are otherwise debilitated (Puar 2017) are poor and working class, BIPOC, queer and trans*, and from the Global South. Meanwhile, taking cues from Eve Kosofsky Sedgwick's theorization of "minoritizing" and "universalizing" arguments (1990), we should also consider that illuminating the normative underpinnings of anthropology, understanding how ableism shapes our lives, and embracing the unbearable possibility that we all might be or become disabled can help us collectively work toward a radical anti-ableist anthropology, that is broadly concerned with power and access in ways that align with decolonial, antiracist, feminist, and anticapitalist knowledge production.

Disabled anthropologists and our accomplices have already been experimenting with creating greater accessibility through ethnographic research methods as well as ethnographic form (photography, creative writing, performance, and sensory experiences).[9] Autoethnography (e.g., Kasnitz 2020) and digital anthropology (Boellstorff 2008) are perhaps better known than the more recently articulated "anthropology at home" (Gibson 2019) and "patchwork ethnography" (Günel, Varma, and Watanabe 2020), but the latter likewise offer rich possibilities for crip ethnography. Queer anthropologists have long conducted research where they already live, for various reasons, including the decolonial turn. While local fieldwork was not necessarily imagined as providing greater accessibility in terms of disability, this was one of our topics for the 2020 AAA Raising Our Voices panel "Disabled Voices in the Field: Towards Reimagining Anthropologists at Work" in which five out of the eight participants—Karen Nakamura, Sumi Colligan, Valerie Black, Rebecca-Eli Long, and I—identified as queer and/or trans*.

In that forum, queer, chronically ill, and disabled anthropologist Valerie Black stated:

One of my fieldsites was "local" to my long-term residence—in the SF Bay Area, and my other fieldsite was in Tokyo. Having a "local" fieldsite made doing fieldwork much more sustainable and accessible for me. But I swiftly recognized the implicit ableism that underpins what counts as a "real" fieldsite. It seemed like to others, my Japan fieldsite was my "real" (properly anthropological) fieldsite. . . . Anthropology is haunted by the figure of the "intrepid" (read: male, white, able-bodied, not a primary caregiver, etc.) anthropologist who can go anywhere at a moment's notice—and I think continuing to dismantle this entrenched figure of the "intrepid" anthropologist is very much an intersectional issue.

We discussed local fieldwork in relation to access to necessary apparatuses of health care and medical providers, the difficulty and additional costs of traveling, and the tremendous labor involved in working through accessibility in new locations (Acevedo et al. 2020). We also discussed the benefits of access technology like video calls to facilitate our fieldwork. During the pandemic, anthropologists have relied on access technology for research more than ever before, experimenting with remote fieldwork or ethnography from afar—though often with the belief that these are poor substitutes for the "real thing." This is a place where anthropology stands to learn in a significant way from disability justice projects.

These experiments are often undertaken as individual endeavors, hacks in accessibility for the lone anthropologist. Working collectively has the potential to create greater accessibility. Sharing the work means that when one or more collaborators are unavailable for a period of time—for any variety of reasons related to being sick, diminishing spoons,[10] caretaking, contending with ableist environments, and so on—there are others who have the capacity to carry things forward. Ideally it also means that people have *complementary capacities* and work together using their strengths as researchers. As anyone who has undertaken it will attest, collaborative research—like mixed ability or cross-disability organizing—is difficult, time-consuming, disorienting (if you are doing it correctly), but also incredibly rewarding.

Without ready examples of how to do cross-disability or even mixed-ability collaborations in ethnographic research, I embarked on an experimental collaborative ethnographic research project during the first summer of the pandemic. My goal was to work toward that (queer) anti-ableist anthropology, relying on what I have learned from cross-disability and mixed-ability organizing, disability anthropology, CDS, and specifically the principles of disability justice (Sins Invalid 2016)—including intersectionality, sustainability, recognizing wholeness, collective access, and interdependence. The accessibility considerations of this project are fluctuating, ongoing, necessarily imperfect, and incomplete. But for the purposes of thinking toward a queer crip ethnography, I want to share some of the collaborative aspects of the research design.

The project is about the University Grove faculty neighborhood of the University of Minnesota. I live in University Grove with my partner, Miranda Joseph, one of the primary collaborators. On the surface, the University Grove project does not appear to pertain to queer anthropology—or disability. University finance and development, land ownership, the racialization of space, histories of dispossession, and white liberalism are our primary objects of analysis. Yet our foundational training in queer anthropology and initial scholarly projects explicitly related to same-sex sexuality and gender transgression (Joseph 2002; Durban 2022), as well as ongoing engagement with queer and feminist studies, shape our inquiries, analysis, and relationships in the field. In this way, the University Grove project is arguably an experiment in accessible ethnography and part of the futures of queer anthropology (Boellstorff and Howe 2015).

Officially the University Grove project was the solution to offer research experience in my "Ethnographic Research Methods" course during the pandemic. This project enabled the continuation of fieldwork training in a way that I hoped would draw attention to dis/ability in the field and begin to interrupt ableist ideas about the right way to do anthropology. It also provided a collective opportunity for students to reckon with institutional racism after the murder of George Floyd in the Twin Cities in the moment of the Black Lives Matter movement and with settler colonialism as students attending a land grant university in the United States.

Enabling students to participate in ethnographic research from their various locations (e.g., "distance ethnography," "remote ethnography," "fieldwork from afar," and "anthropology from home") was the primary accessibility consideration. However, the research design necessarily reflected our access needs with disabilities, chronic illnesses, mental health issues, and a significant increase in caretaking and reproductive labor. Thus, we stayed in bed, at home, and close to home, and access technology facilitated our collaborative research. The student collaborators have accompanied us, and our neighbors, through our daily lives in University Grove and to the

University Archives reading room with the assistance of the internet, an action camera, a digital audio recorder, virtual maps, video chat, and video hosting platforms with captions.

The collective approach is essential to our ethnographic research redesign. Following the disability justice model of cross-disability organizing, the foundational research partnership between Miranda and myself makes the work possible and sustainable for a queer, crip household shaped by the usual impossible demands of the neoliberal university along with additional care labor, doctor's appointments, and time consumed with being sick and contending with ableist institutions. Not only could one person pick up work when the other was not available, the joint project keeps research on the horizon when it could get drowned out by life. We also have more than two dozen students as collaborators, with whom we share the responsibility—appropriately to a limited extent and with mentoring—for data collection and analysis. They collected data from Zillow, Google Maps, the university real estate office; participated in virtual and in-person neighborhood events; and conducted semistructured interviews with more than thirty current and former University Grove residents and people who work in the neighborhood. Through this collectively collected data, we have learned important ethnographic details; for example, the administrator who designed University Grove and was notoriously opposed to racial integration eventually sold his house because of the inaccessibility of its stairs. But we are also putting together arguments about how the University of Minnesota created housing inequality by creating an all-white neighborhood and maintaining a majority white neighborhood through the category of "faculty" as homeowners and that current debates about neighborhood politics tap into deep histories of collective action to maintain exclusive rights to the neighborhood and decrease housing density.

This collaborative approach provides multiple opportunities for researchers to develop a greater awareness of their own positionality. Everyone accounts for what they miss, notice, or understand in the field and the conclusions they draw in relation to their collaborators, as well as to give and receive support for this work. This process was facilitated by everyone having access to the same data and utilizing collective fieldnotes. In addition to recording observations, interpretations, analyses, and questions, the notes let collaborators who are unable to engage a research activity (like a walk around a neighborhood) continue to track the project. And when one of our student collaborators suddenly had to transition to using voice-to-text software after an accident, it smoothed notoriously difficult management of this technology in at least one area of her academic life.

Also in the spirit of collective access, the project centered mixed-ability research, taking into account different bodily capacities. For example, collaborators with greater sight capacity created fieldnotes from video footage from the action camera to provide a transcript for those who are blind/visually impaired to participate in collective analysis. Likewise, those with greater hearing capacity collaboratively created fieldnotes from audio files, notes accessible to those who are deaf/hard-of-hearing as the audio files are not. Because of the primacy of the visual in ethnographic research, the student collaborators found this audio engagement disorienting; they wanted to match the birdsong to the bird, the passing vehicle noise to a car, voices to faces, and so on. They were perplexed by sounds like the wild turkeys taking flight to roost in the oak trees above my house. Though these methods relate to the insights of anthropologists who are experimenting with sensory ethnography (e.g., Pink 2009)—who have argued that attention to senses beyond the visual are important to move past the object "fixes" that trouble our field— here they are specifically taken up as crip hacks for ethnographic research that acknowledge in a more explicit way our interdependence. Centering embodied experiences of research participants *and researchers* in an anti-ableist way, the project has successfully worked toward creating collective access by changing who can participate in ethnographic research. Remote and asynchronous participation in ethnographic research works around a range of immobilities—work schedules, transportation costs, caretaking responsibilities, visa requirements, fatigue, physical disabilities, and more.

Of course, while I have mostly highlighted the benefits and basic structures of anti-ableist collaborative research, we have contended with competing access needs in our project, as is often the case in cross-disability spaces. For example, the fieldwork footage that I recorded reflected changes in my gait from psoriatic arthritis. Flares of pain and stiffness resulted in a kind of Blair Witch Project camera effect: the movements made student researchers nauseous. We approached this without taking this footage that reflects crip embodiments out of the fieldwork experience. I upgraded the technology for greater visual stabilization. And affected students relied on the transcriptlike collective fieldnotes generated by their peers to participate in data collection and analysis. In this way and others, we altered the methods to respond to the unanticipated and shifting needs of ourselves and our collaborators as well as their input about what would positively contribute to the project.

DOING IT TOGETHER   239

11.1 Video still and photograph collage of University Grove project researchers and participants. (Property of author)

Overall, the University Grove project has opened up new spaces for intimacy within our partnership and our queer, intergenerational family as well as among our neighbors and student collaborators. These connections have been enriching for the collaborators' lives, sustaining us through multiple crises: COVID; emergency surgeries; family businesses damaged by white supremacists; intensifications of racialized violence; deteriorating mental health; brief periods of incarceration; unexpected moves; job losses; the loss of reproductive support for ourselves, our children, and parents; the Chauvin trial; and much more. As important as what we have learned from this project about university land development, whiteness, settler land claims, the racialization of space, histories of dispossession, and white liberalism, we have learned even more from the way that we have done this project—collaboratively, together.

Conclusion

I have sought, in this brief chapter, to make the case for a queer anthropology that not only engages crip theory and analytics, from the scholarly center to the quasi-academic edges, but also incorporates the insights of disability justice to make anthropology's knowledge practices more accessible and thus more liberatory. Beyond queer critique "of" disability, then, a queer, crip ethnography might make a queer anthropology for all. In my wildest disability dreams (to quote Leah Lakshmi Piepzna-Samarasinha), queer anthropologists would cultivate unfamiliar intimacies and commit to unraveling ableist models toward more just futures.

Acknowledgments

My collaborators on the University Grove project include Miranda Joseph, Aurelia Tittmann, Fenniver Durban-Albrecht-Joseph, O. Sailer, Haley Olson, Amina Adem, Nicole Bellis, Avery Birt, Greta Copes, Shameela Khan, Lilly Knopf, Zoe Koth, Ashley Laflin, Aarilee Lorenzen, Kendall Mory, Brooke Seaver, Emily Shim, Samantha Torborg, Yeeleng Vang, Ruofeng Wang, Hotho Yussuf, and Yiling Zhang. UMN Liberal Technologies and Innovations Services provided essential research and technology support for the project. Thank you as well to Margot Weiss for the invitation to contribute to *Unsettling Queer Anthropology*, generous engagement as an activist scholar with the ideas in this chapter, and commitment to social justice work in the academy.

Notes

1 Research about the dynamic connections between race/racialization/racism and disability in education articulate their work as disability critical race theory, or "DisCrit" (e.g., Annamma et. al. 2018). Essential reading on this topic is Erevelles and Minear 2010.

2 In "Anthropology and Ableism," I note that Ruth Benedict's "Anthropology and the Abnormal" (1934) can be read in relationship not only to same-sex sexuality (in itself a potential opening to conversation about disability in its pathologization [McRuer 2006]) but also to Benedict's partial deafness and chronic depression.

   Julie Avril Minich claims, "There is also an enormous body of scholarly and activist work that has until recently gone unrecognized by disability scholars *as* critical disability studies, despite advocating a radical politics of corporeal variation and neurodiversity: protests against racialized disparities in health, education, and policing; struggles for environmental justice and reproductive freedom; HIV/AIDS and fat activism; the writings of Audre Lorde on blindness and cancer and of Gloria Anzaldúa on early menstruation and diabetes" (2016, n.p.). Aurora Levins Morales, Qwo-Li Driskill, and Leah Lakshmi Piepzna-Samarasinha (2012) claim Anzaldúa as a queer, crip ancestor. See also Jina B. Kim's (2017) invocation of Audre Lorde.

3 Elizabeth Freeman edited an issue of *South Atlantic Quarterly* with Ellen Samuels on the subject of "Crip Temporalities" (Samuels and Freeman, 2021).

4 Cassandra Hartblay, whose scholarship is shaped by feminist and queer theory, helpfully distinguishes "disability anthropology" from the "anthropology of disability," "wherein the latter suggests a subfield of medical anthropology in which disability is the subject matter." In contrast, disability anthropology "engages the distinctive theoretical concerns and methodological approaches of trans-disciplinary critical disability studies, enacted through a citational politics that foregrounds disability studies texts and scholars. We might also think of disability anthropology as anthropology that draws on and contributes to disability theory and that starts from what Simi Linton has called the 'disability studies perspective' (2005)" (2020, S27).

5 One notable exception related to queer, crip anthropology work is Kulick and Rydström 2015. In queer anthropology, refer to Kennedy and Davis 1993.

6 Beyond published work, consider watching the performances of Sins Invalid, engaging the music and art of Krip Hop Nation, reading the "Leaving Evidence" blog by Mia Mingus, and learning from the extensive resources that Eli Clare has compiled in the "Queer and Trans Disability/Deaf Resources" list. A wealth of recorded interviews and performances is archived on the internet with these activists, a treasure trove of crip brilliance growing steadily during the pandemic. Here are some academic engagements: the Barnard Center for Research on Women's "No Body Is Disposable Series" with conversations between Patty Berne and Stacy Milburn; the CLAGS "Queer Disability Dreams" panel on crip justice with Leah Lakshmi Piepzna-Samarasinha and Sami Schalk; the Ford Foundation exhibition "Indisposable: Structures of Support after the ADA," especially the queerly joyous *#QuarantineLooks: Embracing the Fabulously Mundane* with Sami Schalk and Jina B. Kim; and the American Studies Association Freedom Course "Disability Justice, COVID, and Abolition" with Mia Mingus, Talila "TL" Lewis, and Liat Ben-Moshe.

7 This piece itself reflects such contingencies—written with a challenging deadline through brain fog, joint pain and immobility, GI events, a parent's emergency craniotomy and aftercare in another state, lengthy everyday treatments for Multiple Autoimmune Syndrome, repeated calls and paperwork to justify treatment costs to corporations, attempts to find a primary care provider who will be less of a gatekeeper, a colonoscopy, trips to Mayo Clinic, scheduling and rescheduling appointments with individual health care providers, the spike in

Omicron, COVID-19 entering my pod, and my kid's school closing to transition to remote learning. Under different circumstances, I would have sought to write collaboratively with other queer, crip anthropologists.

8   Both queer and crip theory share an analytic interest in "normativity." The language of "normate" is particular to crip theory, coming from Thomson 1997.

9   For instance, two AAA webinars explore possibilities for performance as disabled and anti-ableist ethnography: "Doing/Undoing Disability Ethnography and Performance" with Arseli Dokumaci, Devva Kasnitz, and Petra Kuppers; and "Collaborative Scripts: Disability and Chronic Illness Through Ethnographic Theatre and Film" with Cassandra Hartblay and Megan Moodie. See also the "Disability as Rupture" issue of the Theorizing the Contemporary series (Wolf-Meyer and Friedner 2022).

10 The disability metaphor of "spoons" to measure capacity comes from Miserandino 2003.

References

Acevedo, Sara M. 2021. "Lifelines: A Neuroqueer Politics of Non-arrival in an Undergraduate Disability Studies Classroom." *International Journal of Qualitative Studies in Education*. 1–5. DOI:10.1080/09518398.2021.2017505.

Acevedo, Sara M., Valerie Black, Mark Bookman, Sumi Colligan, Erin L. Durban, Rebecca-Eli Long, Karen Nakamura, Krisjob Olsen. 2020. AAA Raising our Voices. "Disabled Voices in the Field: Towards Reimagining Anthropologists at Work."

Açiksöz, Salih Can. 2020. *Sacrificial Limbs: Masculinity, Disability, and Political Violence in Turkey*. Berkeley: University of California Press.

Ah-King, Malin, and Eva Hayward. 2014, 232. "Toxic Sexes: Perverting Pollution and Queering Hormone Disruption." *O-Zone: A Journal of Object-Oriented Studies* (1), "Object/Ecology." 1–12.

Alaimo, Stacy. 2010. *Bodily Natures: Science, Environment, and the Material Self*. Bloomington: Indiana University Press.

Annamma, Subini Ancy, Beth A. Ferri, and David J. Connor. 2018. "Disability Critical Race Theory: Exploring the Intersectional Lineage, Emergence, and Potential Futures of DisCrit in Education." *Review of Research in Education* 42: 46–71.

Barclay, Jenifer L. 2021. *The Mark of Slavery: Disability, Race, and Gender in Antebellum America*. Urbana: University of Illinois Press.

Benedict, Ruth, "Anthropology and the Abnormal." *Journal of General Psychology* 10 (1934), 59–80.

Ben-Moshe, Liat. 2020. *Decarcerating Disability: Deinstitutionalization and Prison Abolition*. Minneapolis: University of Minnesota Press.

Boellstorff, Tom. 2008. *Coming of Age in Second Life: An Anthropologist Explores the Virtually Human*. Princeton, NJ: Princeton University Press.

Boellstorff, Tom. 2020. "The Ability of Place: Digital Topographies of the Virtual Human on Ethnographia Island." *Current Anthropology* 61 (21): S109–22.

Boellstorff, Tom, and Cymene Howe. 2015. "Queer Futures." Theorizing the Contemporary, *Fieldsights*, July 21. https://culanth.org/fieldsights/series/queer-futures.

Boster, Dea. 2012. *African American Slavery and Disability: Bodies, Property, and Power in the Antebellum South, 1800–1860*. New York: Routledge.

Burch, Susan. 2021. *Committed: Remembering Native Kinship in and beyond Institutions*. Chapel Hill: University of North Carolina Press.

Chen, Mel Y. 2012. *Animacies: Biopolitics: Racial Mattering, and Queer Affect*. Durham, NC: Duke University Press.

Clare, Eli. 1999. *Exile and Pride: Disability, Queerness, and Liberation*. Boston: South End Press.

Clare, Eli. 2013. "Body Shame, Body Pride: Lessons from the Disability Rights Movement." In *The Transgender Studies Reader 2*, edited by Susan Stryker and Aren Z. Aizura, 261–65. New York: Routledge.

Clare, Eli. 2017. *Brilliant Imperfection: Grappling with Cure*. Durham, NC: Duke University Press.

Cohen Ettinger, Mordecai, Health Justice Commons, and Sins Invalid. 2019. "A Call to Action from Survivors of Environmental Injury: Our Canary's Eye View at the Crossroads of Disability and Climate Justice." In *Skin, Tooth, and Bone: The Basis of Movement Is Our People—A Disability Justice Primer*, 2nd ed., edited by Sins Invalid, 94–106. Self-published.

Disability Research Interest Group. "Doing/Undoing Disability Ethnography and Performance Webinar." https://www.youtube.com/watch?v=hMTL4bfrXp4.

Durban, Erin L. 2017. "Postcolonial Disablement and/as Transition: Trans* Haitian Narratives of Breaking Open and Stitching Together." *TSQ: Transgender Studies Quarterly* 4(2): 195–207.

Durban, Erin L. 2021. "Anthropology and Ableism." *American Anthropologist*. https://anthrosource.onlinelibrary.wiley.com/doi/10.1111/aman.13659.

Durban, Erin L. 2022. *The Sexual Politics of Empire: Postcolonial Homophobia in Haiti*. Bloomington: University of Illinois Press.

Erevelles, Nirmala. 2011. *Disability and Difference in Global Contexts: Enabling a Transformative Body Politic*. New York: Palgrave Macmillan.

Erevelles, Nirmala, and Andrea Minear. 2010. "Unspeakable Offenses: Untangling Race and Disability in Discourses of Intersectionality." *Journal of Literary and Cultural Disability Studies* 4(2): 127–45.

Freeman, Elizabeth. 2010. *Time Binds: Queer Temporalities, Queer Histories*. Durham, NC: Duke University Press.

Fritsch, Kelly, Jeffrey Monaghan, and Emily van der Meulen. 2022. *Disability Injustice: Confronting Criminalization in Canada*. Vancouver: University of British Columbia Press.

Gibson, Hannah. 2019. "Living a Full Life: Embodiment, Disability, and 'Anthropology at Home.'" *Medicine Anthropology Theory* 6(2): 72–78.

Gossett, Che, and Eva Hayward. 2020. "Trans in a Time of HIV/AIDS." *TSQ: Transgender Studies Quarterly* 7(4): 527–53.

Günel, Gökçe, Saiba Varma, and Chika Watanabe. 2020, June 9. "A Manifesto for Patchwork Ethnography." *Cultural Anthropology*, Member Voices edition, sec. Fieldsights.

Hartblay, Cassandra. 2020. "Disability Expertise: Claiming Disability Anthropology." *Current Anthropology* 61(21): S26–36.

Hayward, Eva. 2014. "Transxenoestrogenesis." *TSQ: Transgender Studies Quarterly* 1(1–2): 255–58.

Jain, S. Lochlann. 2013. *Malignant: How Cancer Becomes Us*. Berkeley: University of California Press.

Joseph, Miranda. 2002. *Against the Romance of Community*. Minneapolis: University of Minnesota Press.

Kafer, Alison. 2013. *Feminist, Queer, Crip*. Bloomington: Indiana University Press.

Kasnitz, Devva. 2020. "The Politics of Disability Performativity: An Autoethnography." *Current Anthropology* 61(21): S16–25.

Kennedy, Elizabeth Lapovsky, and Madeline D. Davis. 1993. *Boots of Leather, Slippers of Gold: The History of a Lesbian Community*. New York: Routledge.

Kim, Eunjung. 2017. *Curative Violence: Rehabilitating Disability, Gender, and Sexuality in Modern Korea*. Durham, NC: Duke University Press.

Kim, Jina B. 2017. "Toward a Crip-of-Color Critique: Thinking with Minich's 'Enabling Whom?'" *Lateral: Journal of the Cultural Studies Association*. https://csalateral.org/issue/6–1/forum-alt-humanities-critical-disability-studies-crip-of-color-critique-kim/.

Kulick, Don, and Jens Rydström. 2015. *Loneliness and Its Opposite: Sex, Disability, and the Ethics of Engagement*. Durham, NC: Duke University Press.

Levins Morales, Aurora, Qwo-Li Driskill, and Leah Lakshmi Piepzna-Samarasinha. 2012. "Sweet Dark Places: Letters to Gloria Anzaldúa on Disability, Creativity, and the Coatlicue State." In *El Mundo Zurdo 2*, edited by Sonia Saldívar-Hull, Norma Alarcón, and Rita E. Urquijo-Ruiz. 75–98. San Francisco: Aunt Lute Books.

Linton, Simi. 2005. "What Is Disability Studies?" *PMLA* 120(2): 518–22.

McRuer, Robert. 2006. *Crip Theory: Cultural Signs of Queerness and Disability*. New York: New York University Press.

Minich, Julie Avril. 2016. "Enabling Whom? Critical Disability Studies Now." *Lateral: Journal of the Cultural Studies Association*. https://csalateral.org/issue/5–1/forum-alt-humanities-critical-disability-studies-now-minich/.

Miserandino, Christine. 2003. "The Spoon Theory." https://butyoudontlooksick.com/articles/written-by-christine/the-spoon-theory/.

Morales, Aurora Levins, Qwo-Li Driskoll, and Leah Lakshmi Piepzna-Samarasinha. 2012. "Sweet Dark Places: Letters to Gloria Anzaldúa on Disability, Creativity, and the Coatlicue State," 77–97. In *El Mundo Zurdo 2: Selected Works from the Society of the Study of Gloria Anzaldúa*, edited by Norman Alarcón, Sonia Saldívar Hull, and Rita Urquijo-Ruiz. San Francisco: Aunt Lute Books.

Nakamura, Karen. 2006. *Deaf in Japan: Signing and the Politics of Identity*. Ithaca, NY: Cornell University Press.

Nakamura, Karen. 2013. *A Disability of the Soul: An Ethnography of Schizophrenia and Mental Illness in Contemporary Japan*. Ithaca, NY: Cornell University Press.

Pickens, Therí Alyce. 2019. *Black Madness::Mad Blackness*. Durham, NC: Duke University Press.

Piepzna-Samarasinha, Leah Lakshmi. 2018. *Care Work: Dreaming Disability Justice*. Vancouver: Arsenal Street Press.

Pink, Sarah. 2009. *Doing Sensory Ethnography*. London: Sage.

Price, Margaret. 2015. "The Bodymind Problem and the Possibilities of Pain." *Hypatia: A Journal of Feminist Philosophy* 30(1): 268–84.

Puar, Jasbir K. 2017. *The Right to Maim: Debility, Capacity, Disability*. Durham, NC: Duke University Press.

Samuels, Ellen and Elizabeth Freeman. 2012. *South Atlantic Quarterly* 120(2).

Schalk, Sami. 2018. *Bodyminds Reimagined: (Dis)ability, Race, and Gender in Black Women's Speculative Fiction*. Durham, NC: Duke University Press.

Sedgwick, Eve Kosofsky. 1990. *Epistemology of the Closet*. Berkeley: University of California Press.

Sins Invalid. 2016. *Skin, Tooth, and Bone: The Basis of Movement Is Our People—A Disability Justice Primer*. Self-published.

Taylor, Sunaura. 2017. *Beasts of Burden: Animal and Disability Liberation*. New York: New Press.

Thomsen, Carly. 2021. *Visibility Interrupted: Rural Queer Life and the Politics of Unbecoming*. Minneapolis: University of Minnesota Press.

Thomson, Rosemarie Garland. 1997. *Extraordinary Bodies: Figuring Physical Disability in American Culture and Literature*. New York: Columbia University Press.

Wolf-Meyer, Matthew, and Michele Ilanda Friedner, eds. 2022. "Disability as Rupture." Society for Cultural Anthropology, Theorizing the Contemporary series. https://culanth.org/fieldsights/series/disability-as-rupture.

Wool, Zoë H. 2021. "Disability, Straight Time, and the American Dream: Disabled US Veterans and the Desire for Heteronormative Futures." *American Ethnologist* 48(3): 288–300.

Juno Salazar Parreñas

12

When Our Tulips Speak Together

More-Than-Human Queer Natures

Perhaps you already know that bonobos lubricate their same-sex social bonds by way of what primatologists call "penis-fencing" or "genital-genital rubbing" (de Waal 1995). However, you might not know that a female bonnethead shark doesn't need sperm to make a baby shark (Holtcamp 2009). Together they hint at the kaleidoscopic diversity of life forms on Earth.

If you think about life on a planetary scale, you'll find that the norm for propagating life is not through sex between males and females. Telling you about the "birds and the bees" in the most accurate way possible at this moment would include the story of avian gynandromorphism, in which adult birds can embody colorful intersexuality where half of their bodies are female and the other half male (Pratap 2020). The other half of the story is that bees and a vast majority of other insects experience complete bodily transformation and metamorphosis within their full lifetimes. Bacteria, which vastly outnumber any other kind of living being currently known on this planet, all reproduce asexually (Redfield 2001).

Such celebrations of queer ecologies like the ones that begin this chapter are of relatively recent provenance (Haraway 1989, 2003, 2008; Roughgarden 2004; Willey 2016). A generation ago, queer and feminist anthropologists in the 1970s and 1980s looked to any biological explanation with great suspicion. Why was that, and what has changed?

This chapter explores the relationship of nature and culture as theorized by feminist and queer scholars by thinking with nonhuman life forms: tulips, apes, slime mold, starfish, bears, pigs, and bovines. Thinking with these life forms enables a revisiting of key concepts in the anthropology of gender and sexuality as it relates to queer anthropology. Such concepts include subjectivity underlying pronouns, essentialism, social construction, queer ecology, sociobiology, and representation.

The purpose of this chapter is to consider the possibilities of integrating queer cultural analysis with a kind of biology that is committed to queer diversities. Queer for me is a way to talk about both concepts and embodiments (or theory and practice) that challenge the ideology that heterosexuality, and the male/female gender binary on which heterosexuality depends, is the natural order to which all "life forms and forms of life" must conform (Helmreich, Roosth, and Friedner 2015; Porter 2019, 39). This chapter ultimately argues for a queer harnessing of biology. Biological ways of knowing should not be a forbidden tool in a queer toy chest. Instead, it can be treated as a tool that has the potential to open new and maybe even mind-blowing joy.

Against Essentialism: Tulips

For now, let us think about tulips, but in an indirect way that will have us contemplate what feminist theory of the 1980s teaches us about selves and pronouns. The title of this chapter pays homage to French feminist thinker Luce Irigaray's (1980) germinal essay, "When Our Lips Speak Together." Carolyn Burke (1981), Irigaray's translator into English, explains that Irigaray was writing *against* her earlier teacher, Jacques Lacan, as a patriarch and master of Freudian psychoanalysis, and Lacan's performance of his own concept of the Name of the Father, which is the social identity imposed on selves in a patriarchal, patronymic society. Irigaray was also writing *alongside* her contemporary Jacques Derrida, who critiqued Lacanian psychoanalysis for its "phallogocentrism," a disparaging term Derrida coined to explain how Freudian-Lacanian psychoanalysis obsesses about and sees the phallus as key to a masculinist logocentrism, or the Western philosophical obsession with the Word as containing fundamental, unshakable, and unified truths (and not as signifiers that attempt to signify things, concepts, and impressions that are ultimately absent). Irigaray demonstrates a way of writing that opposes the usual, masculinist logics and carefully plays with innuendo to show "female pleasure" (Burke 1981, 298).

How exactly does Irigaray reject a solid and unified sense of self as a patriarchal, logocentric, and phallic way of thinking? Take, for instance, the following passage. It is written in the first person, addressed to a second person, against a rigidly defined and phallogocentric third person plural they/them:

> We are luminous. Beyond "one" or "two." I never knew how to count up to you. In their calculations, we count as two. Really, two? Doesn't that make you laugh? A strange kind of two, which isn't one, especially not one. Let them have oneness, with its prerogatives, its domination, its solipsisms: like the sun. Let them have their strange division by couples, in which the other is the image of the one, but an image only. For them, being drawn to the other means a move toward one's mirage: a mirror that is (barely) alive. (1980, 71)

In a phallogocentric way of thinking, Man is the self against which Woman serves the narcissism of Man who uses her as a reflection of himself. This way of thinking relies on a core gender binary between Man and Woman, which Irigaray (1980, 71) rejects as a "strange division of couples." Irigaray rejects both the gender binary and heterosexuality on which it depends in favor of something much more open. In this other kind of world between her as the I and her audience the you, there is no "oneness" like the sun in a heliotropic way of understanding cosmologies or any binary that depends on a unified sense of one and zero, either/or, or male/masculine and female/feminine. In Irigaray's cosmology, they are each more than one. They are glittering, luminous, blurry stars in a bigger constellation than a singular solar system.

Some have dismissed Irigaray and French feminist thinkers of her generation as essentialist for attempting to voice an alternative to Western cis- and heteropatriarchy. Essentialism assumes a direct and essential bond between gender and anatomy, that being a woman would mean having two kinds of lips: oral and genital. To say that Irigaray is essentialist requires assimilating the very logic and phallogocentrism that Irigaray is writing against. As her translator, Carolyn Burke (1981, 303), writes: "The lips of 'When Our Lips Speak Together,' for example, should not be reduced to a literally anatomical specification, for the figure suggests another mode, rather than another model. It implies plurality, multiplicity, and a mode of being 'in touch' that differs from the phallic mode of discourse." Irigaray is not biologically essentialist because she refuses to accept the hetero- and cispatriarchal gender binary that structures Freudian-Lacanian psychoanalysis and its impoverished understandings of women as either lacking or as opposites to masculinist identities. Irigaray rejecting Freudian-Lacanian essentialism also rejects structuralism that uses binaries to analyze social and cultural forms, like hot and cold (Lévi-Strauss 1966). Irigaray's alternative to phallogocentrism suggested by her writing is not *the* alternative but *an* alternative to Eurocentric cis- and heteropatriarchy.

Irigaray anticipates arguments made decades later. Take, for instance, Donna Haraway's (2008) explanation that human-dog relations comprise "more than one but less than two" players in a dog agility course. The relationship between canine athlete and human trainer is such that the relationship creates conditions for their becoming something together, but neither is ever independently a complete whole. Irigaray also anticipates Hugh Raffles's (2010, 12) imploring to do away with "Ptolemaic certitude," or the wrongful certainty that the earth is the center of the universe. This evokes Irigaray's stance against "solipsism," or the conceited idea that the self is the only thing that one can know exists. And Irigaray's poetic prose finds an afterlife in the tangibility evoked by Eva Hayward's (2010) *fingery-eyes*, the term she uses to describe the way cup corals sensitively perceive their surroundings.

Yet what might the lips of Irigaray's writing have to do with tulips, stretching their tendrils through the dirt, waiting to explode with the warmth of spring? Like the I and you of Irigaray's writing about lips, there is no easy way to count tulips, which can both be one and potentially many. Tulips are not "couples" but are instead open to a field of asexual and sexual possibilities—as we shall see.

The Social Construction of Gender and Sexuality:
Primates, Hunger, and the Family of Man

Let's turn now to primatology, an essential part of American four-field anthropology, which is the study of "Man" or Anthropos. Macaques and other primates are particularly subjected to projections about humanity that are culturally specific. As Donna Haraway (1989) has illustrated in her perennially important book, *Primate Visions*, nonhuman primates that are classified within the biological Family of Man, since the beginning of the field of primatology, have been shaped by culturally specific ideas of race, class, and gender.

Rhesus macaques were notoriously subjected to cruel torture in laboratories by the psychologist Harry Harlow (1905–81). His "nature of love" project is the stuff of nightmares: he would take vulnerable infants into a cage where they would have to choose between a cold metallic mother mechanism that dispensed milk or an upholstered dummy that did not dispense milk (Haraway 1989). These experiments generated monkeys profoundly deprived of both social bonds and the ability to forge such bonds. His line of experiments was used as scientific evidence to support white middle-class family values of mothers caring full time for their children.

Laboratory studies on monkeys assume that the body and biology are the source of answers and truths about the nature of love and desire. Yet feminist and queer scholarship in the 1980s tells us otherwise: desire, love, and sexuality are all socially constructed. What does that mean? Let us turn to the writings of Gayle Rubin while keeping monkeys and apes in mind.

In "Thinking Sex," the germinal essay that many scholars say founded the fields of queer studies and sexuality studies, Rubin writes against "sexual essentialism," or "the idea that sex is a natural force that exists prior to social life and shapes institutions" (2011, 146) Citing both the work of social historians like John D'Emilio (1983) who have tracked the formation of the identity of the "homosexual" beginning in the 1950s and the work of social theorist Michel Foucault, Rubin writes:

> Sexuality is constituted in society and history, not biologically ordained. This does not mean the biological capacities are not prerequisites for human sexuality. It does mean that human sexuality is not comprehensible in purely biological terms. Human organisms with human brains are necessary for human cultures, but no examination

of the body or its parts can explain the nature and variety of human social systems. *The belly's hunger gives no clues as to the complexities of cuisine.* The body, the brain, the genitalia, and the capacity for language are necessary for human sexuality. But they do not determine its content, its experiences, or its institutional forms. Moreover, we never encounter the body unmediated by the meanings that cultures give to it. (2011, 146–47)

Viewing sexuality and gender as socially constructed doesn't mean that biology doesn't matter. Biology, in this view, is treated as raw materials that are thoroughly mediated by culture, society, history, and politics.

Rubin's word choice makes the case for specifically *human* sexuality. Yet both hunger and sex are experienced by all kinds of creatures that eat and consort with each other. How can we make sense of nonhuman primate sexuality as more than biological? How is all sexuality, including the sexuality of orangutans, slime molds, and tulips, mediated through human cultural and social sensibilities?

Orangutans and Queer Ecology as Critique of Animacy and Heteronormativity

The social lives of orangutans in semicaptive, semiwild conditions show how human ideas of heteronormative sexuality are violently imposed on animals. These impositions have material consequences. By considering primatological and popular literature about orangutans and by sharing the stories of an orangutan whom I personally knew from my ethnographic field research, I show that orangutan individuals have particular experiences and life histories that warrant using "who" or "whom" instead of "that" when referring to them with relative pronouns (Parreñas 2018). I am also showing how queer ecology offers a means to critique heteronormativity.

The question of whether or not to use "who" or "that" is a question of animacy. Animacy is a linguistic term that references how nouns get categorized and treated grammatically (Chen 2012). In English, animacy is distinguished between nouns associated with humans who get a "who" and objects that get a "that" when they are described with a relative pronoun (Guy and Bayley 1995). Grammar is about using language that feels right to everyday speakers of a language. When talking about particular conditions experienced by particular beings and when learning more about their lives, how can it be wrong to talk about them using particular pronouns usually associated with humans?

Take, for instance, the experiences of prepubescent Sadamiah. Orangutans achieve puberty at roughly the same age as humans: around the age of twelve to fourteen. When I met her, she was living in the open-air confines of a place that I call Batu Wildlife Center in Sarawak on the island of Borneo in present-day Malaysia. Bornean orangutans are the least social of all great apes and single female Bornean orangutans in the wild usually have a range of seven square kilometers that barely overlap with other orangutans. This place is 6.5 square kilometers. It is smaller than a typical range for a solitary wild female and yet contains more than twenty orangutans. The density meant that Sadamiah could not avoid contact with others, including pubescent male orangutans whose longer arm spans meant that they, including her brother, could pin her down and force her to copulate. This is precisely what happened when she was eight years old. In the aftermath of the event, rangers and other workers at the site perceived that Sadamiah seemed to be in pain because she moved so slowly days later. But they felt nothing could be done without risk of injuring her further: tranquilizing her and sending her to a vet could lead to her death by a fall from the tree canopy or too much tranquilizer (Parreñas 2018).

Copulation, even if it was prepubescent and ostensibly forced, was seen by park managers as ultimately positive because they highly valued heterosexual sexuality. For the managers in charge of the site, sex under such conditions was "natural" even though the boundaries of the park were quite unnatural and carved by housing developments, a sand mine, a concrete factory, a police training zone, and a hospital. Her potential injury from the incident and her overall welfare or quality of life was not thought to be as important as her potential ability to become pregnant in the future.

To refer to Sadamiah without animate pronouns would deny her particularity, subjectivity, and experiences. She is a member of a kind or species (orangutan) but she also has particular experience of the space of the park and the way that space is literally shaped by humans and their values. Such values are not merely human but are specific to a heteronormative ideology that upholds all kinds of heterosexual sexuality, even prepubescent or violent to behold, as valuable. This ideology was especially apparent when fights between male orangutans entailed bloodshed. It is a common observation in wild settings that male orangutans behave aggressively toward each other (Mitani 1985). However, park managers would intervene and transfer the male who was at risk of fatal injury to another site in Sarawak that looked more like a zoo.

Why would park managers intervene in one kind of natural behavior but not another? The answer is in their heteronormative and patriarchal idea of nature and sexuality and their imposition of what lesbian-feminist theorist Adrienne Rich (1980, 632) described as "compulsory heterosexuality." Even though Rich was referencing American mainstream culture, this ideology underpins conservation biology, which values natalism and population growth for endangered species over welfare or the ethical consideration of what it would take to die well.

Queer ecology, as it was coined by Catriona Mortimer-Sandilands and Bruce Erickson, was about two things: disrupting heterosexist ideas of nature and reimagining environmental, ecological, and evolutionary relations away from cisnormative and heterosexist biases (Mortimer-Sandilands and Erickson 2010; Sandilands 2016; Parreñas and Seymour 2022). Highlighting the way people impose "compulsory heterosexuality" on orangutans does the former. What about the latter? Let us think about the sexy social lives of slime molds.

Slime Molds and a Queer Ecology of Variation

Did you know that slime molds have single cellular bodies and yet are said to have 720 sexes? Or that tulips are *ace*, which is slang for asexual? *Ace* is a term that is usually self-identified (Cerankowski and Milks 2014). Would it be a stretch to use that word to reference how tulips asexually propagate when their bulbs split and generate new tulips? Humans can self-identify, but can self-propagating plants like tulips or parthogenic or so-called virgin-birthing animals like sharks and snakes do so? What signs could people perceive to affirm a nonhuman animal or plant's selfhood that are not stretches of the imagination or solipsistic and narcissistic extensions of human selves?

The regeneration of planetary life is wildly diverse and it may be hard to fathom for people who think in simple binaries between female and male or who obstinately hold on to heteronormative values when confronted with empirical evidence that shows otherwise. Because the life forms that we lump together under the single word "nature" have vast variation, it helps to think about their unique embodiments and ways of being in the world.

12.1 A neon yellow towering slime mold growing on a fallen tree trunk in Berlin. (© Le Bernemi 2020, licensed under CC BY-SA 4.0)

The uniqueness of each of these life forms suggests some kind of self even if they may not identify as selves. The anthropologist Eduardo Kohn (2013) would say that life forms are selves because they engage in sign systems with the world around them by virtue of their existence. Even without going into what such life forms can or cannot communicate through semiotics (or the system of signs), they are already simply selves by being uniquely different enough to be distinguishable from their ecologies. Recognizing the uniqueness of so many different kinds of life forms compels a reimagining of the norms of sex and nature.

Slime molds, for instance, are technically single cellular (Adler and Holt 1975). However, in times of scarcity, they congeal to become a multicellular life form. This ability defies conventions in taxonomy that were first established in the eighteenth century by Carl Linnaeus: they are not fungi nor are they animals or plants. The ability of slime mold to go back and forth between individual and collective inspired the novelist Octavia Butler as she plotted her novel *Dawn* (Bahng 2017). Butler's carefully written notes on December 31, 1989, share the observation of slime mold activity: "when food supply is exhausted, they come together, crawl to a suitable place as a multicellular 'slug' there it builds a 'tower' of its own cells—of *itselves*" (quoted in Bahng 2017, 313). The slime mold's options for singularity and plurality warrant Butler coining a new reflexive pronoun: itselves.

The literary scholar Aimee Bahng interprets Butler's musings about slime molds as a specifically queer approach: "Butler demonstrates a remarkable openness to non-normative biological organization. She does not look to figure the slime mold out. She seems excited to follow it off the script of 1980s evolutionary biology to other possibilities. In slime, she looks for a life model of life that could be, rather than life that already is. It is a speculative fabulation, drawn from life unruly" (2017, 314). Queer in this sense that Bahng offers is about nonnormative biology, one that defied what Bahng describes as evolutionary biology in the 1980s but what should be construed as popular understandings of evolution at the time. Already by the late 1970s, the genomic revolution began to force the reevaluation of species and other taxonomic categories, which then culminated in the demotion of animal, plant, fungi, and protista kingdoms to the domain of eucarya or multicellular life forms by 1990 (Woese and Fox 1977; Woese, Kandler, and Wheelis 1990). What Bahng describes as 1980s evolutionary biology was starting to become obsolete among microbiologists and ecologists, as well as organismic and evolutionary biologists. However, this was also a time in which profoundly sexist and heterosexist ideas of human sexuality undergirded neo-Darwinist, antifeminist ideas of evolutionary psychology and sociobiology. Theories from evolutionary psychology and sociobiology included the idea that rape is a reproduction strategy, that there are fundamental differences between male and female humans, and that behaviors among great apes must be shared across all higher primates—including humans (Symons 1979; Knauft et al. 1991; McKibbin et al. 2008). Darwin never discussed the "survival of the fittest," yet the idea is essential for neo-Darwinists (Claeys 2000, 225). Such ideas did not die with the 1980s but continued well into the careers of evolutionary psychologists and some physical anthropologists as they made efforts to reach general publics while approaching their retirement (Walling 2019; Wrangham 1996; Pinker 2002). Of course, these heterosexist and sexist scientists do not represent the entirety of their fields. Evolutionary anthropologists and biologists have criticized such biases on the terms of the sciences in which they work (Zuk 2002; Travis 2003; Fuentes 2004).

So what about now, when slime molds and their ability to have 720 kinds of sexes and yet still be a single cellular life form are popularized by a world-class zoo like the Paris Zoological Garden and popular media outlets like the *Guardian*, ABC News, and the Canadian Broadcasting Corporation (*Guardian* 2019; ABC News 2019; Thompson Reuters 2019)? Biology today

256 JUNO SALAZAR PARREÑAS

is about variation, which is what makes it possible to converge with feminist and queer studies (Subramaniam 2014). Recognizing the vast diversity of life forms on the planet compels the reckoning that sex as we know it is far more diverse than evolutionary psychologists, heteronormative rape apologists, or neo-Darwinists would have us think.

In addition to the comings and goings of singular/multicellular slime mold, there are parthogenic snakes and sharks, and insects who can spawn eggs without fertilization from males. You now know that tulips can go at it alone and do so reproductively. Taken as a whole, the lives of slime molds, tulips, and snakes all show that the norm for the vast majority of life forms on this planet is asexual and trans. Yet we see them as queer when we think of queerness as a stance against normativity. Their lives resonate with queer values. But would it not be more accurate to call these ecologies trans or asexual instead of queer when their norms are neither heterosexual nor binary? This is where thinking with starfish might help us out.

Starfish and the Materiality of Trans* Embodiments

Some species of starfish can reproduce asexually when a ray is severed from the sea star's body. Out of that severed ray can grow a whole new sea star. Rays are "fingeryeyes," using trans studies scholar Eva Hayward's (2008; 2010, 580) description of their ability to sense the world around them. Hayward (2008) links starfishes' generative power of this transformation to human trans* embodiment with the help of a song from the musical artists Antony and the Johnsons; the Johnsons are named after celebrated activist Marsha P. Johnson who was said to have started Stonewall and who founded the trans rights group STAR (Street Transvestite Action Revolutionaries) in the 1970s.

A simple Freudian-Lacanian interpretation of severing or cutting would be castration or lack. Hayward rejects that analysis to think about what cutting for starfish and trans women enacts. For Hayward, a trans woman, "the cut enacts trans-embodiment—to cut is not necessarily about castration, but an attempt to recast the self through the cut body" (2008, 72). She elaborates:

> To cut off the penis/finger is not to be an amputee, but to produce the conditions of physical and psychical regrowth. *The cut is the possibility*. For some transwomen, the cut is not so much an opening of the body, but a generative effort to *pull the body back through itself*

WHEN OUR TULIPS SPEAK TOGETHER   257

in order to feel mending, to feel the growth of new margins. The cut is not just an action; the cut is part of the ongoing materialization by which a transsexual tentatively and mutably becomes. (2008, 72)

Hayward thinks through the materiality of surgical cuts in the procedure of vaginoplasty, an option for trans feminine bottom surgery, as part of becoming somebody anew. She then brings this materialization to bear when thinking about the possible embodiments of sea stars for whom cuts can start new embodiments. Thinking about the transformation of sea stars and trans feminine people together generates a substantive force behind Hayward and Weinstein's (2015) concept of trans*. Being or becoming trans* is about provisionality and mutability and its emphasis on the prefix of trans-, with the dash substituted with the starfish-like asterisk, readily allows for connection across life forms, whether deep in the sea or on the surface of land.

Taking the materiality of starfish and trans-affirming surgical cuts into mind, is it fair to lump it under the sign of queer, whether queer ecology or queer anthropology? If the life forms that constitute nature were never heteronormative, if their norms were never about heterosexuality, then what indeed is normal and what would it mean to queer that? In the next section, let us think of stretches of queerness so that we may think precisely about the boundaries of what constitutes queerness in a queer more-than-human world.

Figments of (Queer?) Desire: Bears, Pigs, and Bovines

Thus far, we have considered the material lives of nonhuman life forms and what they help us to think about selves (and pronouns), the conflict between essentialism and social construction as it arises in Freudian-Lacanian psychoanalysis and sociobiology, and the concept of queer ecology. This chapter's emphasis on materiality, on actual life forms and how they live, is one technique that emerged in the twenty-first century. However, an older technique in anthropology has been to think of representations. This is especially clear when we think about the cultural representations of certain animals, specifically bears, pigs, and bovines. What is important in what follows is their representation as figments and not necessarily the truth of these life forms. This is especially clear when it comes to bears but is also true when it comes to pigs and cows. Thinking about bears, pigs, and cows compels us to consider the boundaries of what we count as queer.

In 1979, the gay magazine the *Advocate* published an illustrated satirical article that is credited as one of the first sources in which the gay cultural figure of the bear first appeared. Bears, according to the author of the article, George Mazzei, were "hunky, chunky types reminiscent of railroad engineers and former football greats" for whom "beer is their favorite food" (1979, 42). Surprisingly, what is included in this gay zoo of the late 1970s are not cubs (young bears), otters (small-built bears), wolves (medium-built bears), or manatees (hairless bears), but a menagerie of implicitly racialized terms no longer in circulation that referenced gay men and lesbians: owls ("older gay animals" who "are engaged in keeping camp alive" and have "some astounding Ethnic who comes by for a periodic tryst"); gazelles ("who smoke way too many cigarettes, take incredible amounts of drugs and never seem to be stoned"); cygnet swans (who "devote their lives to cultivating perfect bodies and cheap swank"); Pekes [as in Pekinese dogs] and Afghans [as in Afghan hounds] ("who usually come from the Confederate states" [read: white] and "have tawny bodies and large amounts of tawny hair" and "eat three extremely heavy meals a day" and whose "table surfaces are occupied by porcelain this and *cloisonne* that"); pussycats (who are mistaken to be bears, but "keep their freshly pressed chambray shirt tucked" and who "act butch, have an affinity for masculine pursuits, but can't resist a bitchy entendre"); and marmosets ("who look like small, manicured bears but unfortunately incorporate many of the nastier aspects of Pussycats into their personalities") (1979, 42–43). Bear culture has lasted generations, survived the worst of the AIDS epidemic, and continues to flourish in the form of BearRuns, Bear Weeks, Bear Beer Busts, and friendly annual competitions for Mr. Bear, Cub, and even Mama or Ms. Bear titles (Wright 1997).

Are bears so enmeshed in gay culture that desire for a bear is automatically queer? This is a question up for debate when presented with Radhika Govindrajan's argument that women in the Indian Himalayas, who think about the "horizon of sexual possibility that would open up to them through sex with a bear," engage in a "queer archive of desire that hovered between an insufficient present and an unrealizable future" (2019, 162). If a queer of color theorist such as Jose Muñoz said queer is about being insufficiently present and unrealizable, is everything insufficiently present and unrealizable automatically queer? Why is desire for a bear queer and not just feminine desire? Would an aggressively straight woman's desire for a "juicehead gorilla," slang spread by the reality TV show *Jersey Shore* (2009–12) for a cis man who works out and takes supplemental hormones, be queer too

(Zimmerman 2010)? Does arguing that cis women's desire that bears or gorillas be queer suggest that bestiality is queer?

Bestiality was the boogeyman for Christian right activists who fought hard against gay marriage. Many queer activists opposed this and they also opposed the focus of LGBT activism toward marriage equality in the 2000s following the end of sodomy laws (at the expense of other potential foci like employment and housing discrimination or houseless youth). One expression of their unique frustration between mainstream LGBT activism on one hand and right-wing Christian organizing on the other was the parodic creation of the Freedom to Marry Our Pets Society, of which its traces are still online.[1]

It was only recently in the 2000s that many states in the United States added laws against bestiality to their books. In all cases, exceptions are made for agriculture, which relies on sexual contact between humans and animals. Sows raised in the meat industry, for instance, need to be mounted, with human thighs pressed against their sides, for them to be successfully impregnated through artificial insemination (Rosenberg 2017; Blanchette 2020). Because such sexual contact is more than human, includes apparatuses, and transgresses human-animal boundaries, does that make it queer? If a man professes his love for a beautiful cow, particularly in the context of Hindu Right cow protection, does such a transgressive love make it queer (Dave 2014, 2019)? Neither Gabriel Rosenberg (2017), who studied how sex was regulated in state laws by agricultural industrial lobbyists, nor Alex Blanchette (2020), whose ethnographic research entailed sexual contact with pigs, nor Naisargi Dave (2014) who studies animal rights activists in India, explicitly call these relations queer. Yet these different figments open a question for you, reader: What exactly is meant by the word queer, especially when it exceeds the confines of human desire?

Conclusion

More-than-human embodiments include iconic figures like bears, barrier-breaking life forms like slime mold, trans* bodies like starfish, asexual reproducers like tulips, and animals abused like laboratory monkeys or exploited like industrial pigs. Thinking about them together gets us to think about gender, sexuality, and race as social constructs alongside biological matter. This is queer and feminist analysis without sociobiology: biology is not used to support essentialist ideas of gender and sexuality as it does in sociobiology, but instead matters along with the social construction of gender, sexuality, and race. It is the recognition that many kinds of life forms have hunger and sensations. What might we call this approach?

There are different ways to think about this queering of biology for ethnographic and anthropological ends. For instance, we can think of the life forms and the worlds they open as material-semiotic insofar that biological, ecological matter (material) is interpreted through sign systems, including culturally specific sign systems (Law 2009). One other way to think of it is through the idea of "natureculture," which disrupts the false dichotomy in Western thought between nature and culture (Haraway 2003, 3). Concepts like "somatechnics," which combines ideas of the corporeality, techniques, and technologies have also been generative for thinking expansively about diverse embodiments and states of being or becoming (Alm 2013, 307). Another way to think of this combination is the word "onto-epistemology," which combines, instead of compartmentalizes, ways of knowing with ways of being (Barad 2007, 185). Yet another way is offered by scientific funding streams like the National Institutes of Health: "biosocial" is a way to think about the biological markers of social inequality and how social inequalities are perpetuated (Shattuck-Heidorn and Richardson 2019).

For the time being, queer ecology serves as a placeholder that can hold trans* possibilities, ace modes of reproduction, intersex embodiments, and critiques of the violence of heteronormativity. With whatever term we use, we need to remember that "bio" references many kinds of biology. Today, biology is profoundly rooted in a recognition of the planet's diversity, including sexual diversity.

Note

1   See the home page for the Freedom to Marry Our Pets Society, https:// bullybloggers.wordpress.com/freedom-society-page/.

References

ABC News. 2019. "Strange Yellow Organism Known as the 'Blob' Gets New Exhibit at Paris Zoo." https://abcnews.go.com/International/strange-yellow-organism -blob-exhibit-paris-zoo/story?id=66342692.

Adler, Paul N., and Charles E. Holt. 1975. "Mating Type and the Differentiated State in Physarum Polycephalum." *Developmental Biology* 43(2): 240–53.

Alm, Erika. 2013. "Somatechnics of Consensus: Situating the Biomedicalisation of Intersex." *Somatechnics* 3(2):307–38.

Bahng, Aimee. 2017. "Plasmodial Improprieties: Octavia E. Butler, Slime Molds, and Imagining a Femi-Queer Commons." In *Queer Feminist Science Studies: A Reader*, edited by Cid Cipolla, Kristina Gupta, David A. Rubin, and Angela Willey, 310–25. Seattle: University of Washington Press.

Barad, Karen Michelle. 2007. *Meeting the Universe Halfway: Quantum Physics and the Entanglement of Matter and Meaning*. Durham, NC: Duke University Press.

Blanchette, Alex. 2020. *Porkopolis: American Animality, Standardized Life, and the Factory Farm*. Durham, NC: Duke University Press.

Burke, Carolyn. 1981. "Irigaray through the Looking Glass." *Feminist Studies* 7(2): 288–306.

Cerankowski, K. J., and Megan Milks, eds. 2014. *Asexualities Feminist and Queer Perspectives*. New York: Routledge.

Chen, Mel Y. 2012. *Animacies: Biopolitics, Racial Mattering, and Queer Affect*. Durham, NC: Duke University Press.

Claeys, Gregory. 2000. "The 'Survival of the Fittest' and the Origins of Social Darwinism." *Journal of the History of Ideas* 61(2): 223–40.

Dave, Naisargi N. 2014. "Witness: Humans, Animals, and the Politics of Becoming." *Cultural Anthropology* 29(3): 433–56.

Dave, Naisargi N. 2019. "Kamadhenu's Last Stand: On Animal Refusal to Work." In *How Nature Works: Rethinking Labor on a Troubled Planet*, edited by Sarah Besky and Alex Blanchette, 211–24. Albuquerque: University of New Mexico Press.

D'Emilio, John. 1983. *Sexual Politics, Sexual Communities: The Making of a Homosexual Minority in the United States, 1940–1970*. Chicago: University of Chicago Press.

de Waal, F. B. 1995. "Bonobo Sex and Society." *Scientific American* 272(3): 82–88.

Fuentes, Agustin. 2004. "It's Not All Sex and Violence: Integrated Anthropology and the Role of Cooperation and Social Complexity in Human Evolution." *American Anthropologist* 106(4): 710–18.

Govindrajan, Radhika. 2019. *Animal Intimacies: Interspecies Relatedness in India's Central Himalayas*. Chicago: University of Chicago Press.

Guardian. 2019. "The 'Blob': Zoo Showcases Slime Mold with 720 Sexes That Can Heal Itself in Minutes." https://www.theguardian.com/world/2019/oct/17/the-blob-zoo-unveils-baffling-new-organism-with-720-sexes.

Guy, Gregory R., and Robert Bayley. 1995. "On the Choice of Relative Pronouns in English." *American Speech* 70(2): 148–62.

Haraway, Donna J. 1989. *Primate Visions: Gender, Race, and Nature in the World of Modern Science*. New York: Routledge.

Haraway, Donna J. 2003. *The Companion Species Manifesto: Dogs, People, and Significant Otherness*. Chicago: Prickly Paradigm Press.

Haraway, Donna J. 2008. *When Species Meet*. Minneapolis: University of Minnesota Press.

Hayward, Eva. 2010. "Fingeryeyes: Impressions of Cup Corals." *Cultural Anthropology* 25(4): 577–99.

Hayward, E., and J. Weinstein. 2015. "Introduction: Tranimalities in the Age of Trans* Life." *TSQ: Transgender Studies Quarterly* 2(2): 195–208.

Hayward, Eva S. 2008. "More Lessons from a Starfish: Prefixial Flesh and Transspeciated Selves." *Women's Studies Quarterly* 36(3): 64.

Helmreich, Stefan, Sophia Roosth, and Michele Ilana Friedner. 2015. *Sounding the Limits of Life: Essays in the Anthropology of Biology and Beyond*. Princeton, NJ: Princeton University Press.

Holtcamp, Wendee. 2009. "Lone Parents: Parthenogenesis in Sharks." *BioScience* 59(7): 546–50.

Irigaray, Luce. 1980. "When Our Lips Speak Together." Translated by Carolyn Burke. *Signs: A Journal of Women in Culture and Society* 6(1): 69–79.

Knauft, Bruce M., Thomas S. Abler, Laura Betzig, Christopher Boehm, Robert Knox Dentan, Thomas M. Kiefer, Keith F. Otterbein, John Paddock, and Lars Rodseth. 1991. "Violence and Sociality in Human Evolution [and Comments and Replies]." *Current Anthropology* 32(4): 391–428.

Kohn, Eduardo. 2013. *How Forests Think: Towards an Anthropology beyond the Human*. Berkeley: University of California Press.

Law, John. 2009. "Actor Network Theory and Material Semiotics," In *The New Blackwell Companion to Social Theory*, edited by Bryan S. Turner, 141–58. Chichester, West Sussex: Wiley-Blackwell.

Lévi-Strauss, Claude. 1966. "The Scope of Anthropology." *Current Anthropology* 7(2): 112–23.

Mazzei, George. 1979, July 26. "Who's Who in the Zoo? A Glossary of Gay Animals." *Advocate*, 42–43.

McKibbin, William F., Todd K. Shackelford, Aaron T. Goetz, and Valerie G. Starratt. 2008. "Why Do Men Rape? An Evolutionary Psychological Perspective." *Review of General Psychology* 12(1): 86–97.

Mitani, John C. 1985. "Mating Behaviour of Male Orangutans in the Kutai Game Reserve, Indonesia." *Animal Behaviour* 33(2): 392–402.

Mortimer-Sandilands, Catriona, and Bruce Erickson. 2010. *Queer Ecologies: Sex, Nature, Politics, Desire*. Bloomington: Indiana University Press.

Parreñas, Juno Salazar. 2018. *Decolonizing Extinction: The Work of Care in Orangutan Rehabilitation*. Durham, NC: Duke University Press.

Parreñas, Juno Salazar, and Nicole Seymour. 2022. "Afterward: Ecological Inqueeries." *Environmental Humanities*.

Pinker, Steven. 2002. *The Blank Slate: The Modern Denial of Human Nature*. New York: Viking.

Porter, Natalie. 2019. *Viral Economies: Bird Flu Experiments in Vietnam*. Chicago: University of Chicago Press.

Pratap, Aayushi. 2020. "This Rare Bird Is Male on One Side and Female on the Other." *Science News*. https://www.sciencenews.org/article/bird-male-female-grosbeak-gynandromorph.

Raffles, Hugh. 2010. *Insectopedia*. New York: Pantheon.

Redfield, R. J. 2001. "Do Bacteria Have Sex?" *Nature Reviews. Genetics* 2(8): 634–39.

Rich, Adrienne Cecile. 1980. "Compulsory Heterosexuality and Lesbian Existence." *Signs: A Journal of Women in Culture and Society* 5(4): 631–60.

Rosenberg, Gabriel. 2017. "How Meat Changed Sex: The Law of Interspecies Intimacy after Industrial Reproduction." *GLQ: A Journal of Lesbian and Gay Studies* 23(4): 473–507.

Roughgarden, Joan. 2004. *Evolution's Rainbow: Diversity, Gender, and Sexuality in Nature and People*. Berkeley: University of California Press.

Rubin, Gayle. 2011. "Thinking Sex: Notes for a Radical Theory of the Politics of Sexuality." In *Deviations: A Gayle Rubin Reader*, 137–81. Durham, NC: Duke University Press. Originally published in Carole S. Vance, ed., *Pleasure and Danger: Exploring Female Sexuality*. Boston: Routledge and Kegan Paul, 1984.

Sandilands, Catriona. 2016. "Queer Ecology." Keywords for Environmental Studies. New York: New York University Press. Accessed December 31, 2021. https://keywords.nyupress.org/environmental-studies/author/csandilands/.

Shattuck-Heidorn, Heather, and Sarah S. Richardson. 2019. "Sex/Gender and the Biosocial Turn." *Scholar and Feminist Online* 15(2). https://sfonline.barnard.edu/neurogenderings/sex-gender-and-the-biosocial-turn.

Subramaniam, Banu. 2014. *Ghost Stories for Darwin: The Science of Variation and the Politics of Diversity*. Urbana: University of Illinois Press.

Symons, Donald. 1979. *The Evolution of Human Sexuality*. New York: Oxford University Press.

Thompson Reuters. 2019. "The 'Blob,' an Organism with No Brain but 720 Sexes, Debuts at Paris Zoo." https://www.cbc.ca/news/science/paris-zoo-blob-1.5325747.

Travis, Cheryl Brown, ed. 2003. *Evolution, Gender, and Rape*. Cambridge, MA: MIT Press.

Walling, Alexandra. 2019. "Why Jeffrey Epstein Loved Evolutionary Psychology." *The Outline*. https://theoutline.com/post/7956/jeffrey-epstein-evolutionary-psychology.

Willey, Angela. 2016. *Undoing Monogamy: The Politics of Science and the Possibilities of Biology*. Durham, NC: Duke University Press.

Woese, C. R., and G. E. Fox. 1977. "Phylogenetic Structure of the Prokaryotic Domain: The Primary Kingdoms." *Proceedings of the National Academy of Sciences of the United States of America* 74(11): 5088–90.

Woese, Carl R., Otto Kandler, and Mark L. Wheelis. 1990. "Towards a Natural System of Organisms: Proposal for the Domains Archaea, Bacteria, and Eucarya." *Proceedings of the National Academy of Sciences of the United States of America* 87(12): 45–76.

Wrangham, Richard W. 1996. *Demonic Males: Apes and the Origins of Human Violence*. Boston: Houghton Mifflin.

Wright, Les K., ed. 1997. *The Bear Book: Readings in the History and Evolution of a Gay Male Subculture*. New York: Harrington Park Press.

Zimmerman, Edith. 2010. "Jersey Shore Recap: Where Are the Juicehead Gorillas?" *Vulture*. https://www.vulture.com/2010/10/jersey_shore_recap_1.html.

Zuk, Marlene. 2002. *Sexual Selections: What We Can and Can't Learn about Sex from Animals*. Berkeley: University of California Press.

Anne Spice

13

Queer (Re)generations

Disrupting Apocalypse Time

Am I writing at the end of the world? The climate catastrophe looms like an ominous cloud, dropping fire tornadoes and mudslides, sloughing chunks off glaciers, bringing unseasonal storms to unlikely places. The far-flung places anthropologists turned to for stories of exotic "others" are engaged in their own modern cultural salvage projects as a warming climate threatens to destroy their worlds. At the COP27 Conference in 2022, the Pacific Island nations of Vanuatu and Tuvalu lead a call for a fossil fuel nonproliferation treaty. Tuvalu has plans for digitizing its government and culture, a sovereignty without land, as its islands begin to disappear underwater due to the climate-induced rise in sea levels. For some, then, the world is indeed ending, and attempts to mitigate the disaster are made alongside plans to adapt to life beyond it.

As a queer Indigenous anthropologist, I have joined the fight to avert an apocalyptic future in communities whose generational memories include an apocalyptic colonial past and elements of a dystopian present. Through my ethnographic work, I have actively supported the Indigenous land defense movement by living at land defense camps at the front lines of oil and gas extraction and invasion. I have noticed, during this work, both the queerness of the camps and the way that Indigenous temporalities are marked and framed by forms of relational language that connect us to the past and future.

I arrived at Unist'ot'en Camp, in Northern British Columbia, Canada, in the summer of 2015. At the time, the camp was primarily facing the threat of Enbridge's Northern Gateway pipeline, although numerous pipelines had been proposed through the culturally rich valley to get oil and gas to market through the coastal port in Kitimat, British Columbia, Canada. The site had been set up several years before that by Freda Huson (chief Howilkat) and her family as a reoccupation of their traditional territory and a space for their Wet'suwet'en community members to heal from addiction and colonial trauma. I returned over and over again after that first summer and spent the better part of three years there from 2017 to 2020. We faced an ongoing parade of oil and gas companies attempting to access the territory before Coastal GasLink finally obtained a court injunction in 2018, allowing them to begin pipeline construction with the enforcement of police. The checkpoint that allowed Dark House members of the Wet'suwet'en nation to insist on outsiders gaining their free, prior, and informed consent before entering the territory was dismantled during the first police raid in January 2019. Since that time, the territory has become a site of struggle between the energy futures of oil and gas corporations and the lives of Wet'suwet'en people. As the pipeline construction pushes onward without consent, it disrupts and damages the connection to the land, the seasonal cycles that flow through times of harvest and ceremony. In turn, the Indigenous and queer life of the camps (more sites were set up after 2018) disrupts and redirects the work of pipeline construction and also the petroleum-fueled future that the pipeline leads us to. We fight against the inevitability of environmental and cultural destruction by deepening connection to the land, by living in community and resisting industrial invasion, and by doing so we create possibilities for alternative futures in which Indigenous peoples can live and thrive.

The flow of time, the sense of Indigenous history and future possibility, is often captured by the language of "generations," as we reckon with the traumas we inherit from our ancestors and the decisions we make that will affect our children, our grandchildren, and beyond. At first glance, the language of future generations and the image of the Indigenous child appear to exclude queer relations and queer politics, especially in the "no future" thread articulated by Lee Edelman (2004). So too does the queerness of camp life, the many queer, Two Spirit, trans, poly, and nonbinary folks at the front lines of organizing, sit aslant the sometimes conservative traditionalism of Indigenous reservations and communities. And yet brought together, queer *and* Indigenous temporalities as they are lived in land defense camps reject the linearity of straight time, of colonial time, the relentless push of capitalist progress, and instead imagine alternative possibilities for collective life together. In this chapter, I outline apocalypse time—settler colonial and capitalist temporality—before taking up some of the alternative possibilities I saw and experienced in Indigenous land defense camps, including temporal sovereignty, generational kin- and future-making, and queer utopic/collective futurity to show how queer Indigenous ethnography can surface other ways of living that might reject and disrupt apocalypse time.

Apocalypse Time

Infrastructures of resource extraction exemplify the catastrophic linearity of apocalypse time. The teleology of resource extraction orders and governs pipeline construction activities toward the end goal of transporting oil and gas products to market. This temporality, driven as it is toward project completion, is shot through with colonial intent. The logic of elimination here is deployed against any source of delay, complication, or uncertainty. Indigenous people from Standing Rock to Wet'suwet'en Territory and beyond continue to contest the construction of new oil and gas infrastructures. When this happens, industry and police move swiftly to remove Indigenous people from the path of the pipelines. The fact that the "blockaders" are Indigenous people with long-standing relation to their homelands is obscured and overwritten by the project's timeline and goals. What appears to be a logical, profit-driven motive to meet construction timelines and targets hides a more insidious eliminatory outcome. The specter of genocide, the deep history of Indian removal, the threat of land theft, the assertion of control and dominance over unceded lands: all these hide within project timelines like soldiers inside a trojan horse. This settler colonial temporality is oppressive, as it seeks to overcome and dominate other ways of understanding the link between land and time. There is a sense of inevitability and urgency that parallels early colonial invasions. The well-being of future generations, the will and wishes of the ancestors, and current Indigenous uses of the territory are pushed aside to accommodate urgent construction timelines. Pipeline infrastructures invade our lands and our futures.

Kevin Bruyneel (2007) describes how "colonial time" writes Indigenous people out of the present by positioning them as either "static" (anachronistic/outside of modern time) or "advancing" (occupying a place on the cultural evolutionary timeline imposed by the colonizers). When Indigenous sovereignty appears to require a performance of authenticity rooted in the distant past, this performance makes Indigenous people ineligible for claims on the modern present (Bruyneel 2007; Barker 2011). Mark Rifkin (2017) expands on these settler colonial temporalities to argue against the reification of a singular present, asking, "How does conceptualizing time as itself a mutual experience for those initiating and subject to such violence make temporality into an extension of settler colonialism?" (9). Tom Boellstorff (2007) identifies "straight time" as being characterized by "strict linearity . . . evolutionary and millenarian connotations, and . . . paranoid relationship to futurity" (237). The apocalypse, in this formulation, lies at one end of a straight line, and between past and future lies a series of normative (and heterosexual) reproductive relations. The evolutionary trajectory imposed by colonization overlaps also with the heteropatriarchal temporality of straight time.

Colonial time is deeply tied to capitalist time. If capitalist accumulation drives market expansion at all costs, ecological and cultural damage to Indigenous lands will continue to make economic sense. In the case of oil and gas production, expansion of production is legitimized by pressure to get oil and gas to market, even as a drastic reduction/moratorium on fossil fuel production becomes necessary to avert the most disastrous climate-change futures. As Naomi Klein argues in *This Changes Everything* (2014), the biggest barrier to addressing climate change is the capitalist economy itself and its aggressive expansion despite the ecological and social effects. Capitalist temporalities play out on the ground in pipeline disputes as unchangeable and inevitable construction timelines. Potawatomi scholar Kyle Whyte (2020) argues that the language of "crisis" obscures the colonial roots of climate change and favors solutions that may further challenge Indigenous sovereignty. The urgency of the response to climate change may traffic in the same colonial epistemology as climate change itself, as both problem and response emerge from the same colonial historical context. Klein, too, notes that the roots of the current "crisis" are historical—if global warming had been addressed in the 1960s, an incremental approach may have been possible. The fact that climate change is a "crisis" at all, then, is due to the relentless push of capitalist production, in which market cycles are severed from natural processes of ecological renewal. Now, the crises compete, with the urgency of climate change solutions up against a social reliance on capitalist structures. There is argument about which systems maintain social well-being, as both environments and economies are urged to be "resilient," as land defenders insist that the oil and gas industry is killing Indigenous people and the industry argues that land defenders are killing jobs. Economic processes merge with the crisis itself, as the clock ticks down to the point at which catastrophic species loss and natural disaster will make life as we know it unlivable on earth. Despite attempts to slow the conveyor belt of capitalist production, it continues in the same direction, toward the same dystopian future, while activists push for just-in-time climate solutions.

This climate apocalypse is propelled by a destructive teleology, an aggressively linear temporality aligned with the capitalist process that brings oil and gas products to market. Capitalist time and colonial time coalesce in spaces of Indigenous resistance to oil and gas pipelines, as the construction schedules and timelines push relentlessly along a linear path to project completion, displacing and criminalizing Indigenous people who dare to stand in the way. The accumulation of resource wealth necessitates adherence to these capitalist timelines, even when they disrupt the seasonal cycles of Indigenous life, even when they lead us further along the path to climate catastrophe. Extractive industry refuses to abandon these timelines because profits depend on them, even as we face repeated warnings that continuing warming will lead to large-scale disaster for all life on this planet.

Temporal Sovereignty

Indigenous blockades like the Wet'suwet'en Indigenous land defense camps I lived in are an attempt to disrupt the linear infrastructures through which oil and gas flow to market, to disrupt the apocalyptic teleology that the industry continues to fuel. The camps make possible/live toward a different relationship to time, an Indigenous temporality that might embrace different possible futures. In Tlingit, the phrase *haa shagóon* refers to a sense of the past-and-future in the present. I've seen it translated as "our ancestors," "our family history," "our story," or "past, present, and future generations." In the 1983 short documentary film *Haa Shagóon*, Daklaweidi Tlingit elder Austin Hammond introduces the phrase: "It is hard for our Tlingits to explain to others what we mean by haa shagóon. Haa shagóon—it is what we are now, what we have been since the beginning, and everything that our children must become. Haa shagóon, that is the way it is with us." The film contains speeches and songs from a peace ceremony held to draw attention to the destruction and theft of Tlingit lands. It is a call to action for Tlingits, a patient and generous entreaty to "the white man" to honor and respect the lands of our ancestors and future generations. *Haa shagóon*, as "the way it is with us," is more than a description of events. The phrase doesn't simply reference a group of people (the ancestors) or a narrative (our history). It is an orientation to time that brings ancestors past and future into the actions taken in the present. It is both a critique of colonial time and an alternative to it. As a form of "prophetic temporality" (Rifkin 2017), *haa shagóon* does not just predict possible futures, it alters them. When we hold past and future generations so closely, when we treat both with respect, they shape the decisions we make in the present. This is the revolutionary possibility of Indigenous temporalities—our understandings of time offer passage into deep ancestral knowledge, which is brought to bear on future possibilities. Temporal sovereignty, then, would allow Indigenous peoples to bring our ancestors with us into future worlds, would allow our knowledge and experience to matter, would open new possibilities for liberation.

In *Our History Is the Future* (2019), a citizen of the Lower Brule Sioux tribe, Nick Estes, discusses the connections between land, time, history, and resistance. "Indigenous notions of time," Estes says, "consider the present to be structured entirely by our past and by our ancestors. There is no separation between past and present, meaning that an alternative future is also determined by our understanding of our past. Our history is the future" (14). Estes describes how the resistance to the Dakota Access Pipeline is an enactment of Indigenous time and temporality. The Oceti Sakowin have always pulled their future and history into the present through resistance. Through this movement, a tradition of resistance is created, a living and changing continuation of their long history of fighting colonial invasion and occupation. The Standing Rock resistance, Estes notes, is prophesied. Oceti Sakowin people have long warned of a "black snake" come to threaten the water and the lifeblood of the people. He goes on to explain, "But prophets and prophecies do not predict the future, nor are they mystical, ahistorical occurrences. They are simply diagnoses of the times in which we live, and visions of what must be done to get free" (14). Here, prophecy is actionable. Water protectors and land defenders are agents of history, enacting the liberatory vision of those who came before. They pull their history into the present to create a livable future.

Indigenous resistance projects itself backward and forward in time. Here, altering our present moment becomes a historical project. Generations of Unist'ot'en have cautioned their family to protect the land. The inspiration for the land occupation that would become the Unist'ot'en Camp can be traced through Freda to her aunties, grandmothers, and great-grandmothers, who told their children and grandchildren never to sell the land, to remember what it offered them. The head Dark House hereditary chief name "Knedebeas" has been passed through the generations along with the responsibility for protecting Unist'ot'en land from invasion. Now, four generations of land protectors are represented on a mural that faces the road through the Unist'ot'en Camp. Freda stands to one side, fist raised, joined by three generations of chiefs who carried the title of Knedebeas. In 2019, before the territory was raided by armed police, Freda's niece explained to her five-year-old daughter that it wasn't safe to stay on their *yintah* (land/territory). The child's name, translated, means "our ancestor, returned." When told that the police were coming and that she would have to leave, she told her relatives, "Don't let them take our yintah," echoing the advice of her ancestors. The work of resistance is to challenge the completion of the project of settlement, to open future worlds shaped by Indigenous ancestors (who are here with us). The work of resistance is to stop the completion of the pipeline, to push back against the creation of closed epochs and eras, to let our ancestors speak through us, to build a future with their hands, with our hands.

The practice of *haa shagóon*, and other Indigenous orientations to time, is an act of resistance. With the help of our past and future relatives, we refuse to consent to our destruction as peoples. While we still attempt to prevent destruction, we also insist that colonial destruction does not signal our inevitable decline or elimination. We refuse the colonial timeline that ends with extinction, for Indigenous peoples and for the earth. We return to a seasonal round that is inherently reciprocal and relational. We try to break out of the colonial timeline that constrains our future, that predicts more of the same colonial control, that limits alternatives. We open possibilities for livable futures on our lands. "The work of prophesy," Mark Rifkin says in his analysis of Indigenous temporalities in Sherman Alexie's *Indian Killer*

(1996) and Leslie Marmon Silko's *Gardens in the Dunes* (1999), "lies in its ability to stimulate and coalesce a nonsuccessive relation between persistence and potential—the ability of *was, is*, and *will be* to enter into complex exchanges with each other that do not follow an inherent progression from one to the other" (2017, 177). The foretold does not equal the inevitable.

Futurity/Generations

In daily life on Wet'suwet'en Territory, we often turned to the language of "generations" to emphasize our claims to our own autonomous futures. Indigenous land defenders use generational language to articulate the temporal claims of our political projects. We talk about the stakes of the fight by emphasizing what we're doing for the "next generation," for our children and our children's children. We protect the land and water for the next generations, and we entreat others to make decisions with a seven-generation timescale in mind. We lean into the leadership of matriarchs, who are celebrated as water-bearers and life-givers and mothers. This reproductive language pushes against a colonial project that attempted to eliminate us, including our capacity to reproduce future generations. The forced sterilization of Native American women, a foster system that removes native children from native homes, and the residential and boarding-school systems that embedded sexual shame in generations of children after stealing them from their families: all these structures challenge Indigenous reproductive futurity. American blood quantum laws and the "out marriage" clauses of the Canadian Indian Act remove forms of recognition, protection, and status from Indigenous children born below the imposed purity threshold of the settler government. These are genocidal structures and policies, and the insistence that we keep future generations in mind makes sense after such a violent and concerted attempt by the colonizers to make the reproduction of Indigenous nations impossible.

Add this to the continued environmental degradation of Indigenous lands and the erosion of Indigenous autonomy and governance under colonial occupation and you have a recipe for future disaster. Healing from the generational wounds of colonialism while land continues to be stolen and degraded from underneath our feet is no easy task. The fight against extractive industry and environmental destruction, given the context of catastrophic climate change, is a fight on behalf of everyone, for the right to clean water, good food, clear air, and weather events that we have the capacity to adapt to and not flee. This fight too we connect back to prior resistance to colonialism. A sign at a Tahltan blockade reads "They stole the children from the land, now they steal the land from the children," linking the horrors of residential schools to the land theft required for capitalist expansion and the accumulation of resource wealth. The colonial thirst for land that drove early colonial efforts in North America continues today as a quest for profit—capitalism reproduces and maintains colonial dispossession through resource extraction. As the land is surveyed, claimed, bought, leased, and exploited, the violent property relation that severed our ancestors from their territories is replicated. Colonial capitalism masks its genocidal intent with the promise of future wealth and prosperity for all, at the continued expense of Indigenous lives, lands, and livelihoods. Our grandmothers and grandfathers were denied happy childhoods, forced instead to leave their families, forced into manual labor, separated from their siblings, subjected to multiple forms of abuse. Hundreds of children who attended residential schools died in those spaces and were buried on schoolgrounds in unmarked graves that are still being "discovered." These childhoods, these children, figure prominently in present calls for justice, as they mark starting points for trauma that carries through future generations in other forms: addictions, domestic violence, poverty, unstable housing. The processes that deny Indigenous children of the present access to their lands and cultures threaten to echo these generational traumas. We hold the image of our future children in our minds, as we make decisions that shape the world in which they will live. We want them to have clean water, to be able to live freely on their ancestral lands. I've heard matriarchs and land defenders speak passionately about how they don't want to have to describe the taste of moose, of salmon, to their great grandchildren after the land has been destroyed. We fight to preserve the relationships with our lands that shape us as peoples and to project those forward into the future.

The language of future generations is a powerful call to change course, to resist, to sacrifice for the sake of children not yet born. In an era of catastrophic climate change, it is a call that could speak deeply to all people who want to imagine a less destructive future on this planet. Do the Indigenous temporalities that challenge the apocalyptic future of colonial capitalism rely on a heteronormative reproductive futurity? Or, as Boellstorff suggests, is there a way to "queer" temporalities to resist the straight apocalyptic time that's taking us on a linear path to disaster?

Queer Utopia

When I first arrived at the Unist'ot'en Indigenous land defense camp in 2015, I was struck by how *queer* it was. To start, *the people* who showed up to volunteer to support Indigenous sovereignty were queer as hell. Young queer anarchists and punks from the city, Two-Spirit and queer Indigenous folks, middle-aged lesbians, multiamorous family groups, trans and nonbinary people—everyone was there.[1] And more than simply being included, queer folks were at the center of organizing support for the Indigenous front lines, the ones who kept showing up, year after year, to volunteer at the camps. The culture of the camps took on a queer cast, from the common language and in-jokes that emerged, to the local traditions formed, such as a weekly "femme Friday" that encouraged gender-bending, campy makeup, and flamboyant clothing. This culture existed alongside more conservative Indigenous elements and also transformed them. Direct action camps included workshops on gender and sexuality, and Indigenous leadership worked with elders to encourage use of people's preferred pronouns. After living with a particularly homophobic but also slightly oblivious Indigenous man for months, we joked about anonymously letting him know that "everyone he loves is gay." One of the chiefs noted (with a laugh) that a nearby cabin had multiple beds, which could be good for accommodating "the . . . what's it called when there's many partners? Poly people." This openness to queer life at the camps was hard won, after a falling out with a large environmental organization because of their trans-exclusionary policies, and the everyday learning curve of making sense of new words for queer relationships and identities. Nonbinary and trans friends (both Indigenous and non-Indigenous) told me that they were sometimes misgendered by Indigenous community members, but, even so, most insisted that the collective work of protecting Indigenous sovereignty and stopping the pipelines took political priority over the recognition of individual gender expression. Life at the land defense camp itself is queer, oriented as it is against the straight, capitalist time of pipeline construction.

The queer life of Indigenous land defense presents a contradiction to the formulations of queer politics advanced by queer theorists such as Lee Edelman. Edelman (2004) contests the centrality of the figure of the child in a narrative of reproductive futurism that drives the dominant order of civil society, suggesting that queerness be an embrace of the death drive of that order: "In a political field whose limit and horizon is reproductive futurism, queerness embodies this death drive, this intransigent jouissance, by figuring sexuality's implication in the senseless pulsions of that drive" (27). Edelman's ethical project, then, is a queerness that pronounces "that the Child as futurity's emblem must die; that the future is mere repetition and just as lethal as the past" (31). The dedication to "no future" that Edelman espouses is an uneasy fit with Indigenous political movements that insist on a resistance to colonial occupation through a kind of reproductive futurity that also traffics in the heteronormative: we want to survive, we want our children to survive, we want to look to the future and see Indigenous families and cultures and ways of life. We reject the completion of the genocidal project of colonization, and we insist on the reproduction of our cultures. In another way, however, the "no future" framework fits with Indigenous opposition to the colonial worlds that have supplanted our ancestral ways of being, and we can get on board with a project that advances the death drive of destructive ways of life. In Nick Estes's words, "for the earth to live, capitalism must die" (2019, 257). Capitalism promotes a fundamentally destructive relationship to the land, and the global proliferation of capitalist production has brought the earth's ecosystems to a tipping point. The fight against colonial governance is intertwined with resistance to capitalism, as both combine to threaten the planet. Put another way by the radical Indigenous organization the Red Nation, "Indigenous people understand the choice that confronts us: decolonization or extinction" (2021, 108). The issue might be in the singularity of the future we are either claiming or rejecting, and for that matter the past and present we position ourselves in relation to. We can embrace the death of the dominant order without celebrating our own demise. We can refuse some futures while imagining others, and this may mean accepting the reality of the climate apocalypse while also insisting on our survival.

What form does that survival take? How do we build that future while hastening the decline of the empire that's taken hold of our ancestral lands and torn them apart for profit? Here too we can look to queer theory for an orientation to time that, as José Esteban Muñoz puts it, insists "on the essential need for an understanding of queerness as collectivity" (2009, 11). Muñoz responds to "Edelman's assertion that the future is the province of the child and therefore not for the queers by arguing that queerness is primarily about futurity and home. That is to say that queerness is always in the horizon" (11). Muñoz theorizes a relationship to time that places queerness in the future, a utopian possibility of reaching beyond the anxieties and fears of the present. "Queerness's time is a stepping out of the linearity of straight time," Muñoz writes. "Straight time is a self-naturalizing temporality. Straight time's 'presentness' needs to be phenomenologically questioned, and this is the fundamental value of a queer utopian hermeneutics. Queerness's ecstatic and horizonal temporality is a path and a movement to a greater openness to the world" (25). Muñoz gestures to a "collective futurity" that is rooted in the past, as what he calls "queer utopian memory" mobilizes queer memories of utopia and moments into a longing, a desire for another world, a different future. This future may reach beyond the nation-state and collide with the revolutionary, which also imagines, without blind optimism, other ways of relating to each other. Reading Muñoz alongside Indigenous temporalities that hold the past and future together without glorifying the present, I see an alignment, a rhythm. Indigenous peoples look to our ancestors, to precolonial times, not for wistful nostalgia or naïve hopes of returning to ways of life that have been lost. We see future possibilities in our connection to the past; our ancestors are with us now and in the future also, helping us to imagine something different than the world of the conquerors. Queer futurity draws on a similar sense of political imagination, against the apocalyptic threat of colonial time.

Colonial/capitalist time and straight time converge as resource extraction is cast as a by-product of reproduction. Former prime minister Stephen Harper once referred to Canada's natural resources as a "national inheritance," turning generational links to property relations that pass along generational wealth for a prosperous future.[2] For Indigenous peoples, the land is not an inheritance, and it is our relationship with the land that is passed along through the generations. Queer Indigenous time looks to a future where all people take up relations of care with the earth, decommodifying our connection to the land and recognizing the life and agency of the nonhuman world. We can love the land, get to know it, commit to it, tell it our secrets.

Here, queer anthropology, and more specifically queer ethnography, is well positioned to shift from the symbolic to the material, from the realm of literature or performance studies that is the wheelhouse of queer theory to the networks of social relations that congeal in anticolonial political movements. The front lines of Indigenous land defense, the spaces where pipeline construction meets Indigenous resistance—these are the spaces where the battle over the future, apocalyptic or otherwise, is waged. At land defense camps, the linear progression of colonial capitalism meets the cyclical temporality of Indigenous resistance meets the imagination of queer utopia. Queer and Indigenous people lead the path from "no future" to "no pipelines" and push against the apocalyptic timelines that collect wealth for some on the way to catastrophe for all. Indigenous blockades work as a strategy to interrupt commodity flows, disrupting the circulation of capital (Pasternak and Dafnos 2017). The interruption of capitalist processes and timelines is materially realized in the form of the blockade. Before the February 2020 police raids, I helped to organize a camp that blocked access to the road to Unist'ot'en Territory. The blockade was in place for a month—a time of deep winter beauty and renewal during which industry and police could not access the territory. That said, we were under heavy surveillance from police helicopters and drones, and we feared the potentially lethal violence of the impending police raid. I was extremely anxious, not only for my own safety but for the lives of those around me. As the end of the month neared, an Unist'ot'en matriarch and friend visited me at the blockade. "Take your anxiety and your fear," she told me, "and give it to the land. Give it to the river. The land can hold it." Despite knowing that the police raid was imminent, despite the fear and uncertainty, the land continues to offer to care for us. This reciprocal relationship—one fundamentally opposed to the extractive relations of colonial capitalism—is key to the work of land defense, and it is grounded in a sense of time that is larger than all of us. The river knew our ancestors, and the river will know the next generations also. Turning to the river in the face of colonial invasion is to embrace these queer relations, to reject straight time, to see beyond apocalypse.

Queer Indigenous temporalities deftly balance realism and hope. Yes, the climate is changing. Yes, it may be too late to change course. Yes, we're going to fight like hell anyways. We can be utopic in apocalyptic times, by making space for noncapitalist, noncolonial ways of relating even in the spaces of siege created by resource extraction and industrial invasion. In spaces of Indigenous land defense, queer and Indigenous land defenders and water protectors do just that, by modeling collective forms of living that, however imperfect, challenge the legitimacy of the colonial state, challenge the inevitability of environmental decline, challenge the primacy of profit, and challenge the completion of the prior apocalypse of colonization. If it is possible to live in spaces of relative freedom, spaces that turn to Indigenous governance and jurisdiction, that value collective autonomy, that encourage better caretaking of each other and our environment, then a future that scales up these spaces is also possible. We do so in defiance of police violence, of corporate greed, of liberal apathy. Queer and Indigenous ways of relating *align* through land defense to challenge the destructive teleology of extractive capitalism. There is an expansiveness to Indigenous relations that is reaching for that queer horizon, that draws queer people into spaces of Indigenous land defense because of the possibility of community and a more robust care for each other and the earth.

All Our Relations

None of this is to say that relations on the front lines of Indigenous land defense are idyllic. Life under siege, under constant surveillance, under threat of criminalization, is hard, even when that life is collective. Moments of joy and freedom give way to interpersonal drama and heartbreak and broken promises. As Kai Cheng Thom argues in *I Hope We Choose Love: A Trans Girl's Notes from the End of the World* (2022), the tension between our chosen family, as queer people, and the nuclear families that form as our queer kin have children is enough to shake our idealism to its very core. She asks, "Who is going to share my life with me? Who is going to fight with me, take care of me, grow old and die with me? Who will I take care of? Who would I die for? I think about these questions all the time these days. I still have a chosen family, but I think queers are confused about what we mean by the word 'family,' unsure of where we are going and what we hope to become" (118). There are other questions of belonging that surface in emerging Indigenous communities, including the role of non-Indigenous people in the future of the community and movement, the dangerous and sacrificial quality of the work to be done, the commitments people maintain to the movement and the "outside world" and whether these are sustainable. For Indigenous nations that are still organized, primarily along lines of blood relatives, where do queer people, and non-Indigenous people (or even Indigenous people from other nations) fit in? And how do we practice our commitments to each other within the kinship structures of Indigenous life while facing the oppressive force of the colonial state? Here, the answer may lie in our future imaginings, not in present reality. What I am sure of is that the relational expansiveness of Indigenous cultures makes queer futurity distinctly possible, even "at the end of the world." When Indigenous people pray, it is common to add the phrase "all my relations" to the end of the prayer. These relations are not just our blood relatives or even our human relatives, but also our plant and animal kin, and I would add our chosen families here as well. The challenge for Indigenous political movements is to live into this openness and to embrace the queer utopian futurity that makes honored space within our networks of relations for queer people. We can recommit, also, to our nonhuman relatives, who are facing genocides of their own as we lose species at an unprecedented rate. We can make decisions with not only future generations, but all our relations in mind.

For queer Indigenous people, liberatory futures are still within imaginative reach. Indigenous temporality is tangible and expressed in kinship relations to land and responsibility/accountability to land and nonhuman relations. We hold the reality of climate apocalypse and colonial occupation alongside the dystopian present and insist on our place in the future. In the anthology *Love after the End* (Whitehead 2022), Two-Spirit and queer Indigenous writers tell new stories about a future within and beyond apocalypse. The stories are funny, touching, sexy, and sad. All together they take up the responsibility of utopia, the necessity, at this moment of planetary catastrophe, to build livable worlds even as the old ones crumble around us. These moments of queer love and care and tenderness animate spaces of Indigenous land defense. I promised to care for the river even if she has a pipeline beneath her. We love the lands that shape us as peoples even if they are toxic. We create welcoming spaces for queer life in the pipeline's path. We have not abandoned the fight for future generations, for our children and our children's children. We know we can live beyond apocalypse—"after the end"—because we have done it before, are doing it now. We know it is our responsibility to fight as hard as we can against an apocalyptic future that leaves this earth in ruins. But we believe, also, in the power of re-generation, in the memory that makes possible a future utopia, in the renewed connection to our nonhuman relatives, in the return of balance in a deeply unequal world. A way out of the straight timeline. Despite the reproductive gloss of generational language, in this current moment of environmental crisis, a queer kind of love and kinship is generating future possibilities for life on this planet. By building relations beyond compulsory heterosexual monogamy, and even beyond the human itself, we create ruptures in the linear capitalist temporalities that are bringing us all to the cusp of catastrophe. We commit to a future of (re)generations, for all our relations.

Notes

1 Here, the term *Two Spirit* can refer to alternative Indigenous gender identification, or sexuality, or both. I retain the language of *queer* not to contrast it with *Indigenous*—to assume that queer and Indigenous people at the camps are two separate demographics would be a mistake—but to maintain language that is primarily about *a way of relating* as opposed to an individual identity. For more on Indigenous gender and sexuality, see Laing 2021; Pyle 2018; Davis 2014, 2019; and Wesley 2015.

2 David Johnston, "Speech from the Throne to Open the Second Session of the Forty-First Parliament of Canada," October 16, 2013, Parlinfo, Parliament of Canada, transcript, https://lop.parl.ca/sites/ParlInfo/default/enCA /Parliament/procedure/throneSpeech/speech412.

References

Alexie, Sherman. 1996. *Indian Killer*. New York: Warner Books.

Barker, Joanne. 2011. *Native Acts: Law, Recognition, and Cultural Authenticity*. Durham, NC: Duke University Press.

Boellstorff, Tom. 2007. "When Marriage Falls: Queer Coincidences in Straight Time." *GLQ: A Journal of Lesbian and Gay Studies* 13(2–3): 227–48.

Bruyneel, Kevin. 2007. *The Third Space of Sovereignty: The Post-colonial Politics of U.S.-Indigenous Relations*. Minneapolis: University of Minnesota Press.

Davis, Jenny. 2014. "'More Than Just 'Gay Indians': Intersecting Articulations of Two-Spirit Gender, Sexuality, and Indigenousness." In *Queer Excursions: Retheorizing Binaries in Language, Gender, and Sexuality*, edited by Jenny Davis, Joshua Raclaw, and Lal Zimman, 62–80. Oxford: Oxford University Press.

Davis, Jenny. 2019. "Refusing (Mis)Recognition: Navigating Multiple Marginalization in the U.S. Two Spirit Movement." *Review of International American Studies* 12(1): 65–86.

Edelman, Lee. 2004. *No Future: Queer Theory and the Death Drive*. Durham, NC: Duke University Press.

Estes, Nick. 2019. *Our History Is the Future: Standing Rock versus the Dakota Access Pipeline, and the Long Tradition of Indigenous Resistance*. New York: Verso.

Klein, Naomi. 2014. *This Changes Everything: Capitalism vs. the Climate*. New York: Simon and Schuster.

Laing, Marie. 2021. *Urban Indigenous Youth Reframing Two-Spirit*. New York: Routledge.

Muñoz, José Esteban. 2009. *Cruising Utopia: The Then and There of Queer Futurity*. New York: New York University Press.

Pasternak, Shiri, and Tia Dafnos. 2017. "How Does a Settler State Secure the Circuitry of Capital?" *Environment and Planning D: Society and Space* 36(4): 739–57.

Pyle, Kai. 2018. "Naming and Claiming: Recovering Ojibwe and Plains Cree Two-Spirit Language." *TSQ: Transgender Quarterly Review* 5(4): 574–88.

The Red Nation. 2021. *The Red Deal: Indigenous Action to Save Our Earth*. Brooklyn, NY: Common Notions.

Rifkin, Mark. 2017. *Beyond Settler Time: Temporal Sovereignty and Indigenous Self-Determination*. Durham, NC: Duke University Press.

Silko, Leslie Marmon. 1999. *Gardens in the Dunes*. New York: Simon and Schuster.

Thom, Kai Cheng. 2022. *I Hope We Choose Love: A Trans Girl's Notes from the End of the World*. Vancouver: Arsenal Pulp Press.

Wesley, Dana. 2015. "Reimagining 'Two-Spirit Community': Critically Centering Narratives of Urban Two-Spirit Youth." MA thesis, Queen's University.

Whitehead, Joshua, ed. 2022. *Love after the End: An Anthology of Two-Spirit and Indigiqueer Speculative Fiction*. Vancouver: Arsenal Pulp Press.

Whyte, Kyle Pows. 2020. "Against Crisis Epistemology." In *Handbook of Critical Indigenous Studies*, edited by Brendan Hokowhitu, Aileen Moreton-Robinson, Linda Tuhiwai-Smith, Steve Larkin, and Chris Andersen, 52–64. New York: Routledge.

Martin F. Manalansan IV

14

The Queer Endotic

Experiments on the Infra-ordinary
(Or seeds for a worlding)

If this essay is a house, it would be a makeshift shelter, flimsy, open to the elements, yet harboring unruly wobbly aspirations and "gnarled" memories.[1] It is a shaky structure that grows, expands, contracts, meanders, and collapses. This essay is an invitation to dwell in the tentatively sutured and messy reflections on and stories about what it means to "live (and survive) queerly" and to "profess queer anthropology." Despite its improvisational veneer, the architecture of this essay is founded on the strong undercurrents of queer of color critique, women of color feminism, critical race theory, and the pioneering works of queer anthropology.[2] These frameworks form a contingent yet lively mix of ideas and stories that enliven initial misgivings and forlorn ideas that may have found its way to the essay due to the current context of its conception—the COVID-19 global pandemic. I wrote this essay in the middle of this ongoing pandemic that seemed, at least during that moment, to be insurmountable and endless. Some of the following vignettes are from another (still ongoing but now less virulent) global pandemic, AIDS/HIV. The other stories are about episodes of daily life in various mostly domestic settings. I aim to offer an embodied sense of queerness as a vulnerable refuge, a refusal, a placeless nowhere-ishness, and a hopeful elsewhere-ishness—all constituting a queerness that is tacitly embedded in these uncertain scenes and precarious times. I do this to reflect on the practices and variant forms of something we can call "queer anthropology." This essay engages with queer paradoxes of the endotic, the infra-ordinary, the small, the contingent, and the visceral through their exhaustive and expansive archives and how they can be used to invigorate a queer anthropology. In this essay and as I will further discuss, I use *endotic* and *infra-ordinary* interchangeably to refer to the complexities, fertile grounds, and possibilities of the ordinary, the mundane and the banal.

Toward a Queer Infra-Ordinary

Queerness is infra-ordinary. Following the French novelist, filmmaker, documentalist, and essayist Georges Perec (1997, 2010), I understand the infra-ordinary as everyday rituals, behaviors, and scenes that are often optically unmarked and fall below the ordinary (Phillips 2018, 181). Perec was a member of Oulipo, French writers who were devoted to exploring experimental form in writing. He writes:

> How should we take account of, question, describe what happens every day and recurs every day: the banal, the quotidian, the obvious, the common, the ordinary, the infra-ordinary. The background noise, the habitual.
>
> To question the habitual. But that's just it, we're habituated to it. We don't question it, it doesn't question us, it doesn't seem to pose a problem. . . . This is no longer even conditioning, its anesthesia. We sleep through our lives in a dreamless sleep. But where is our life? Where is our body? Where is our space? How are we to speak of these "common things," how to track them down rather, flush them out, wrest them from the dross in which they remain mired, how to give them meaning, a tongue, to let them, finally, speak of what is, what we are. What's needed perhaps is finally to found our own anthropology, one that will speak about us, will look in ourselves

for what for so long we've been pillaging from others. Not the exotic anymore, but the endotic. (1997, 210)

Like Perec, I center the endotic and conceive it not as a dreary quotidian repetition of rituals, postures, enactments, or a static, anesthetized state. Rather, it is an alternative and dynamic form of social and ontological incipience. I insist on repositioning endotic or infra-ordinary moments into a central space, to give them rhythmic palpable intensity and visibility in thinking about queer and queerness.

Therefore, I depart from the popular ways queerness is considered to be akin to the exceptional or the spectacular, always located outside the banal. In fact, it is very much part of the life of the ordinary. Queering, here, is not about a competition for discovering the most outrageous, scandalous, and extraordinary. It is not as a static state but a worlding and unworlding that could possibly veer toward "bent," wayward paths. The infra-ordinary impinges and weighs on the body. This unstable and shifting pressure is precisely the moment of queer potential. We need to attend to how small thoughts, fleeting gestures, and scenarios do not necessarily lead to an anesthetized state but to a compositional process or an attunement that may possibly temper, disrupt, unravel, or alter time, space, and/or being (Stewart 2011). On the contrary, it is about a brave struggle to notice and represent the resonant energies obscured by habit and the "common sensing" of things and processes that blind us, leaving us unaware of where we stand and how we are drenched and awash in the shifting liquidity of the normative and the queer. Thus, my thinking around the queer endotic focuses on the errant potentials and possibilities of what could arise if we labored, attended to, wallowed in, or lingered on the banal, the regular, the habitual, and infra-ordinary. In other words, the queer endotic is about the remarkability of the unremarkable.

Perec admonishes critical social observers from creative writers to ethnographers to pay close attention to things, people, and events by conducting a rigorous audit of what is "out there." Unfortunately, Perec's notion of the endotic and the infra-ordinary does not explicitly engage with power inequalities. These dimensions are virtually absent in his writings. His prose might seem to reek of the classic male white flaneur of Europe, on the prowl to claim and own the spaces of modernity. Others may conceive Perec's notions of the endotic and infra-ordinary as acts of colonizing and domesticating the wildness of the everyday by offering a scrubbed-down version rendered by an imperial eye. Yet I catch a sense of humility and vulnerability in his work that might nuance this initial surface reading of his work.

Perec's work (2010) gestures to significant emotional and affective investments inherent in what initially might be read as clinical observations and descriptions of a Parisian street (Hall 2020). His use of "exhaustion" goes beyond literal physical meaning when, in fact, to exhaust something is to both invest in and release emotional energies. To be more specific, exhaustion in this case is both cathectic and cathartic in the pursuit of the endotic and the infra-ordinary.

I consider the endotic and the infra-ordinary not as the antipodes to the exotic, the outlandish, and the exceptional but as nodes of vitality in a continuous process of tidal shiftings and evolving undercurrents, of worldings where repetitions are part of an accretion, a surge of mounting energies and intensities. At the same time, as in other organic processes, these are also part of co-constitutive "unworldings," of destruction, loss, diminution, and breakdown. In other words, these repetitions and accretions are part and parcel of an (un)worlding that forms "the context or background against which particular things show up and take on significance: a more mobile but more or less stable ensemble of practices, involvements, relations, capacities, and affordances" (Anderson and Harrison 2010, 8).

I follow Perec's lead as part of a larger juxtapositions of current ideas about the ordinary. For example, I read Perec's endotic with and against Berlant and Stewart's (2019, 17) "new ordinary," which is a "collective search engine" and an incipient "energy circuit" from a smirk to a facial tic (among others) that impinges and "impacts" your body. These are "seeds for a worlding." The new ordinary then (to paraphrase the authors) is a concatenation of the transitory and the habitual that fuels the creation of textures, surfaces, and encounters, and blends "the material and the semiotic" as "jumping off points" "to construct composures, worldviews, stances and bodily orientations" (17). They suggest that the new ordinary involves labor, a constant working over, working through, and working beyond the thing(s) at hand.[3]

It is precisely the labor and work inherent in the ordinary that have led anthropologists John Jackson (2013) and Omar Kasmani (2019, 2021) and the literary scholar Heather Love (2013) to challenge the notion of Geertzian thick description where a wink or a cockfight involved layers of observations and hermeneutic maneuvers. All three came out with their versions of "thin description" that explore the contingency and messiness of fieldwork and anthropological knowledge formation. Danilyn Rutherford (2012, 469) suggests that there is a "kinky empiricism" inherent in the anthropological enterprise that takes on the tensions between the empirical and the ethical, which form "the messy realities in which ethnography lives."[4] Thin description then is an attempt to display and perform awkwardness, uncertainty, mess, uncomfortable proximities, and palpable vulnerabilities both in ethnographic fieldwork and in its writings.

Veena Das (2020) offers another equally fascinating notion of the ordinary that parallels if not exceeds Perec. Far from conceptualizing the ordinary as singular or bilevel (ordinary vs. infra-ordinary), Das sees the ordinary as an organic process where vulnerable subjects survive through not an escape from the everyday but rather "a descent into the ordinary" as a way to inhabit even the very spaces of destruction, decay, and defeat. She writes, "A politics of the ordinary [which is] a stitching together of action and expression in bringing together a different everyday . . . the birthing of the eventual everyday from the actual everyday" (58). I would like to consider Das's notion a queer one, suggestive of the recuperation of a mercurial queer infra-ordinary that animates action, forces, and energies that have been repeatedly dismissed, forgotten, or left unnoticed to fester and peter away into cultural oblivion.

A queer anthropology of the infra-ordinary is about the workings of the granular.[5] The granular are rough sediments of fleeting events and episodes that do not fully escape the bounded, hurried flow of routinized everyday life and habituated ways of living. I think of the infra-ordinary when I am on the beach and scoop sand under shallow waters with my bare hands, going underneath the water, grabbing as much as I can hold, but almost always, most of my gray bounty escapes my grasp. Cold, rough, and shimmering in the light, the remaining sand grains left in my palm are precisely those that I intently examine. They are remains of what seems to be insignificant matter, but they fascinate me and arrest my attention.

It is important to consider these coarse life kernels not as mere minor constitutive elements of bigger and grander stories or of more encompassing spheres of human behavior.

The infra-ordinary is not something on its way to something bigger than itself nor is it a simple microcosm or a cog in a macromechanical universe. The infra-ordinary is not a background or a prelude to some spectacular event that will give it significance and coherence. Instead, the infra-ordinary is about the power of the small, the contingent, and the visceral on their own bare terms, without regard to embellishments or a rigid teleology. The infra-ordinary is queer with its odd, frayed, loose, and untethered character, brimming with possibilities, glimmering in its own light. The granular is not an isolated unit or moment but rather is a frictive product of grains rubbing against, clashing, fusing, and breaking apart of other granules, other moments. It is not the fine-grained, "micro" level of sensing the world.[6] It is, in fact, a coarse unfinished moment always brushing against previous, ongoing, and future scenes. I deploy the idea of "small" as not a definitive and bounded unit of measure, but rather a contextual, shifting, and mercurial "scale." I think of scale not as a scientific unit of measure but as a multivalent, unstable ideological construct produced by structural forces, affective atmospheres, and historical conditions (Carr and Lempert 2016).

A queer anthropological perspective on the endotic and the infra-ordinary reorients our sensual attention on wayward possibilities and forms of messy narrative unfoldings, even as these are fleeting and fragmentary records of things coming into or about to come into being. They do not need a resolution, a conclusion, or a summation. Considered on their own, they travel across the specificity of the experience and merge into resonant and palpable tonal echoes of unconnected, often distant memories and events. Such mnemonic tableaus juxtapose the specificity of infra-ordinary events and their mnemonic (dis)connections with various triggers, impulses, and desires—not always in an upward progressive way, but oftentimes in unruly, scattered directions and (dis)orientations.

This queer endotic is constitutive of the horizon that Jose Esteban Muñoz (2009) has astutely suggested. I think of Muñoz's queer horizon where the line between land and sky are blurred and escape ocular capture. I would further qualify that queer horizon is not literally the "over there"; it is not a separate geographic or temporal marker but rather is an intrinsic part of a sprawling and persistent nonlinear flow of time and space that can be fractured or "out of joint." The queer horizon is oftentimes wobbly, linked through various forms of life, beings, relationships, and energy. In addition, the queer horizon of the infra-ordinary offers an embodied space and time for longing, wonder, expectations, aspirations, and hope. Its instability allows for both serious contemplation and lusty playfulness.

The queer endotic is enmeshed in the workings of power, of human activity—it is not a ready-made "thing." As a queer anthropologist of color, I refuse to flatten and universalize the infra-ordinary. By queer, I also think of my own ambivalent location and emplacement in a traditionally colonialist academic field. There is no generic unmarked banality, but rather relative significance and banality are evoked and made possible or impossible through one's social location in the power structure. Therefore, considering my own particular social and biographical emplacement, I am interested in minoritarian infra-ordinary.

Juxtapositions

To give substance to my account of the queer infra-ordinary and the queer endotic, I offer a series of unwieldy and messy fieldnotes (from my two ethnographic projects: my first published monograph, *Global Divas*; and a forthcoming book entitled "Queer Dwellings"), itinerant musings, and diary entries. These fragmentary accounts are from various times and places, all centered on episodes of the contingent, the small, and the fleeting. They are not statements of facts. Rather, they form a set of impressionistic events or jumping-off vantages involving unfolding scenes, energies, and bodies. They constitute loose, muddled, and untamed stories and scenes that follow what Perec suggests when he writes, "It matters little to me that these questions should be fragmentary, barely indicative of a method, at most of a project. It matters a lot to me that they seem trivial and futile, that's exactly what makes them just as essential, if not more so as all the other questions by which we've tried in vain to lay hold to our truth" (1997, 211). I suggest reading these accounts as if one were entering divergent atmospheres of unfamiliar rooms of a strange house and being adventurous by not expecting a logically ordered set of arguments. To read them is to attune to their particular conditions and to be affectively and viscerally engaged. It is also to ask what forms of attention and representation might we need to know to apprehend the queer endotic?

Queer anthropology is not just the work that I do but also the way I am in the world. That is, I am less interested in "thinking like a queer anthropologist" than in "feeling and living as one." I am interested in the forms of intellectual and quotidian labor that combine if not blur the borders of the personal and the professional. The juxtaposed fragmentary events that follow reveal tensions between these two realms. These vignettes or narrative fragments are moments from my own personal diaries and professional fieldnotes written between 1990 to the present.

These vignettes are a series of small, episodic quotidian histories—they are suffused with affects, feelings, and emotions. My purpose is not merely to highlight my personal life and my fieldwork but to illustrate and give flesh to the workings of the queer endotic in playful fragments in keeping with the unfinished nature and aspirational workings of queer anthropology.

To create a nonlinear, itinerant chronicle of both professional and personal odysseys, I juxtapose ethnographic field stories and diary entries with popular cultural texts to flesh out the possibilities and limits of the queerness of the infra-ordinary or the endotic as a theoretical approach, a methodological stance, a political conviction, and as a set of embodied affective and sensorial stances in the everyday.

Moving away from the blaring misleading "truths" of numbers and "stats" of deaths and infections, I turn to annoyance, shock, bliss, discomfort, and boredom as immeasurable yet productive emergent states of queerness—a queerness always unfolding and in process. Using inspirations from and encounters with affective experimental texts like Lauren Berlant and Katie Stewart's *The Hundreds* (2019), trashy makeover television shows like *Tidying up with Marie Kondo*, as well as everyday encounters, professional intrigues, and banal boredom, I aim to extract from diary pages of seemingly incoherent scribblings some vital moments of world-(un)making, living, detachments, attachments, intimacies, refusals, and disaffections. Focusing on unlikely fieldsites and life's flotsam, such as a cramped apartment, a pile of clothes, dust motes, face masks, stale air, and trash, I limn the pivotal value of the visceral, the fleeting, the contingent, the small, and the infra-ordinary to possibly nurture transient yet vital thoughts about being and becoming queer in the early twenty-first century. My hope is that by intently focusing on the unfinished, the ongoing, the fleeting, and the insignificant in the everyday as they move between ethnographic research and everyday lives, we might learn to see queer anthropology less as a finished, complete set of methods, concepts, theories, and arguments, and more as an experimental and inspirational resource for thinking, building, and living.

A contextual note: I "came of age in" or "arrived at" queer anthropology in the 1980s during the early explosion of the AIDS pandemic. With the tidal waves of deaths, illness, violence, and struggle, I was swept away by events that were mostly out of my control. I often wonder whether my first ethnography, resulting in my book *Global Divas*, was a way to gain some control, attain some mastery, and acquire some consolation from the grief and trauma of the AIDS pandemic. Now, I wonder what it means to write my second book, "Queer Dwellings," under somewhat similar circumstances. There are many unanswered questions and unfinished scenes.

Diary Entry: March 12, 2021. Minneapolis.

The eyes looked gentle at first. But the mask transformed the gaze into a menacing one. The Scruff profile declared that the masked guy was "fully vaccinated" along with single or married or open relationship—I forget which one. I am tempted yet repelled. Fearful yet horny.

I am so bored and exhausted with the COVID lockdown. It seems like forever. I rarely leave the house except to go to a grocery store that does not deliver. Besides, it has been too cold. I Zoom, I phone, I text. Nothing seems to be enough.

The pandemic has magnified my solo status. I am alone and I have lived alone since I turned eighteen. Singletons in the pandemic have become more the norm than the queer. What makes it any different from pre-COVID days? Different viruses? Different fears?

During the first few months, I felt my apartment was a cocoon and a warm refuge but news of family members and friends who have died in Manila have disabused me of that illusion. My exhaustion from being confined has been further weighed down by grief.

Fieldnotes: Global Divas, February 23, 1994, New York.

He was a gay Filipino immigrant in his thirties. He could not look at me in the eye as he told the story. He said he was ashamed. He was in the hospital for more than a week for AIDS-related pneumonia. He had to be rushed to the hospital by a friend. When he was discharged, he hurriedly went home. He was frantic because he left things in his small New York City apartment in disarray. When he opened the door to his Lower East Side studio, the sharp scent of rotting rice attacked his nostrils like a sharp thrust of a knife. He felt sick. He felt very ashamed. When I asked him why he felt ashamed, he said that had he died in the hospital, someone else, probably a stranger, would have been a witness to his domestic foibles and failings. I understood what he meant about the smell of rotting rice, uncontained, that touches not only the nostrils but seems to attach if not attack one's body— especially the skin.

Diary Entry: July 20, 2016. Chicago.

I was eating my usual roast chicken dinner at my neighborhood diner in Chicago when I heard a tap on the window. It was a colleague of mine from the university who was in the city for shopping. She hurriedly went in and in a sudden rush of words, blurted that she was in a hurry to pick up her daughter from the train station. She apologized. And I was puzzled. She quickly followed with the fact that she would have readily sat down to keep me company and prevent me from suffering from the trauma of eating alone. I wanted to tell her that I love eating alone in the city. But she was so engrossed with her own domesticity and good intentions, she did not hear me.

Fieldnotes: Queer Dwellings. April 11, 2009. New York City.

Natalia was always talking about her childhood. I wanted to follow up on her stories, so I scheduled a short chat. But, as always, we were in her small apartment she shared with five others. It was cramped and typically dark with one or two yellow lights. Often, another roommate was there either sleeping or doing some kind of housekeeping activity so we kept our voices low and would lie or sit in one corner. This time, we were looking out into the middle of the room and somehow a ray of light from a slightly open slit from the thick curtains uncovered the slow movements of dust motes in the air. The kind of haze that is visible if you look hard enough. There were enough specks to punctuate the sight that we took notice. Natalia noted that the slow dance of these dust motes reminded her of other places. The relaxed atmosphere was in sharp contrast to what was happening outside the apartment—the crazed choreography of bodies, avalanches of smells and sounds going in their immigrant working-class neighborhood. Our brief chat reminded her of the times she would have these slow languid discussions with her sisters and friends back in Colombia. The sessions happened in the wide verandah of her home and there will be some flies— or at night, some mosquitoes dancing in the air. She loved those leisurely, blissful moments, and our rather dreamy and unhurried "interview" made her nostalgic. These moments made her forget her frenetic life working as a maid in Manhattan.

Fieldnotes and Post-fieldwork Reflections: Queer Dwellings. Sections from October 11, 2011, and September 12, 2020. New York City.

Watching an episode of Marie Kondo's homestyle show makes me envious and annoyed at the same time. The Konmari folding method is especially excruciating (for me). I hate folding clothes.

Folding clothes for the three women, Isabel, Natalia, and Imelda, are sensorial experiences that open up fleeting moments of "small joys." When I asked them if they had specific folding techniques for various types of garments and if aesthetics or "looking good" was a factor, the three of them laughed. Imelda said that in the dark, the manner and beauty of one's fold is unimportant. As long as one folded a scarf or a shirt in a neat rectangle or small neat bundle to be small enough to stash away easily and to efficiently pile them to withstand any strong movement, then they were happy with the fruits of their labor. They would gossip in whispers while their hands were busy tucking the clothes into manageable sizes. The shifting texture of the fabric, the smell of freshly cleaned laundry, and the ability temporarily placed some order in the disorder. Sometimes, the folding of clothes was a partial reparative activity when those small accidents happen of colliding bodies causing stuff to spill over. Folding activities happened in the dimly lit room where two small lamps emitted a weak jaundiced light in particular corners. Imelda said that folding was mostly tactile, about efficient hand and finger movement. After the dailiness of this activity, it first seems that it has become part of their kinesthetic habits and body memory when folding clothes does not require vision nor does it require a mindfulness.

Isabel confessed that folding was an enjoyable activity that was soothing and comforting. The tempo and habituated hand movements assuaged and alleviated the pain of some events during that day. At the same time, folding involves the enfolding of their lives with the past as memories of smells, textures, and images of home come in together. Isabel noted that there is a smell of cleanliness that she learned from her grandmother when she was a child. She apparently found a detergent that approximates those childhood aromas, so nostalgia is evoked. Natalia took folding similar to her memories of kneading bread in her family's bakery back home. The feel of soft fabric imitating the fine smooth texture of the dough dislocates her sometimes. She loses a sense of time and place in the dark especially as she dealt with the mountainlike piles of clothes. The piles representing the mountain of where she grew up, slowly disappearing as she finishes folding the batch of clothes. Being busy in the dark lends a sense of comfort to Imelda as she has experienced homelessness before and the fact that she can wash and store her clothes without fear of it being stolen and the blanket of the darkness covering her was soothing.

But what is it about the repetitive quotidian act of folding and its sensorial underpinnings? What are the fabulous underpinnings of the folding techniques between the three Queer Six women's approach with that of the Konmari method?[7] *In Kondo's how-to manual, the act of folding does not contain any of the exuberant affective flourishes and improvisational impulses of the Queer Six. Kondo's operating mode is total control where she imposes a definite script for folding angles and storing tactics for shirts and handkerchiefs. The Queer Six's style is constituted by flexibility, improvisation, and playfulness. Folding for the Queer Six includes a touch of whimsy and an undercurrent of affective impulses—small haptic joys, surges of memories, the attitude of "making do" and an awareness of the fragility of one's surroundings.*

Diary Entry: April 2, 2021. Minneapolis.

I started writing this page after a turbulent month of COVID deaths in my immediate family. Ensconced in what I thought would be a cocoon of comfort, aloneness, and distance, I kept walking around my three-level apartment with the only sign of an-other life or lives were the stray rabbits in my backyard, which I fed carrots every day. This was the scheduled daily activity in my quarantine life—but bunny-feeding time was always somewhat erratic and sometimes I forget until I see their aggressive faces pressed against my floor-to-ceiling window facing the yard. Wanting, demanding, and begging. So, I would usually rush to the refrigerator and grab a few carrots from the vegetable compartment that was bursting at the seam with the root crop. One such time, I held the carrots in my hand when I was suddenly triggered by the memory of a bombastic political figure. I threw the carrots violently into the barren ground of my nongarden, almost crushing them. I snickered a bit, I closed the sliding-glass doors, then I sat down to my coffee and toast watching the rabbits (were there two? Or was my mind playing tricks?) munching on their neon-colored ration. Not hearing the crunch of their teeth against orange flesh, I bit into my toast noisily and looked away.

Eating, they say, is a source of solace during the pandemic. Eating alone, they say, is a recent pandemic affliction—we all must adjust to playing and living solitaire in various forms. But my gustatory adventures have mostly been solitary. I think I have been eating alone since I left my family home in the '80s. There is nothing valiantly romantic or heroic about it. It is what it is.

The Promise of the Queer Endotic

I suggest that the queer endotic necessitates an ethnographic I/eye and skin or a raw embodied engagement, vigilant to the potentialities and alternative messy imaginings of things that often remain in mindless subterranean normativities. The stories I have presented talk about spaces and times that go beyond their specific historical and spatial emplacement. This is what I mean by what I called (at the beginning of this essay) "elsewhere-ishness" and "nowhere-ishness," where the details of the stories can be read as wayward descriptions that do not "toe the line" of literal factuality and physical geographies. The stories subtly gesture to things and events that have remained outside one's bodily powers, where visceral or gut reactions and fleeting sensorial experiences can be ways to trouble the ideas of professing queer anthropology and living a queer life. I am calling for forms of intellectual and affective labor that create the queer endotic or infra-ordinary to seriously consider lingering emotions and itinerant thoughts such as unfulfilled desires, boredom, grief, loss, and nostalgia as chronic unpredictable emotions and affects that resist easy aphoristic conclusions and "thick" description (Jackson 2013; Love 2013), and refuse adherence to semantic depth and interior truth, and resilient formidable attachments (Love 2013; Kasmani 2019, 2021).[8]

The juxtaposed narratives above signal the various ways in which details of visceral, fleeting, and small life adventures do not always cohere or easily add up to something grand and spectacular—even as they connect and speak to each other. In fact, the vignettes and this whole essay foreground these dangling, partial, and loose granules of potentials and "could-bes." I offer these autoethnographic and ethnographic juxtapositions as details that can lead to quixotic and unpredictable routes on surviving and living queerly. Queerness is not the destination but rather the process in which these infra-ordinary details, strands, and moments come alive, acquiring a cultivating function where life, death, denial, pleasure, growth, and decay unfold. The queer endotic then is about the nurturing of a quixotic and intense attention to the shifts and turns, textures and details of the infra-ordinary and their sometimes unconventional outcomes or futures by suspending judgment or adherence to a finished form. In other words, to focus on the queer endotic means to dwell in these various mercurial moments and inhabit these unsettled states of being and becoming.

A queer anthropology of the infra-ordinary and the endotic should be considered very seriously during these times of global uncertainty and vulnerability. With the ways we live "now," we need to recognize the power of the queer endotic as a much-needed stimulating force in the face of isolation, fear, and loss. This may seem impractical and dreamy for many readers, but I believe it offers a way to rouse people from the stupor of dailiness in order to discover, within its confines, more expansive and capacious views of the banal and the mundane. Far from being solipsistic, these stories and the framework of the queer endotic demand a critical dialogical openness, a porous form of embodiment and a fleshy attention to a quirky turn of events that may prove to be vital for our future survival and for the expansion of a queer anthropology. This is not at all prescriptive—I do not know the "right" form that queer anthropology should take—but I do believe anthropologists need to stay with and inhabit these kinds of stories, moments, and energies as part of our own quotidian and professional survival.

As I finished the first draft of this essay, I received a text from my friend Gerry informing me of the COVID death of our buddy Joey. An emoji of a yellow face holding a heart punctuated the news. A few months ago, I had a chat with Joey about his plans to retire to Europe with his partner. We talked about the future and its uncertainty with the ongoing pandemic, but he appeared to have very firm plans about how his retirement years would look. This story might appear to be an illogical or even a self-aggrandizing final statement of the essay, but I offer this event because I believe it is important to center the messy feelings I was having right at that moment to consciously avoid a sense of self-satisfied completion. This life episode is not meant to wind up and wrap up the discussion. Rather, I offer this dangling thread of a mundane episode of loss to invite the readers to dwell in and inhabit the various scenes and episodes. I leave this essay unfinished and open-ended to enable it to be exposed to the queer resonant unfolding power of the infra-ordinary, the unpredictable yet vital energy of the visceral, and the palpable significance of the small.

Notes

1 I am indebted to and inspired by Joseph Russo's (2018) notion of the "gnarled."

2 I am acknowledging the works of Esther Newton, Ellen Lewin, Liz Kennedy, Kath Weston, Ralph Bolton, Evie Blackwood, Bill Leap, and many others.

3 For her notion of the "queer ordinary" and the labor that goes into it, see Love 2015.

4 See Billio and Hiemstra 2013.

5 I wrote this idea about what I call the "ethnographic granular" or the "endotic granular" a year before Lauren Berlant's last book *On the Inconvenience of Other People* where they talk about the "granular everyday." When I read it, it was obvious that we were fellow travelers. I am honored to be in synch with Lauren's brilliant ideas. I acknowledge their brilliance and generosity through the years.

6 For a more expansive reading of the micro, see Love 2016.

7 The Queer Six is an affectionate name I gave to a household of six undocumented queer immigrants, who are the focus of my work in "Queer Dwellings." I understand that, for some people, the idea of naming a group in terms of its number might trigger "bad" connections with historical events that used similar appellations such as the Chicago 7 or the Central Park 5. I did not intend that. My aim was both an emotional shorthand but also a theoretical stance since the name implies a particular normative form of togetherness and collectivity that I interrogate in the "Queer Dwellings" book project.

8 See Love 2015.

References

Anderson, B., and P. Harrison. 2010. *Taking-Place: Non-representational Theories and Geography*. Farnham, UK: Ashgate.

Berlant, Lauren. 2022. *On The Inconvenience of Other People*. Durham, NC: Duke University Press.

Berlant, Lauren, and Kathleen Stewart. 2019. *The Hundreds*. Durham, NC: Duke University Press.

Billio, Emily, and Nancy Hiemstra. 2013. "Mediating Messiness: Expanding Ideas of Flexibility, Reflexivity, and Embodiment in Fieldwork." *Gender, Place and Culture: A Journal of Feminist Geography* 20(3): 313–28.

Carr, E. Summerson, and Michael Lempert, eds. 2016. *Scale: Discourse and Dimensions of Social Life*. Berkeley: University of California Press.

Das, Veena. 2020. *Textures of the Ordinary. Doing Anthropology after Wittgenstein*. New York: Fordham University Press.

Hall, Sarah Marie. 2020. "Revisiting Geographies of Social Reproduction: Everyday Life, the Endotic, and the Infra-ordinary." *Area: Royal Geographical Society* 52: 812–19.

Jackson, John L., Jr. 2013. *Thin Description: Ethnography and the African Hebrew Israelites of Jerusalem*. Cambridge, MA: Harvard University Press.

Kasmani, Omar. 2019. "Thin Attachments: Writing Berlin in Scenes of Daily Love." *Capacious: Journal for Emerging Affect Inquiry* 1(4): 34–53.

Kasmani, Omar. 2021. "Thin, Cruisy, Queer: Writing through Affect." In *Gender and Genre in Ethnographic Writing*, edited by E. Tauber and D. Zinn, 163–188. Cham, Switzerland: Palgrave Macmillan.

Love, Heather. 2013. "Close Reading and Thin Description." *Public Culture* 23(5): 401–34.

Love, Heather. 2015. "Doing Being Deviant: Deviance Studies, Description and the Queer Ordinary." *differences: A Journal of Feminist Cultural Studies* 26(1): 74–95.

Love, Heather. 2016. "Small Change: Realism, Immanence, and the Politics of the Micro." *Modern Language Quarterly* 77(3): 419–45.

Muñoz, Jose Esteban. 2009. *Cruising Utopia: The There and Then of Queer Futurity*. New York: New York University Press.

Perec, Georges. 1997. *Species of Spaces and Other Pieces*. New York: Penguin.

Perec, Georges. 2010. *An Attempt at Exhausting a Place in Paris*. Cambridge, MA: Wakefield Press.

Phillips, Richard. 2018. "Georges Perec's Experimental Fieldwork." *Social and Cultural Geography* 19(2): 171–91.

Russo. Joseph. 2018. "Gnarled Ecologies: Postindustrial Affects of Southeast Texas." Unpublished doctoral dissertation, University of Texas, Austin.

Rutherford, Danilyn. 2012. "Kinky Empiricism." *Cultural Anthropology* 27(3): 463–79.

Stewart, Kathleen. 2011. "Atmospheric Attunements." *Environment and Planning D: Society and Space* 29: 445–53.

CONTRIBUTORS

Jafari Sinclaire Allen is Professor of African American and African Diaspora Studies at Columbia University, where he is the director of the Institute for Research in African American Studies, and editor-in-chief of *Souls: A Critical Journal of Black Politics, Society, and Culture*. Allen's latest book, *There's a Disco Ball Between Us: A Theory of Black Gay Life* (Duke University Press) was published in 2022. He is also the editor of "Black/Queer/Diaspora," a special issue of *GLQ: A Journal of Lesbian and Gay Studies* (2012), and author of *¡Venceremos?: The Erotics of Black Self-making in Cuba* (Duke University Press, 2011) and numerous research essays.

Tom Boellstorff, Professor in the Department of Anthropology at the University of California, Irvine, is author of many articles and the books *The Gay Archipelago: Sexuality and Nation in Indonesia* (2005), *A Coincidence of Desires: Anthropology, Queer Studies, Indonesia* (2007, Duke University Press), and *Coming of Age in Second Life: An Anthropologist Explores the Virtually Human* (2nd edition, 2015). They are coauthor of *Ethnography and Virtual Worlds: A Handbook of Method* (2012) and *Intellivision: How a Videogame System Battled Atari and Almost Bankrupted Barbie* (2024), and coeditor of *Data, Now Bigger and Better!* (2015) and *Speaking in Queer Tongues: Globalization and Gay Language* (2004).

Erin L. Durban is a queer, nonbinary, disabled/chronically ill interdisciplinary scholar with a PhD in Feminist Studies. Durban is Associate Professor of Anthropology at the University of Minnesota, and affiliated with American Studies and Gender, Women, and Sexuality Studies. They are currently cochair of the Association for Queer Anthropology and the UMN Critical Disability Studies Collective. Durban is the author of *The Sexual Politics of Empire: Postcolonial Homophobia in Haiti* (2022), which won the National Women's Studies Association–University of Illinois Press First Book Prize, and coeditor of *"Nou Mache Ansanm* (We Walk Together): Queer Haitian Performance and Affiliation," a special issue of *Women and Performance* (2017).

Elijah Adiv Edelman is Associate Professor of Anthropology at Rhode Island College. As a Public Anthropologist focusing on trans rights, their research takes an ethnographic and community-centered approach in addressing how transgender and gender nonconforming communities become organized and managed through cultural, social, and political processes. They are the author of *Trans Vitalities: Mapping Ethnographies of Trans Social and Political Coalitions* (2021), the first ethnography focused on Washington, DC-based trans coalitional social justice work. This work highlights meaningful life-making practices as responses to traumas produced by mainstreamed racialized, classed, and bodily pathologizations.

Lyndon Gill is Associate Professor in the Departments of African and African Diaspora Studies, Anthropology, and Women's and Gender Studies at the University of Texas at Austin. He received his PhD in African American Studies and Anthropology from Harvard University, and has received postdoctoral fellowships from Princeton University, the University of Pennsylvania, and the Ford Foundation. His first book, *Erotic Islands: Art and Activism in the Queer Caribbean*, was published by Duke University Press in 2018. He is also a poet and installation artist.

Marshall Green is a shape-shifting Black Queer Feminist nerd; an Afro-Future, freedom-dreaming, rhyme-slinging dragon slayer in search of a new world; a scholar, poet, facilitator, filmmaker; and an Assistant Professor of Africana Studies at the University of Delaware. He earned his PhD from the Department of American Studies and Ethnicity with specializations in Gender Studies and Visual Anthropology at the University of Southern California. He is completing his memoir, *A Body Made Home: They Black Trans Love*, with the Feminist Press. He is a proud founding member of Black Youth Project 100 (BYP100). Instagram and Twitter: @drDrummerBoiG

Brian A. Horton is Assistant Professor of Anthropology at Brandeis University, where he is also affiliated with the Department of Women's, Gender, and Sexuality Studies, the Department of African and African American Studies, and the South Asian Studies Program. His areas of scholarly interest span queer anthropology/queer theory, South Asian anthropology, digital anthropology, and global studies of (anti)Blackness. Across each of these broad domains, his research and teaching explore the thresholds between pleasure and violence, wherein he asks how gender, sexual, and racial minorities experience and endure myriad forms of violence while simultaneously enacting possibilities for pleasure, fun, and creativity.

Nikki Lane is Assistant Professor in Gender, Sexuality and Feminist Studies at Duke University. An interdisciplinary scholar trained as a Cultural and Linguistic Anthropologist, her work broadly explores issues related to American popular culture, African American language practices, and sexual cultures in the United States. Emphasizing analyses of race, gender, sexuality, and class, her work examines contemporary Black queer life and language. She is the author of *The Black Queer Work of Ratchet: Race, Gender, Sexuality, and the (Anti)Politics of Respectability* (2019) which explores the use of the word "ratchet" in a community of Black queer women in Washington, DC.

Martin F. Manalansan IV is Professor in the Department of Women's, Gender, and Sexuality Studies at Rutgers University, New Brunswick. He is the author of *Global Divas: Filipino Gay Men in the Diaspora* (Duke University Press, 2003) and the forthcoming *Queer Dwellings: Mess, Mesh, Measure*. He has edited several collections, including *Q&A: Voices from Queer Asian North America* and *Beauty and Brutality: Manila and Its Global Discontents*. He is the president-elect of the Association for Asian American Studies.

Shaka McGlotten is Professor of Media Studies and Anthropology at Purchase College-SUNY, where they also serve as Chair of the Gender Studies program. They are the author of *Dragging: Or, in the Drag of a Queer Life* (2021) and *Virtual Intimacies: Media, Affect, and Queer Sociality* (2013), as well as coeditor of *Black Genders and Sexualities* (with Dána-ain Davis, 2012) and *Zombies and Sexuality* (with Steve Jones, 2014). Their work has been supported by Data and Society, the Alexander von Humboldt Foundation, Akademie Schloss Solitude, and the Andy Warhol Foundation.

Scott L. Morgensen is Associate Professor of Gender Studies at Queen's University, where he cofounded and co-organizes the Queen's Feminist Ethnography Network and is a former cochair of the Association of Queer

Anthropology. His essays and edited special issues have been published in the fields of anthropology and queer, feminist, Indigenous, American, and critical race and ethnic studies. He is the author of *Spaces between Us: Queer Settler Colonialism and Indigenous Decolonization* (2011), which was awarded the Ruth Benedict Book Prize Honorable Mention in Queer Anthropology. His current work examines queer and feminist ethnography as contributions to anti-colonial and liberatory theory, method, and pedagogy in gender studies and interdisciplinary fields.

Kwame Otu is Associate Professor of African Anthropology at Georgetown University's Walsh School of Foreign Service. His book, *Amphibious Subjects: Sasso and the Contested Politics of Queer Self-Making in Neoliberal Ghana* (2022), is part of the New Sexual World Series published by the University of California Press. Currently, he is working on his second monograph entitled, *The Salvage Slot: Technology and the Ecologies of the After-afterlife in Postcolonial Ghana.* In this ethnography, he explores how e-waste workers in Ghana navigate the toxicity of urban mining to illuminate Africa's paradoxical location as a site of extraction and deposition.

Juno Salazar Parreñas is Associate Professor of Science and Technology Studies and Feminist, Gender, and Sexuality Studies at Cornell University. Her research is driven by the question of how embodied human-animal relations reveal the social, cultural, and political dimensions of contemporary global environmental crises. She is the author of *Decolonizing Extinction: The Work of Care in Orangutan Rehabilitation* (Duke University Press, 2018), which received the Michelle Rosaldo Prize from the Association for Feminist Anthropology and honorable mentions from the Association for Asian Studies and the American Anthropological Association. She also edited the book *Gender: Animals* (2017).

Lucinda Ramberg is Associate Professor in Anthropology and Feminist, Gender, and Sexuality Studies at Cornell University. Her research projects in South India have focused on the body as an artifact of culture and power in relation to questions of caste, sexuality, religiosity, and projects of social transformation. She wrote *Given to the Goddess: South Indian Devadasis and the Sexuality of Religion* (2014, Duke University Press) which won the Ruth Benedict Book Prize in Queer Anthropology among other prizes. She is currently working on a manuscript entitled "We Were Always Buddhist: Dalit Conversion and Sexual Modernity."

Sima Shakhsari is Associate Professor in the Department of Gender, Women, and Sexuality Studies at the University of Minnesota. They hold a PhD in Cultural and Social Anthropology from Stanford University and an MA in Women, Gender, and Sexuality Studies from San Francisco State University. Shakhsari's book, *Politics of Rightful Killing: Civil Society, Gender, and Sexuality in Weblogistan* (Duke University Press, 2020) received the Fatema Mernissi Book Award Honorable Mention from the Middle East Studies Association. Their current project focuses on the racial politics of gender and class in uneven geographical/geopolitical moves and social movements in diaspora.

Savannah Shange is Associate Professor of Anthropology at University of California, Santa Cruz, where she also serves as principal faculty in Critical Race and Ethnic Studies. She earned a PhD in Africana Studies and Education from the University of Pennsylvania, a MAT from Tufts University, and a BFA in Experimental Theater from Tisch School of the Arts at New York University. Her first book, *Progressive Dystopia: Abolition, Anti-Blackness and Schooling in San Francisco* (Duke University Press, 2019) is an ethnography of the afterlife of slavery as lived in the Bay Area. She is a proud alumna of BYP100 and is currently working in collaboration with organizers to document and amplify the practice of abolition in everyday life.

Anne Spice is Tlingit, a member of the Deisheetan clan and Kwanlin Dun First Nation. She is Assistant Professor in the Department of Anthropology at the University of Toronto, Mississauga. An activist anthropologist and land defender, she studies the confluence of colonialism and racial capitalism and seeks to resist its damaging effects on Indigenous communities.

Margot Weiss is Associate Professor of Anthropology and American Studies at Wesleyan University, where she coordinates Queer Studies, and former cochair of the Association for Queer Anthropology. She is the author of *Techniques of Pleasure: BDSM and the Circuits of Sexuality* (Duke University Press, 2011), which won the Ruth Benedict Book Prize in Queer Anthropology and was a finalist for the Lambda Literary Award in LGBT Studies, and coeditor of *Queer Then and Now: The David R. Kessler Lectures* (with Debanuj DasGupta and Joseph Donica, 2023). Her current book project explores the politics of institutional knowledge production and the place of desire in queer/left activism.

Ara Wilson is Associate Professor of Gender, Sexuality, and Feminist Studies and Cultural Anthropology at Duke University. Her long-term ethnographic work is focused on Thailand (*The Intimate Economies of Bangkok*, 2004) and on transnational sites such as the World Social Forum. She has published analytical articles on key terms for queer feminist analysis, such as *infrastructure, intimacy*, and *gender*. A former cochair of the Association for Queer Anthropology, she is currently on the advisory board of *Meridians* journal.

INDEX

Bold page numbers refer to figures

abolition, 7, 17, 191–92, 195
Access Denied (survey summary), 218
accessibility, 18, 228, 230, 234–41
accountability, 6, 14, 46, 222, 280; and ethnography, 13, 16–19, 192, 198–99; and queer anthropology/ queer theory, 54–55, 59–60, 65, 67, 69–70
Acevedo, Sara M., 231
Açiksöz, Salih Can, 231
activism: AIDS, 55; animal rights, 260; and anthropology, 10, 18, 198; and Black anthropology, 192–95, 198, 200; Black lesbian, 33–34, 37, 41, 47; environmental, 232–33, 241n2, 275; gay rights, 11, 84, 89; Indigenous LGBTQ2S, 92n3; language, 122, 128n12; lesbian Delhiite, 107; minoritized gender and sexualities, 82, 89, 211; and queer studies, 64, 117; same-sex marriage, 102–3, 106; trans, 11, 17, 180–81, 210,

213–22, 231, 247, 257. *See also* LGBT rights
Advocate (magazine), 259
aestheticization, 33, 36–37, 134–37, 144, 147, 293
affect, 89, 146, 158, 286, 288–90, 294–95; and anthropology, 18, 33, 145; and marriage, 104, 106
Afghan refugees, 178
Africa, 54, 101; and queerness, 44–46, 69, 160; and slavery, 6, 39, 103, 107, 154, 204, 230; West, 163
African diaspora, 42, 100, 164, 202–4. *See also* Black Atlantic
African female husbands, 110
African queer studies, 69, 160
African studies, 200, 203
Agard-Jones, Vanessa, 69, 232
Alexander, M. Jacqui, 48, 199
Alexeyeff, Kalissa, 137
Alexie, Sherman, 272
Allen, Jafari Sinclaire, 7, 13–14, 33, 55, 58, 78, 191
Allport, G. W., 87

alterity, 2–3, 21n9, 41, 152; consumption of, 17, 71n11, 82, 101, 194; and cultural difference, 2, 15, 81; exoticizing, 8–10, 12, 21n9, 57–59, 266; and LGB politics, 214–15, 247, 261; racialization, 4–5, 57, 63, 87, 237, 240, 241n1; and transnational queer anthropology, 16, 152–54, 157, 164. *See also* antinormativity

Altman, Dennis, 156–57

Amar, Paul, 182

American Anthropological Association (AAA), 10–12, 21n11, 46, 92n3, 183n7, 196, 234, 243n9; "Disabled Voices in the Field" (AAA panel), 235. *See also* Association for Queer Anthropology (AQA, formerly Society of Lesbian and Gay Anthropologists (SOLGA) and Anthropology Research Group on Homosexuality (ARGOH))

American Dialect Society, 122

American studies, 68, 175–76, 197

Amin, Kadji, 12, 54

Amini, Mahsa Jina, 183n8

Amory, Deborah, 4, 7, 21n6, 46–47

ancestors, 194, 202, 267, 269–74, 277–78

animacies, 126n3, 232, 252–53

Anthropocene, 232–33

anthropology at home, 235

Anthropology Research Group on Homosexuality (ARGOH), 10–12. *See also* Association for Queer Anthropology (AQA, formerly Society of Lesbian and Gay Anthropologists (SOLGA) and Anthropology Research Group on Homosexuality (ARGOH))

anti/ableism, 9, 15–18, 123, 125, 228–29, 233–39. *See also* cripping ethnography

anticapitalism, 18, 229, 235

anticolonialism, 38, 277. *See also* decolonization; postcolonialism

anticure (Clare), 231

antinormativity, 60, 63, 70, 169, 257; of queer theory, 5, 54, 70n5, 118, 139–40, 172, 229

antiracism, 18, 89, 229, 235

Antony and the Johnsons, 257

Anzaldúa, Gloria, 33, 142, 228, 242n2

archives, 33, 46–47, 60, 80–81, 238, 242n6; of queer research, 33, 106, 145, 259, 284

area studies, 56, 68–69, 175–76

Arondekar, Anjali, 57, 175

artists, 69, 194–95, 198, 200, 205, 232; Black lesbian intellectual, 13, 34–37, 47

asexual reproduction, 18, 248, 250, 254–57, 260

assimilation, 125, 155, 169, 171, 175

Association for Queer Anthropology (AQA, formerly Society of Lesbian and Gay Anthropologists (SOLGA) and Anthropology Research Group on Homosexuality (ARGOH)), xii, 1, 4, 7, 10–12, 21n6, 46; T-shirts, 2–3, 6

asylum, 156, 177–81, 214

Atis Rezistans, 232

attunement, 193, 285

Austin, J. L., 65

autoethnography, 31, 213, 235, 295

autological subject (Povinelli), 103

Babb, Florence, 2

Bahng, Aimee, 256

Bailey, Marlon, 107, 110

ball culture, 110

Bandung era, 161

Barrett, Michèle, 102

Batu Wildlife Center, Borneo, 253

BDSM cultures, 63, 111. *See also* kink
  cultures
Beal, Francis, 39
bears, 258–60
beauty pageants, 158–59
Behar, Ruth, 34
Beirut, Lebanon, 182
Benedict, Ruth, 9, 80, 92n2, 183n7,
  228, 241
berdache, 20n1, 141
Berlant, Lauren, 286, 290, 297n5
Berne, Patricia (Patty), 229
Bérubé, Allan, 91
bestiality, 105, 173, 260
Biden, Joe, 178
Biehl, João, 223
binaries, 3, 116, 118, 120–23, 180;
  gender/sex, 137–38, 153, 157–58,
  210, 248–49, Z., 254; nature/culture,
  108–10, 247–61; state/civil society,
  171, 182, 183n8
biological relatedness, 108–9, 111
biological sex, 109, 117
biology, 18, 108–9, 248, 251–52, 254–58,
  260–61
Black, Valerie, 235–36
Black Atlantic, 69, 107, 160
Black Box, xi
Blackdacting, 192
Black LGBT folx, 110, 197–98; Black
  lesbians, 13, 33–36, 107, 204
Black Lives Matter, 237
Black Power, 154
Black queer studies, 13, 69, 160, 164;
  Black queer anthropology, 17, 19,
  31–49, 91, 191–205
Black radical intellectual traditions, 14,
  31–36, 48n1, 49n5, 195
black snake prophesy, 271–73
Black study (Moten and Harney), 17,
  191, 201
Black/trans (Snorton), 5

Black women, 37–39, 45, 106–7, 125,
  142; personhood of, 39–40, 49n5
Blackwood, Evelyn, 11, 212
Black Youth Project (BYP100), 195,
  201
Blanchette, Alex, 260
Boas, Franz, 92n2
Boellstorff, Tom, 12, 15, 35, 57, 118,
  158, 230; on critical empiricism, 54,
  59; and straight time, 269, 274
Bolles, A. Lynne, 38
Bollywood, 146
Bolton, Ralph, 6
borderlands epistemology (Anzaldúa),
  118, 160
Borneman, John, 100, 105–6
Brainer, Amy, 104
Brazil, 105, 109, 143
Brown, Lydia X. Z., 229–30
Bruyneel, Kevin, 269
Burke, Carolyn, 248–50
Butler, Judith, 53, 60, 105; *Gender
  Trouble*, 55, 117, 135–36, 140; and
  performativity, 65–67, 146–47; and
  trans figure, 67, 69, 139, 141
Butler, Octavia, 255–56
Byrd, Jodi, 182

Camminga, B, 213
camp, 136–37, 259, 275
Canada, 45, 178–79, 267, 277
Canaday, Margot, 172
capitalism, 9, 123, 229, 268; and apocalypse time, 18, 268–72, 276–78;
  global, 57, 154, 162, 171–72, 184n14;
  homo-, 177, 184n14; racial, 78–79,
  232. *See also* colonialism; liberalism;
  neoliberalism
Card, Claudia, 105
care, 83, 91, 278–80
carework, 19, 100–101, 104, 230,
  236–39, 242n7, 251

Carpenter, Edward, 9

Center for LGBTQ Studies, CUNY (CLAGS), 56

Chambers-Letson, Joshua, 135

Changing Our Minds (film), 84–**85**

Chaudhry, V. V., 141

Chen, Mel Y., 232

Chiang, Howard, 69

Chika, x

China, 161–62, 182

Christian, Barbara, 47

Christianity, 9, 101, 161, 177, 229, 260

chronic illness, 232–37, 241n2, 242n7

chrononormativity (Freeman), 228

cisnormativity, 9, 15, 18, 82, 254

citation practices, 33, 38, 142, 175, 233, 242n4

#CiteBlackWomen, 38

civilization discourse, 10, 15–16, 81, 101, 179; and LGBT rights, 155, 170–72, 176–77; and reproduction, 105, 108

civil society, 170–73, 183n2–3, 275; and queer geopolitics, 177, 182; transnational, 164n3, 184n8

Clare, Eli, 228, 230, 231, 242n6

class, 47, 86–88, 102, 106, 120, 127n6, 141, 197; and intersectionality, 2, 20n4, 38, 56, 58, 61–64, 111, 210–12; middle- and upper-class people, 181, 233, 251; and queerness, 3–5, 45, 67, 179–81; and race, 14–17, 37, 83, 107; working-class people, 40, 45, 197, 235, 292. *See also* Marxism; poverty

climate change, 269–70, 273–76

Coastal GasLink, 267

Cohen, Cathy J., 4, 34, 64, 173

Cohen, Lawrence, 3, 56

collaboration, 13, 32, 57, 202, 236–40

collective futurity, 268, 277

Collier, Jane, 100

Colligan, Sumi, 235

colonialism, 14–18, 68, 126, 171, 182, 229–32; and anthropology, 6–10, 12, 80, 118; and apocalypse time, 18, 268–72, 276–78; and genocide, 268, 273–74, 276; and Indigenous Peoples, 267, 273–74; Israeli, 174; and kinship, 103, 109, 111–12; neo-, 175; and plastic pollution, 109, 232–33; settler, 8–9, 103, 182, 237, 268–70; and sexuality, 78–82, 89, 101, 176. *See also* capitalism

Combahee River Collective, 38

comparative methodologies, 15, 71n6, 118, 126, 153, 160–61, 181–82

compulsory heterosexuality, 18, 65, 153, 253–54, 280

Conner, Randy, 212

Cook Islands drag, 137

COP27 Conference (2022), 266

Cornejo, Giancarlo, 68–69

COVID-19 pandemic, 19, 199, 202–3, 237, 240, 283–84, 291, 294–96; and ethnography, 233, 236–37, 242n7

Crenshaw, Kimberlé, 38

criminalization, 86, 88, 211, 213–14, 217, 270, 279

crip of color critique, 7, 228–29

cripping ethnography, 17–18, 227–43

crip theory (McRuer), 5, 227–31, 234, 240, 243n8

crip time (Kafer), 228, 233

critical anthropology, 33, 153

critical area studies, 69

critical cultural studies, 38

critical disability studies (CDS), 228–29, 232, 237, 241n2, 242n4

critical empiricism (Boellstorff), 54, 59

critical race feminism, 103

critical race theory, 70n4, 99, 105, 283

308 INDEX

cross-cultural study, 2, 9, 11, 13, 20n1, 141, 211

crosscurrents (Fajardo), 57

cross-dressing, 137–38

Cuba, 39–40, 43, 46, 49n5, 161

cultural anthropology, 13, 134; socio-cultural, 32, 229

culture theory, 153, 162–64

Currah, Paisley, 213

Currier, Ashley, 69

customary, the (Fiereck, Hoad, and Mupotsa), 69

Cvetkovich, Ann, 56

Dakota Access Pipeline, 271

Das, Veena, 287

data: collectively generated, 216, 218–20, 223, 238–39; producers of, 32, 59; versus queer theory, 14, 54, 68–69, 70n4, 71n6; as "raw," 12, 47, 57–60. *See also* ethnography

Dave, Naisargi, 58, 107, 260

Davis, Angela, 107

Davis, Dána-Ain, 107

Davis, Jenny L., 6

Davis, Madeline D., 3

DC Trans Needs Assessment (DCTNA), 216–21

Decena, Carlos, 143–44

decolonization, 78, 91, 103, 154, 171, 276; and anthropology, 7–8, 21n10, 32–34, 38, 43, 57–59; and language, 118, 124, 126; and queer, crip ethnography, 229, 234–35; and queerness, 18, 111, 175

de Lauretis, Teresa, 55

Delhiite lesbian activists, 107

Deloria, Ella Cara, 92n2

D'Emilio, John, 251

Derrida, Jacques, 55, 249

Detroit Black queer and trans* house culture, 107, 110–11

devadasis, 110

Devereux, Georges, 9

deviance, 4, 58, 60–65, 79, 87, 103, 170

Dickemann, Jeffrey, 6

DiFranco, Ani, xii

digital anthropology, 235

dis/ability, 2, 5, 17, 117, 125, 180, 214. *See also* cripping ethnography

disability anthropology, 228–31, 234, 237, 242n4

disability critical race theory (DisCrit), 241n1

disability justice, 228, 230, 233–38, 241, 241n2, 242n6

disability studies, 182, 228–29, 231, 241n2, 242n4

"Disabled Voices in the Field" (AAA panel), 235

disciplinarity, 34–35, 41, 195, 203

Dixit, Madhuri, 146

domesticity, 111, 211, 292. *See also* house cultures

Dominican gay and bisexual men, 143–44

double consciousness (Du Bois), 118

drag, 16, 39–40, 134, 137–38, 140; in *Gender Trouble*, 66–67, 136, 139, 141

Drake, St. Clair, 32

Driskill, Qwo-Li, 228, 230

dubbing culture (Boellstorff), 57

Du Bois, Cora, 9

Du Bois, W. E. B., 118

duCille, Ann, 46

Duggan, Lisa, 5, 63, 105

Dunham, Katherine, 192

Durban, Erin L., 17–18, 231

Dutta, Aniruddha, 158, 212

Earth, Barbara, 212

Edelman, Elijah Adiv, 17, 213

Edelman, Lee, 53, 56, 67, 268, 275–76

INDEX   309

Elliston, Deborah, 3, 56, 92n3

embodiment, 5, 40, 100, 137, 146, 202, 248; and ableism, 234; and Black feminist narrative theory, 31–32; body vs. flesh, 38, 142–43; gendered, 67, 109, 138; more-than-human, 18, 247–61; and performance, 67, 133–35; and the queer endotic, 18, 284–95; and somatechnics, 261; trans, 3, 18, 56, 108, 139, 257

Embodiment Institute, 202

empiricism, 83, 254; anti-empiricism, 58–60; kinky, 59, 68, 287; and queer theory, 14, 34, 53–71

Empress Of, x

Enbridge Northern Gateway pipeline, 267

Eng, David L., 5, 57, 106

environmentalism, 194, 232–33, 241n2, 275

ephemerality, 46, 145–46

epicene languages, 120, 125–26, 127n7. *See also* pronouns

Erickson, Bruce, 254

erotic autonomy (Alexander), 48

erotic subjectivity (Allen), 58

essentialism, 10, 248–50, 258, 261; anti-, 65, 117, 136, 140, 251

Estes, Nick, 271, 276

ethnicity, 33, 61, 86–88, 155, 212

ethnocartography (Weston), 2, 78, 81, 83, 92n3, 141, 174; and queer anthropology, 8, 11–15, 59, 70, 90

ethnographic sensibility, 33, 42

ethnography, 145–46, 157, 179–80, 212, 216–20, 231–32; and activism, 18, 192–95, 198; and the archive, 45–46, 70n1; and being in relation, 40–43; of Black gender, 142; and creative practice, 192–98; for depathologizing sexuality, 82–90; of

drag queens, 39–40, 66, 136; and embodiment, 13, 202; participant observation, 33, 40, 83, 153, 194, 198, 204; patchwork, 235; and primitive sexuality, 9, 78, 80–82, 90–91, 92n1, 101; and queerness, 7, 104, 290–95; sensory, 18, 239, 286–96; thick description in, 8, 21n9, 46, 71n12; thin description in, 194, 286–87; transnational queer, 154–58, 162–63. *See also* cripping ethnography; fieldwork

eugenics, 79, 229–30, 232–33

Eurocentrism, 13, 16, 35, 56, 154, 179, 211, 250

Evans-Pritchard, E. E., 9

everyday life, 34, 101, 119, 134, 143, 145, 163, 284. *See also* queer endotic

evolutionary biology, 256–57

evolutionary psychology, 256

exile, 100, 105, 107, 228

exoticizing, 8–10, 12, 21n9, 57–59, 101, 266, 285–86

extractive industries. *See* oil and gas industries

Fabian, Johannes, 80

fabulousness, 138, 144, 146, 294

Fajardo, Kale Bantigue, 57, 159

family, 43, 199–200; chosen, 101, 110, 279–80; "Family of Man," 251–52; "Family of Nations," 171–72. *See also* kinship

Fanon, Frantz, 163

Female Desires (Blackwood and Wieringa), 3

feminism, 7–8, 19, 56–59, 64, 68, 99, 135, 229; and anthropology, 11, 18, 21n10, 74n5, 108, 118, 234–37, 248; Black lesbian, 13, 31–41, 47–48, 55, 59, 204; and gender, 65, 122,

125–26, 128n12, 140; and intersectionality, 63, 160, 228; and kinship, 102–3, 105, 107; postcolonial, 70, 79, 109; queer, 15–17, 70n4, 175, 242n4, 283; and sexuality, 248–51, 254–57, 261; trans-exclusionary radical (TERF), 117, 126; white, 49n4, 214

Ferguson, James, 153

Ferguson, Roderick, 14, 64, 90–91

Fielder, Brigitte, 108

fieldwork, x, 3, 44, 103, 153, 199, 235–36, 286–87; Black gay feminist, 33, 40–41; cripping, 17–18, 227–43; and the queer endotic, 290, 293. *See also* ethnography

Fiereck, Kirk, 69

Fitzgerald, Thomas, 10, 20n1

Floyd, George, 237

Foucault, Michel, 9, 55, 61, 65, 118, 171, 228, 251

France, 37, 41, 248–49, 284

Freedom to Marry Our Pets Society, 260

Freeman, Elizabeth, 228

Fritsch, Kelly, 230

From, Sam, 84

futurity, 53, 146, 268–69, 273–80

Garber, Marjorie, 137

garotos, 143

Gaudio, Rudolph, 66

Gay, Jan, 92n4

Gay American Indians, 92n3

gay and lesbian anthropology, 2, 5, 11–12, 20n2, 21n9, 53, 92n3

The Gay and Lesbian Studies Reader, 60

gay whiteness (Bérubé), 91

gender affirmative health care, 139, 179–80, 212, 214, 258

gender identity, 16, 156, 179; globalized definitions of, 137, 210–11, 223n1; Indigenous, 215, 281n1; in *It Gets Messy in Here* (film), 197–98. *See also* identities

gender identity disability (GID), 231

gender-liminal people, 211–12, 214, 222. *See also* trans people

gender normativity, 66, 136, 138, 157, 210

genealogical society (Povinelli), 103

genealogies, 37, 68–69, 100, 108, 191; of queer anthropology, 1–12, 77–78, 81, 90–91; of queer theory, 14, 55–58, 153

generations, 273–74, 277, 280; decolonizing generation (Allen and Jobsen), 34, 43, 47

genocide, 268, 273–74, 276

geopolitics, 3, 159, 180; and LGBT rights, 16, 161, 176–82, 213; and queerness, 57, 68, 172–76, 181–83; sexual, 13, 16, 101

Ghana, 191, 193–94, 203

Ghetto Biennale, 232

Gill, Lyndon, 17, 69, 194

Gilliam, Angela, 39

Gilmore, Ruth Wilson, 195

globalization, 2, 5, 13, 57, 152, 154–57, 162

Global North, 54, 68, 70, 143, 159, 213

Global South, 17, 59, 68, 154, 157–63, 170, 235

GLQ (journal), 56

governmentality (Foucault), 171, 182, 183n4

Govindrajan, Radhika, 259

granular, the, 2, 287–88, 297n5

Green, Marshall, 17

Grenada, US invasion of, 42

Grindr, 157

Gumbs, Alexis Pauline, 202

Gupta, Akhil, 153

haa shagóon, 270–72

Haa Shagóon (film), 271

Haiti, 42, 231–33

Halberstam, Jack, 5, 57

Hall, Clyde, 92n3

Hames-García, Michael, 12, 54, 55, 63

Hammond, Austin (Tlingit elder), 271

Haraway, Donna, 250, 251, 261

Harlow, Harry, 251

Harney, Stefano, 201

Harper, Stephen, 277

Harrison, Faye V., 7, 34, 59

Harrison, James, 85

Hartblay, Cassandra, 231, 242n4

Hawaiian sovereignty, 182

Hayward, Eva, 109, 232–33, 250, 257

healing, 195, 201–2, 207, 273

health care, 213–14, 230, 236, 242n7, 243

Hegarty, Benjamin, 158

Heintz, Ren, 107

Hemphill, Prentis, 202

heteronormativity, 4, 18, 62, 155, 164, 173–74, 176; of anthropology, 11; and queer ecology, 252, 257–58; and the state, 169, 172–74

heteropatriarchy, 9, 157, 182, 229, 232, 250, 269; and kinship, 15, 104, 108–9

heterosexism, 123, 254, 256

heterosexuality, 64, 102, 104, 110; compared to homosexuality, 86; compulsory, 18, 65, 253–54, 280; as natural order, 248–49, 258; as normative, 38, 49n5, 140, 153, 229, 233, 269

heterosexual matrix, 15, 101–2, 112, 140

hijra, 16, 66, 110, 134, 141, 157–59, 163; and domestic units, 106, 111, 163; as exotic, 57, 141

Hines, Sally, 213

HIV/AIDS, 156, 198, 230, 259, 284, 290–91; and quality of life, 214, 220; and queer research, 6, 55, 105, 227

Hoad, Neville, 69

Holland, Sharon, 63, 69

homocapitalism (Rao), 177, 184n14

homonationalism (Puar), 5, 53, 63, 175–77, 182, 184n14

homonormativity (Duggan), 5, 63, 105, 155, 173, 175

homophobia, 6, 21n11, 123, 163, 164, 170, 275; in AAA, 10, 21n11; states accused of, 174, 179; universal definitions of, 176–77, 181

homosexuality, 81–91, 105, 227, 230; as analytic category, 2–3, 10–12, 20n1; Gayle Rubin on, 251–52

Hooker, Evelyn, 78, 82–91, 92n5

Horton, Brian A., 16, 147

Hossain, Adnan, 159

house cultures, 107, 110–11

Howe, Cymene, 15

human-dog relations, 250

human rights, 13, 16, 155, 172, 179–80, 202, 211, 213. *See also* LGBT rights

Hurricane Hugo, 42

Hurston, Zora Neale, 92n2, 192

husbians, 106

Huson, Freda (chief Howilkat), 267, 272

hyper (in)visibility (Reddy), 57

identities, 38, 62, 142–44, 147, 154, 159, 221, 228, 248–49; of ethnographer, 40–41, 83–84; and LGB politics, 156, 214–15; and queerness, 2, 4–5, 55, 92, 134–36, 140, 145, 215; and state rights, 169–70; and trans people, 138–39, 157–58, 180, 209–11; western, 156–57, 174, 179, 181

illiberal states, 156, 172–73
immigrants, 19, 143, 154, 182, 221, 291–92, 297n7
imperialism, 41, 57, 79, 154, 172, 175–76, 229–32. *See also* capitalism; colonialism
incarceration, 60, 183n8, 230, 240
India, 3, 101, 146, 159, 163, 174, 178, 260; queer communities in, 106, 163; sexuality in, 181, 259
Indian Act (Canada), 273
Indian Residential Schools (Canada), 273–74
Indigenous sexualities, 79, 90, 92nn2–3, 103
Indigenous sovereignty, 21n10, 103, 182, 266–71, 275
Indigiqueer identities, 92n3. *See also* Two Spirit people
Indonesian queer communities, 117, 158
infra-ordinary. *See* queer endotic
interdisciplinarity, 34, 78–80, 91, 211, 227–34
International Gay and Lesbian Association (ILGA), 170
International Gay and Lesbian Human Right Commission (IGLHRC), 170, 183n3
intersectionality, 1–2, 17–18, 38, 47–48, 63, 117, 164, 210; and crip theory, 228–37; and embodiment, 13, 38–40; and Western universality, 47–48, 69
intersex people, 214–15, 247, 261
interstices (Spiller), 39
intimacies (Lowe): 14, 21n8, 77–80, 83, 89, 91
intimacies of empire (Stoler), 77–79
intimate economies (Wilson), 57
Irigaray, Luce, 248–50
Iran, 172–81, 183n8, 212
Isherwood, Christopher, **85**

Islam, 63, 155–56, 173–74, 179, 180, 212
Islamophobia, 154
Israel, 155, 174–75, 184n11, 213
It Gets Messy in Here (film), 197–98

Jackson, John, 194, 286
Jackson, Zakiyyah Iman, 5
Jacobs, Sue-Ellen, 92n3
Jain, S. Lochlann, 230
Japan, 66, 138, 231, 236
Jobson, Ryan Cecil, 21n8, 35, 71n14
Johnson, E. Patrick, 67, 141, 142
Johnson, Marsha P., 257
Jones, Delmos, 43
Joseph, Miranda, 237–38

Kafer, Alison, 228
Kandaswamy, Priya, 106
Käng, Dredge Byung'chu, 160
Kashmiris, 174
Kasmani, Omar, 286
kathoey, 141
Kauanui, J. Kēhaulani, 80, 182
Kennedy, Elizabeth Lapovsky, 3, 11
Khan, Faris, 212
Khubchandani, Kareem, 146
kink cultures, 67, 111. *See also* BDSM cultures
kinky empiricism (Rutherford), 59, 68, 287
kinship, x–xii, 48, 99–101, 134, 146, 153, 157, 169; in anthropology, 5, 10, 15–16, 66, 99–112; of Indigenous life, 273–74, 279–80; queer, 2, 144, 280. *See also* family
Kitimat, BC, 267
Klein, Naomi, 269
Kohn, Eduardo, 255
Korea, 160
kothi, 157
K-Pop, 160

INDEX 313

Krip Hop Nation, 242n6

Kulick, Don, 66, 138, 230

Lacan, Jacques, 55, 248–49

laelae, 137, 141

LaFortune, Anguksuar Richard, 92n3

Lamm, Nomy, 230

Landes, Ruth, 9

Lane, Nikki, 17

Lang, Sabine, 92n3

language activism, 117, 122, 128n12

Lara, Ana-Maurine, 69, 111

Latin America, 49, 69, 160, 184n13

Latinx people, 41, 117, 160, 164, 220

law, 163, 172, 211, 215, 260, 273; anti-discrimination, 169; and LGBT geopolitics, 174, 181. *See also* recognition (state, legal); *individual statutes*

Leap, William, 3

legitimacy, 10–11, 47, 91, 123, 136, 145, 221; and kinship, 102, 104–7, 110; of queer scholars, 6, 15; state, 155, 278

lesbians, 102, 110, 135, 142, 181, 254, 259, 275; and anthropology, 2–5, 11–12, 22n12, 53–56, 92n3, 152, 174; Black, 13, 31–41, 44–45, 47–48, 59, 107, 204; and geopolitics, 43, 170, 211; and queer studies, 20n2, 21n9, 61–62. *See also* Association for Queer Anthropology (AQA, formerly Society of Lesbian and Gay Anthropologists (SOLGA) and Anthropology Research Group on Homosexuality (ARGOH))

Lévi-Strauss, Claude, 104, 108

Lewin, Ellen, 3, 11

Lewis, Talila "TL," 230

LGBT rights, 16, 155–56, 161, 176–82, 213; model of, 163, 214–15; and trans vitalities, 17, 221–22

liberalism, 103, 117, 155, 162, 169–77, 182, 232, 237, 240; liberal intimacy, 77–92

liberatory anthropology, 229, 241. *See also* decolonization, and anthropology

liberatory futures, 267–74, 280

Liboiron, Max, 109

Lil Nas X, xi

linguistic anthropology, 15, 56, 66, 116–29, 211

Linnaeus, Carl, 255

Little Thunder, Beverley, 92n3

Locke, Peter, 223

logocentrism, 249

Long, Rebecca-Eli, 235

Long, Scott, 174

Lorde, Audre, ix, 41, 46, 55, 192, 204, 228, 242n2; on qualities of light, 36–37, 41; "The Master's Tools Will Never Dismantle the Master's House," 49n4; on US invasion of Grenada, 42–43

Los Angeles, California, 83–87, 197–98

Love, Heather, 58, 61, 286

Love after the End, 280

Lowe, Lisa, 77–80, 83, 91

Lucumí (Santería) practice, 111

Luibhéid, Eithne, 172

Luis, Keridwen, 107

Lyons, Andrew, 9–11

Lyons, Harriet, 9–11

Macharia, Keguro, 54, 68

Madison, Soyini, 133

Malinowski, Bronislaw, 9, 80, 81–82, 90

Manalansan, Martin F., IV, 3, 18–19, 56–57, 143–44, 159, 192, 220; *Global Divas,* 289–90; *Queer Dwellings*, 289–90, 297n7; on mess, 4, 145, 163–64

Manayath, Nithin, 106
Marable, Manning, 36, 48n1
Marhoefer, Laurie, 87
Marmor, Judd, 88
marriage, 9, 102–6, 108, 169, 211–13, 260, 273
marriage/death (Borneman), 105–6
Marxism, 38, 102, 154, 165n4
masculinity, 101, 117, 125, 138, 143, 159–60, 217, 259; dominant spaces of, 59, 146, 249–50; and performativity, 137–38; trans, 67, 143, 220, 232
materialism, 38, 103; feminist, 102
Mattachine Society, 84
Mazzei, George, 259
McGlotten, Shaka, 17
McIntosh, Mary, 102
McRuer, Robert, 5, 228, 231
Mead, Margaret, 9, 71n11, 80, 92n2, 153
Meiu, George Paul, 104
mental health, 44, 84, 88, 92n5, 237, 240. *See also* pathologization; psychiatry; psychoanalysis; psychology
mess: Black gay mess, 33; *It Gets Messy in Here* (film), 197–98; and queer anthropology, 4, 145, 163–64; and the queer endotic, 283, 286–89, 295; and trans vitalities, 17, 210, 215–16, 221–23
mestizos, 40, 49n5
Middle East, 174, 176, 184n13
Migraine-George, Thérèse, 69
Mikdashi, Maya, 68, 175–76
Milbern, Stacey, 230
Mingus, Mia, 230, 242n6
Minich, Julie Avril, 241n2
minoritarian subjects 33–34, 144–45, 289

minoritizing/universalizing (Sedgwick), 10, 62, 235
Mintz, Sidney, 35
misogynoir, 47. *See also* racism; sexism
misogyny, 221, 229. *See also* sexism
Mitchell, Gregory, 143
mixtape, ix–xii
Moore, Leroy F., Jr., 230
Moore, Lisa Jean, 213
Moore, Madison, 144
Moore, Mignon, 107
Moraga, Cherríe, 142
Morales, Aurora Levins, 230
Moreau, Julie, 159
Morgan, Lewis Henry, 102
Morgensen, Scott L., 5, 14, 61, 103, 141
Morris, Rosalind, 56, 66, 141
Mortimer-Sandilands, Catriona, 254
Moten, Fred, 201
Mother Camp (Newton), 20, 54, 66–67, 136–37
Moussavi, Ghassan, 182
mulata figure, 40, 49n5
mundane, the, 13, 18, 284–85, 289–90, 296, 297n3. *See also* queer endotic
Muñoz, José Esteban, 4, 5, 57, 145–46, 164, 276, 288
Mupotsa, Danai S., 69

Najmabadi, Afsaneh, 180–81, 212
Nakamura, Karen, 21n6, 231, 235
Namaste, Vivian, 67, 139, 141
Nash, Jennifer, 38
National Center for Transgender Equality, 217
National Gay and Lesbian Task Force, 217
National Institute of Mental Health, 84, 88, 92n5
National Institutes of Health, 261
natureculture (Haraway), 8, 261
neocolonialism, 175

neo-Darwinism, 256–57

neoliberalism, 170, 183n2; and the academy, 17, 191, 221, 238; and geopolitics, 154, 161, 177–79; and homonormativity, 63, 169–70, 172

New Jewel Movement, 38

Newton, Esther, 11; *Mother Camp*, 20, 54, 66–67, 136–37

New York City, 44, 65, 83, 92n4, 146, 191

Njena Reddd Foxxx, x

nonbinary people, 116, 122, 128n12, 197, 268, 275

nongovernmental organizations (NGOs), 156–58, 163, 170–71, 177, 180–82, 209–10

nonnormative heterosexualities (Cohen), 64

normate (Thomson), 17, 234, 243n8

nostalgia, 46, 277, 292–93, 295

Obama administration, 178

Ocean, Frank, xii

Oceti Sakowin people, 271

Ocha, Witchayanee, 212

Ochoa, Marcia, 158–59

oil and gas industries, 18, 266–70, 274, 277

one-dimensional queer (Ferguson), 14, 90

onto-epistemology, 261

ontological choreography (Thompson), 109

orangutans, 252–54

Ortner, Sherry, 108

Otu, Kwame, 17

Oulipo, 284

Out in Theory (Lewin and Leap), 3

Outright (IGLHRC), 170

Palestine, 174, 213

Papantonopoulou, Saffo, 213

Paris Zoological Garden, 256

Parker, Pat, 33

Parreñas, Juno Salazar, 18, 252–53

participant observation, 33, 40, 83, 153, 194, 198, 204

passing, 138–39, 180

pastiche, 164

Patel, Geeta, 175

pathologization, 63, 82, 86–90, 100, 217, 227–28, 241n2. *See also* mental health; psychiatry; psychoanalysis; psychology

Patil, Vrushali, 101

patriarchy, 117, 121–22, 125, 249. *See also* heteropatriarchy

pedagogy, 2, 34, 84, 194, 198, 201–3, 237–40

Peña, Susana, 213

Perec, Georges, 284–87, 289

Pérez, Elizabeth, 111

performance studies, 16, 66–68, 134–35, 141, 277; queer anthropology of performance, 16, 133–48

performativity, 13, 48, 70, 110, 134, 142–43; Butler on, 53, 60, 65–67, 117n4, 135–40, 147

phallogocentrism, 249–50

Phelan, Peggy, 56

Philippines, 3, 143

Piepzna-Samarasinha, Leah Lakshmi, 230, 241

pinkwashing, 155, 174, 184n10, 213

plastics, 109, 232–33

pleasure, 8, 46, 100, 111, 138, 146, 160, 192, 295; female, 44–45, 249

Plemons, Eric, 139

police violence, 143, 212, 267–68, 272, 278–79. *See also* state violence

postcolonialism, 3, 7–8, 15, 59, 63, 68–70, 78, 99; and anthropology, 33, 82, 172, 176; and disablement (Durban), 231; queer, 12, 16–17, 55–56, 118, 161, 175, 182

316   INDEX

poststructuralism, 37, 65

poverty, 86, 219–20, 232, 235, 274

Povinelli, Elizabeth, 56, 57, 103, 155, 182

power, 91, 99–100, 123, 142, 235; centering analyses of, 2, 5–8; discursive, 37, 126, 159; and queerness, 11–12, 46, 55, 60–63, 163, 285, 288–89, 296; systemic, 48, 154–55, 162, 171–72, 176–77, 180–82, 183n4; and trans people, 136–38, 140, 220–23, 257. *See also* civilization discourse; recognition (state, legal); state violence

predominantly white institutions (PWIs), 197

prescriptive intellectual work, 36, 39, 41, 48, 70n4, 127n11, 296

primatology, 247, 251–54

primitive sexuality, 9, 77–82, 90–91, 92n1, 101

private property, 102–3, 274, 277

Probyn, Elspeth, 56

promiscuous methodology, 18, 71n6, 133–34, 146, 229

pronouns, 15, 116–29, 252–53, 275.

psychiatry, 10, 82–84, 87–89, 92n5, 231. *See also* mental health; pathologization

psychoanalysis, 39, 248–50, 258

psychology, 78–82, 180, 251, 256–57

Puar, Jasbir, 68, 155, 173, 175–76, 231; on homonationalism, 5, 53, 63, 182

public intellectual work, 11, 58, 88, 196–97, 213, 221, 233, 256

Puri, Jyoti, 181

quality of life, 220–23, 253. *See also* trans vitalities

queer (term), 1–5, 11–12, 164n1, 222

queer asylum, 156, 177–81, 214

queer, crip theory, 228. *See also* cripping ethnography

queer diasporas, 57, 91, 160, 177, 213; Black, 34, 107, 164, 202, 204; in transnational queer studies, 69, 159

queer ecology, 18, 247–61

queer endotic, 18, 283–97

queer ethics (Dave), 58, 107

queer horizons (Muñoz), 5, 276–77, 288

Queerly Phrased (Livia and Hall), 3

queer of color critique, 8, 16–19, 54–59, 63–64, 106, 140, 164, 214, 259, 283

queer regionalism, 69, 159–60, 209–20, 212. *See also* transnationalism, and queer anthropology

queer theory, 4, 70n4, 153, 175–76; and antinormativity, 5, 54, 70n5, 118, 139–40, 172, 229; normative whiteness of, 63–64, 67, 141; origin stories of, 2, 12, 14, 55–58, 153; SOLGA/AQA T-shirts, 2–**3,** 6; theory of the flesh, 141–42; as theory/universal, 14, 34, 53–54, 58–60, 64–65, 68–69, 71n6, 140, 159; US-centrism of, 14–15, 55, 60, 68–70, 176, 182

queer turn, 14, 56

queer utopia, 275–80

racial analogy, 7, 21n6, 63, 87–88

racial capitalism, 78–79, 232

racialization, 38, 42, 49, 67, 87, 237, 240, 241n1; and anthropology, 13–14, 17, 86, 154, 233; and disability, 241nn1–2; and queered states, 174, 180; and queerness, 4–5, 20n4, 57, 106–8, 118, 141, 155, 259; and sexuality, 63–64, 78–91, 100, 143, 146 racism, 12, 14, 63, 78–79, 154, 179, 232; and ableism, 229, 241n1; in anthropology, 6, 8–9; anti-Black, 5, 81, 88, 100, 107, 143, 195, 230; antiracism, 18, 89, 229, 235; and homonationalism, 53, 63, 155; structural, 47, 48n1, 123, 237. *See also* white supremacy

Radcliffe-Brown, A. R., 105

Radical Fairies, 103

Raffles, Hugh, 250

Ramberg, Lucinda, 15

Rao, Rahul, 176–77

rape, 41, 256–57

Reagan, Ronald, 170

recognition (state, legal), 63–64, 103–7, 110, 121–22, 169–70, 217

Reddy, Gayatri, 57

Red Nation, 276

refugees, 156, 177–81, 214

relationship: being in (or not), 17, 40–43, 199–201, 204–5; building, 195, 197–98; with the land, 278. *See also* accountability

representation, xii, 3, 7, 101, 154, 182, 232, 289; and anthropology, 21n9, 34, 46, 100, 198, 248, 258; and queer studies, 56, 67, 258

reproduction, 105–9, 237, 253, 276–77

reproductive futurity (Edelman), 53, 274, 276

reverse discourse (Foucault), 118

reworking anthropology (Harrison), 34

rhesus macaques, 251–52

Rich, Adrienne, 254

Rifkin, Mark, 269, 272

Riggs, Marlon, ix, 31, 33–34, 192

Robertson, Jennifer, 66, 138

Rodríguez, Juana María, 145–46

Rofel, Lisa, 33, 34, 56, 161, 182

Rosenberg, Gabriel, 260

Ross, Diana, ix

Roy, Raina, 158, 212

Rubin, Gayle, ix, 11, 65, 71n9, 111; charmed circle, 60–**61;** on sex/gender system, 56, 102; "Thinking Sex," 54, 60–65, 251–52

Rutherford, Danilyn, 59, 287

Rydström, Jens, 230

Sadjadpour, Karim, 173

Saint, Assotto, 36

salvage anthropology, 58, 81

Sanabri, Emilia, 109

sanctions, state, 172, 174, 178, 181, 184n11, 184n18

San Francisco, California, 6, 83, 92n3, 110–11, 170

Sangodare, 202

Santos, Ana Cristina, 213

Sari, Elif, 179

Sarwak, Borneo, 253

Saudi Arabia, 174

savagery, 42, 101, 108, 156; savage slot (Trouillot), 10; savage sexualities (Kauanui), 80

#SayHerName, 38

Schechner, Richard, 66

Schneider, David, 99

Scientific Humanitarian Committee (Germany), 92n4

Sedgwick, Eve Kosofsky, 4, 10, 53, 55, 62, 235

settler colonialism, 18, 109, 156, 160, 182, 237, 240; and sexuality, 78–79, 103, 174, 176; shaping anthropology, 7–9, 71, 81, 153; and temporality, 268–70

settler homonationalism (Morgensen), 5, 103

sex hormones, 109, 259–60

sexism, 119, 121–23, 128n12, 179, 256. *See also* misogynoir; misogyny

sexology, 9, 82

318 INDEX

sexual dimorphism, 108

sexual economies, 104, 143, 161, 212, 217

sexuality, 153, 157, 161, 173–79, 211, 230; primitive, 9, 78, 80–81, 90–91, 92n1, 101; and racialization, 63, 78–79, 82–89, 101; and "Thinking Sex," 60–65, 251–52

Shakhsari, Sima, 16, 173, 210

Shange, Savannah, 7, 142, 191

shimmers (Horton), 147

Silko, Leslie Marmon, 273

singletons, 105–6, 180, 249, 291

Sins Invalid, 227, 242n6

situated theory, 47, 54, 57–60, 64–70, 162

slavery, 6, 39, 78, 103, 107, 154, 204, 230

slime molds, 254–57

Smalls, Krystal A., 6

Smith, Christen, 38, 143

Snorton, C. Riley, 5, 139

social death, 105–6

social evolutionism, 9, 101, 256–57, 269

social justice. *See* activism

social sciences, 2, 14, 56, 58, 77–78, 118

Society of Lesbian and Gay Anthropologists (SOLGA). *See* Association for Queer Anthropology (AQA, formerly Society of Lesbian and Gay Anthropologists (SOLGA) and Anthropology Research Group on Homosexuality (ARGOH))

sociobiology, 248, 256, 258, 260–61

solipsism, 249–50, 254, 296

somatechnics, 261

Somerville, Siobhan, 172

Southeast Asia, 43, 157–58, 162

sovereignty, 13, 21n10, 89, 103, 111, 182

Soviet Union, 161, 170, 183n3

Spade, Dean, 213

Sparks, David, 212

Spice, Anne, 18

Spillers, Hortense, 36–40, 63, 69, 103, 107, 142

Stack, Carol, 100, 107

Standing Rock, 268, 271

starfish, 109, 257–58

"State of Trans Organizing," 214

state, queer anthropology of, 16, 169–87

state violence, 155, 171, 174, 177–81, 214. *See also* police violence

Steedly, Margaret, 153, 162

Stewart, Kathleen, 194, 286, 290

Stoler, Ann Laura, 79

Stout, Noelle, 161

Strathern, Marilyn, 56

Street Transvestite Action Revolutionaries (STAR), 257

structuralism, 108, 250

Stryker, Susan, 212

subversion, 67, 136, 138–39, 147, 169

Suriname *mati*, 3, 157

surveillance, 40, 60, 63, 87, 194, 278–79

Sylvester, ix

Syrian refugee crisis, 179–80

Taboo (Kulick and Willson), 3

Tahltan blockade, 274

Taiwan, 104

Takarazuka Revue, 138

Taliban, 178

TallBear, Kim, 103, 109

Tallie, T. J., 159

Taylor, Clark, 10

Tellis, Ashley, 106

territoriality, 182

terrorism, 155, 170, 174, 176, 179, 182

Thailand, 3, 8, 66, 160, 212

Thatcher, Margaret, 170

theory in the flesh (Moraga), 142

thick description, 8, 21n9, 46, 71n12, 286, 295

thin description, 194, 286–87

third world, 16, 33, 36–38, 47, 161, 176–77. *See also* Global South

Thom, Kai Cheng, 279

Thomas, Wesley, 92n3

Thompson, Charis, 109

Thomsen, Carly, 231

Tidying up with Marie Kondo (TV show), 290, 293–94

Tlingit language, 270–71

Tongues Untied (Riggs), 31

tongzhi, 110

toxicities, 109, 232–33, 280

trans (term), 20n1, 209–10

trans exclusion, 214–15, 275; trans-exclusionary radical feminism (TERF), 117, 126

transnationalism, 3, 19, 202, 210, 228–29; and adoption, 106; and ethnography, 33; and geopolitics, 170–84, 209; and queer anthropology, 16–17, 54–56, 152–65; and queer studies, 16, 68–70, 175

transnational turn, 13, 56–57, 70, 152

trans object-making, 209–10, 221–22

trans* ontology, 109, 258

trans people, 67, 138–39, 212; and AAA panel, 235; in Bombay, 147; and disability theory, 231–32; and gendered pronouns, 116, 120, 124–25; in geopolitics, 177–82; in Indonesia, 158; in Iran, 180; in Istanbul, 182; in the Philippines, 158–59; and queer theory, 139, 141; starfish becoming, 257–58; structural exclusion of, 214–15, 275. *See also* gender-liminal people

transphobia, 1, 10, 156, 174, 179–81

trans rights, 11, 17, 180–81, 210, 213–22, 231, 247, 257

trans studies, 8, 135, 160, 182, 213, 231–32, 257; Black, 69, 139; trans anthropology, 1, 20n1, 209–12, 222. *See also* trans vitalities

trans vitalities, 17, 209–23

trauma, 122, 141, 146–47, 199–200, 267, 274, 291

travesti, 16, 66, 69, 109–10, 134, 138, 160

Trobriand Islands, Papua, 81

Trouillot, Rolph, 10

Trump administration, 178

TSQ (journal), 160

Tuck, Eve, 21n10

tulips, 248–50

Turkey, 163, 177–79; Istanbul, 182

Tuvalu, 266

Two Spirit people, 110, 215, 280, 281n1

Two-Spirit People (Jacobs, Thomas, and Lang), 92n3

Uganda, 177

Ulysse, Gina, 195

Unist'ot'en camp, 18, 267, 272, 275, 278

United Nations, 44, 156, 164, 171, 180

United Nations High Commissioner on Refugees (UNHCR), 177–78

United Nations Human Rights Council Report (UNHCR), 212, 223n1

University Grove project, 237–**40**

US-centrism, 14–15, 55, 60, 68–70, 176, 182

US Department of State, 174

US Muslim ban, 179

USSR. *See* Soviet Union

Valentine, David, 3, 56, 216

Vance, Carole, 10, 11, 37, 63, 158

Vanuatu, 266

Vider, Stephen, 111

Vincent, Louise, 213

Virginia Transgender Health Initiative Study, 218

vulnerability, 19, 146, 192, 284, 287

waria, 158

Warner, Michael, 4, 55, 58, 62

war on terror, 170, 182

Washington, DC, 45, 92, 215–21

Washington Transgender Needs Assessment Survey, 218

water protectors, 18, 272

Weheliye, Alexander, 142

Weiss, Margot, 5, 14, 111, 140

Wekker, Gloria, 3, 56, 57, 91, 157

welfare, 41–42, 64, 106, 155, 183n2

Western hegemony, 8, 15–16, 118, 155–59, 162, 171, 213

Westermarck, Edward, 9

Weston, Kath, 9–10, 56, 58, 68, 77, 79–80, 92n1; on ethnocartography, 8, 11–12, 59, 78, 81, 92n3, 141, 174; on kinship, 100, 110

West Sumatra, 212

Wet'suwet'en territory, 18, 267–68, 270, 273

"What's Queer about Queer Studies Now" (Eng, Halberstam, and Muñoz), 57, 71n7

white feminism, 37, 49n4, 214. *See also* feminism

white innocence (Wekker), 91

whiteness, 21n6, 84, 144, 155, 159, 238, 251, 285; and ableism, 233–36; and anthropology, 15, 19, 57–59, 71n11, 78–81, 141, 203; and BIPOC genealogies, 106–7, 108, 112; and

Blackdacting, 192; and feminism, 37, 49n4, 214; institutional, 48n1, 146, 192, 197, 204, 231; and liberalism, 232, 237–38, 240; and queer theory, 12–14, 17, 54–55, 60, 63–70, 164, 175; and sexuality, 82–91, 101. *See also* alterity

white supremacy, 14, 21n8, 64, 79, 154, 195, 240; and anthropology, 6–9, 57, 91, 156, 221, 228–29; and cultural hegemony, 118, 159. *See also* racism

white women, protection of, 39, 49n5, 101

Whyte, Kyle, 269

Wikan, Unni, 11

Wilchins, Riki Anne, 3

Willey, Angela, 109

Williams, Brackette, 40–41

Wilson, Ara, 16, 57

Wong, Alice, 230

Wong, Alvin, 69

Wool, Zoë H., 231

worldings, 285–86, 290

xanith, 141

xenophobia, 9, 178–79, 229

Yanagisako, Sylvia, 100

'yan daudu, 66

Yang, K. Wayne, 21n10

yintah, 272

Yogyakarta Principles, 211

Zebra Katz, x

Zengin, Aslı, 182

Printed and bound by CPI Group (UK) Ltd, Croydon, CR0 4YY
16/06/2024

14515362-0001